Graced CROSSROADS

Pathways to Deep Change

&

Transformation

TED DUNN

Graced CROSSROADS

Pathways to Deep Change
&
Transformation

TED DUNN

CCS Publications
www.CCSstlouis.com

Copyright© 2020 by Ted Dunn

Published in the United States by CCS Publications, Comprehensive Consulting Services, St. Charles, Missouri: www.CCSstlouis.com

Permissions

Unless otherwise stated, Dr. Ted Dunn uses his own translation and/or paraphrase of Scripture. Dr. Dunn draws from a variety of sources, especially the New International Version and the New Living Translation. His practice is to reference chapter and verse for scriptural sources, but not to identify precise translations.

William Stafford, "The Way It Is" from Ask Me: 100 Essential Poems. Copyright © 1998, 2014 by William Stafford and the Estate of William Stafford. Reprinted with the permission of The Permissions Company LLC on behalf of Graywolf Press, Minneapolis, Minnesota, graywolfpress.org.

Library of Congress Cataloging-in-Publication Data

Dunn, Ted

Graced crossroads : pathways to deep change and transformation / Ted Dunn

ISBN: 978-1-09830-567-3
ebook ISBN: 978-1-09830-568-0

Printed in the United States of America

First Edition

Endorsements

"Ted Dunn's remarkable and insightful work demonstrates how, at a critical moment in human history, faith-based communities (including religious congregations) are invited to go beyond 'adapting to change' in order to engage in the challenge of 'deep transformation'. Our time is clearly a moment of grace for those of us who can respond courageously to the promptings of the Holy Spirit. Dunn artfully integrates key insights from spirituality, psychology, and organizational processes in an effort to provide a holistic and humanizing path leading into the future. A must-read!" **Mary Beth Ingham, CSJ. Author and Professor of Philosophical Theology, Franciscan School of Theology, San Diego**

"Ted invites men and women religious to explore how God is working through them to find meaning, purpose, and new life for their institutes. I've appreciated his facilitation style as it is grounded in both spirituality and humor! In these times of major transition and change, Ted inspires both leaders and members to choose a path that holds the potential for deep change and transformation. Throughout this work, he demonstrates a profound understanding and appreciation of the unique challenges facing Religious Life today." **Patrick Del Ponte, Director of Planning at Hoffman Planning, Design and Construction, Inc.**

"As Ted's professional partner and wife of 30 years, I know Ted from the inside out. I have witnessed his tenacious commitment to choose life in the midst of profound loss, confusion, and unwelcomed change. This book is a culmination of his personal journey of transformation, extensive contemporary research, and decades of walking deeply with religious women and men in many countries. This work is not for those seeking quick fixes and easy answers to the dilemmas and challenges facing Religious Life today. However, this work is for you, and for your community, if you have the courage to embrace the soulwork necessary for personal and communal transformation." **M. Beth Lipsmeyer, Ph.D. Clinical Psychologist, Consultant, and President of Comprehensive Consulting Services**

DEDICATION

This book is dedicated to individuals and communities who are at a graced crossroads in their lives and are looking to transform their lives in a way that holds meaning, purpose and the promise of new life.

ACKNOWLEDGMENT

This book is the culminating result of over 30 years of practice as a clinical psychologist and guide to religious communities. I want to thank all those individuals and communities who allowed me into the living room of their lives in order to accompany them through processes of deep change. I especially want to thank the religious men and women who invited me to guide them through a Journey of Transformation. I am grateful for the deepening of my own spiritual journey you have afforded me through our work together. It is my greatest hope that the wisdom gained from our collective experiences and what I am sharing in this book will enlighten others who wish to take this road less traveled.

I wish to also thank Diarmuid O'Murchu whose writings I have read throughout my professional career and for encouraging me to publish. I wish to also thank Richard Rohr, Joan Chittister, Parker Palmer, Margaret Wheatley and Ronald Rolheiser whose writings I have also relished over the years. These authors have that rare and uncanny ability to describe the spiritual journey, in all its beauty, complexity and nuances, with tremendous clarity. I wish to thank Theresa LaMetterey, a Sister of St. Joseph of Orange, whose feedback has been enormously helpful as she read, studied and edited my manuscript.

Thirty years ago, Beth and I vacationed on the north shore of Kauai with our family enjoying the island beauty and laid-back lifestyle. Over the years Kauai has become our spiritual home, a place where we have been able to rejuvenate ourselves, body, mind and soul. In the recent years, Beth and I have spent winters in Kauai as a kind of mini-sabbatical. It has provided me with the time and the soul-centeredness to put this book together.

The Aloha spirit of Kauai has been imparted to me through two people in particular. Reneé Janton has been our spiritual companion, a woman who is the incarnation of Aloha. She is the *real deal* who relies completely on the abundant providence of grace in the Universe. I also wish to thank Noah Peragine, our Yoga instructor who taught me the discipline of mind, body, spirit integration. He would end every session with prayers of gratitude and his mantra: "May we be a beacon of light and forklift unto humanity." His mantra has become mine as well.

I wish to especially thank my wife, professional partner and soulmate, Beth, whose love has sustained me through my own graced crossroads. While in the darkest moments of my own crossroads, when I had could no longer permit myself to hope because I could not stand the pain of disappointment, she said, "I'll carry the hope for you." Never have I felt so loved. Her love, companionship and encouragement have sustained me in my personal life and professional work. Beth's own insights regarding the integration of psychology and spirituality have been a constant source of wisdom for me and all those who have had the privilege of working with her.

CONTENTS

PREFACE

"Yearning for a new way will not produce it. Only ending the old way can do that. You cannot hold onto the old, all the while declaring that you want something new. The old will defy the new; the old will deny the new; the old will decry the new. There is only one way to bring in the new. You must make room for it." Neale Walsch

---

We cannot travel to the future without honoring our past, our ancestors and traditions, but these cannot lead us there. We need to include and transcend the past, loosen our grip on time-honored traditions and make room for the new. What leads us into the future is our courage, creativity, and tenacity to give life to our deepest longings called forth by the lure and love of God. Honoring the past cannot mean living in the past. And honoring our ancestors cannot mean living as they lived. If we truly honor those who have brought us to today, we must do for the next generation what our ancestors did for us: We must make room for the new. "For our lives to be meaningful," said Pierre Teilhard de Chardin, "they must succeed in continuing the creative work of evolution."

Intentions Of This Book

This book will address four central questions:

1. What are the graced crossroads religious communities are now facing and the deeper invitations calling them to the inner work of transformation?

2. What are the challenges and opportunities in our world and within Religious Life that have brought communities to these graced crossroads?

3. How might communities assess their capacity to engage in communal transformation, what will it ask of them, and what can they expect to come from it?

4. What does a Journey of Transformation truly involve and how can communities proactively engage in this Divine Mystery?

Our entire globe is going through a Great Turning, a massive transition which we, as a species, are partially responsible for creating. The fate of the planet, humanity, and the 20 million other species that inhabit our common home are all tied together. We are at a tipping point at which we will either evolve into a new way of being or devolve toward a sixth great extinction in the 4-billion-year history of our planet.

Religious Life, as well, is going through a seismic transition due to both external global changes and internal changes taking place within the Church and Religious Life. The demographic changes alone are demanding enormous change. Beneath these surface changes, though, communities are facing any number of crises related to survival, identity, integrity and relevancy. These crises, in turn, are challenging the very soul of communities at the crossroads.

Religious communities are at a graced crossroads facing existential decisions that will determine their fate. Beyond the obvious need for organizational change, many communities are discovering a *deeper invitation* as they discern God's call to new life. They are searching for ways to navigate this transition. Many hope to bring forth a new spirit as they work toward completion. Others hope to bring forth not only a new spirit but new life by transforming their own lives and creating new pathways to the future.

It seems everyone is talking about "transformation," not just the Catholic religious communities, but civic communities, other mainline religions, corporations, and institutions of all kinds. If you search Amazon for books on transformation you will find over 50,000 titles. It is a term used so often today it has become a kind of buzzword, glibly tossed about and used synonymously and erroneously with "change." This obfuscates its true nature and glosses over the depth of its potential. I hope to add both clarity and depth to our understanding of what transformation is and how communities can engage in this work.

Despite all the books on transformation, few take an in-depth look at how transformation occurs, and even fewer describe how to engage in this type of work as a community. There are those who write about personal transformation from a religious, faith or psychological perspective. And there are those who address systemic change and transformation from a business or corporate perspective. Very few authors cross-over and integrate both personal and organizational transformation from an integrative multidisciplinary perspective. My desire is to bridge this gap and draw upon the wisdom of not only faith traditions, but of contemporary understandings in psychology, spirituality, systems theory and cultural evolution.

Communities who wish to engage in transformation need to have a better handle on what it is and what they can expect from it in terms of its promise and its peril. They need to know how to approach this work, what it will require of them and have ways to assess their capacity to do this kind of work. The hard truth is the vast majority of communities and organizations fail in their efforts to transform their lives and give birth to new life. The good news is that the research tells us why. Those who engage in this work need to know these pitfalls ahead of time so they can proactively address them and improve their odds of success.

Many communities are approaching their planning and visioning efforts during these times of transition in much the same manner as they had when their lifecycle was on the upswing. What the research tells us is that these conventional approaches (e.g., strategic planning) have a dismal track record, especially when applied to organizations on the downside of their lifecycle and the goal is transformation. Conventional approaches used during unconventional times, such as these, will not work. Some communities have experimented with alternative approaches (e.g., Theory U, Open Space Technology, World Café, Appreciative Inquiry) and these can certainly add tools to the process toolbox. However, by themselves, in the way these are typically used, they will also not result in communal transformation.

The Journey of Transformation that I am introducing is a comprehensive, multidimensional and multilayered approach to communal transformation. It is comprehensive in addressing every facet of community (e.g., spirituality, mission and ministries; community life and the relationships among members; and stewardship of personnel, financial and material resources). It is multidimensional, addressing three primary dimensions of community: personal (emotional and spiritual), interpersonal (relational and communal) and organizational (structural and systemic). It is also multilayered in that it not only addresses what you see on the surface (e.g., land, buildings, finances, ministries), but the layers of life that lie beneath the surface (e.g., norms, patterns, practices, structures, culture and soul of community).

What will you have at the end of all of your downsizing and rightsizing, if you have not attended to the inner work of transformation? A primary reason most communities fail in their efforts to transform their lives is fear. They rely upon conventional methods, focus on surface changes and neglect the inner work. Most religious communities are too afraid to take the kinds of bold actions necessary to bring about transformation. Most will use strategic planning and give it a spiritual label, hoping that it will somehow connect with their members and foster more depth. Most will avoid the kind of intimate and in-depth conversations necessary for genuine transformation.

The Journey of Transformation is a new way of integrating planning and visioning efforts along with the inner work of transformation. What I'm referring to here is a way of transforming your lives and planning your future, not so much in terms of writing a grand plan, but by engaging one another in the discipline of dreaming, dialogue and discernment in order to co-create your community's future. This is a way of shaping your future together that transforms your way of thinking, relating, and serving our world. It is a means for creating new mind-sets, heart-sets and skill-sets needed for the work of transformation.

It is widely known that religious are becoming older, fewer and more diverse, with fewer institutionalized ministries. This is the *official future* we all hear about, see happening and is predicted by every actuarial. It is the basis for planning that most communities will use, thus, making the official future an inevitable outcome. The official future is a self-fulfilling prophecy by those who offer no alternative prophetic stance against such predictable outcomes.

What I am offering here is a way to shape an unofficial future using unconventional approaches providing new ways to bring your longings to life. It is a means for opening other possible futures than the one we all read about. The official future is not a fait accompli, unless you follow the well-worn path of least resistance. Ultimately, no one can truly predict the future, but you have the freedom to shape it. In freedom there is possibility, and in possibility there is hope.

Most of us yearn for the freedom to create a life of purpose and possibility, the chance to commit ourselves to something larger than our own ego, that we might transcend the limits of our own selves. The most fundamental expression of our freedom, it seems to me, is to create a future of our own choosing, informed by God, and comprised of our gifts, our deepest longings and our greatest aspirations. The Journey of Transformation is a communal faith journey, not a new name for strategic planning. While the end goal may well be a prophetic vision, the power of this journey lies more in how you walk it than in any vision claimed.

The Journey of Transformation is a journey that will test your readiness to live authentically out of your deepest beliefs and leave behind all that has become bereft of meaning or is made more of nostalgia than of your call to further the reign of God. It is a journey that seeks to transform the very culture of community through holy and intimate conversations, loving and reconciling exchanges and communal discernment of God's call. It is less about the future that awaits you than the sort of people you are, who you are growing to become and the very purpose you claim for your existence.

For Whom this Book is Written

This book focuses on Catholic religious communities and, even though I will be addressing them, it is well suited for any value-based or faith-based organization facing similar crossroads. While I will be referencing a number of specifics regarding Religious Life, my experience with other organizations in the United States and internationally has also informed the material in this book. Thus, the foundations, principles and approaches involved in the Journey of Transformation can readily be applied to other religious or civic communities and organizations seeking transformation.[i]

The Journey of Transformation is not for everyone and certainly not for the faint of heart. It is for those communities and organizations who have come to realize that they are in an unsustainable and unacceptable situation and, therefore, must radically change the way they live life now and into the future. It is for those who have come to realize that they cannot do this work alone, by committee, or from the top-down, but only through collaboration and partnership. It will serve those who are lost in a quagmire of ambiguity, uncertainty and complexity in their efforts to forge a future in a rapidly changing world. It will aid those who suffer from *paralysis by analysis*, stymied by entrenched conflicts, and blocked by resistance to change. Finally, it is for communities who, rather than adapting to our world, wish to transform both themselves and the world in which they live.

The Journey of Transformation, then, would not work well in communities or organizations who are focused solely on their bottom line and do not have a value-base or faith-base that drives their mission. It will not work well for those do not wish to learn how to work through conflicts and chaos, or open up creative conversations, and cannot see the generative value in it. This book, then, would not appeal to those looking for some kind of quick-fix, formulaic program or sanitized solutions.

---

i For the most part, throughout the book I will use the term "community" generically, representing any religious institute, church, value-based or faith-based community, their affiliated organizations, or other organizations for whom mission and the meaning of their lives and work lies well below the "bottom line." I will be explicit when referring only to "religious communities," meaning Catholic institutes, congregations or communities.

While I provide many examples to illustrate approaches, I would not consider this a field book that provides detailed instructions. While there are common themes across communities, each community has a unique culture with its own language, stories, circumstances, opportunities and constraints. There is no one-size-fits-all approach to transformation. Any approach that is used, including this one, must be tailored specifically to a community. Please know that although the examples and illustrations I offer throughout the book are real, I have used fictitious names of individuals and communities in order to protect their identity.

The material in this book will assist leaders, planners and all those helping to guide communities through the challenging and rewarding work of deep change and transformation. It will help you build upon what you already know about planning and visioning. It will add a comprehensive framework for understanding, integrating and implementing your efforts to guide communities through the work of transformation. It will provide new insights, broaden your repertoire of approaches, and strengthen your overall capacity to do this work.

Additional resources

This book will assist those who want to deepen their understanding of transformation and how they might engage in the inner work of transformation. I will be publishing a companion book, *The Inner Work of Transformation* (working title), that will supplement the material presented in this book. This supplement will offer a series of reflections and exercises for personal reflection, journaling and sharing in small groups. My intention is to help individuals engage in their personal and communal work of transformation. It will help leadership teams, local communities and other small groups to engage in intimate conversations that have transformative potential. The website for Comprehensive Consulting Services, www.CCSstlouis.com has additional supplemental materials, including videos and articles.

What's In The Book?

Part I: A Great Turning

Part I – *A Great Turning* – includes chapters 1 through 5. Chapter 1 introduces the notion of *Graced Crossroads* as the place in which we realize there is no way to continue as we have been, and we must choose a new path to the future. It is a bend in the road which will be an end in the road for those that fail to make the turn. It is a crossroads in which we realize that what got us to today, will not get us to tomorrow. It is graced crossroads for those who listen to the deeper invitation: God's call to choose life. The graced crossroads is an existential crossroads in which communities will either deliberately choose life or follow a path of least resistance. Graced crossroads is a place of discernment, a place for making choices that will determine a community's fate and shape its destiny. We will explore this Divine Mystery of transformation and what it means to cooperate with grace and actively participate in personal and communal transformation.

Chapters 2, 3, 4 and 5 provide the context for the graced crossroads and examine the transitions taking place in our world and in Religious Life. Understanding this Great Turning will help you address these kinds of questions: Given that Religious Life is always transformed in response to societal needs, what are the most pressing societal needs today? Given that Religious Life is also transformed by internal changes, what are those changes and challenges? What will be the relevance, role and distinctive contribution of vowed religious in our rapidly changing world? How might communities become agents of transformation for Religious Life and our world?

Chapter 2 – *The World in Which We Live* – looks at the global and U.S. context. It examines the major changes taking place and the trends that are shaping our future. These are the signs of the times that will inform how communities can become either relevant or obsolete, proponents of change or the status quo. Communities that remain an analogue culture in our digital world will fall into obsolescence. Those that transform and become agents of transformation will have a hand in shaping the future of Religious Life and our world.

In *Chapter 3 – Cycles of Religious Life* – places the current transition of Religious Life in an historical context. I will briefly review the research showing that Religious Life is going through a cyclical transition, just as it has many times in the past. I will discuss the remarkable parallels between the cycles of Religious Life and the cycles of organizational life. These parallels offer a convergent validity to what is known about how communities might move through these transformative times and how they might fail or succeed.

Chapter 4 – *The Changing Religious Landscape* – provides a detailed picture of the changing landscape of religions across the globe and in the United States. I will describe the demographic shifts across all religions, the emergences of "Nones" (those with no religious affiliation) and the likely causes for the decline among mainline religions. I will then describe the shifts taking place in the religious values, beliefs and practices within the United States. These are all additional signs of the times that will hopefully influence how communities see themselves and the people they serve. I will highlight the diversity that exists within and across religions and offer ways to restore the dignity of difference.

Chapter 5 – *Challenges Facing Religious Communities* – zeroes in on the cascading crises communities are now experiencing. The demographic changes themselves are daunting and are having a major impact on communities. Still, these changes are only the tip of the iceberg. This chapter will look at the cascading crises of survival, identity, integrity and relevancy that so many communities are facing. These crises lie beneath the surface of communities and are the types of things most communities will fail to adequately address with their conventional approaches to planning and visioning. These subterranean issues must be addressed if communities are to transform their lives and bring forth new life.

Part II: Assessment, Options, and Considerations for Discerning Your Chosen Path

Having set the context, I will invite you to look at your own community. Chapter 6 – *Assessing Viability* – invites you to assess your current state of health or diminishment. Without this kind of grounding, assessment of the challenges you will face, and your capacity to deal with them, you could easily make choices based upon fear, denial or wishful thinking. Engaging in a collective self-assessment of your strengths and liabilities as a community, along with an initial appraisal of the challenges and opportunities, is a helpful starting point. I will offer several ways to go about these crucial assessments to help you get a better handle on your capacity for change and transformation.

Chapter 7 – *Discerning Your Options* – helps you to look at your choices. There are a number of options for communities at the crossroads and each one carries its own set of implications and consequences. Each has its own mixture of pros, cons and potential outcomes. None of them are black and white or have only one standard approach for implementation. While it is impossible to predict or guarantee the outcomes of any one option, you can claim your desired outcomes and learn from others who have been down these roads. I will share what other communities, who have taken these different paths, have discovered are the ten most important learnings. These will help you make more informed decisions about options and paths you might wish to take.

Chapter 8 – *What Does It Take?* – addresses what it takes to pursue a Journey of Transformation in light of your realities. The strength of your community's determination to do this work is key, but goodwill alone is not enough. It is important to honestly assess your collective capacity to do the work required of any option. Otherwise, it could be a set-up for failure. I will address a number of questions communities typically have when exploring the possibility of transformation (e.g., costs, benefits, timeline).

Chapter 9 – *Conventional Approaches to Planning and Visioning* – examines the strengths and limitations of different approaches to change and transformation. I will highlight what I call the "Dirty Dozen," the twelve most likely pitfalls that communities encounter when engaged in the work of transformation. We will look at the research showing that conventional approaches to organizational change are only marginally effective during the more mature phases of an organization's development and entirely ineffective as means of transforming organizations. The Journey of Transformation incorporates some of these conventional and unconventional approaches but integrates these into its more comprehensive framework.

Part III: Journey of Transformation

Part III – *Journey of Transformation* – brings us to the heart of this book describing the nature of transformation and what it requires to engage in communal transformation. Chapter 10, *The Nature of Transformation,* provides the foundation for what transformation truly is. We will glean what we can from current understandings of human development in psychology and spirituality, along with systems theory, organizational development, and our evolving culture and universe. All of this will provide us with the 10 most important learnings about the nature of transformation: five key principles and five dynamic elements. These, in turn, will form the foundation for the Journey of Transformation.

Chapter 11 – *The Journey of Transformation* – provides an overview of the approach to communal transformation. While transformation is a Divine Mystery, and the inner workings of grace are beyond our understanding, there are ways we can dispose ourselves to the workings of grace. There is a great deal we can know about transformation through our own experience, modern science, as well as faith traditions. Transformation does not happen without our active participation. It happens by our willing and active *cooperation with grace*. We cooperate with grace through the virtues of faith, hope and love and by engaging the five dynamic elements of transformation. These dynamic elements woven together, infused with the virtues of faith, hope and love, are what constitute the Journey of Transformation. The next five chapters then describe each of the five dynamic elements that are key to the work of communal transformation.

Chapter 12 – *Shifts in Consciousness: Creating a New Narrative* – is about looking toward the future through new lenses. These shifts in perspective reinforce what we so often hear quoted from Albert Einstein: "No problem can be solved from the same level of consciousness that created it." This is the same message Jesus gave us when he said we need new wineskins for new wine (Matthew 9:17). Ultimately, it is a shift or transformation of consciousness that enables communities to imagine and write a new narrative of the future. We will explore ways of not only changing perspectives (e.g., reframing) but also of transforming and awakening new levels of consciousness (e.g., mindfulness).

Chapter 13 – *Reclaim Our Inner Voice: The Seat and Source of Everything that Lives* – is the soulwork of community. This chapter explores what is the soul of community, what some call the true self, and distinguish it from the charism of a community. We will look at how easy it is to lose touch with the soul and the challenge of reclaiming it. It is an heroic journey to come home to our true selves and it takes heroic communities to do this work together. If communities plan for their future based upon surface conversations and not honest, intimate expressions of their inner voice, they risk building a house of cards. We will look at ways that communities might come to claim their inner voice and enliven their collective soul.

Chapter 14 – *Reconciliation and Conversion: The Womb of Our Becoming* – addresses the hard work of healing individually and communally. This is the crucible of transformation and the Achilles' heel of every group with whom I have ever worked. Our avoidance of conflict is universal, a tragic gap in our ability to reach across our differences and welcome the stranger. We will see what it might take for communities to learn how to do this work and walk through the narrow gate of forgiveness.

Chapter 15 – *Experimentation and Learning: Acting Our Way into a New Way of Being* – invites your community to become a learning community. It will require that you adopt a beginner's mind and become learners again. It will require that you reclaim the green space in community where members can feel safe again to risk growing together, rather than going off to other green spaces outside of community to grow. We will look at what creativity is and what it takes to raise your communal IQ. Communities need to incubate and foster the development of new, creative approaches to the future.

Chapter 16 – *Transformative Visioning: Gather the Wisdom, Weave a Dream* – is the visioning and planning element into which the other four dynamic elements are woven. It is this element that drives the entire process. It continually invites you to listen to your deepest longings and greatest aspirations. It is an organic, emergent and iterative process. It is a process that continually invites you to cooperate with grace, and respond to the lure and love of God as you transform your lives and create your future. It incorporates both conventional and unconventional approaches into the larger Journey of Transformation, with an emphasis on depth, integration and partnership.

I will provide some specific ways in which you might organize your efforts to engage in the Journey of Transformation and Transformative Visioning in particular.

Epilogue: Ever Ancient, Ever New offers some final reflections on the four questions we have sought to address and on the ancient path of transformation.

Perspectives from a Guide to Communities Seeking Transformation

I am an "outsider" to Religious Life and consequently bring a different lens and set of experiences than those of you who live it. The work of deep change and transformation has been my ministry, a calling I came to appreciate and embrace midway through my career. I offer consultation, but don't call myself a "consultant." I offer facilitation, but don't call myself a "facilitator." If there is a name for what I do, I suppose it would be: "Guide to communities seeking transformation." Although it doesn't fit neatly on a business card, this is essentially what I do.

I suppose I am much like a Sherpa who knows the terrain and guides others who wish to take the journey. I can guide communities in their search for transformation because I am familiar with its ways. However, I also know and honor the fact that the journey is yours, not mine. The reasons you might take it, what you hope to get out of it, where and how far you wish to go is entirely up to you. It is your life and you must live with the consequences of your choices, not me. My role is to offer guidance based upon my experience as to what your choices might involve and how to go about the challenging and rewarding work of communal transformation.

My work with men and women of faith has evolved along with my understanding and appreciation of Religious Life: the gifts that you bring to our world, the challenges you face, and the opportunities you have on the horizon. The experiences I have had accompanying so many through processes of deep change and transformation has enabled me to deepen my own spiritual journey. Over the years I have offered presentations and articles hoping to pass along the insights I have gained from these experiences. I am grateful to have this time in my life to integrate and pass along these learnings in this book. I hope it will aid you in understanding your own graced crossroads and, should you choose, engaging in the Journey of Transformation.

Part I:
A Great Turning

"You need only claim the events of your life to make them yours. When you truly possess all you have been and done, you are fierce with reality."
Florida Scott-Maxwell

Part I, *A Great Turning*, describes the massive transitions taking place in Religious Life and our world. We start our journey by appreciating the profound nature of these transitional times, which I call a *Graced Crossroads*. In this first chapter, I will discuss the role of grace during these times of transition and how our *cooperation with grace* is key to the inner work of transformation. We will also explore the *deeper invitations* you might discover at these graced crossroads and the dynamic forces of life and death that you will encounter.

The transformation of Religious Life, as with all life, takes place in response to two primary forces: changes occurring outside of Religious Life and those occurring within Religious Life. Gerald Arbuckle spoke of this dual interaction this way: "There must be an interaction between the Gospel and the culture, a process whereby both poles of the interaction are open to insights from each other… a living exchange between the Church and the diverse cultures of people."[1]

Chapter 2, *The World in which We Live*, looks at global societal changes. It examines the major changes taking place in our world and the trends that will likely shape our future. Chapters 3, 4 and 5 explore the cyclical nature, current landscape and pervasive challenges within Religious Life, respectively.

The purpose for contextualizing the Journey of Transformation in these internal and external realities is two-fold: 1) to challenge the denial and misinformation that prevents so many communities from dealing with their current realities; and, 2) to ground your discernment and plans for the future based upon reality. The purpose here is not to take away hope; it is to instill hope by becoming "fierce with reality." Understanding and owning your particular circumstances can bring you substantial relief, especially knowing that your story is part of a larger story.

These are the signs of the times that inform how communities might become either increasingly relevant or obsolete. Communities that remain an analogue culture in our digital world will become obsolete. Those that transform and become agents of transformation will themselves have a hand in shaping the future of Religious Life and our world.

Chapter 1:
Graced Crossroads
A deeper invitation

"All ages end – from the Iron Age to the Bronze Age, from the age of the Renaissance to the Reformation.... No era – no matter how influential or how far-reaching – lasts forever."
Peter Senge

Introduction

There is a Great Turning taking place across our planetary home. A mixture of natural and manmade circumstances has brought our planet to a tipping point – global warming, rising sea levels, species extinction, waves of migration resulting from famine, war and terrorism, a consumption of earth's resources beyond her capacity to regenerate and more – all threatening our common home and humanity's future. Pope Francis, Margaret Wheatley, Al Gore, Barbara Marx Hubbard, John Haught and many other luminaries have suggested that we are on the brink of a sixth great extinction of our planet. It is an existential evolutionary crisis in which our species will either evolve into a new consciousness and a new way of being, or devolve into an abyss of death and destruction.

Hope for our species and our planet lies in our willingness and determination to collaborate in taking the next evolutionary leap to a new level of consciousness. Eckhart Tolle, put it this way: "When faced with a radical crisis, when the old way of being in the world, of interacting with each other and with the realm of nature doesn't work anymore, when survival is threated by seemingly insurmountable problems, an individual life-form – or species – will either die or become extinct or rise above the limitation of its condition through an evolutionary leap.[2]

The world in which we live has radically changed in recent decades. It is far more complex, interdependent, uncertain and volatile than ever before. Global giants, such as Google, Amazon and Alibaba, now dwarf the wealth and power of once sovereign nations. In a matter of moments, the Dow can drop 1000 points when Twitter rumors trigger computer sell-offs. A cartoon published in a Danish newspaper can spark a global eruption of violence among radical Islamics. Global connectivity, technology, and climate change are forces accelerating and amplifying this Great Turning. The world is evolving faster than most of us could have ever imagined, and it seems no one is in charge.

Within this Great Turning are the tectonic shifts taking place across the religious landscape. Here in the United States, for example:

1. There is a rise in the hunger for spirituality and a decline in all mainline religions, especially Catholics;

2. While mainline religions are declining, there is a rise in two ends of the spectrum, Evangelical Protestants and those with no religious affiliation (Nones);

3. Nones are now the largest subgroup, outnumbering Catholics and trending larger; and

4. Hispanics will soon comprise the majority of Catholics, though they too are filling the ranks of Nones and Evangelicals.

And within the Catholic population, Religious Life itself is facing its own set of crises. In the United States, sisters and priests are approaching 40,000 and brothers around 4,000. In 2020, for the first time, there will be more priests than sisters. The average gain of only 150 new members per year will not offset the larger wave of declining numbers of religious for decades to come. These demographic shifts represent only one small portion of the many challenges facing communities, but the practical impact of these demographic changes on the life and mission of communities is demanding enormous time, energy and resources. Adding to the loss of members, a diminishing pool of leaders, advancing age and financial strains are a host of deeper issues related to identity, integrity and relevancy that strike the very soul of communities.

Good news

The good news is that Religious Life is not dying. It is transforming just as it has through many lifecycle changes since the time of Jesus. It is on the leading edge of an evolving consciousness in support of our planetary evolution. This is the context and impetus giving rise to the transformation of Religious Life. To their credit, most communities are now fully engaged in trying to make sense of their future and plan for it. The denial that persisted in recent decades is finally giving way to more proactive efforts to adapt and change.

The good news is that you are a part of this Great Turning and you are in good company! The vast majority of communities are in the same boat. It is not a character flaw of your community or a failure on the part of past leaders that you are facing such daunting challenges. Your community, along with all of Religious Life, is facing the same crossroads. Everyone is searching for the answers and *together* you will find them.

The good news is that death is neither inevitable nor the last word. We know that Religious Life has gone through many cycles. Religious life has been in crisis before and, having faced similar challenges, has come through them to birth a new way of being. This is a natural movement of all living systems. Death is not the last word; it is a new beginning. This is *God's promise*: "I am the resurrection and the life. Those who believe in me, even though they die, will live; everyone who lives and believes in me will never die. Do you believe this?" (John 11:25-26).

Hard choices, hard work, no matter what

"Enter through the narrow gate; for the gate is wide and the way is broad that leads to destruction, and there are many who enter through it. For the gate is small and the way is narrow that leads to life, and there are few who find it." Matthew 7:13-14

Religious Life will rise again, but there are hard choices ahead, and there are no quick fixes, simple or off-the-shelf solutions. No one can give you the answers. All of the options you have will require hard work. There is no escaping it. Even if you just wanted to close down your community, there would be tough decisions and complex plans to implement in order to take care of business, to say nothing of grieving the losses and negotiating the inevitable differences of opinion regarding all of the decisions you must make. You're right – it isn't fair! The only solace, perhaps, is that God is with you and will not abandon you. This is *God's covenant:* "Be strong and courageous. Do not be afraid or terrified because of them, for the Lord your God goes with you; he will never leave you nor forsake you" (Deuteronomy 31:6).

Most communities, predictably, will "die by default" as a consequence of choosing the well-worn path of least resistance. Fear will be their primary driver, not faith or hope or love. Fear will be their downfall, preventing them from taking the types of bold actions required of transformation: fear of experimenting and failing, fear of losing financial security, fear of taking risks and jeopardizing their civic or canonical status, fear of the conflict and chaos and, ultimately, a fear of dying.

No matter what option you choose, to reconfigure, restructure, "die with dignity" or some other choice, you cannot go on as you have in the past. No matter what you choose to do at this point, there is hard work ahead that cannot be avoided. At a minimum, even if your choice is to shut down, someone will have to do the work involved. This work is time consuming, complex, expensive and painful. There is no avoiding it. The only question is: What path will you take and who will join you in the endeavor?

There are many options from which to choose but, absent your willingness to engage in the *inner work of transformation,* these will amount to little more than surface changes meant to ease the administrative burdens and make for a smoother path to completion. Those who do the inner work of transformation will have more success in generating new life than others who simply plan for organizational change.

Transformation offers hope for new life beyond the numbing narrative of "aging and diminishment" that is reinforced daily by what members are experiencing. Transformation is driven first by the urgent need for change, but ultimately impelled by a *deeper invitation,* a beckoning by the lure and love of God. Transformation requires deep, not incremental, change and a paradigmatic shift to a new level of consciousness. This, in turn, demands that communities take a different approach to planning, visioning and shaping their future than what they have used in the past. The different approach I am offering religious communities is to discern God's call to new life through what I call the *Journey of Transformation.*

Standing at a Graced Crossroads

> *"This is what the LORD says: 'Stand at the crossroads and look; and ask for the ancient paths, where the good way is; and walk in it, and find rest for your souls.'" Jeremiah 6:16*

When I have asked communities, "Do you a desire to transform and bring forth new life?" they invariably say, "Yes!" Unfortunately, the vast majority of communities, despite their enthusiasm, will not put forth the concrete resources, or exert the emotional grit and spiritual discipline needed to make the hard choices and transform their lives. They will not calendar the time, commit their money, or engage their members in the hard work required. They will choose, instead, the path of least resistance. Unwittingly, bit by bit, they will make choices driven more by fear than courage, choices that all but guarantee their demise.

Some communities, a smaller percentage, will discover and embrace the fullness of grace at these crossroads. They will recognize a deeper invitation by discerning God's call to new life and go all-in on a Journey of Transformation. This Journey of Transformation, as we will see, involves planning for the external, practical changes in community (e.g., finances, buildings, healthcare), but includes far more than these practical changes. It is an inward journey, as well, a pilgrimage through the dark night of the soul lured by the love of God. It is both a perilous and promising journey to be sure and only the most courageous communities will be able to embrace its fullness. However, for those who do, God's covenant of fidelity and promise of new life will not disappoint.

There are a great many things about the current status of Religious Life and its future prospects that are uncertain and hard to grasp. No one can predict an "unpicturable"[3] future. However, a few things have become very clear to me as a result of my work with communities around the globe. Here is what I know to be true for communities standing at a graced crossroads:

1. A bend in the road is not an end in the road, unless you fail to make the turn;

2. What got you to today, won't get you to tomorrow;

3. Adaptation and change are necessary but will not, by themselves, transform you;

4. There is, still, a deeper invitation; and,

5. The Divine Mystery of transformation is one in which we participate by cooperating with grace and the ongoing story of creation.

A bend in the road...

"When the way comes to an end, then change – having changed, you pass through." I Ching

Helen Keller once said, "A bend in the road is not an end in the road, unless you fail to make the turn." The vast majority of communities will fail to make the turn. Some will wait until it is too late and, by the time they wake up,

Do it too late for us?

they will have exhausted their resources and their will to change. Others will make only incremental changes, believing they are doing what's needed, only to discover their safe, small changes are not enough. And some of the most resilient communities will successfully make this bend in the road and bring forth new life. They will have a hand in birthing the future of Religious Life.

Communities who will not make the turn are those who will not respond soon enough or courageously enough. For some of these communities the urgency of the situation simply does not register. The parable of the boiling frog, while a bit graphic, drives the point home. They say that if you put a frog into a pot of boiling water, it will leap out right away to escape the danger. But, if you put a frog in a kettle that is filled with cool water, and then gradually heat the kettle until it starts boiling, the frog will not notice the threat until it is too late. The frog's survival instincts are wired to detect sudden, not gradual, changes. Apparently, the same is true for humans.

Changes occurring within religious communities are, for the most part, gradual. People die off, property is sold, and ministries are let go, a bit at a time. The gradual nature of these changes, however, reinforces the tendency to minimize or deny the cumulative impact. It makes it less likely for communities to take bold steps in order to adjust to what looks like minor changes. Yet, when facing this bend in the road, the riskiest choice of all is to make minor adjustments. It will be too little, too late and the end of the road for these communities.

Other communities are aware of the urgency, but their manner of coping gets the better of them. Some tell their members to look at all the good that is happening and stop all this talk about *aging and diminishment*. It's depressing. They are tired of it and they want to focus, instead, on the life and opportunities that exist. It's true, aging and diminishment will not be the narrative that rallies Religious Life. You need a *plan for life*, not death. However, whitewashing the impact of these hard realities – aging and diminishment – is also not a plan for life. It only leads to more suffering.

It is important to take a long, loving look at the real. The reality is that aging and diminishment are dramatically affecting the number of willing and able people available for leadership, boards, key ministry positions and active participation in the life of community. The bench is thinning out! The few, already *busy* people, are overwhelmed with responsibilities, yet are asked to take on even more. The changing demographics are affecting virtually every aspect of community: your finances and healthcare needs; vocation and formation efforts; utilization and maintenance of your land and buildings; your members' energy and capacity to plan and make wise decisions; as well as your mission and vision for the future. Avoid these realities and you will not make that bend in the road.

Other communities recognize the urgency; they see the bend in the road up ahead, but their fear gets the better of them. They will succumb to *paralysis by analysis*, and will continually search for more information, more clarity, and more assurances of success before acting. Others will close in on themselves, fearing their loss of independence and eschewing assistance from *outsiders* (laity or religious). The bend in the road is the end of the road for those who are unwilling to accept the reality of their circumstances and respond courageously.

What got you to today...

"Loyalty to a petrified opinion never yet broke a chain or freed a human soul." Mark Twain

What got you to today, won't get you to tomorrow. Your numbers alone won't permit it. While numbers are not the heart of the matter, it is obvious that life cannot continue as it has been in the past because of rapidly changing demographics. Imagine a very large round table upon which is placed everything about your life as a community: Your mission, along with individual, corporate and sponsored ministries; your life in community as members, leaders and other companions (e.g., associates); and, your stewardship responsibilities for your human, financial and material resources. Think of your healthcare needs, management of all your staff and employees, responsibilities on boards and toward all of your partners in mission. Think of all the land and buildings you own and manage. Visualize putting all of your life on the table.

Now imagine that each member of your community is standing around this large table holding up all of your life. Say the total load, if evenly dispersed, weighs around 25 pounds per person. Now imagine that every other person, half of your membership is gone from the table, as they will likely be in the next 10 years or so. Now how much does it weigh? The answer, obviously, is twice as much as before. Can you carry twice the load you are carrying today? Is your calendar half full? Most members and leaders I know are already over-worked. You simply cannot do in ten years what you are doing today, at least not in the same way you are doing it now. By the numbers alone, tomorrow has to be different than today.

Your members will be not only fewer, but also older with significantly less energy and cognitive capacity to do what they are doing now. Your capable people are no doubt already carrying a heavy load and will be spread too thin to handle it all in the years ahead. Increasingly, your buildings will be underutilized and more in need of maintenance. Your membership, because of aging, will need more healthcare. There will be fewer people to handle the current ministry responsibilities. You will have fewer members who are willing, able, electable and compatible to be in leadership. Your income from working members will be reduced. By these demographics alone, you will be forced to do life differently. Even if you wanted to stay the same, you cannot. What got you to today, will not get you to tomorrow.

Trying harder to get a few more vocations, even if successful, won't stem the enormous tide of diminishment. Downsizing to one less building, one less ministry, or one less person on a leadership team, won't resolve the strain, let alone open up new life for mission. Making more Chapter decrees to amend your Constitutions, study your vows, initiate a new ministry, or recruit vocations, when there is no one with the wherewithal to do all these things, will only be demoralizing. Meeting once a year as a total group and leaving the rest to leadership or committees doesn't work. Strategic planning using business-as-usual methods and mindsets won't get you to tomorrow.

Too many communities are looking at life in the rearview mirror, instead of looking forward toward the future. I have said before, "when communities have more memories than dreams, they are dying."[4] Focusing on your dreams of a future requires letting go of the past. You need to let die what needs to die in order to let live what wants to live. Communities need new approaches to transform their lives and plan for their future, and they need new mind-sets, heart-sets and skill-sets to implement them. "New wine is stored in new wine-skins so that both are preserved" (Matthew 9:17).

John Gardner once said, "The last act of a dying organization is to get out a new and enlarged edition of the rule book."[5] Communities that are dying tend to fall back on the old rules, not only their Constitutions and Directories, but that great big book of unwritten rules (i.e., "the way we've always done things"). The norms, the way things have always been done, the tried and true, may have worked in the past, but you'll need to risk experimenting with new approaches to pave the way toward a viable future.

Too often, when communities are facing the prospect of change, someone will stand up in defense of the past. They interpret any plea for something new as an implied condemnation of a failed past. They will defend their traditions, Constitutions, and prior leaders for their efforts. What happened in the past may have been successful, but assigning credit or blame is not the point. *Change is not an indictment of the past; it is simply its natural evolution.* The challenge is to learn from the past what is relevant for today and what might be a better approach for tomorrow. Stand upon the shoulders of those who came before you and honor their efforts by celebrating the past and creating a viable future. That's what all successful leaders do. That is what got you to today and that is what will help you get to tomorrow.

Adaptation is necessary, but...

> *"Consecrated persons therefore must keep themselves as intellectually open and as adaptable as possible, so that the apostolate will be envisaged and carried out according to the needs of their own time, making use of the means provided by cultural progress." Vita Consecrata*

The amount of change we will experience in the next 100 years is on track to exceed the change experienced in the entire human history. Our capacity to adapt to this accelerating rate of change is being greatly challenged. Trying harder doesn't work. We must become smarter and more agile in adapting to these changes.

David Wechsler developed the Wechsler Intelligence Tests for adults and children, the most widely used tests for measuring a person's IQ (Intelligence Quotient). His definition of a person's intelligence is the ability "to act purposefully, to think rationally and to deal effectively with his environment."[6] Essentially, the smarter a person is, the more effective is his or her capacity to adapt to the environment. Smarter communities will do the same and adapt to changing circumstances.

When was the last time you bought a book at Border Books or rented a video from Blockbuster? These companies failed to adapt to changing circumstances. Gone are the stalwart businesses that once were household names, such as: General Foods, TWA, Sears, Montgomery Ward, Woolworth and RCA. Gone are the darlings of Wall Street, such as Enron, Paine Webber, and E.F. Hutton (I guess people stopped listening). Even the famed Motor City, Detroit, filed for bankruptcy in 2013, the first large city in the United States to do so. Communities that survive will adapt to their changing circumstances and those that don't will not survive.

The window of opportunity is closing rapidly. It may be impossible to predict how long the larger transition might be for Religious Life but, for specific religious communities, it is more reasonable to calculate the amount of time remaining. With the life expectancy for men in the United States being 74, and for women 81, you do the math. If yours is a men's community, and the average age of your members is 70, how much time do you think you have left to adapt? If you are a women's community, and the average of your members is 80, how long do you think you have left? Whatever time you think you have left, cut it in half. Most groups overestimate the time available to them and wait too long to begin to act. Adapt now before it is too late!

What doesn't work

Adaptation is necessary, but how you adapt is key. The vast majority of communities will become extinct during this cycle of Religious Life because their efforts to adapt will be unsuccessful. Fortunately, there are identifiable reasons why their efforts are unsuccessful. Seven of the most common misguided efforts are:

1. **Make new improved versions of the past.** Just like the new improved versions of Tide or Crest, communities will make new improved version of themselves. They will attempt to do what they have always done, only better.

2. **Focus on external change, rather than the inner work.** Communities will focus on changing what's on the surface of their lives (e.g., buildings, finances, land, and ministries), and ignore what's underneath, the inner work of personal and interpersonal transformation.

3. **Try harder, not differently.** Communities will try harder to tighten their belts, reduce expenses, postpone retirement, downsize, rightsize, and repurpose buildings, hoping for a different outcome (Einstein's definition of insanity).

4. **Play it safe, rather than innovate.** They will play it safe, rather than innovate out of fear of making bad investments, losing their reputations, or experimenting and failing. As it turns out, playing it safe is the riskiest choice of all.

5. **Engage in incremental, rather than deep change.** Communities favor small changes in which the outcomes are predictable, conversations are manageable, and things are more controllable, rather than choose to engage in deep change.

6. **Avoid something bad, rather than create something good**. Fear drives communities to worry more about making mistakes, rather than focusing their attention and resources on innovating new possibilities.

7. **Download the same information, rather than create a new operating system**. Communities will download the same information using the same operating system, rather than create a new operating system. Without a transformation of consciousness (new wineskins), no truly novel possibilities will emerge.

Communities must adapt, rather than persist in doing more of the same. Purposeful, rational and effective adaptation is a necessary part of forging a future. It is necessary but insufficient, *if* your desire is to also transform. There is, still, a deeper invitation.

A deeper invitation

"Therefore, I am now going to allure her; I will lead her into the wilderness and speak tenderly to her." Hosea 2:14

We have all been here in our adult lives, at least once: Alcoholics Anonymous calls it "hitting bottom," the point at which we are forced to admit that there is a grave problem and we need to reach out for help. It is not a time to throw in the towel, but a recognition that, alone, we are not enough to bring about our own healing or path to the future. People of a Christian faith might call this a "come-to-Jesus" moment. For communities, as in our personal lives, this can be a *graced crossroads.*

As painful as it is, once we finally hit bottom, there is a feeling of liberation and relief. We can stop fighting and *let Jesus take the wheel.* We are released from all the unnecessary suffering that comes from denying our suffering, fighting against it, resenting it, or blaming ourselves and others for it. When we hit bottom, we let go of all the exhausting and futile attempts to cling to what is not working, and we finally accept the hand we have been dealt. We begin to ask questions for which there are no immediate answers but for which answers must be found.

With our denial gone, we can begin to listen and search for these answers. We can begin to hear that still, small voice (1 Kings 19:11-13). The Celtics call this a "thin" time or place where the veil between the two worlds of heaven and earth is thin. Christine Paintner, in *The Soul's Slow Ripening,* calls this a "threshold time," when we are moving from one time and one awareness to another. It is a place, says Paintner, where we can make "deeper connections with the divine."[7]

A graced crossroads, as I call it, is a place in which we must let die what needs to die in order to let live what wants to live. It is a place wherein God continually puts before us choices between life and death. God urges us, lures us, summons us to choose life, but these choices are always ours to make. There is a poignant awareness that whatever choices we make will be life-altering. Our lives will never be the same from this point forward. Here, in the agony of our own Gethsemane, there is a profound awareness that we are not alone. Jesus, God, or whoever is your Higher Power, is accompanying us. The crossroads is a holy place, a thin place where grace does more abound (Romans 5:20).

Grace flourishes in every nook and cranny of creation, but never are we more aware of its presence and amenable to its ways than when we are at such a crossroads. Grace comes bidden and unbidden, whether we are aware of it or not. When we arrive at a crossroads, the pain we must endure hollows us out. We are emptied of all hubris and stripped of our defenses. It is here, in the deep quiet of our own soul's searching, that we come face to face with those parts of ourselves we have rejected, hidden from ourselves and those we loved. It is here, at the crossroads, that grace works its way into every nook and cranny of our being.

A graced crossroads, while it is a painful place to be, is simultaneously a profoundly freeing place to be, a place of refuge. "Come to Me, all you who are weary and burdened, and I will give you rest. Take My yoke upon you and learn from Me; for I am gentle and humble in heart, and you will find rest for your souls. For My yoke is easy and My burden is light" (Matthew 11:28-30). At the graced crossroads, we gladly take the yoke. It is easy. It is liberating to let go of exhausting and futile attempts to cling to what is not working, to control what is outside of our control, and to deny, blame and shame ourselves and others for our suffering. It is freeing to finally accept the truth, however painful it might be (John 8:32).

Religious communities are now at a graced crossroads. It is a thin time, a liminal time, a threshold between what was and what is yet to come. Here, at these graced crossroads, is a *deeper invitation*: "Today I have given you the choice between life and death, between blessings and curses. Now I call on heaven and earth to witness the choice you make. Oh, that you would choose life, so that you and your descendants might live!" (Deuteronomy 30:19).

Choose life so that your descendants might live. *Choose life* so that you might live more fully in whatever time you have left. *Choose life* so that you might have a hand in the transformation of Religious Life and our planet through the reign of Love, Mercy and Justice.

The Divine Mystery and Cooperation with Grace

"Love doesn't just sit there, like a stone; it has to be made,
like bread; remade all the time, made new." Anonymous

If your community is listening for a deeper invitation and discovers a yearning to choose life, the question becomes: What does *new life* mean, and how can you transform your lives in order to give birth to it? How do you walk through this divine paschal mystery together? Ronald Rolheiser describes the process well in in his book, *The Holy Longing*: "The paschal mystery… is a process of transformation within which we are given both new life and new spirit. It begins with suffering and death, moves on to the reception of new life, spends some time grieving the old and adjusting to the new, and finally, only after the old life has been truly let go of, is a new spirit given for the life we are already living."[8]

In so far as the workings of grace is concerned, the Divine Mystery of transformation may be beyond our comprehension, but it surely does not happen without our active participation. Sitting in a prison cell, a young Martin Luther King, Jr. wrote that, "Human progress never rolls on the wheels of inevitability; it comes through the tireless efforts of men willing to be co-workers with God."[9] You can either try to plan your future or create the conditions for grace to intercede. To do the former, you must presume to know what the future is. To do the latter, you need to learn how to cooperate with grace and do the inner work of transformation.

Dynamic elements of transformation

In my work with men and women religious across different cultures, both individually and congregationally, I have come to identify five dynamic elements that are key to cooperating with grace and doing the inner work of transformation. As I will describe throughout this book, these elements are supported by our faith traditions, life experiences, and by contemporary studies on personal, interpersonal, and organizational transformation. These are:

1. **Shifts in consciousness: creating a new narrative**

2. **Reclaiming our inner voice: the seat and source of everything that lives**

3. **Reconciliation and conversion: the womb of our becoming**

4. **Experimentation and learning: acting our way into a new way of being**

5. **Transformative visioning: gather the wisdom, weave a dream**

The key here is in *integrating* the inner work of transformation (these dynamic elements) with the outer work of organizational change. In other words, the conventional methods, like strategic planning, which of course are needed to set goals, objectives, timelines and budgets, must be integrated with processes that engage members in the inner work of transformation.

Bottom line: While you must plan and adapt, *you cannot plan your way through transformation*. It is, at its core, a faith journey. It is not a *heady* experience. It is a visceral and holy experience requiring a willingness to embrace the paschal mystery of life, death, resurrection and new life – not just in theory but in practice. And, although prayers are needed, *you cannot only pray your way through transformation*.

For a community to create the conditions for grace to intercede, it will need to do the personal, interpersonal and organizational work of transformation. Admittedly, the personal and communal work of transformation are far more delicate and difficult than organizational change. It's easier to talk about money, ministries, buildings and healthcare, than it is to address directly and comprehensively the challenges of community living. Yet, members, and the communities they create, are the glue that holds it all together. If there is no concentrated focus upon personal and communal transformation, *what will you have, and who will you be, at the end of all your organizational changes*?

How can you be sure that if you engage in all this work, you will get what you want in the end? Sorry, there are no guarantees. I will describe for you what this journey involves, how you might stumble, what it asks of you, how you can improve your odds of success and what you might get out of it. However, there are never any guarantees as to what comes from this kind of pilgrimage. You never know ahead of time where a passage through the dark night will lead. Ultimately, this kind of journey is always a leap of faith. The Journey of Transformation is an ongoing journey of faith that continually places before you the choices between life and death.

Love pulls us through

It is pain that brings us to a graced crossroads, but it is Love that pulls us through. I do not know of any individual or community that can succeed in this kind of work without the profound lure of love. Why else would anyone go through such an ordeal? And never are we so lured than when we, and the relationships that matter to us, are broken and we are brought to our knees. No longer able to stand on our own two feet, we hear more clearly a deeper invitation: "I am going to lure her and lead her out into the wilderness and speak to her heart" (Hosea 2:14). It is by the luring love of God, your community, its mission and your yearning to make things whole again that you will gain the strength to step further into the spiral of transformation.

What *pushes* communities are realities they can no longer escape. For most, it is the diminishing numbers, advancing age, the maintenance responsibilities that cast a larger and larger shadow over mission. What pushes most is the fact that funerals outnumber new vocations 20 to 1, that the pool of willing and able members available for leadership is shrinking, that they have more building space and property than is utilizable or justifiable. What pushes them is the brokenness so many have named over and over and the pain that cries out for healing.

What beckons communities toward life and spurs them on is their faith in the great mystery of life, death and resurrection. At a crossroads, you are invited to surrender to the ultimate of all tests of faith – the paschal mystery. You know deep down inside that in order to be made whole again, real again, you must let die what needs to die. In order to choose life, you must let go of what no longer gives life. You must let go of the treasured people, places, practices, mindsets, ministries and institutions you were once called to embrace because they were life giving, but now no longer are.

Forces of death that seduce us

Yet, amid all the forces that push and lure us toward life, there are forces of death, fear and doubt that seduce us toward a path of least resistance, a choice for *death by default*. We play hide and seek with the truth we know could set us free. When push comes to shove, we have a thousand reasons to justify our avoidance of painful truths, uncomfortable experiences and hard choices. Without efforts to counter it, entropy takes over and we gravitate toward the path of least resistance. Instead of doing the hard work we know is required, we say, "We're too old, too few, too poor, too busy, too tired, too set in our ways," too whatever to change. We wait, equivocate and postpone until the slippery slope of a weakening resolve carries us to inertia.

We start enthusiastically and quickly grow weary when more tangible results do not come quickly enough or coincide with what we thought we would get from all our hard work. We want immediate results, progress we can measure, quick relief, and are seduced by easy, less costly solutions. And yet we know that transformation is a lifelong marathon, not a sprint. We know from our past efforts that the work of deep change is slow in coming, onerous and tiring.[10]

Graced crossroads is a thin place where we come face-to-face with choices between life and death. It is the place to which we are lured by the forces of life and seduced by the forces of death. It is where we struggle to say "yes" to a deeper invitation or maintain our illusions of independence, power and control. Yet, it is in this very struggle that we are transformed. It is in this struggle that we can learn to cooperate with grace and find our way home. Thomas Merton tells us that "grace is granted us in proportion as we dispose ourselves to receive it by the interior activity of the theological virtues: faith, hope, charity."[11] We have only to create the conditions for grace to intercede and dispose ourselves to receive it.

The Journey of Transformation is for communities who are courageous enough to listen and respond to a deeper invitation at their own graced crossroads. Transformation is not something we can engineer or bootstrap ourselves into accomplishing. However, we can participate in this Divine Mystery by cooperating with grace and doing our own inner work. Communities who participate in these ways will have the opportunity to not only transform themselves but will help to transform Religious Life and our world. They will put their mark on this Great Turning and add a meaningful page to the ongoing story of creation.

CHAPTER 2: THE WORLD IN WHICH WE LIVE

Who are you called to become?

"Humans have a responsibility to find themselves where they are, in their own proper time and place in the history to which they belong and to which they must inevitably contribute either their response or their evasions, either truth and act, or mere slogan and gesture."
Thomas Merton

Introduction

Religious Life has gone through many evolutionary cycles, each time transforming itself in response to the dual forces of *external* societal changes and changes from *within* Religious Life itself. This chapter focuses upon the external changes, the Great Turning taking place across the globe. This is the medium through which Religious Life is now evolving. The world in which we live is not just the context for Religious Life, it is the ground from which it springs and the object of all its endeavors. As Ilia Delio once said, "Creation is not a backdrop for human drama but the disclosure of God's identity."[12]

Understanding the rapid nature of change which our planetary home is experiencing is key to understanding the transformation of Religious Life, its evolving identity and relevancy for our world, and its mark in the ongoing story of creation. Communities who are responsive to, and evolve with, these changing societal needs will transform and become increasingly relevant. Those communities who continue to see and respond to the world as they have in the past, will become irrelevant and cease to exist.

We will begin this chapter exploring the accelerating rate of change and five global trends contributing to this Great Turning. I will invite your reflections on each of these with a refrain of sorts: *So what? Now What?* In other words, what difference, if any, does understanding these *signs of the times* actually make for you and your community? And, given these signs of the times, what different choices, if any, might you and your community now want to make?

Because each community is embedded within its own environmental circumstances, I will not attempt to describe every trend across the various locales in the United States. I will leave it to each community to further reflect upon the trends within your own civic community. Such a critical analysis of your local signs of the times would add greatly to your collective discernment regarding what different choices your community might want to make.

After reflecting upon the world in which we live, we will return to the big picture, the Great Turning. I will then invite you to go further in your reflections: Does the way you understand your *presence* and *partnership* in the world, and, therefore, the way you serve the world, need to change or transform? Or, is the path you are on precisely the path you need to be on for as long as you possibly can? Who are you called to become?

A Great Turning

> *"When the stories a society shares are out of tune with its circumstance, they can become self-limiting, even a threat to survival. That is our current situation."*
> *David Korten*

There is a Great Turning taking place across our planetary home. Do you perceive it? Al Gore, Barbara Marx Hubbard, John Haught, Ilia Delio, Pope Francis, and many other luminaries tell us that we are on the brink of a sixth great extinction of our planet, an existential, evolutionary crisis in which our species will either evolve into a new consciousness and a new way of being, or devolve into an abyss of death and destruction.

Scientists and futurists agree. We are at a tipping point. Our globe has gone through five mass extinctions in its 4.5 billion year history and we are facing a sixth. According to Al Gore: "There is no prior period of change that remotely resembles what humanity is about to experience."[13] We are experiencing it now! Of the 45 million centuries, this one is different. Previously, it was asteroids and earthquakes, but now it is our species leading the planet to the brink of an abyss, and it will be our species that will determine its fate.

Brian Swimme tells us: "The future of Earth's community rests in significant ways upon the decisions to be made by the humans who have inserted themselves so deeply into even the genetic codes of Earth's process."[14] What role will Religious Life, your community, and you have to play in all of this, and who do you choose to be in the midst of it? Between "fake news," "alternative facts" and "parallel universes," how can you even read the signs of the times with any clarity? Truths and untruths all seem to have the same authority. There is a cloud of confusion swirling among these truths and untruths, and it is up to each one of us to sort it out.

The Future is Arriving at Warp Speed

"We are living in the greatest revolution in history, a huge, spontaneous upheaval of the entire human race. Not a revolution planned and carried out by any particular party, race or nation, but a deep elemental boiling over of all the inner contradictions that have ever been in people, a revolution of the chaotic forces inside everybody. This is not something we have chosen, nor is it anything we are free to avoid." Thomas Merton

It took 400 years from the innovation of the printing press to the first billion books in print. It took only 12 years from the innovation of cell phones to reach 1 billion subscribers.[15] The future is arriving at warp speed and outpacing our capacity to adapt and cope. Throughout human history, the future arrived at a relatively slow pace, giving us time to adapt and change. Only in the last century has this change exceeded our capacity to cope. This is challenging all of us to find new ways to cope, adapt and participate in shaping our future.

The rate of change in our world is truly mind-boggling. According to Eric Schmidt, CEO of Google, from the beginnings of human civilization until 2003, five exabytes of data were amassed and we are now creating five exabytes of data every two days![16] By the way, an exabyte is 1,000,000,000,000,000,000 bytes of information. He made that statement way back in 2010, so imagine what we are accumulating now. According to Moore's Law,[ii] our world's computer capacity doubles every 18 months. You do the math (I can't).

It is astounding to contemplate the exponentially accelerating rate of change. A generation ago, my father worked at Remington Rand on Park Avenue in New York. At that time, in the 1950s, Remington Rand was home to one of the most cutting-edge mainframe computers, one that took up an entire room. Now, a smartphone we can hold in the palm of our hand has more capacity than the computers that sent Apollo 13 to the moon. According to Ed Stone, smartphones today have computers with over 240,000 times the memory, and 100,000 times more speed than the computers on the Voyager spacecraft launched in 1977.[17]

We not only have smart phones, but smart homes. Three years ago, my wife and I got a Roomba that can vacuum our floors when we are sleeping and neatly tuck itself back in its storage module before we wake up. Two years ago, our daughter gave us Alexa for Christmas, a computerized personal assistant who does whatever we ask, while talking to us in a calm, melodious voice. She can tell us the weather, sports scores, and anything else we might find on the internet. She can play music, read us stories and tell us jokes. She can turn our lights on, dim them, or turn them off, lock and unlock our doors, and manage

---

ii Moore's law, put forth by Gordon Moore in 1965, originally suggested that computer capacity would double every two years. This was later adjusted to every 18 months and has been validated over the years.

our heating and cooling. She can start our car and send it a google map of our upcoming trip – all of this, at our beck and call.

We have smart cars, as well, that can talk to one another and drive themselves. There are already 2.5 million self-driving cars on the road. Five years from now, driverless cars will be standard fare. Much of the technology is already available in cars. My car can park itself and stay in its own lane, free from my having to steer it. With adaptive cruise control, it can track the car in front of me, accelerate, hold its speed, decelerate or stop itself, all hands and foot-free. If I fail to stop when a car, person or animal darts in front of me, it will take over and stop the car for me. With the push of a little blue button, I can access a person (who resides in the cloud) who will download directions for me, order tickets to the ball game and make dinner reservations, all at my verbal request. Ready or not, flying cars are now being tested for urban air travel in Germany, Japan and the United States!

We have virtual worlds complete with virtual glasses and avatars. Maybe you saw the ad showing a woman wearing virtual glasses gyrating on the couch while she took a virtual rollercoaster ride. No need to go to the mall or surgery center when you can have virtual shopping from your couch and virtual robotic surgery done in a remote location. We have virtual boardrooms, class-rooms, businesses and communities. We have refrigerators that can order food and drones that will deliver it. We have 3D printers that can make anything from manufacturing and building materials to bandages, guns and body parts.

Quantum computers can solve certain problems in a few milliseconds that, just a short time ago, it would have taken the fastest supercomputer millions of years to calculate. They have the potential to create new materials and medicines, as well as solve long-standing scientific and financial problems. If you don't understand the technical aspects of quantum computers, not to worry. Most mere mortals don't. The bottom line is this: quantum comput-ers are more powerful than anything built to date and will further escalate the already mind-boggling speed with which the future is arriving. Can you perceive it? Imagine it? Does it matter?

The Future Arrives through Chaos

The changes occurring in our world are not only accelerating exponentially, they are becoming much more volatile and harder to predict. Novelty is the new normal, not more of the same. Yet, we are not programed to see novelty. We are programed to see what *has been, and* what we are used to seeing, making the future very hard for us to imagine, let alone predict. Yet it is precisely the unlikely, unpredictable and unimaginable that shapes our future. Nassim Taleb dubbed this phenomenon the "black swan:"

> "Our world is dominated by the extreme, the unknown, and the very improbable (improbable according to our current knowledge) – and all the while we spend our time engaged in small talk, focusing on the known, and the repeated. This implies the need to use the extreme event as the starting point and not treat it as an exception to be pushed under the rug…. the future will be increasingly less predictable, while both human nature and social 'science' seem to conspire to hide the idea from us."[18]

We are programed, in other words, to believe that black swans do not exist. Taleb suggests that the computer, internet, and laser were all examples of black swans. "All three were unplanned, unpredicted and unappreciated upon their discovery, and remained unappreciated well after their initial use."[19] The reasons black swans are so hard to see are the same reasons it was so hard to see and prevent from happening 9/11, Pearl Harbor, or the financial market collapse of 2008. Even though we had the information, we could not connect the dots. We expect to see in the future what we've always seen in the past.

Yogi Berra once quipped, "It's tough to make predictions, especially about the future" and he was right. In 1973, a Princeton University professor, Burton Malkiel claimed that a blindfolded monkey throwing darts at the financial pages of the newspaper could select a portfolio that would do just as well as one carefully selected by the experts.[20] He was wrong. The monkeys consistently did far better than the experts! The finding came from studies simulating the comparison of brokers' predictions to those of monkeys from 1964 to 2010. Monkeys randomly threw darts onto the stock listings. They then compared the monkeys' random picks to those of the brokers. Despite (or more likely, because of) the brokers' vast knowledge and experience, the monkeys consistently outperformed the experts.

No longer is our world dominated by the predictable forces of the few dominant nations or companies. The hierarchical power structures of companies and nations, alike, are being toppled by the internet and social media. As a result, the world is more chaotic than it has ever been. When Thomas Friedman wrote his best-selling book, *The World is Flat*,[21] he described a world of globalized interdependence, wherein everyone is now on a level playing field. Everyone has access to the world's knowledge and can compete in the global market place, largely because of the internet. The world is flattening out.

Chris Anderson, in his book, *The Long Tail*,[22] describes today's world as having a global marketplace with a long tail, no longer dominated by only a few. He sees the long tail as a much larger share of the market, one that is more accessible by means of the internet, and one that spawns endless niche markets. This shift from the dominant few to the markets of many allows for greater diversity. It has also upended the status quo and added to the market chaos.

Future shock

When Alvin Toffler wrote *Future Shock* nearly 50 years ago, he predicted that the technology of the future would be a revolutionary sea change that would shock, disorient, and fragment our society. The revolutionary shift from the Industrial Age to the Information Age has been chaotic. Attempting to navigate these volatile times is like rowing a dingy through a hurricane with the ferocious winds blowing through the financial markets, the tumult of terrorism and the frightening effects of climate change.

The impact of this rapid change and chaos is shocking, especially to those who struggle with change and who thrive on familiarity – in other words, most of us. According to Daryl Conner, "future shock" is here. Conner defines future shock as "the point at which humans can no longer assimilate change without displaying dysfunctional behavior."[23] In other words, we become less effective in our work and less able to function in our personal lives. Among Conner's long list of symptoms of future shock were these:

- Poor communication and mistrust;

- Reduced directness and honesty;

- Increased defensiveness, blame and conflict;

- Reduced propensity for risk-taking and poor decision-making;

- Low morale, apathy, and resignation;

- Non-compliance and undermining of leadership;

- Feelings of victimization and disempowerment;

- Psychological and physical distress.

Conner believes that we are like sponges absorbing the enormous stress of the world. Most of us will not cope well, but some of us will. He earmarks five basic characteristics of "resilient" people and organizations. The ones most capable of handling the rapid pace of disruptive change are:

1. Positive: Displaying a sense of security and self-assurance;

2. Focused: Having a clear vision of what they want to achieve;

3. Flexible: Demonstrating pliability amidst uncertainty;

4. Organized: Using structured approaches to ambiguity;

5. Proactive: Engaging change, rather than defending against it.[24]

Reflection: The Accelerating Rate of Change

---

1. *How are you affected by the rapid speed and chaos of change? What symptoms of future shock from Conner's list are you and your community experiencing?*

2. *What characteristics of resiliency do you and your community seem to possess? To what degree are you and your community coping with, and adapting to, the speed and chaos of change?*

Five Drivers of Global Change

"No founding or refounding can succeed if it is divorced from its environmental context. For today's refounding attempts to succeed, therefore, the leaders and member-ship of religious congregations must know which trends in the surrounding society are likely to support or hinder their efforts." Patricia Wittberg

Chaos theory tells us that there is not one future out there, but multiple, unpre-dictable futures.Don't throw up your hands just yet. As unpredictable as the future might be, there are a handful of discernable trends. Amidst the chaos and information overload, there are some macro trends that might inform our future. Amy Webb describes how the trending signals are talking to us:

"The future doesn't simply arrive fully formed over night, but emerges step by step. It first appears at seemingly random points around the fringe of society, never in the mainstream. Without context, those points can appear disparate, unre-lated, and hard to connect meaningfully. But over time they fit into patterns and come into focus as a full-blown trend: a convergence of multiple points that reveal a direction or tendency, a force that combines some human need and new enabling technology that will shape the future [25]

Those who take the long view, like Amy Webb, Thomas Friedman, Al Gore, Peter Senge, Barbara Marx Hubbard, Pope Francis and others, have identified a handful of trends that are likely to have the greatest impact upon our globe in the coming years. There is remarkable convergence among these scientific, religious, political and business leaders. Here are five of the most important trends impacting our globe in the near future:

1. Environment and climate change;
2. Our interconnected world;
3. Demographic shifts and inequalities;
4. Revolutionary technology; and,

5.   Power and violence.

1.   Environment and climate change

"It was a spring without voices. On the mornings that had once throbbed with the dawn chorus of robins, catbirds, doves, jays, wrens, and scores of other bird voices there was now no sound; only silence lay over the fields and woods and marsh." Rachel Carson

My first awakening to the notion of climate change and damage to our environment came during biology class my sophomore year in high school. On the first day of class, the teacher handed each of us a copy of Rachel Carson's *Silent Spring*[26] as our first reading assignment. Carson vividly detailed a dystopian view of the future based upon the impact of pesticides and pollutants. It was a poignant and prescient glimpse into the future. Published in 1965, the political backlash was enormous and unrelenting. The struggle between environmentalists, who seek sustainability, and corporations, who work to gain profits at the expense of the environment, has only intensified and continues to this day.

The combination of rapid, unsustainable growth in our population, resource consumption, depletion of topsoil and freshwater supplies, as well as pollution, is putting our globe at risk. Here are just a handful of examples:

- We consume over 100 billion tons of raw materials per year, more than 90% is waste, equaling 1 ton of waste per person, per day, most of which is dumped into lakes, rivers, oceans or soil;
- More than 20% of the world has no access to clean drinking water;
- 70% of the fisheries are overfished;
- More than 1/3 of the forests have been destroyed in last 50 years;
- Over half of the wetlands have disappeared in the last 100 years;
- Overproduction of farmland has resulted in 2.5 billion acres of degraded soil in the last 100 years;

- CO_2 levels are 1/3 higher than they have been in the last 650,000 years.[27]

In the late 1970s, Love Canal (near Niagara Falls) gained national notoriety for the public health problem originating from the disposal of 22,000 barrels of toxic waste. In 2000, the Academy Award winning film, *Erin Brockovich,* reawakened people to the corrupt and damaging practices certain corporations have on our environment and human safety. Erin Brockovich, despite her lack of legal education, became instrumental in building a case against the Pacific Gas and Electric Company. The governing officials of Flint, Michigan came under fire for exposing thousands of its citizens to lead poisoning as a result of using contaminated water. Most recently, Time Magazine's 2019 Person of the Year, 16-year-old Greta Thunberg brought renewed attention to our climate crisis.

Despite the fact that over 97% of the world's scientists have warned of the catastrophic effects of climate change, and 84% of them attribute this to human practices, skepticism abounds, particularly among those with a vested interest in our fossil-fuel dependent economy. According to Pew Research, a global median of 51% say climate change is already harming people around the world. However, those countries with the greatest emissions of carbon dioxide; namely, the United States and China, have the least concern.[28]

Reflection: Environment and Climate Change

---

1. *How are you and your community being affected by climate change? What impact is it having on your way of living and your environment?*

2. *In what ways are you and your community conforming to the challenges of these trends (i.e., becoming drawn into them) versus transforming these challenges (i.e., demonstrating an alternative way of being in our world or harnessing the potential power of these global trends and helping to shape it constructively)?*

2. Our interconnected world

Global connectivity has been evolving ever since travelers ventured beyond their local villages and brought back new goods, technologies, and arts, as well as ways of understanding ourselves and the world in which we live. Thomas Friedman describes three of the more recent Great Turnings in our globalized world:

- **Globalization 1.0** lasted from when Columbus came to the new world in 1492, until about 1800. This was the age where human muscle was augmented by wind, steam and horsepower and where nations (often inspired by religions) led the way in breaking down walls.

- **Globalization 2.0** lasted from roughly 1800 to 2000. The driving forces of globalization that shrank the world from medium to small during this era were multinational companies. These railroad, telephone, computer and fiberoptic companies moved the world through the Industrial Revolution toward a mature global economy.

- **Globalization 3.0** began in 2000 and continues to this day. The driving forces that shrank the world from small to tiny, and leveled the playing field, were the software and hardware that made it possible for individuals to compete and collaborate globally.[29]

It is only when Microsoft came out with Windows III in 1995 that ordinary persons had access to a nascent World Wide Web. This was a game-changer that literally opened windows to the world. It put the world's knowledge at the fingertips of everyone who had access to a computer. For example, the Library of Congress is the largest library in the world, holding some 32 million books (of the 130 million books in existence across the globe).[30] The Internet, by contrast, is estimated to have around 5 zettabytes of information (or 4 X 1022 bits),[31] and nearly every byte of it is available to most people on the planet.

Although not everyone is connected, we are close to having a planet-wide electronic communications grid. We are using drones, satellites and lasers to deliver the internet to everyone. Even now in 2020, there are, on average,

80 billion connected devices and 5 billion people surfing the internet. It won't be long before every one of the world's 7.5 billion people have access to the internet.

Nearly a century ago, Teilhard de Chardin introduced the idea of the "noosphere" to describe what he believed to be a global consciousness. He was convinced that the next evolutionary leap in humanity was the development of an interconnected web of consciousness, linking the minds, hearts and souls of every human being together. He introduced this idea nearly a half century before the internet became a reality. His ethereal noosphere – a superhuman, evolutionary consciousness – is now a virtual reality.

Remember the New Year's celebration across the globe in 2,000 and the planetary euphoria that erupted? Remember the 2008 United States market crash that sent markets plunging around the world? From the Arab Spring uprising in 2011 to the 2016 Russian hacking of the DNC, our interconnected world is our inescapable new normal. Social media quickly amplifies human events in one part of the planet and, if they go viral, they reverberate around the globe. Twitter, Facebook, Snapchat, Pinterest, and the like, are all part of our global nervous system.

For good or for bad (and there is plenty of both), we are now living in an interconnected, if not hyperconnected, world. More than ever before in history, our fates are linked together politically, economically, socially and spiritually, as well as through science and technology. While there will be enormous resistance (e.g., attempts to build walls; efforts to unilaterally control and exploit parts of the globe; jingoistic warfare of all kinds), there will be no stopping this massive trend toward greater connectivity, collaboration and interdependence. As many have suggested when reflecting upon our Great Turning: We will either all hang together, or we will all hang separately.

Reflection: Our Interconnected World

---

1. *How are you and your community being affected by this trend toward greater interconnectivity (e.g., opening your boundaries and partnering with others)? What impact is it having, good and bad, on your way of living and ministering?*

2. *In what ways are you and your community conforming to the challenges of these trends (i.e., becoming drawn into them) versus transforming these challenges (i.e., demonstrating an alternative way of being in our world or harnessing the potential power of these global trends and helping to shape it constructively)?*

3. Demographic shifts and inequalities

"The future is already here – it's just not evenly distributed."
William Gibson

There are approximately 7.5 billion people on the earth today, 6.5 percent of the roughly 108 billion humans that ever existed on the earth. Only 200 years ago, there were a mere 1 billion. In the 20th century alone our global population grew from 1.5 billion to 6.1 billion. Every day, across the globe, there are 360 million births and 150 million deaths. The rate of growth has slowed over the last 50 years and is projected to level off. Even so, by 2050 the earth's population will be close to 10 billion!

Taking the long view, we are much better off as a species than we were in previous centuries. On average, based upon life expectancy and child mortality rates, we are living longer and are much healthier than in previous centuries. In 1800, no country had a life expectancy over 40 years of age and today it has nearly doubled. While there is global convergence toward greater life expectancy, there is inequality as these shifts vary greatly across nations. For example, a century ago the life expectancy in South Korea and India was only around 23 and now it has tripled or quadrupled. Those in sub-Saharan Africa still only live as long as 50 years of age, while life expectancy in the United States is 79 and Japan is up to 80.[32]

In the last one hundred years, maternal mortality rates are down from 500-1000 deaths per 100,000 to around 10. Child mortality rates are down from premodern times of 300-500 deaths per 1,000 births to below 5 per 1,000 in industrialized countries. Deaths due to disease, disability, war and famine are all down. Again, while these are averages across the globe, the inequality across nations persists and is largely attributed to the disparities in financial wealth of countries.

It is no surprise that countries spending more on healthcare tend to have a higher life expectancy, although this reaches a point of diminishing returns. Health care expenditures have grown enormously over the last 100 years and are projected to continue to grow, albeit at a slower rate. Bottom line, countries with greater overall wealth have greater overall health.

There is a demographic shift of the balance between young and old. The older population is the fastest growing demographic segment. By 2050, there will be twice as many older citizens than children. In the United States, between 2003 and 2013, the 65+ population increased from 35.9 million to 44.7 million. By 2060, this number is expected to reach 98 million. The "silver tsunami" will result in tremendous demands on healthcare, especially dementia care, on a smaller working-age population.

Today, 244 million people live outside of their birth countries—three times the rate in 1960. If the world's migrant population lived as one country, it would rank as the fifth largest country in the world. Migrants and refugees from Africa and the Middle East continue to arrive in Europe in unprecedented numbers. Those from Latin American continue to come to the United States and Canada. Forecasts suggest that this large-scale migration from poor countries to richer regions will continue as a trend for the foreseeable future. Jim Yong Kim as President of the World Bank Group, said:

> "With the right set of policies, this era of demographic change can be an engine of economic growth. If countries with aging populations can create a path for refugees and migrants to participate in the economy, everyone benefits.

> Most of the evidence suggests that migrants will work hard
> and contribute more in taxes than they consume in social
> services."[33]

It's estimated that 40 percent of the global population could be African by 2100. Increasingly, Africans will leave their continent. As they migrate throughout the world, they will take their churches and religious practices with them, greatly influencing the spread of faith. African churches are thriving in Europe, leading four of the largest megachurches in Britain. Houston is home to at least 25 African churches.

Poverty levels, on average, have also gone down across the globe as these are highly correlated with health, life expectancy and education. According to the World Bank, as of 2015, a person is considered to live in extreme poverty if he or she is living on less than 1.90 international-dollars per day. While the percentage of the population living in extreme poverty has gone down, the absolute numbers, due to population growth, have remained steady for the past three decades.

Prior to the Industrial Revolution, most of the globe (85 to 90%) lived in absolute poverty. This changed dramatically in the last 200 years, especially in the last 30 years. Currently, about 10% of the global population lives below the poverty line. More than 90% of global poverty is concentrated in lower-income countries with young, fast-growing populations who will have an increased number of working-age people. At the same time, more than 75% of global growth comes from higher-income countries with rising numbers of elderly and fewer working-age people. These aging countries will need to boost their social safety nets.

The gap between the rich and poor is widening among advanced economies, while mixed among developing countries. President Obama referred to the widening income inequality as the "defining challenge of our time" and Pope Francis has frequently challenged the "economy of exclusion." Beyond the moral unfairness of it all, income disparity dampens overall growth and causes social unrest.

Almost half of the world's wealth is now owned by just 1 percent of the population. During the July 25, 2016 Democratic National Convention, Bernie Sanders said, "It is not moral, it is not acceptable, and it is not sustainable that the top one-tenth of one percent now owns almost as much wealth as the bottom 90 percent." It is true that America has more income inequality (twice as much) than any other developed country. The top 0.1 percent of people in the U.S. takes in over 184 times the income of the bottom 90 percent.

Reflection: Demographic Shifts and Inequalities

---

1. *How are you and your community being affected by these global demographic shifts and inequalities? What impact is this having, good and bad, on your way of living and ministering?*

2. *In what ways are you and your community conforming to the challenges of these trends (i.e., becoming drawn into them) versus transforming these challenges (i.e., modeling an alternative way of being in our world or harnessing the potential power of these global trends and helping to shape it constructively)?*

4. Revolutionary technology

Aside from Alexa, Roomba and self-driving cars, things will get even more exciting in just a few years. Robots, nanotechnology, biotechnology, and machines that learn from one another, even feel and create art, are realities shaping our future. Just a few years ago, the emergence of this technology was hard to imagine. It is still hard to fathom.

Nearly half of the working class, and even technology professionals, expect their jobs to be automated within ten years. We are educating our children today for jobs that don't even exist, nor can we imagine what they will be in 10 or 20 years. According to Sir Ken Robinson, a distinguished educator and author, we have an "education crisis" that is equal to or greater than our "climate crisis."[34] Our educational systems teach children how to regurgitate information on tests, but are unable to teach children how to think, feel, problem-solve, resolve conflicts, and create, the very skills needed to adapt to our changing world and meet the challenges of tomorrow.

By the 2030's we will have *hybrid thinking*. Our thinking will be a hybrid of biological and non-biological thinking. We'll have nanobots that will connect our neocortex to a "synthetic neocortex" in the cloud. In other words, our brains will have direct access to billions of computer modules on the internet. Would you like to know how many bytes in a zettabyte? No need to Google it, your brain can just connect to the cloud and you'll know.[35] The bionic man and woman are becoming a reality.

We don't recognize it as such, but we are living in an age of digital telepathy, where we can send information directly to each other's brains via the internet. Scientists at the University of Southern California have been working on a cognitive neural prosthesis that can restore and enhance memory function. This research has a practical and altruistic purpose: to help victims of stroke or traumatic brain injury regain their cognitive abilities and motor function. Rather than having to relearn, they need only reload those memories.

For the roughly 100,000 years of modern existence, the *Homo sapiens'* genome has been shaped by the twin forces of random mutation and natural selection. Now, for the first time ever, we possess the ability to edit not only the DNA of every living human but, also, the DNA of future generations. We can direct the evolution of our own species. This is unprecedented in the history of life on earth. Jennifer Doudna and Samuel Sternberg, in their book, *A Crack in Creation,* ask us to confront an essential question: "What will we, a fractious species whose members can't agree on much, choose to do with this awesome power?[36]

Reflection: Revolutionary Technology

---

1. *How are you and your community being affected by these revolutionary technologies? What impact are these having, good and bad, on your way of living and ministering?*

2. *In what ways are you and your community conforming to the challenges of these trends (i.e., becoming drawn into them) versus transforming these challenges (i.e., evidencing an alternative way of being in our world or*

harnessing the potential power of these global trends and helping to shape it constructively)?

5. Power and violence

Global powers are shifting eastward and are altering the dynamics of the world's superpowers. This, in turn, is intensifying old rivalries and spawning new hotspots for violence and corruption. Here is a sampling of the kinds of geopolitical shifts taking place:

- Accelerating proliferation of weapons of mass destruction and missiles (e.g., Iran, Russia, North Korea);

- Transnational terrorism, organized crime, and drug trafficking (e.g., ISIS, al-Shabaab, al-Qaʻida; West African, Russian, and Latin American drug cartels);

- Human and weapons trafficking;

- Cyberwarfare and identify theft;

- Military developments challenging the superiority of the United States and encouraging regional aggression (e.g., Pakistan, North Korea, Russia);

- Authoritarian rule in major countries, coupled with militarism and imperialism (e.g., Syria, Ukraine, Russia);

- Clashes over resources could cause a global economic collapse that would produce widespread conflict and less political cooperation;

- Disintegration of the Western Alliance system and renewed nationalism.

While it may be hard to believe, especially if you listen to the news on a regular basis, the world is less violent today than it has ever been in its history. While terrorism, domestic violence, and regional conflicts are on the rise in certain countries, mortality rates are significantly down as a result of military conflicts.

While 9/11 was the single deadliest terrorist attack in history, most terrorist attacks have been in other countries. Iraq, Afghanistan, Nigeria, Pakistan and Syria top the list, while the risk of terrorism in the United States remains low. According to the Global Terrorism Database, 80 Americans were killed in terrorist attacks from 2004 to 2013, the majority of which are combat-related and are outside U.S. soil. Since 2006, 98 per cent of all deaths from terrorism in the US resulted from attacks carried out by lone actors, resulting in 156 deaths. Deaths from terrorism decreased in 2015 to 29,376. This is the first decrease in the number of deaths recorded since 2010.

There are nine countries that have nuclear weapons: United States, United Kingdom, Russia, France, China, Pakistan, India, Israel and North Korea. Iran is knocking on the door. The United States is still considered to have the strongest military power, but China and Russia have developed new nuclear strike capability for which we have yet to develop a viable defense.

The surge of populism and nationalism has toppled governments and international cooperation (e.g., Brexit or Britain's exit from the European Union). The Trump administration unilaterally broke off international trade agreements, nuclear agreements and the Paris climate agreement. As the United States and the western world retreats from the global stage, China, Russia and others are filling the void.

Reflection: Power and Violence

---

1. *How are you and your community being affected by these socio-economic and military power shifts? What impact are these having, good and bad, on your manner of living and ministering?*

2. *In what ways are you and your community conforming to the challenges of these trends (i.e., becoming drawn into them) versus transforming these challenges (i.e., demonstrating an alternative way of being in our world or harnessing the potential power of these global trends and helping to shape it constructively)?*

Who are You Called to Become?

"We stand at a critical moment in Earth's history, a time when humanity must choose its future. This future holds at once great peril and great promise. To move forward we must recognize we are one human family and one earth community with a common destiny."
Earth Charter, Preamble

During the most recent lifecycle of Religious Life, religious men and women built hospitals, schools and other large institutions to serve the poor and marginalized. They provided direct service in a multitude of ways at home and in remote corners of the world. Their decades of faithful service unquestionably deserve laudatory praise. Ironically, religious men and women have worked themselves out of a job. Gone are the days of large, flagship institutional ministries. Yesterday's needs are not the same as today's or tomorrow's.

The Great Turning taking place today tells us that societal needs are changing rapidly. Communities will need to not only adapt but transform their lives if they are to remain relevant in the future. How does this Great Turning taking place across our globe inform the next evolutionary movement for Religious Life? In light of this Great Turning, who are you and your community being called to become?

Each community will certainly need to discern their own answers to these questions and choose their path accordingly. However, as I look at global chaos amidst this Great Turning, and our own chaos here in the United States, I see two themes of emergent needs that could potentially make for a critical, if not prophetic, role among religious: *presence* and *partnership*.

Presence and partnership

I believe that loneliness is perhaps the deepest suffering of our time. Even though we are texting and emailing for hours, even though we have global connectivity, it does not reduce our loneliness. We are not connected to others because we are not connected to ourselves. We are not taking the time to breathe, to sit in silence, and get in touch with what we are truly feeling, or to know our bodies and our minds. We need to come home to ourselves, to our souls, and to our God. We need to quiet and free ourselves from dwelling in the past and fretting about the future. We need to be *present* in the here and now, to ourselves and one another, in order to be truly free, as this is the very foundation of our happiness.

What could be more needed now than your compassionate presence? Our virtual worlds have ensconced us in echo chambers of self-reinforcing belief systems. Despite our advanced technology and global connectivity, we are increasingly siloed and estranged from one another. The most pervasive disease now is not one that needs a hospital to treat; it is loneliness, a sad irony and a pervasive byproduct of all our connectivity. You could, if you believe yourselves to be called, bring a compassionate presence to this global disease of loneliness.

What could be more needed now than wisdom, and who better to offer this than you, in a world that increasingly discounts facts and truth in favor of alternate universes? What could be more needed now than models of living community, and who better to offer this than you, in a world that seems more interested in building walls than bridges? What could be more needed now than the presence of those who live gospel values of compassion, kindness, inclusivity, justice, forgiveness and mercy in world so polarized and prone to violence? Who better than you?

Islands of sanity and gospel living

In 2016, the Leadership Conference of Women Religious (LCWR) invited Margaret Wheatley to give a keynote presentation. During her talk, she showed a familiar image: concentric circles of water rippling gently outward across otherwise tranquil water as waterdrops fell upon its center. Her message was that leadership is easiest, and its impact more obvious, when the waters are calm. She then showed another image: a dark and stormy ocean, a maelstrom of clouds, wind and waves. Her message: It is much harder to lead, and know the difference it makes, in the times of upheaval in which we find ourselves today.

Scientists agree that we, humanity and our entire planet, are at a tipping point. We are at a point in which we will either devolve into a dark abyss or evolve into a new way of being, a new planetary consciousness. In looking at this big picture, Margaret Wheatley minces no words, warning us that the situation is going to get worse before it gets better. In order to support this claim, she cites the work of Sir John Glubb,[37] whose research on the cyclical rise and fall of civilizations paints a grim picture of where we are today and the darkness we have yet to face.

Wheatley lays out the case, rather convincingly, that we cannot fix or plan our way out of this mess. It's going to happen. Our world will continue its downward spiral. As depressing as it all sounds, she asks an important question, the title of her most recent book: *Who do we choose to be?* The best we can do, she suggests, is to face the realities, claim our voice and create islands of sanity to preserve the seedbed from which humanity might someday take root, transform and ascend once again.[38]

Now, whether or not you believe that our planet is on the verge of collapse, most would agree that our world is in turmoil. And many of us experience that our efforts to *fix* things amount to little more than a drop in the bucket that has little impact upon the global tumult. I find both hope and challenge in Wheatley's question – Who do we choose to be? – and I find resonance with her three-pronged answer – *face realty, claim our voice, and create islands of sanity.*

A few years ago, a Franciscan Sister invited me to help a group of associates develop some skills and strengthen their community. Maggie Slowick, OSF formed a group of associates in Cuernavaca, Mexico to support and nourish their spiritual journey, and their commitment to assist children and families suffering from poverty, drugs and violence. I wondered, when I traveled down there, what possible difference could Maggie and her small band of associates make in a country drowning in a sea of needs?

Starting with one, then a few, and now 14 Associates, they have not yet fixed the poverty, violence or drug problems in Cuernavaca, but they have touched hundreds of souls and given hope and hands-on help to hundreds of people.

Yes, it is a drop in the bucket in the grand scheme of things, but it is more than an island of sanity. It is a community of men and women living side-by-side, praying together, and supporting one another as they look reality in the face, claim their voices and plant the seeds of Gospel values (love, truth, generosity, and the corporal works of mercy) so that humanity might ascend once more. Ultimately, it is not about fixing. It's about *presence.*

Partnership

"You know how to interpret the appearance of the sky, but you cannot interpret the signs of the times." Matthew 16:3

LCWR, in searching for a new path forward, recently invited those who work with women's religious communities for their input to help them plan for their future. One of the questions that emerged in my focus group was: "Are we on a fool's errand?" In other words, they wanted to know if LCWR's efforts to change, transform and plan for their future were a waste of time. It was a question that brought all of us on the conference call to silence, reflection and substantive sharing. It is a great question, and one I'd like to turn back to you.

In the midst of this Great Turning, are you, or your community, on a fool's errand to even attempt to transform your lives and the world in which you live? Just our brief overview of this Great Turning is overwhelming: an accelerating rate of change and increasing chaos; climate change, demographic shifts and migration; revolutionary technology, global connectivity and power shifts; all of which are bringing us to the brink.

It is impossible to keep up with it all and adapt to it, let alone find a niche and make a difference. There is a sea of needs in our world that is ever-changing. It is impossible to predict or even imagine where it is all going. How can religious communities adapt to these changes, let alone transform their lives and make a difference in our world on the brink? What we know is that the dominant systems are insufficient to face the challenges of today: declining moral standards with the rise in narcissism, cynicism, populism, nationalism, racism, ageism, political polarization and violence, climate change, financial inequities, trafficking, terrorism and all the rest. If there is one errand amid this Great Turning that I know to be a fool's errand, it is to believe that "I alone can fix it."

This Great Turning, like all others, is bigger than any one leader, one community, or nation can navigate on their own. Cross-disciplinary and cross-cultural partnerships and collaboration are the only way to solve the planetary crises of today. Partnership and collaboration are the only way that communities will be able to thrive, strengthen their identity, live with freedom and find relevance in our world. Pope Francis urges everyone to participate: "All of us can cooperate as instruments of God for the care of creation, each according to his or her own culture, experience, involvements and talents.[39]

Ninety percent of all the scientists who have ever lived are alive today. We accumulate more knowledge in a year than was produced in prior centuries of scientific study. We have the information to do what it takes to solve these planetary challenges. What we are in need of now is greater wisdom more than knowledge. We cannot Google our way out of this. What we need now is to try differently, not harder, and to pull together before we pull apart. We need collective, interdependent efforts, not siloed ones. Our world needs your willingness, as religious men and women, to face reality, raise your voices of morality and faith, and to be a compassionate presence. Our world needs your willingness to create sanctuaries of sanity and communities of authentic Gospel living that can offer our world an alternative way of being.

Reflection: Presence, Partnership and Call

---

1. Does the way you understand your presence and partnership in the world, and, therefore, the way you serve the world, need to change or transform? Or, is the path you are on precisely the path you need to be on for as long as you possibly can?

2. In light of this Great Turning, who are you being called to become?

Chapter 3: Cycles of Religious Life
Reassuring and Disconcerting

"Religious Life did not die as a result of renewal, did not evaporate, did not abandon its compass points. It simply became more of what it was meant to be: a way of life in search of the God of the Daily, whatever the situation, whenever the era, whatever the shape of the system in which they now found themselves."
Joan Chittister

Introduction

Within the Great Turning of our world, Religious Life is going through its own great turning, a transition going on now for over a half century. It is a transition in response to shifts taking place within Religious Life and the Church, as well as external pressures from a rapidly changing world. Having explored the changes taking place in the external world, we now turn our attention to the transitions taking place *internal* to Religious Life. The good news is that such transitions have occurred many times before and, if history is any indicator, Religious Life is not dying – *it is transforming.*

49

The challenge for Religious Life and each community is to successfully navigate this transition when all roads ahead are inherently risky and ambiguous. I will begin this Chapter by looking at the cycles of Religious Life. There are many lessons to be gleaned from looking at the evolution of Religious Life and its cyclical patterns of transformation. Gathering the learnings from these patterns will help you better understand and meet the challenges of today.

Adding to these lessons are what can be learned from the corporate world. There is a great deal of research shedding light on how businesses succeed or fail, far more than there are studies available on religious communities. The research describing the life, death, and new life cycles of the corporate world is strikingly similar to what we know about religious communities. The convergence is remarkable and enables us to tap this richness in both domains of study, organizational and religious.

I will then address the question of whether or not the current decline in Religious Life is "normal" or is a symptom of something wrong. Some authors have suggested that the peak numbers of religious in the 1960's was an anomaly and that the current decline in numbers is a return to normal. Some have urged communities not to dwell so much upon "aging and diminishment" as this is not the new narrative. While these assertions have merit, there is also a great danger if these are interpreted to mean that the realities of aging and diminishment are of minimal concern. Those who deny or minimize these challenges will only bring about more suffering.

Religious Lifecycles

Gerald Arbuckle, was among the first to address the work of refounding in his 1966 publication, *Out of Chaos: Refounding Religious Congregations.*[40] While insisting that refounding was essentially a faith journey (i.e., an Exodos journey of purification), he integrated lessons from organizational theory and practice into his approach to refounding. The primary theme woven throughout his essays centered around the need for communities to reclaim and renew their founding myth, meaning the archetypal expression of their charism.

"Refounding is not a search for an increase in vocations,"[41] said Arbuckle. Rather, it is the creative working through the chaos and resistance to change that ultimately generates new life. The resistance to change among the larger corporate body, he believed, was too great for the entire community to overcome. He held that only an "extremely rare" subgroup of members had the requisite passion, creativity and courage to regenerate an institute's founding myth.[42] He advocated that it was leadership's job to provide this type of small group with the resources they needed to engage in this challenging work of refounding. Conversion, creativity, and radically new contemporized expressions of the Gospel were among his keys to successful refounding.

Like Arbuckle, Lawrence Cada and his colleagues also believed that refounding was essentially a faith journey, a process of redemption in graced persons and the community. Cada believed that renewing the myth and prophetic role of a community was such an arduous journey that it could only be endured by persons with "deep personal love for Religious Life and for the community."[43] Unlike Arbuckle, who spoke of refounding as the work of a small subgroup of people, Cada emphasized that it is the work of the entire community. They believed that communal (systemic) change was necessary, through personal and communal learning, experimentation, and discernment, in order for a community to transform and give birth to a new cycle of life.

Cada and his colleagues offered a wider lens for these refounding efforts, placing them in the context of the evolution of Religious Life over two millennia. They described several great turnings, life-death-new-life cycles, of Religious Life occurring since the time of Jesus (see Figure 1: Cada, cycles of Religious Life). In reviewing these cycles, they observed that "religious communities arose in response to dramatic social changes in the Church and in the larger cultural and political arena."[44] Their basic premise is that Religious Life is going through another cyclical transformation as a result of changes within the Church (Vatican II) and the Church's dissonance with emerging social norms.

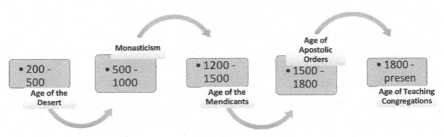

Figure 1: Cada, Cycles of Religious Life

In examining the evolution of Religious Life, Cada and colleagues developed a sociological model depicting the five phases that religious communities experience through the life of what they called, the "vitality curve": 1) founding; 2) expansion, 3) stabilization; 4) breakdown; and, 5) a critical phase.[45] The critical phase is the one in which communities will either choose a path that leads to life or a path that leads to death.

They conclude by saying, "most religious communities in the Church today will eventually become extinct."[46] They believed that the experience of decline among religious is one in which members have lost contact with the founding vision, their espoused values are no longer congruent with their lived behaviors, and their overall sense of belonging has been eroded. They believed that most communities would continue on a path toward death.

They further suggested that the "small percentage" of communities that do survive and revitalize will have these three characteristics: 1) transforming response to the signs of the times; 2) reappropriation of the founding charism; and, 3) profound renewal of the life of prayer, faith and centeredness in Christ. Personal and communal transformation, new models of living community, and a positive communal vision for the future were also seen as key to successful revitalization.[47] Those that choose a path of transformation would need to discern a new, risky Gospel venture more aligned with the exigencies of the world, a new way of organizing and structuring their lives, and a new way of attracting, inviting, accepting and integrating members into community.

In the largest study of its kind, *The Religious Life Futures Project*, David Nygren and Miriam Ukeritis surveyed 9,999 religious priests, sisters and brothers and shared their findings in 1990. They sought to better understand the values, beliefs and practices of religious men and women as well as to glean insights about the future. Their study reinforced what others had surmised anecdotally: Religious Life was in crisis, especially regarding leadership. Among the major findings were these:

- Loss of conviction about the vows and members were challenged to remain faithful to them, especially chastity for men and obedience for women;

- Lack of sufficient clarity about the role of religious and a coherent corporate approach to action (i.e., personal and collective relevancy);

- Lack of clear corporate identity, while personal identity was more connected to an individual's ministry;

- Despite the espoused preferential option for the poor, many felt little or no personal commitment to the poor;

- High degree of assimilation into the mainstream culture (e.g., of materialism, workaholism, individualism);

- Younger members had the greatest involvement but least impact upon the life of community;

- Behavioral competencies lagged behind the changing values and emerging focus on mission;

- Personal discernment and authority trumped communal discernment and congregational authority.[48]

Nygren and Ukeritis believed that authority within congregations, or the magisterium, was highly contested and conflictual, and saw it as among the most important issues congregations ought to face. They warned communities that they had a "10-year window" to turn things around before it would be too late. They, too, called for a radical response to the Gospel and a life more aligned with serving those who are poor and living on the margins.[49]

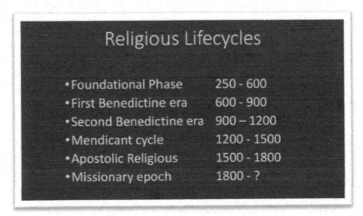

Figure 2: O'Murchu, Religious Lifecycles

Diarmuid O'Murchu, also among the most prolific and prophetic voices addressing the transformation of Religious Life, calls for a shift in the existing paradigm of Religious Life (see Figure 2, O'Murchu, Religious Lifecycles). Looking back at the history of Religious Life, like Cada, he also saw a pattern of Religious Life having six cycles of shifting paradigms.[50] The ebb and flow of each lifecycle was spurred on, he believed, by not only changes occurring within Religious Life, but especially those in the outer world to which it was responding: a world in turmoil, political and social unrest, spiritual atrophy and moral decadence.[51] He observed that each cycle of growth and decline lasted around 300 years before the next major paradigmatic shift occurred.[52]

O'Murchu, in his most recent reflections on refounding and the transformation of Religious Life described what he saw as the next evolutionary shift in paradigms. He described this shift by contrasting the existing paradigm with one seeking emergence:

> "Our prayers, hymnologies, and devotions insinuate a co-dependent allegiance to an all-powerful deity, a king-like hero above the sky, who alone can rescue us from our depraved plight 'down here.' This is a long way from the Jesus who invited us to be friends and not servants (Jn. 15:15), the Jesus who pointed the finger away from himself toward the new companionship (kingdom), inviting us to co-discipleship in co-creating a better world characterized by gospel liberation."[53]

Like others, O'Murchu describes this evolutionary movement as a "paschal" journey of life-death-rebirth which he thought to be a natural, organic movement.[54] Throughout his publications, he continues to emphasize refounding as a "divine prerogative," one best illuminated through personal and communal discernment.[55] Like others, he envisions a return to the spirit of the Gospel and release of the spirit from the confines of fossilized structures and outdated worldviews. In his book, *Inclusivity: A Gospel Mandate*[56], he offers new frames for understanding the vows in light of the Gospel, and intimations of the future paradigm emerging within Religious Life (i.e., communities of compassion).

In order to give life to new paradigms Michael Crosby calls for dissent from the hierarchical structures of the Church and return to the core message of

Jesus and the Gospel. Addressing the message of Pope Benedict XVI, regarding the "crisis of faith in the church," he reframes the crisis as a "lack of faith in the institutional Church itself." He views the crises within the Church as evidence of its "structural sins, including: a lack of relevancy; sexual scandals; lost credibility; hemorrhaging numbers; abuse of power and intolerance of criticism."[57]

Crosby points to the Church's "deep contradiction between its mystical, organic identity that is living and adapting (like any open model) and its organizational identity that is becoming increasingly closed and no longer open to its originating power."[58] He calls for a new Christology (i.e., a Cosmic Christ), a shift in consciousness (i.e., an awakened, understanding heart), and authentic community life (i.e., one expressing mutual interdependence). He believes that contemplation, connection, and compassion are central dynamics for becoming a "kindom" Catholic.

Patricia Wittberg, who has also written extensively on refounding, concluded: "No founding or refounding can succeed if it is divorced from its environmental context."[59] She goes on to add a number of "ifs," contingencies to be met in order for refounding to occur:

> "If a group freely chooses to do so, if its leaders do not betray its goal by fostering cults of personality around themselves and infantilizing their followers, if its chosen goal meets a pressing societal need, if its lifestyle and philosophy resonates with that of the surrounding culture, and if no serious opposition derails it, then perhaps a new religious community may be born or part of an existing one refounded."[60]

Along with the authors just mentioned, Barbara Fiand, Ronald Rolheiser, Sandra Schneiders, Richard Rohr, Joan Chittister, Walter Brueggemann, and many others, are seeding new narratives for the next evolutionary shift in Religious Life. These *agents of transformation* are planting seeds for creating new paradigms of Religious Life. They are urging a new, more awakened consciousness and are providing new language and frames for understanding the values and vows of Religious Life. They are providing new understandings for what it means to be a consecrated religious in today's world. They are moving past the structures, languages, and emphasis on religious dogma of the past, and focusing on the spiritual messages of today's Gospel. All of them are imparting new insights contributing to the mosaic picture of Religious Life emerging from this current transition.

How long will it take?

Cycles in Religious Life

No one knows how long it might take for Religious Life to move through this transition and give birth to its new form. In 1975, Fitz and Cada predicted that it would take 25 years to run its course.[61] In 1985, Cada and colleagues said that religious were 15 years into the transition and had another 15 years to go.[62] Both estimates would have put the completion of this transition in the year 2000. In 1990, Nygren and Ukeritis, warned of a 10-year window, also marking the year 2000.[63] We are now two decades past these predictions.

O'Murchu, in 1998, estimated that the current paradigm of Religious Life would last another 70 years before "refounding in any serious sense" might occur.[64] By his calculation, it will be 2068 before we reach the other side of this transition. It would appear that we are on God's time, not ours, and any attempt to pin down or forecast its completion is mere conjecture. We will know it only in hindsight.

Cycles of religious communities

While it might be impossible to predict how long it will take for Religious Life to transform, if we focus on individual communities, we can get a better fix on the length of time it typically takes to work through communal transitions. In my research surveying communities engaged in refounding, restructuring, or reconfiguring, I found that most groups spent, on average, about 10 years to work through these structural changes. This did not include the time it takes building up to the decision. As you can imagine, most communities can talk about these issues for years before they begin such efforts in earnest.

On the other side of these decisions are the additional years working through the implementation, evaluation and ongoing reshaping of these efforts. A congregation may make a Chapter decision to merge, for example, and take another 10 years to implement the practical, structural, financial, legal, and governmental changes. However, it takes many more years to merge cultures, if this is achieved at all. All told, these endeavors take decades, not years.

The enormous amounts of time, energy, and resources that are needed to make the decisions, implement and continue working through these decisions, is one reason why mergers, for example, have become less frequent in recent decades. The result of spending all the time, energy and resources rarely fixes the problems they set out to fix. Often times, the result is a larger pool of the same demographic profile, a larger "gerontocracy." Another major reason for the decrease in the number of mergers is the difficulty in finding other compatible communities with sufficient resources to take in more senior members.[65]

What are the odds?

No living organism, company, nation or era lasts forever. Religious Life and religious communities are no exceptions. In fact, no religious order has continued a path of growth and expansion over 200 years.[66] Life emerges, lives for time, declines and gives way to death only to reemerge in a new way, as a new lifeform.

The vast majority of religious communities that ever existed are now extinct and the vast majority of communities that currently exist will succumb to the same fate.[67] Most communities, despite their prayers, hopes and ardent efforts, will fail to transform their lives and bring forth a new cycle. O'Murchu believes that upwards of 85% will fail. Of the remaining 15%, some will continue at some low level of functioning, while only 10% will come to birth a new cycle. Only 10%!

Patricia Wittberg reviewed the research on the survival rates of religious communities. She reported that most studies found that only 10% of communities lasted 25 years or more. The historians that reported higher rates, she opined, excluded hundreds of fleeting attempts that never attained official status."[68] Thus, 90% of communities that are successfully launched will not survive past 25 years and 90% of those that complete one lifecycle will not succeed in birthing another.

Cada and others have made similar claims based, it seems, primarily on the historical patterns over the last two millennia. Fitz and Cada put it this way: "From an historical perspective, then, a reasonable expectation would seem to be that most religious communities in the Church today will eventually become extinct. A religious community which does not die out may go into a long period of low-level or minimal survival."[69] Thus, your community's odds are roughly 1-in-10 that it might successfully transform and birth a new cycle of life.

Reflection: Cycles of Religious Life

---

1. *In reviewing the cycles of Religious Life:*

2. *What new insights have you gleaned that affect how you understand the future of your own community and Religious Life as a whole?*

3. *How might these insights influence your approach to planning the future of your own community?*

Corporate World Comparisons

These 1-in-10 odds of a religious community birthing a new cycle are remarkably consistent with businesses in the corporate world. Most businesses, like most religious communities, will fail to get off the ground. About half of all new businesses survive five years or more, and about one-third survive 10 years or more. The average life span of a fortune 500 company is between 40 and 50 years.[70]

While businesses might forecast the need to change, their traditional approaches to organizational change, such as downsizing, rightsizing and strategic planning, have a dismal failure rate of up to 85%. Gone are the stalwart businesses that once were household names, such as General Foods, TWA, Montgomery Ward, Woolworth and RCA. Gone are the darlings of Wall Street, such as Enron, Paine Webber, Bear Stearns and E.F. Hutton (I guess people stopped listening). Even the famed Motor City, Detroit, filed for bankruptcy in 2013, the first large city in the United States to do so.

Just as religious communities went through a period of reconfiguration efforts (i.e., unions and mergers), corporate mergers grew 100-fold between 1980 and 2000.[71] And just as most of the reconfiguration efforts failed to birth new life, most of the mergers in the business world also failed.[72] In 1955, Forbes published its first Forbes 500, a list of the 500 largest and most powerful companies. In its fifty-year anniversary issue, only 13% of these companies were still on the list. Despite their size and wealth of resources, they either ceased to exist or toppled from the list.[73] Continuity cannot be the assumption. Discontinuity is the norm. Barely 10% of religious communities and 10% of businesses are likely to rebirth a new cycle of life when facing a crossroads.

We now use iPhones and digital cameras to take pictures, not film cameras. We now use computers and digital printers, not typewriters or mimeograph machines. We listen to music through iTunes, Spotify and Pandora, not record players. We communicate predominately through texting and social media with Facebook, Twitter, LinkedIn, Pinterest, to name a few. Too many organizations are still run by analogue leaders trying to function in a digital world. And these organizations will not make the turn. They will go the way of the dodo bird.

Disconcerting And Reassuring Realities

Although the denial of *aging and diminishment* that persisted for decades continues to melt away, there are still pockets of denial among some members of nearly every community. Some members believe that the decline in numbers is *normal* and conclude, therefore, that everything is fine and there is no need for radical change. Labeling the decline in numbers as normal somehow reinforces their belief that life can, and ought to, continue as it has in the past.

Others believe that a person's age (no matter how old) does not result in diminished capacity. Despite all evidence to the contrary, they do not see age as having any bearing on a member's capacity to participate in ministry, to drive or to serve in leadership. Somehow, the talk of aging and diminishment is seen as an affront to their own experience of aging or their hope for the future.

There are three messages commonly echoed among members today that subtly reinforce this denial and minimization of aging and diminishment:

1. The peak numbers in the 1960's were an anomaly and the current decline is normal;

2. Aging and diminishment are not the new narrative; and,

3. "We only had three when we started. What's the big deal?"

These messages have been taken out of context and coopted by those who persist in denial, do not want to address the realities of aging and diminishment, and believe that life can go on as it has in the past. This denial or minimization only serves to confound and thwart a community's needed adaptations and increases their likelihood of greater suffering. Let me briefly address each of these three messages.

Normal for Religious Life, but not for those experiencing it

Some have suggested that the peak numbers in Religious Life during the 1960's were actually an "anomaly" and that the numbers are now returning to what is, from an historical perspective, "normal."[74] Indeed, what we have seen is that Religious Life has cycled through peaks and valleys. Religious Life is now in a downward cycle, one of at least five such cycles in its history. Thus, the peaks and valleys of its evolutionary path are generally viewed as normal.

Schneiders, like others who have written extensively on reasons for the decline in numbers, believes that the decline in numbers is largely due to the combined effects of internal changes in the Church (i.e., the upheaval following Vatican II) and external societal changes (e.g., families having fewer children and women having more options).[75] She, like others, believes that Religious Life "is a charismatic lifeform, called into existence by the Holy Spirit, to live corporately the prophetic charism in the Church. It is not a workforce gathering recruits for ecclesiastical projects." Thus, its primary role is to be prophetic, and size is of no concern: "No congregation 'needs' more members than are actually called to it by God."[76]

On the one hand, this perspective on the decline ought to be enormously reassuring for those who might be inclined to see the current decline as the death of Religious Life. Thus far, each decline has been followed by a reemergence of a new form of Religious Life. This decline is not a harbinger of death. Rather, it is signaling the end of Religious Life as we have known it and the birthing of a new form of Religious Life that is still emerging.

On the other hand, while the current decline may be normal for Religious Life, it is not at all normal for the people and communities going through it. In fact, the effects of aging, diminishment and the death of so many members are all very challenging and painful realities. Unfortunately, those who wish to deny these hard realities and minimize the need to change have misappropriated this *normal* cycle in Religious Life. They use it to *normalize* and, thus, minimize and deny these realities within their own community.

Part of the story, but not the new narrative

Others have suggested that aging and diminishment ought not be the narrative for what is happening in Religious Life today. Mary Pellegrino, for example, spoke of this "diminishment narrative" as a simplistic and narrow narrative that implies an "epic failure of the paschal mystery."[77] I agree completely. Aging and diminishment are not the new narrative for Religious Life, not the full story nor the end of the story. Such a narrow focus on aging and diminishment will not instill hope for the future, attract new members or foster new life.

That said, some have misappropriated this message to rationalize their avoidance of aging and diminishment. Instead, they wish to focus on recruiting new vocations and starting new ministries, or continuing the path they are on, rather than dwell on matters of aging and diminishment. And they have a point. While aging and diminishment are among the most pressing matters, they can become all-consuming issues for communities. These must not overshadow the many other challenges that exist, not the least of which is how to nurture new life and a new mission. Neither denial of these realities, nor being totally consumed by them, will serve the best interests of communities who wish to plan for their future.

"We only had three when we started. What's the big deal?"

When leaders stand up at assemblies and share the mind-numbing demographics, I will often hear members say, "Well, we only had three to begin with. What's the big deal?" While I see the logic, I believe it is mostly another effort to minimize or deny their disturbing reality. It is a comparison that is taken out of context and is misleading.

The number of members that originally accompanied your founder or foundress was fewer than the number you have now. They were likely half your age (if not younger) and in much greater health. Additionally, they had little "baggage" to carry, other than the clothes they brought with them, which was a much less complicated picture than today. They did not have the baggage of aging buildings, aging members, a complex and fragile network of lay partners, the responsibility of sponsored and other established institutions, property, and complex legal and financial structures. And they did not have the emotional baggage from years of living together.

Furthermore, the founding phase of a community is vastly different from a declining or transitional phase. The energy is different, the tasks and challenges are different, and so is the nature of mission, life in community and responsibilities for stewarding resources. The founding phase brings the excitement of new energy, new members and new possibilities. While the refounding or completion phase brings these possibilities, it also brings the certainty of many funerals, closures and letting go. Thus, you may have had a small number to begin with, however, the phase you are in now is different, more complex and more challenging.

What, if anything, is wrong?

The Apostolic Visitation of Institutes of Women Religious in the United States, and the investigation into the Leadership Conference of Women Religious (LCWR), focused in on the declining numbers of women religious as a pretext for their investigation.[78] The Church's focus on declining numbers as evidence of the failed leadership among women Religious evoked strong rebuke. Sandra Schneiders likened it to a "medieval Inquisition" and believed that, like Jesus, women Religious were being "scapegoated" by the hierarchical Church's need to regain control.[79]

At the very least, the "inquisition" obfuscated the serious and complex challenges facing Religious Life and the Church. No one reason, or set of reasons, can definitively be ascribed as causing this decline. However, we must identify the challenges (causal or not) that need to be addressed if there is ever to be a renewal and transformation of Religious Life. I will leave it to those living Religious Life to provide these kinds of critical analyses of what is *wrong*. I am better positioned to talk about the *challenges* facing Religious Life, the subject of our next two chapters.

In summary, aging and diminishment are a big deal. They are a big part of the story, but not the new narrative. They may be normal in the grand scheme of things, but they are also an indication that times are changing and so, too, must Religious Life change. They are realities that every community must face.

Aging and diminishment are neither the new narrative nor the heart of the matter regarding the transformation of Religious Life. Nonetheless, these are urgent matters for every community that will require an enormous amount of their time, energy and resources to address. The challenge in addressing these realities, is for them not to become the sum total of a community's attention, such that they eclipse any focus on the future life and mission of a community. A further challenge is to neither live in denial, nor become utterly disheartened by all of the letting go that must occur. Grieving the loss of youth and the loss of members will be key to working though the denial or pain and opening up new possibilities for the future.

Reflection: Disconcerting and reassuring realities

Regarding the realities of aging and diminishment:

1. *What do you find disconcerting or reassuring?*

2. *How has your community balanced the need to attend to these realities and, simultaneously, the future of your life and mission?*

Conclusions

Having surveyed the cycles of Religious Life, there are factors that are both reassuring and disconcerting regarding its current status. Here are ten of the most important conclusions we can glean. These provide insights into the current transition of Religious Life as well as the challenges, opportunities, and what might be required of communities seeking to transform their lives and mission.

1. **Within the Great Turning of our planet, Religious Life is going through a profound and natural, evolutionary transition of its own, spurred on by both internal changes happening in Religious Life and the Church, as well as external changes taking place in our world.**

2. **Survival, identity, integrity and relevancy are among the many challenges facing Religious Life today.**

3. **Religious Life has evolved through several cycles of life, death, transformation and new life – a pattern most believe will continue into the future.**

4. **Although there are no guarantees, most people expect that a new cycle of Religious Life will emerge once this decline reaches its nadir.**

5. **We don't know how long this current transition in Religious Life might take, but history suggests that it will be decades before we recognize, in hindsight, the *new life* that has emerged.**

6. **If history repeats itself, 90% of existing communities will not survive this current life cycle transition and give birth to a new cycle of life.**

7. **While the current cyclical decline of Religious Life may be considered "normal" from an historical perspective, it is nonetheless a painful reality affecting individuals and their communities.**

8. **While "aging and diminishment" is not a narrative that will inspire new life, it is one challenge among many that is having**

a tremendous impact upon the life and mission of communities. It is dangerous to deny or minimize these realities.

9. The communal transformation needed during these transitional times is not about becoming larger in size, but larger in faith, hope and love.

10. The communal transformation, like the Exodus journey, is a paschal journey of faith requiring:

    a. a shift in consciousness and the creation of new narratives;

    b. personal and communal conversion;

    c. reappropriation and renewed expressions of your archetypal myth and charism;

    d. creativity and experimentation in order risk new ventures;

    e. radically new visions for the future that give authentic expression to the Gospel more fully in touch and aligned with the world today.

CHAPTER 4:
THE CHANGING
RELIGIOUS LANDSCAPE

A source of division or catalyst for change

"You know how to interpret the appearance of the sky, but you cannot interpret the signs of the times."
Matthew 16:3

Introduction

The religious landscape across the globe and within the United States has changed dramatically in the last fifty years. Catholics, in particular, are not who they were when Vatican II encouraged communities to study and adapt to the signs of the times. The trends in Religious Life and the general Catholic population are there for all of us to see. What do you see and what difference does this make on your understanding of your own community, the broader community, the Catholic Church? What implications do these changes have regarding your efforts to transform your life and mission? Being uninformed or misinformed about the changing religious landscape will leave communities behind, in the dark, and unable to evolve into the future.

This Chapter offers three perspectives regarding the changing religious landscape. The first is an overview of the demographic changes taking place among all religions across the globe before focusing on the United States. Following a panoramic worldview, we will then drill down and focus particularly on the demographics related to Catholics in the United States, both laity and religious.

The second perspective is a description of the trends regarding religious attitudes, beliefs and practices in the United States. We will look at comparisons across religions, then, once again, hone in on the Catholic culture, in particular. The shift in attitudes, beliefs and practices that lies beneath the surface is less often examined, perhaps a little harder to measure, but is no less impactful upon Religious Life than the changing demographics.

The third perspective offers a reflection on *restoring the dignity of difference*. Having surfaced the changes and differences that exist across the religious landscape, and the judgments that these too often bring, we will explore four ways to restore the dignity of difference. This diversity across the religious landscape can be either a source of judgement and division or a catalyst for change and transformation. I will invite your reflection upon both of these possibilities.

Demographics Shifts

The demographic shifts among religious populations around the globe and in the United States have a direct impact on our world, from a rise in fundamentalism, to our polarizing politics and our increased hostilities and violence. As we explore these demographic changes, I would invite you to reflect upon what these say to you with regard to your future planning. What is the impact of these demographic changes upon the future life and mission of your community?

Across the globe

By the numbers

Of the nearly 7 ½ billion people currently inhabiting the earth, 84% of them are affiliated with some form of religion. Roughly one third of the world's population are Christian and half of these are Catholic. One quarter of the global population are Muslim, and 16% are "Nones" (non-religious or unaffiliated). Hindus account for 15%, Buddhists 7%, and 6% are affiliated with folk, indigenous, or other traditional religions (e.g., African traditional religions). Jews account for only .2% of the world's population.[80]

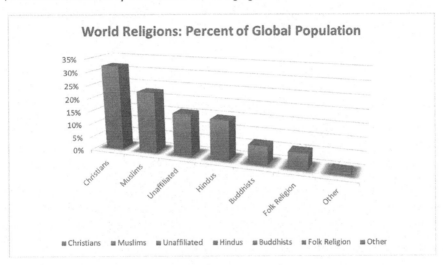

Figure 3: World Religions

Roughly a quarter of all Christians live in Europe, a quarter live in sub-Saharan Africa and a third live in the Americas. A third of all Christians live in only three countries (United States, Brazil and Mexico). Most Muslims live in the Asia-Pacific regions (62%), while the majority of others live in the Middle East and Africa. Most religious groups (73%) live in countries in which their religious group makes up a majority of their country's population. Most of the religiously unaffiliated (76%) live in the Asia-Pacific regions.

The median age of two major groups, Muslims (23 years) and Hindus (26 years), is younger than the median age of the world's overall population (28). Christians have a median age of 30, followed by members of other religions (32). Jews have the highest median age (36), more than a dozen years older than the youngest group, Muslims. Jews are more highly educated than any other major religious group around the world (averaging 13.4 years), while Christian's are the second most educated group (9.3 years). Muslims and Hindus have the fewest years of formal schooling (5.6 years), but are gaining faster than any other group.[81]

Women, across the globe, tend to be more religious by most measures (e.g., religiously affiliated; and pray more frequently). Women attend religious services more often among Christians, but among Muslims and Orthodox Jews, men attend more often.[82]

Trends

Muslims are the fastest growing religion in the world. By 2050 the number of Muslims will nearly equal the number of Christians around the world. By 2050, Muslims will make up 10% of the overall population in Europe and India will be home to their largest number (surpassing Indonesia). Four out of every 10 Christians in the world will live in sub-Saharan Africa. Nones across the globe will be on the decline, while Christians will remain about the same.[83] Surprisingly, Christianity is growing the fastest in Iran and Afghanistan, partly due to the backlash against extremist violence.[84]

While government restrictions on religious practices are lessening, there has been a rise in religious hostilities around the globe which have become increasingly more violent. Religion-related terrorist activities occurred in 82 countries in 2016 compared to 73 in 2013. Among the world's 25 most populous countries, the highest overall restrictions on religion in 2014 were in Egypt, Indonesia, Pakistan, Russia and Turkey. Christians and Muslims were harassed in the most countries in 2014.[85]

Catholics

Of the 2.2 billion Christians in the world, just over 1.1 billion of these are Catholic. In raw numbers, across the globe, Catholics have more than tripled over the last century because of population increases. However, the percentage of Catholics in the world population has remained relatively stable, around 17% of the world's population.

Over the last century, there has been rapid growth in the Catholic population in Sub-Saharan African and Asia-Pacific regions, while Europe's share has decreased sharply (now at 24%). Brazil has more Catholics than any other country with around 127 million Catholics and is home to 11.7 percent of the world's Catholic population. Brazil is followed by Mexico (96 million), Philippines (76 million), United States (75 million) and Italy (49 million).[86]

Vowed religious men and women

In 2013, Rome indicated that there were 300,000 fewer women religious and priests in religious orders than there were 40 years earlier with a marked decline in Europe, the United States and Oceania (e.g., Polynesia, Micronesia, Malaysia and Melanesia). While the total number of priests (in both diocesan and religious orders) held to 413,418 in 2012, the number of women religious fell from one million worldwide in 1973 to just over 700,000 in 2013.[87]

In 2014, worldwide, there were nearly 1.2 million women religious, religious brothers and priests (religious order and diocesan) in the world:

- 705,529 women religious;
- 279,561 diocesan priests;
- 134,752 order priests;
- 55,314 brothers.[88]

Across the United States

Of the 320 million people in the United States, 83% say they belong to a religion and 71% are Christian. Protestants, as a whole, are the majority of the population at just over 50%. Evangelical Protestants, the largest subset among Protestants, are 25% of the U.S. population. Catholics are the largest single denomination at 21% (70 million).

Trends

The United States remains home to more Christians than any other country in the world with seven-in-ten affiliated with some branch of Christianity. However, there is a significant downward trend, especially among Mainline Protestants and Catholics. If it were not for the influx of Latinos, the number of Catholics in the United States would be down significantly more than it is. According to Putnam and Campbell, "roughly 60% of all Americans today who were raised in America as Catholic are no longer practicing Catholics."[89]

"Nones" are the fastest growing group and are now more numerous than any other religious group, surpassing even Catholics.[90] The rise in Nones has been dramatic, from 7% in 1984, to 24% in 2017.[91] Projections to 2050 indicate that the downward trend among Christians, and the rising trend of Nones, will continue.[92] Interestingly, Mormonism is the fastest growing religious group, albeit from a small base.[93]

The downward trend in the number of Catholics is not new. In 2007, Catholics were 24% of the population and in 2014 they were 21%.[94] According to the Pew Research Center, "No other major faith in the U.S. has experienced greater net losses over the last few decades as a result of changes in religious affiliation than the Catholic Church."[95] And no other religious group in the survey has such a lopsided ratio of losses to gains."[96] Putnam and Campbell put it this way: "Except for the timely arrival of Latino immigrants, the future of the American Catholic Church might appear bleak."[97]

The population of Catholics in the United States is moving more south and west, largely influenced by the immigrant population.[98] On average, as of 2014, U.S. Catholics have a median age of 49 (and growing older) and have slightly more women (54%) than men (46%). Nones, on the other hand, are growing younger (median age 36). Jews and Hindus are the most highly educated and have the highest incomes while Catholics mirror the general population in education and income. While 52% of Catholics are married, non-married Catholics are at an all-time high with 21% never having been married. Interfaith marriages, at 39%, are also at their highest.[99]

While most Catholics (55%) are white, they are increasingly more ethnically and racially diverse. Four in ten Catholics are of a racial or ethnic minority.[100] Additionally, four in ten Catholics are either first or second-generation Americans. Currently, 41% of Catholics are Hispanic. By 2050, Hispanics will constitute the majority of Catholics in the United States.

While most Hispanics (55%) in the United States continue to belong to the Catholic Church, they are leaving the Catholic Church nearly as much as whites (non-hispanic).[101] The primary trend among those leaving is a bimodal distribution. They are either becoming evangelical Protestants or religiously unaffiliated. Despite the fact that fewer Hispanics are remaining Catholic, the enormous influx of Hispanic immigrants continues to make up an increasingly larger share of U.S. Catholics.[102]

Trends among vowed religious

The number of women religious in the United States has dropped dramatically from its peak, in the mid-1960s, of 185,000. There are currently under 45,000 with a median age of 75 (less than 1% are under 40). They are declining in number by an average of 2,051 per year. Barring any major disruption in this trend, and projecting the trend out to 2030, there will be around 17,600 women religious. For women's communities, the average annual number of *new vocations* across the United States is one. However, with a retention rate hovering around 50%, the average annual number of *new members* (i.e., those who make perpetual profession) is zero! The half-life for women's religious communities is 10 to 12 years. In other words, most will be half the size they are today within the next decade or so.

The number of priests has also dropped, though not as dramatically as for women religious. The number of priests in 1970 was close to 60,000 and now is around 35,000. The trend line is much the same going forward. In raw numbers they are losing an average of 506 men per year. Barring any major disruption in the trend, and projecting the trend out to 2030, their total number will be just over 29,800. By that time, most of these men will be either infirmed or retired.

The number of religious brothers shows a similar decline. Their peak number in 1965 was just over 12,000 and they are now hovering around 4,000. In raw numbers they are losing 102 members per year. Barring any major disruption in the trend, and projecting the trend out to 2030, their total number will be around 2,400.

Although there are plenty of numbers published suggesting an *interest* in Religious Life (e.g., hits on websites, inquiries, expressed interest by younger persons, number in formation, etc.), the fact remains that the annual totals for new *perpetually professed* members across the 800 institutes have averaged around 150 (men and women combined) for the past several years. In the 2011 CARA study, 82% of responding institutes reported no one professing perpetual vows, 14% reported one, and only 4% reported having 2 or more.[103] Fewer and fewer institutes have any new perpetually professed members.

With yearly combined losses averaging over 2,650, and yearly gains averaging only 150, there remains a net loss of over 2,500 religious men and women across the United States per year. The trend line remains steep in the coming years. Despite the numbers of those expressing interest, this trend shows no signs of letting up. In 2022, for the first time, there will be fewer women religious in the United States than priests! If we project out to 2030 with the same trendlines, there will be fewer than 17,600 women religious, 29,800 priests, and 2,400 brothers in the United States. In her review of the literature, Mary Johnson concluded that, with the exception of a small majority of institutes that have successfully recruited new members, "the future of Religious Life in the United States would appear to be in peril."[104]

A popular myth has emerged claiming that the more traditional institutes (e.g., those wearing a traditional habit) are growing, while the less traditional institutes are declining. However, others have debunked this myth stating that these numbers are "about equal."[105] Despite anecdotal reports that the trend may be reversing, only a half-dozen religious institutes of women and 13 institutes for men have substantially increased their membership in recent years.[106] Over two-thirds of the increase among the men can be attributed to one institute (Legionaries of Christ).[107] The Center for Applied Research in the Apostolate (CARA) concluded that "Whatever these institutes have done or are doing is unlikely to offset losses in the tens of thousands elsewhere.[108]

The number of Catholic schools, hospitals, and parishes with a priest are all significantly down since 1965. Participation in the Mass and sacraments are all significantly down, as well. For example, baptisms are half of what they were in 1965. Mass attendance, marriages and annulments have all declined by more than half over the past 50 years.

What about new and emerging communities? In 1999, CARA reported on new and emerging communities in the United States since 1965. They repeated their survey in 2006 and again in 2016. Their most recent data indicated that there were 159 new or emerging communities in the past half century. The vast majority of these were public or private Associations of the Christian Faithful, along with a few Societies of Apostolic Life. Only 28 (18%) of these were Religious Institutes.[109]

Since 2006, nearly twice as many of the emerging communities had declined (fewer members, or now disbanded, suppressed, or no longer affiliated with the Catholic Church), compared to communities that had grown in number. Among those reporting significant growth, their numbers were very small (most fewer than 7 members). The exceptions to these were the highly publicized Dominican Sisters of Mary Mother of the Eucharist, along with the Sisters of Life, each with over 100 members.[110]

Urging the reader to maintain perspective, the report concluded, "None of the current groups came close to matching the rates of growth routinely experienced by the religious institutes that were merging in the United States in the nineteenth century."[111] Thus, while new and emerging religious institutes may provide seeds of the future, they have not yet swelled in numbers enough to abate the larger wave of declining numbers.

Age

The average age for all religious in the 1960's was around 35. The average age now for all religious is 70 (68 for men and 75 for women). In the next ten years, for the most part, women's communities will be in their 80's and men's will be in their 70s. The age distribution is highly skewed toward the upper age range. According to a 2014 CARA report, there were more women over 90 than under 60 and less than 1% were under 40.[112]

Associates

According to CARA's 2016 special report on Associates in the United States and Canada, six-in-ten of the 378 responding institutes have Associates, 79% in the United States, 21% in Canada. The 55,942 Associates were more than double the number in 2000, 90% women and 10% men. Their average age is nearly that of sisters with 82% over 60 years of age.[113] The demographic challenges facing Associates parallel those of religious communities (e.g., aging and lack of new Associates, leadership and financial sustainability).

Summary

If you have lost the forest through the trees and found yourself getting dizzy with all of these statistics, let me boil it down and summarize the top ten U.S. trends for you:

1. **While mainline religions are declining, there is a rise in two ends of the spectrum; Evangelical Protestants and Nones.**

2. **Nones are the largest subgroup, outnumbering Catholics and trending larger.**

3. **Lapsed Catholics now outnumber practicing Catholics and are trending larger.**

4. **Catholics in the United States are moving more South and West.**

5. **All Christians, including Catholics, are aging and becoming more racially diverse.**

6. **Catholics, and Catholic institutions, are declining in the United States and would be hemorrhaging if not for the influx of Hispanic immigrants.**

7. Hispanics will soon comprise the majority of Catholics, though they too are filling the ranks of Nones and Evangelicals.

8. Catholic women religious, priests and brothers are dramatically older and fewer. In the next 10 years most communities will be half the size they are today.

9. There is a small stream of new members and a few new communities, but these will not stave off the larger wave of declining numbers of aging religious for decades to come.

10. Associates roughly parallel vowed religious in their demographic changes.

Reflection: How do you interpret the signs of the times? (Matt. 16:3)

---

1. Why do you believe there is a tremendous increase in the spiritual hunger among Americans while, simultaneously, there is a radical decline in those who attend mainline Churches, especially Catholics?

2. What difference do these changing demographics make for you and your community as you plan your future and explore the deeper invitations for transformation?

Culture Shifts among U.S. Catholics

"Institutes of consecrated life are thus invited courageously to propose anew the interposing initiative, creativity and holiness of their founders and foundresses in response to the signs of the time emerging in today's world." Vita Consecrata

The Christian Church provides an experience of community centered in Jesus with all of its traditions, codes, creeds, organizational structures and ways of educating the faithful. The Catholic Church of today, however, is radically different than the community of faithful at the time of Jesus. However slowly and painfully, it has evolved over the course of 2000 years.

The infant Church had no parishes, churches, schools, catechism or Bible as we know it today. The early disciples were Jews who were married (even St. Peter) with families and trades. The early Church was a table-like affair. Everyone participated in a strong community spirit. By the year 160 a system of priests and bishops was organized.[114] It wasn't until the Church was legalized in 313 by Emperor Constantine that it became formalized (Edict of Milan). Priests were then given high social ranking and began wearing distinctive clothes. Pope Leo I (440-461) was first to claim universal authority. Between 400 and 1100 the altar moved away from its central position until it faced the back wall and the priest had to celebrate mass with his back to the congregation.[115]

Christians had always engaged in some form of penance for their failings, but it wasn't until 1000 that there was absolution for sins. In 1215 the Church instituted annual confession, in 1551 it became a sacrament and in 1614 the ritual called for a screen between the confessor and penitent.[116] The first record of a law pertaining to Sunday observance dates back to 506, but it wasn't until the eleventh century that the Decree of Gratian made Sunday observance a universal law of the Church. Celibacy was not required until the 12th century.[117]

In 325, the Council of Nicaea gave us the Nicene Creed. Between 1545-63, the Council of Trent, initiated in response to the Protestant Reformation, revised Church doctrine on a variety of issues, from original sin and salvation to the profession of faith (Tridentine Creed). The Immaculate Conception was defined in 1854 and Papal infallibility during Vatican I (1869-70). Vatican II (1962-65) ushered in the modern era of the Church focusing on a community of covenanted people committed to God and God's mission.

The times, they are a changing

While changes were slow in the first two millennia, changes in the beliefs and practices of Catholics in the United States have shifted dramatically over the past 50 years. Prior to Vatican II, in the United States, Catholics were at the bottom of the socioeconomic ladder and faced prejudice and discrimination. Catholics stuck together and found solace in parish life and in their common ground of attitudes, beliefs and practices.

In the 1950's, Catholics believed in doctrinal authority, papal infallibility, and understood that noncompliance with basic Church teachings was a mortal sin. The Church was a refuge where unity prevailed over diversity. For example, the vast majority of Catholics attended Mass, supported taxes for social welfare, agreed with Church teachings on divorce and agreed that God punished people for their sins.

The sixteen documents produced by the Second Vatican Council created a sea change within the Church dispensing many of its traditions (e.g., the Latin mass and meatless Fridays) and bringing increased diversity.[118] This sea change took place within the context of tremendous social, political, economic and religious changes across the globe. The 1960s in the United States was marked by assassinations, the Vietnam War, Watergate, civil rights, gay rights, environmental activists, women's liberation, the pill, free love and rock and roll. Adding to the cultural upheaval and institutional mistrust were enormous advances in technology, science, medicine and globalization.

The Catholic Church was viewed as no longer the one true Church, no longer infallible, and no longer held together by a solid set of common beliefs and practices. The codes and creeds could no longer contain the emerging Church. The attitudes, practices and beliefs among Catholics were changing and have continued to evolve to this present day. The fact is that the majority of Catholics today disagree with the Church's teachings regarding premarital sex, gay marriage, contraception, women's ordination, married priests and a host of other issues. Most people who were raised Catholic are no longer practicing Catholics.

Amidst this ongoing evolution, the men and women in Religious Life carried the diversity that exists within their own communities and among the laity often awkwardly, if not contentiously. "Unity in diversity" was a common rhetorical aspiration but a reality seldom achieved. What are your beliefs as vowed religious? How well do you tolerate, accept or embrace these differences among yourselves and the people with whom you serve? How judgmental and painfully divisive have these differences been in your community, or do you even talk about them?

From the surveys I have done, I have come to see that most men and women religious have only a vague grasp of the beliefs and practices among the broader population, and even less of an understanding regarding the beliefs and practices of their own members. Yet, most religious present an outward image of support for the Church's teaching. When assembled together, few will skip Mass, or give voice to their opposition to Church teachings, even though privately (i.e., when away from the Motherhouse), their beliefs and practices are quite different. This appearance of conformity belies the diversity that exists and diminishes the authenticity of community.

Unity and diversity, judgement and division

What judgments do you hold toward the people you serve, or others in community, whose beliefs and practices differ from your own? What judgements have been made of you? Are your beliefs and practices as vowed religious mirroring the cultural trends or offering an alternative?

How well do you know the members of your own religious community or the wider civic community within which you live and minster?

Because many men and women religious know very little about what their own members believe or practice, I have encouraged them to open up these conversations. When they do so, it is an eye-opening and edifying experience. When I have surveyed communities and facilitated their assemblies aimed at exploring their diversity of beliefs and practices, four themes have emerged:

1. Members of religious communities are nearly as diverse as the general population. They are not a monolithic homogenous group that tows the party line. While on average, they are a bit more aligned with the Church's teachings than their lay cohorts, and have proportionally fewer people on the extremes, they

are more diverse than even they themselves would imagine. The richness of their diversity, for the most part, has yet to be fully embraced.

2. In addition, any one member's beliefs cannot be neatly categorized as belonging to one of two camps, either "conservative" or "liberal." For example, someone might strongly oppose premarital sex but support gay rights. Another might believe in women's ordination but oppose serving communion to divorced Catholics. Labeling members as "conservative," "liberal," "traditional" or "progressive" not only stifles conversation, it white-washes the reality of individual differences that exist. It keeps members naive as to their own reality, perpetuates false images and perpetuates divisive judgements.

3. The fear of judgment or reprisal leads members to be more reticent than the general population to speak openly about their beliefs. They are fearful of the judgements and reprisals not only from the Church, but from publics who may be, themselves, ardent supporters of the Church. They are afraid of risking their reputation, donor support, or being "reported to the bishop" should they speak publicly about beliefs that differ from the Church. For women religious, this fear was reinforced as a result of the LCWR investigation and apostolic visitations.

4. Perhaps even more disturbing is the fear many have of the judgments and reprisals from among members of their own community. I've had many occasions, while facilitating assemblies and Chapters, that a member might come to me and say, "How can she call herself a 'good Catholic' if she does not go to Mass?" "How can he be the face of the congregation if he is openly gay?" Some members are aghast when other members speak or act in ways that deviate from the Church's party line, when, in fact, the variance around this line is nearly as wide as the publics'. Members judge and reprimand other members who have the courage to claim their differences with the Church. They do so, often, with little awareness as to the diversity that exists among

their own members and, sometimes, with little personal insight regarding their own beliefs or practices that are not aligned with Church teachings.

Without honest conversation about members' genuine differences in attitudes, beliefs and practices, a community remains uninformed as to its true identity and lacks authenticity. Without a solid ground on which to stand, communities risk diminishing their integrity and, consequently, their future survival. It makes it hard for them to accompany other laity in their questions about Church teachings. A community's identity, integrity, relevancy and survival rest on its willingness to not just tolerate its diversity, but to understand and embrace it. When communities can have honest and open conversations, they at least give themselves the possibility of transformation; but without this, it is impossible. Thus, I offer the following trends with the hope that this might provide a catalyst for more open and honest discussion among community members.

Attitudes, beliefs and practices

In the 1950s, "In God we trust" was added to our American currency and the *Pledge of Allegiance* was amended to include, "under God." Current surveys indicate that a lot has changed since the 1950s. However, trying to assess these changes by comparing one survey to the next is a challenge. The attitudes, beliefs and practices among Catholics vary greatly across surveys due to the characteristics of the population sampled in a given survey (e.g., frequency of Mass attendance, ethnicity, age, gender, education, family upbringing and birth order, socioeconomic status, degree of religiosity, politics, etc.).

For example, survey results vary widely depending upon whether the population is loosely identified as Catholic or *practicing* Catholic. When asked, "What is your present religion, if any?" one-in-five U.S. adults say they are Catholic. Within this group, some say they attend Mass at least once a week (39%), while others say they rarely or never go to Mass (16%).[119] Catholics who say they attend Mass regularly (at least once a week) are consistently more in agreement with Church teachings than are Catholics who attend Mass less frequently.[120]

Keeping in mind these caveats, let me offer the results of a number of surveys that describe the kinds of changes taking place among Catholics today.

Premarital sex and cohabitation

Seventy-seven percent of Catholics disagree with the Church on premarital sex.[121] While the Catholic Church does not favor premarital sex, the vast majority of Americans still engage in it (84% of those between 18 and 23). Fewer than four-in-ten Americans (38%) view premarital sex as wrong. Only about a quarter of adults under age 30 (27%) say living with a partner outside of marriage is sinful, compared with roughly four-in-ten older adults. Eighty-four percent of Catholics say it is acceptable for unmarried parents to live together to raise their children.[122]

Homosexuality and same sex marriage

Over two dozen countries now allow gay marriages. Seventy percent of Catholics disagree with Church on homosexuality.[123] Support for same-sex marriage has steadily grown in recent years. In 2015 the U.S. Supreme Court ruled that the Constitution guarantees gay marriages throughout the land, 11 years after same-sex marriage was first made legal in Massachusetts. While the Catholic Church remains opposed to gay marriage, roughly six-in-ten Catholics now support it.

Interfaith marriage

While many still marry within their religion, fewer Americans hold this as important as it once was. Now, about half of Americans marry outside of their religion. One-in-five Catholics were raised in interfaith marriages. Over eighty percent of Americans, as well as Catholics, approve of interfaith marriages.[124]

Divorce

While Jesus, himself, taught that marriage is permanent, and the Church has reinforced this, one-quarter to one-third of Catholics are divorced, and about one-in-ten have remarried. Most U.S. Catholics (66%) believe that divorce is acceptable (depending upon circumstances). Only one-in-five Catholics, and Americans as a whole, believe divorce is a sin. Most (62%) also think the

Church should allow Catholics who have been divorced, and remarried without an annulment, to receive Communion. Only 15% of divorced Catholics have sought an annulment.[125], [126]

Abortion

Despite the fact that Americans remain split regarding their personal beliefs on abortion, most Americans (70%) do not want to see Roe v. Wade overturned and wish to preserve a woman's right to choose.[127] Most Catholics (56%) believe abortion should be legal compared to 83% of the general population.[128] Sixty-one percent of Catholics disagree with the Church on abortion.[129]

Death penalty

There is rising opposition in the U.S. to the death penalty (37% opposing), with Catholics mirroring this general trend (34% opposing). In a recent change in the Church's position, Pope Francis decreed that the death penalty is "unacceptable in all cases." White Catholics, like the general public, are almost evenly divided in their views with 45% expressing support for the death penalty and 50% in favor of life in prison. In contrast, only 29% of Hispanic Catholics favor the death penalty for people convicted of murder, while 62% prefer they serve life in prison.[130]

Assisted suicide

While the Catholic Church strongly opposes assisted suicide, about six-in-ten adults (62%) say that a person suffering a great deal of pain with no hope of improvement has a moral right to end their own life. Catholics, in general, mirror this belief.[131]

Women's ordination

Although the Catholic Church opposes it, over 75% of Catholics now approve of women's ordination.[132] Most every other religion (except Mormon) approve of women clergy.

Married priests

Since 1139, the Church has favored celibacy. Despite the Church's ban against married priests (since the First Lateran Council, 1123), most Catholics in the U.S. favor the idea of married priests.[133] There are currently about 80 married priests in the U.S. (mostly former Episcopalian priests). In the CARA survey of Catholic women, six-in-ten support ordaining women as permanent deacons. [134]

Mass attendance

On average, 23% of Catholics attend Mass at least once a week (45% for pre-Vatican II down to 18 % for Millennials, and women more than men).[135] Catholics who say they attend Mass regularly (at least once a week) are consistently more in agreement with Church teachings than are Catholics who attend Mass less frequently.[136] In a survey of Catholic women, over half (53%) attended Mass only a few times a year or less, while one-in-five attended weekly.[137] Fifty-Seven percent of practicing Catholics believe that you can be a "good Catholic without going to Mass" [138] and most do not see missing Mass as sinful.

Confession

Despite the fact that confession (reconciliation) is one of the Church's seven sacraments, only about 2% of Catholics go to confession regularly.[139] In a recent CARA survey of Catholic women, only 3% went to confession regularly and 70% never went or went less than once a year.[140]

Contraception

Sixty to 90% of Catholics disagree with the Church on birth control. While the Church teaches that contraception is "intrinsically evil," half of all Catholics use the pill and 70% use, or would use, condoms. Eighty-four percent of Catholics say the Church should modify its ban on the use of artificial birth control.[141]

Evolution

While Pope Francis does not see any inherent contradiction about the science of evolution and the Church's teachings, and most Americans and Catholics believe in evolution, about one-third of Americans, including Catholics, do not believe in evolution. They believe that humans and other beings have existed in their present form since the beginning of time. Roughly two-thirds of white evangelical Protestants do not believe in evolution.[142]

Bible literalism

Thirty-three percent of Americans believe that the bible is "literally" the word of God, down from 65% in 1960. Among Evangelicals, 60% hold this belief, while among Catholics only 23% hold this belief.[143] In fact, few practicing Catholics read the Bible (22%) or go to Bible study groups (14%).[144]

Prayers

Roughly 35% of practicing Catholics pray weekly devotions to Mary or a special saint. Twenty-seven percent of practicing Catholics pray the Rosary weekly.[145] When asked how they pray, about half of Catholics say they use mainly memorized prayers like the Hail Mary and the Lord's Prayer (21%) or a combination of memorized prayers and personal conversations with God (31%). More than four-in-ten Catholics (44%) say their prayers consist mainly of personal conversations with God.[146] In a CARA survey of Catholic women, half pray daily, mainly for the wellbeing of family and friends, or simply have conversations with God. A relatively small percentage participate regularly in Eucharistic Adoration, Bible Study or Lectio Divina (13% and 12%, respectively). The vast majority (71%) of these women do not participate in a group prayer outside of Mass.[147]

Helping the poor

Catholics are split on their beliefs about closing the gap between the rich and poor and whether it is a sin to buy luxury items without helping the poor. However, over ninety percent of Catholics believe in helping the poor.[148]

God's hand in the elections and the Super Bowl

A majority (57%) of white evangelical Protestants say God played a major role in determining the outcome of the 2016 election, a view shared by one-in-five Catholics. One-quarter of the general population believes that God will determine the next Super Bowl winner, and nearly half say God rewards devout athletes.[149]

Summary

Most Catholics in the United States:

- don't go to Mass, yet see themselves as good Catholics;
- disagree with the Church's position regarding women's ordination and married priests, gay marriage, interfaith marriage, divorce and annulments;
- disagree with the Church's position on sexual morality, including abortion, homosexuality, cohabitation, premarital sex, and the use of contraception;
- believe in helping the poor, but not necessarily closing the gap between rich and poor;
- believe in evolution, not bible literalism;
- oppose the death penalty but approve of assisted suicide;
- no longer say rote prayers, devotional prayers, or the Rosary; and few parishioners read the bible;
- no longer go to confession.

Reflection: Impact of changing and diverse beliefs and practices

---

1. *What impact do these diverse and rapid changes in beliefs and practices have upon you and your community?*

2. *What difference does this make for you and your community as you plan for your future and explore the deeper invitations for transformation?*

What is the glue that holds us together?

The vast majority of Americans believe in God and an afterlife, and view religion as an important part of their life and identity. Beyond this large swath of common ground, diversity prevails both within and across the religious landscape. The Catholic Church is no exception. The attitudes, beliefs, and practices of its members, as well as its priests, brothers and sisters, are far more diverse than most might imagine.

Is there any unity amidst this diversity or is the Catholic Church a house divided? Robert Putnam and David Campbell, who wrote *American Grace*, sought to answer the question of whether or not religious pluralism can coexist with rising religious polarization. They provided an exhaustive review of the literature related to the religious landscape and concluded by saying America's grace lies within its ability to reach across its differences with a "web of interlocking personal relationships."[150] It comes down to our relationships and our willingness to honor the diversity that exists, rather than trying to change how others practice or what they believe.

Putnam and Campbell described the futility of trying to convince others to change their beliefs and practices. "Disagreements over religion," they said, "are often disagreements over fundamentals: the immovable object of one person's belief meeting the irresistible force of another's."[151] Not only is it impossible, it is misguided, if not morally offensive. What divides us is not our differences. Rather it is our condemnations and attempts at coercion that are the cause of our polarization, rising tension and violence.

John Allen, who wrote, *The Future Church: How Ten Trends are Revolutionizing the Catholic Church*, gives a detailed description of the future trends within the global Catholic Church. In probing the challenges of divisions and polarization that exists within the Catholic Church he, too, concludes by encouraging a stronger web of relationships:

> *"Fostering holiness in the upside-down Church of the twenty-first century will require special courage – the courage of humility, of patience, of perspective. Above all, it will require the courage to think beyond the interests of one's own Catholic tribe, conceiving the Catholic future not in zero-sum terms but as a bold synthesis of the best of each of the Church's constituencies."*[152]

The glue that holds us together is not a uniform set of codes and creeds. It is our willingness and ability to tolerate, accept, understand and, ultimately, embrace our differences. What divides us is not our differences, but our judgements and attempts to force people to believe as "I" believe or fall in line with the Church's code for what constitutes a good Catholic.

Restoring the Dignity of Difference

Life that ceaselessly unfolds throughout the universe with its boundless diversity is, in God's eyes, all "good" (Genesis 1:31). Thus, for us to reject, ignore, or even minimize life's diversity would be to cast off the very seedbed and offspring of creation. It would be sacrilegious. In light of the goodness of all creation, how can we meet the challenge of following our own spiritual path in the context of community, while at least tolerating, if not respecting and, ideally, embracing the dignity of difference? How can you, as religious men and women, remain true to yourselves and your own religious beliefs and practices, while mutually honoring the differences among all of your members, mission partners and the people you serve?

Let me ask you to reflect for a moment on a few scenarios:

- How would you advise a Catholic family member who is divorced and wants to take communion while at Mass?

- What would you tell a parishioner who is struggling to accept his or her identity as gay or lesbian?

- What would you say to a Catholic friend who confides in you about an abortion and is racked with shame?

- What would you say to a member of your community who was sexually abused by a priest and too frightened to report it?

Reflect for a moment about one of these scenarios and think of a particular person who could be in one of these scenarios. Imagine what your spoken or unspoken judgements might be. Try to put yourself in the other's shoes. Would you accompany them to find their own way, guide them according to yours, or tell them what the Church says they *should* do? Would you let what they say enter into your own soul and influence how you see them, the issue or yourself? Now reverse roles and put yourself in their shoes. Imagine that you were the one struggling. What would you want from others in order to feel safe, understood and empowered to make a discerned decision?

It is a terrible irony that the Eucharistic Liturgy (Mass), which is intended to be a renewing and unifying communal experience of our faith is, for many, an experience of boredom, alienation and division. It is disturbing that our Catholic creeds and codes have alienated so many of our own, and rebuffed so many would-be seekers, because of the Church's fixation on dogma, our insistence upon one *right* way to be Christian, or one *right* way to be Catholic. How can we accompany others in their questions, doubts and differences if we are unable to authentically accompany one another with dignity in the differences we experience in community?

How can we restore the dignity of difference? One thing is sure: goodwill alone is not enough. You will need to make conscious and deliberate *choices*, bring the right *intentions*, develop and hone your *skills*, and apply them with *discipline*. Here are four things that would help to restore the dignity of difference:

1. Bridge the tragic gap and by reaching across our differences;

2. Shift from the hypocrisy of conformity to the integrity of authenticity;

3. Move from denial and intolerance to integration and acceptance; and,

4. Work toward transformation through the crucible of conversion.

Maybe, if you make good choices in how you speak and listen, ground yourselves with good intentions, bring the best of your skills for listening actively and empathically, you can help restore the dignity of difference. Let me speak briefly to each of these.

Bridge the tragic gap by reaching across our differences

It is not our differences that divide us but our *judgements*. It is our judgements that lead us to make insensitive and cruel remarks. We need to replace judgment with understanding, cruelty with compassion, avoidance with engagement, and our need to tell others what to believe and how to behave with empathic listening, in order to understand and learn to appreciate what others believe and why they behave as they do. We need to learn how to reach across our differences, bridge what Parker Palmer calls our "tragic gap" or our fear of the "alien other,"[153] and lean toward one another with understanding and compassion.

Without such self-examination, reflection and dialogue, you run the risk of wounding one another out of naiveté and misunderstanding or, worse, out of arrogance and misguided attempts to proselytize. Without honest reflection, exploration and conversation you will more easily judge one another rather than understand one another, and avoid each other rather than engage each other.

In his recent book, *Living Mission Interculturally*, Anthony Gittins suggests: "One reason for our xenophobia and less than human approach to diversity is what can be illustrated as the 'cultural flaw': our human tendency to divide and conquer, to oppose and confront, to separate and discriminate. But another may well be our tendency to religious intolerance, self-righteousness, and the aggressive defense of 'my truth' against all comers."[154] We need to redeem this cultural flaw and strengthen our capacity for mutual respect and appreciation of our differences.

Shift from the hypocrisy of conformity to the integrity of authenticity

Second, we need to redeem our sense of integrity by living authentically and more in sync with our true beliefs than with the expectation others have of us. If diversity is not accepted, we will feel pressured to conform outwardly – going to Mass, reciting rote prayers, kneeling, standing, sitting and speaking the Catholic party line – simply to avoid the scrutiny and judgment of others. When we conform outwardly in a manner that betrays our own authenticity, we pay a terrible price. It costs us our personal integrity. We don't feel right with ourselves. Others see it, know it and judge us accordingly.

Our hypocrisy alienates us from ourselves, from family and friends, and from those who are seeking a real Church or an authentic religious community. We want to live in communities where we know we *belong*, where we feel at *home*, where we can *explore our doubts* so that we can *grow in our faith*. Communities will remain a house divided if members outwardly conform and hide their true selves, or if they are true to themselves and judged unacceptable by others. We need to reclaim our true selves and support the fragile web of inclusion modeled by Jesus in order to restore the integrity and dignity of difference.

Move from denial and intolerance to integration and acceptance

Third, we need to explore the diversity among our religious beliefs and practices for the same reason it is wise to explore and unearth the treasures in any area of diversity. Without an honest self-examination and candid exploration, our ignorance, fears and prejudices will fan the flames of systemic racism, sexism, ageism, homophobia, xenophobia and all manner of tribalism. Ignorance of our diverse religious beliefs and practices will only lead to denigrating and dehumanizing others. It will stunt our own growth and stymie the growth in others.

Shakil Choudhury, the author of *Deep Diversity: Overcoming Us vs. Them*,[155] tells us that our fear of alien others is hard-wired into us, part of our primitive brain structures. He offers hope, however, saying that our implicit biases, blind spots and prejudices can be overcome through the development of skills. Among these skills are self-awareness, meditation, education and empathy. He believes that if these skills are intentionally developed, then it is possible to transform the brain's instinctually fearful response to differences into one of compassion and understanding.

Milton Bennet describes a developmental model of intercultural living. He suggests that we need to work hard to move from seeing, judging and interpreting community through *my* own eyes, and acting as if *my* beliefs are the only acceptable beliefs (Ethnocentrism) to seeing community through the context of other belief systems. We need to adapt our approach to others by constantly monitoring our own reaction to others (Enthnorelativism). In this way, we grow in:

- accepting that *my way* is not the *only way*; distinguishing my beliefs from others and seeing both as human;

- following our own conscience without imposing our views or convictions on others;

- seeing from the other's viewpoint with respect in order to learn, incorporate, and adapt our views and behaviors, but not at the cost of our own identity.[156]

Each person in community, each difference expressed, then, has a mutually influential and beneficial impact upon community, creating a new intercultural community.

Work toward transformation through the crucible of conversion

Finally, the fourth reason to explore your diverse religious beliefs and practices is to work toward personal and communal transformation. In one community, following a reflection I offered on Eucharist, a member responded saying, "My theology is fixed. I don't need any new theology." He was closed to any other perception but his own and was in a state of what might be termed *arrested spiritual development*.

Jesus calls us to change: "Unless you change and become like children, you will never enter the kingdom of heaven." (Matthew 18:3). Cardinal Newman is known to have said, "To live is to change; to be perfect is to have changed often." The cost of avoiding change is arrested spiritual development. We might age, but we will not mature spiritually or otherwise.

Admittedly, there is a cost, too, for maturing and engaging in this work of transformation. We might want transformation, but most want it without the cost of personal conversion. It stretches us, often painfully, to grow and evolve. It will cost you to welcome diversity in your community. Restoring the dignity of difference cannot happen without the pain of conversion and transformation. We cannot transform and evolve if we are to insist upon being right rather than being human, if we close our eyes to differences among us, if we choose to "live and let live," "agree to disagree" and avoid the hard work of growth and maturation. If we transform, it will cost us.

Our spiritual and religious practices evolved for thousands of years before, and since, the time of Jesus. No single faith or religion can serve all humanity for all time. We were never a Church of one mind, or traveling on one spiritual path made of one set of beliefs and practices. However slowly and painfully, the Catholic Church continues to evolve and transform. By restoring the dignity of difference, and seeking the conversion required of us to do so, we honor God and allow for the continued evolution of the Church.

Reflection: Restoring the Dignity of Difference

Which of these efforts to restore the dignity of difference poses the greatest challenge for your community and why?

1. *Bridge the tragic gap and embrace the dignity of difference.*

2. *Shift from the hypocrisy of conformity to the integrity of authenticity.*

3. *Move from denial and intolerance to integration and acceptance.*

4. *Work toward transformation through the crucible of conversion.*

CHAPTER 5:
CHALLENGES FACING
RELIGIOUS COMMUNITIES

From the surface to the soul

"The system is broken."
Barbara Marx Hubbard

Cascading Crises

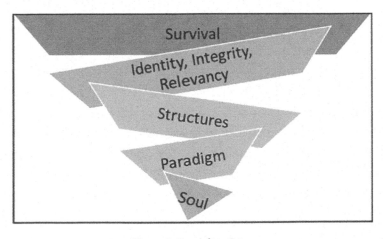

Figure 4: Cascading Crises

Religious communities are facing a cascade of crises from the surface of their lives down to their very soul. On the surface are the demographic changes adversely affecting personnel, leadership and finances, and putting the operational *survival* of communities in jeopardy. These challenges are where most communities focus their time, energy and resources. However, beneath these challenges are crises pertaining to the *identity, integrity* and *relevancy* of religious communities. And below these are the *structures* that undergird life in community that are no longer adequate for the challenges facing communities today. The very *paradigm* for Religious Life is in flux. These challenges cut across all levels of life down to the very *soul* of communities.

The combined effect of these cascading crises is placing the future of communities, and Religious Life as a whole, in jeopardy. Communities will need to successfully address each of these in order to make the bend in the road. They will need to create a new identity, reduce the gaps in integrity and make themselves more tangibly relevant in the world. They will need to create new structures in support of a new paradigm more in line with their deepest longings and the urgent needs of the world. To the degree that these are brought into alignment, the possibilities for new life improve. This work of realignment is the work of transformation.

This chapter describes in detail the challenges that religious communities must face if they are to transform their lives and mission. These crises will not be fixed with simple solutions. The system is too broken and cannot, nor should it, be restored to what it once was. These crises, if successfully addressed and worked through, can become the gateway to transformation.

Crisis of Survival

I agree with those who suggest that the size, per se, of a community is "insignificant."[157] However, I believe it is the *change* in size, the demographic shifts of rapidly decreasing numbers, and the advancing age of members that is having a tremendous impact. These demographic shifts are increasing the financial stress, shrinking the pool of potential leaders, and bringing communities to their knees.

The next ten years is *crunch time* for nearly every religious community in the United States. Many communities are already in a crisis of survival simply because their resources are stretched too thin and getting thinner. My research indicates that the demographic changes creating this crisis of survival are related to three areas: 1) a limited number of willing and able members to carry out both internal and external ministries; 2) a shrinking pool of members who can provide viable leadership; and, 3) financial burdens.[158]

Personnel crunch

Communities with rapidly declining numbers and advancing age will soon, if they haven't already, reach the breaking point. They will have no members left to replace all those who leave key positions. There will be too many positions to fill, too many needs to address, with too few personnel to maintain life as it is currently lived. In short, the bench is thinning out!

I see it all the time, members in key positions becoming ill: a vocation director breaks a hip, the healthcare director has a stroke, the treasurer has a heart attack, the communications director gets diagnosed with cancer, a congregational leader becomes too cognitively impaired or emotionally overwhelmed to carry the heavy load. When members can no longer function in key positions, leadership teams scramble to fill slots. They draw upon those who may, or may not, be well trained. They draw upon those who may, or may not, want the position (let alone feel *called* to the ministry). They draw upon those who are already in other positions of responsibility but are needed in a more critical position, or they might ask someone to pull double-duty. At some point this triaging approach fails and the system breaks down.

Shrinking pool of recycled leadership

Increasingly there is a shrinking pool of members to provide adequate leadership. Let's say you have a community with 100 people and 20 of them are *willing* to discern the call to leadership. Of the 20 that are willing, let's say 15 think they are *able* to provide leadership (i.e., physically and cognitively capable). Of the 15 that are willing and able, maybe 7 are potentially *electable* (i.e., they

97

have enough credibility and regard in the community such that they could be elected). Of the 7 that are remaining, who is *compatible* enough to form a viable leadership team? In other words, although it may look like you have the numbers, after you consider who is *willing, able, electable,* and *compatible,* the real numbers shrink considerably.

Often, those who are willing are not so able, electable, or compatible with others who might also be elected. They may be kind and generous in offering their services, but their skills, cognitive capacity, health or wellbeing are not strong enough for the complex demands of today's leadership. Or they might be among the best and brightest, but they don't "play well with others," or have the trust and respect of the membership enough to be elected. When communities were larger and younger, there were many willing, able, capable and electable members to go around. Not anymore.

Many communities, doing the best they can with who they have, elect leadership teams that are greatly challenged simply because of limitations related to age. While there are many people who are vibrant, capable, and work full time in their 70's and 80's, it is no secret that the older we live, the more limitations we face both physically and mentally. Our energy, bodies and brain power diminish, not strengthen, with age. For example, as we age, the brain's executive functions diminish. These functions include problem-solving, cognitive flexibility, abstract thinking, reasoning and judgement. These executive functions are the very capacities needed in leadership today to contend with the complex and rapid changes.

I see people elected who no longer have the cognitive capacity to carry out the complex tasks of leadership. I see others who simply do not have the energy or emotional resilience for the demands of leadership. Of the last ten leadership teams with whom I have most recently worked, nine of them lost at least one member during their term. Recognizing the frequent risks of losing someone along the way, one team created a "pre-nup." It was a written contract stating their wishes should they become impaired, resign, or be forced to leave office during their term – a sign of the times!

A leadership team with whom I recently worked had only one member with a firm grasp on, and the ability to address, what the community was facing. The others, as generous as their offerings were, could not perform ordinary functions of leadership (e.g., compose a well-written letter, present or lead a discussion at a community gathering, decipher financial statements or supervise staff). It was impossible for them to address the complex planning for healthcare, properties and ministries, contribute meaningfully on boards, or facilitate the handling of delicate interpersonal matters in community.

Through no fault of their own, they no longer had the wherewithal to deal with the many urgent and complex matters in community, and they knew it. They felt personally embarrassed and frustrated by their limitations. Knowing the community was counting on them only added more pressure. They were frightened for their community's sake and knew it needed more help than they could provide. Yet, knowing all this, they remained reluctant to explore other options or seek outside help.

Communities recycle leaders because there is no one to replace them. These limitations are real, and the consequences are painful for leaders and members alike. The shrinking pool of competent leadership is making it impossible to continue in the same way as they have in the past. Reducing the number in leadership by one or two does little to solve the problem. The system is broken.

Financial and healthcare challenges

The third most common threat to survival caused by the demographic shifts is the financial challenge. The problems here include diminishing revenues, rising healthcare costs, buildings that are increasingly underutilized or need to be repaired, renovated, repurposed, or sold, as well as land that needs to be divested. These financial issues are complex, interrelated, and emotionally loaded. They present a major hurdle to leaders who, for the most part, are not formally trained in the legal, financial, medical, architectural or real estate competencies needed to address them.

Belt-tightening is not enough. Communities are simply too strapped to continue as they have in the past. Currently, according to the National Religious Retirement Office (NRRO), only 33% of reporting institutes are "adequately funded" for retirement.[159] The total underfunded retirement liability for men's and women's institutes is only expected to rise in the coming years.

With fewer members in remunerative ministries, revenue streams are drying up. Members, feeling an increased pressure to work, are postponing retirement and working well into their 70s and 80s. While some want to work, and are capable of working, others are struggling to keep up with the demands of work. Still others are disappointed, or resentful, for having to work at this stage in life. Some, feeling like "I've paid my dues," decide for themselves to retire regardless of the pressure. Others, despite failing heath, press on out of duty.

With more senior members needing healthcare, and insurance reimbursements tightening, costs are skyrocketing. Some communities have their own licensed healthcare facilities. Many more communities have developed their own home-grown, unlicensed healthcare facilities. As more members need help, and fewer members are available to provide it, communities hire more lay assistance. Communities are increasingly struggling to finance, supervise, and manage their personnel and the facilities.

Only the most sophisticated healthcare communities can stay afloat amid the turbulent times in a competitive healthcare industry. Communities with fewer resources, and whose mission is not healthcare, are trying to hand over management of healthcare to professional management companies. If they cannot afford that option, their next step is to let go of ownership all together. If there are no buyers, then they are left to close their facilities and send their members needing care to outside facilities. Not only is the letting go of ownership and operations complex, it is time consuming, costly, and emotionally taxing.

In addition to the cost of care for aging members, is the care for aging buildings. Many of these buildings were built in the 1950s and 1960s, when numbers swelled among religious. These cinder block buildings typically have high maintenance costs. As members decline in number, and when existing members resist coming back to the motherhouse, these massive buildings are left increasingly underutilized. A building with forty rooms may have a handful of people living there. Selling, deconstructing, renovating or repurposing these buildings is costly and, in some remote areas, not even possible. They become white elephants impossible to offload.

Reflection: Crisis of Survival

---

1. *How would you describe your community's challenges to survive?*

2. *What impact are these having upon your mission and the lives of your members?*

3. *How are you addressing these as you plan for your future?*

Crisis of Identity

> *"Until we can articulate who we are and why we are, and until we can do so in a way that is attractive to twenty-first century Christians, we will not be able to refound our communities." Patricia Wittberg*

What would you say to a prospective candidate about how being a vowed member of your community differs from members of any other religious community, or from other philanthropic or faith-based organizations? Communities are struggling to define their identity and clarify their mission. If members are not clear on who they are, why they exist, and their primary purpose for being in community, it makes it very hard to articulate a vision, sacrifice to make it real, prioritize and align resources, or attract new members.

Some suggest that religious communities have become more like faith-sharing groups or intentional communities, wherein identity is derived primarily from the individual spiritual quest, rather than a common institutional service. Members live and minister apart from each other and gather for shared prayer and socializing. New entrants are attracted by the spirituality of the group rather than by its distinctive institutional identity.

According to Margaret Wheatley, "The most powerful organizing dynamic in life is identity. The first act of life is to define a self, whether a micro-organism or a human being. In humans, how we define ourselves determines our perceptions, beliefs, behaviors, values."[160] Yet, this self-organizing capacity is in jeopardy and communities are struggling to define who they are, their purpose for existence and their vision for the future. This identity crisis is exacerbated by: 1) boundaries confusion, 2) mission drift, and 3) maintenance responsibilities that leave little time, energy or resources available to nurture new life or plan for the future.

Boundary confusion

All living things require two things in order to maintain a solid identity: 1) clear and permeable boundaries, and 2) a sense of purpose. For many religious communities, both elements have been compromised leaving them wondering: *Who are we and what do we stand for?* Canon law very clearly defines what constitutes a religious or secular institute, what qualifies as vowed membership, who are clerical, laity and associates in mission. While these are clear in the canons, it is less clear in the lived reality of communities.

Some communities opened their boundaries to include more laity. As the numbers of members were declining many looked to their associates to carry the torch of their mission and charism into the future. In some cases, lay associates and other mission partners might participate in all matters of the community, not just ministries. They might be on committees, live in local communities, or participate in assemblies and weigh in on matters of governance and finance. Some communities have sought to develop new forms of membership, both vowed and non-vowed (e.g., Agrégées). In 2016, even LCWR opened its boundaries to include lay consultants and facilitators in their annual assemblies.

Other communities, in an effort to distinguish their identity from non-members have clarified their boundaries and made them less permeable. Associates are no longer invited to "member-only" conversations, especially related to governance, formation and finances. Associates, if they participate at all in Chapters, might be invited as "observers" (without voice), or as "guests" who could come to only special presentations or opening and closing celebrations.

A religious community that does not have clear and permeable boundaries will fail to thrive. It will lose a solid sense of identity. Patricia Wittberg said it this way: "Establishing clear and appropriate boundaries, so that the difference between being and not being a member is readily apparent, is an essential step in any group's construction of its identity. Unless a group has boundaries, it cannot long exist."[161]

Mission drift

Though it helps to distinguish the nature of participation among members and non-members, it still leaves the question: *What is the essence of vowed membership?* What is the distinctive role of vowed members and how is that any different from the lay partners. When Vatican II pronounced the universal call to holiness, it chipped away at the uniqueness and specialness of vowed life. Wittberg said: "In one stroke, it nullified the basic ideological foundation for eighteen centuries of Roman Catholic religious life."[162]

Member satisfaction that used to come from an *esprit de corp* and pride in community ministries is now more derived from personal ministry and spiritual growth. Communal identity, once marked by flagship ministries, is no longer distinguishable from other communities or the services provided by laity. What's left is a potpourri of spiritualities.

In the absence of a clear and coherent identity, vision and mission, institutes have become increasingly secularized, losing not only their recruitment base but their distinctive voice and impact upon society. What is the mission and vision of your community in today's world and what impact are you having? Does your mission inspire you, energize you, and compel you to sacrifice to see it become a reality? How is your community's mission uniquely different than any other community?

Most communities, by now, have created beautiful mission and vision statements. They are on everyone's websites, brochures, and hung on the walls in and around the Motherhouse. Especially in the 1980s and 1990s, in sync with corporate America, nearly every community sought to put words to their mission hoping to coalesce their energies, solidify their identity and attract new members.

Unfortunately, most mission statements (i.e., *why* you exist) and vision statements (i.e., *what* you hope to accomplish) are written in vague, general, and highly spiritualized terms. Most mission and vision statements do not have sufficient clarity, and may not inspire sufficient passion and ownership among members or provide enough direction to help solidify a sense of identity. Perhaps in an effort to have every voice heard, no one's words are left unrepresented or, to reach a consensus, these statements are morphed into broad abstractions. They do little to inspire members or prioritize the allocation of resources.

Perhaps too much was asked of a printed document. Or perhaps the mission statements represent the reality for most communities: that their mission has drifted from what it once was and remains a confusing amalgam of interests. As members were encouraged to find their own ministries, the diversity diffused any focus making it harder to define mission and focus a vision. Perhaps the vision statements also reflect the reality for most communities: that what they hope to accomplish has branched out in so many directions there is no longer a clear and cogent picture holding it all together.

Maintenance overshadowing mission

"Failure to articulate overall strategy leads to an incrementalism that emphasized maintenance concerns over organizational revitalization." Patricia Wittberg

Maintenance demands of today are literally smothering the life out of any possibility for a future life and mission. They are sapping the energy, finances, and time from leadership. The day-to-day realities of leadership simply hold too many demands. Despite Chapter promises to focus upon mission and create new visions, the immediate and urgent maintenance responsibilities inevitably overshadow and supersede the Chapter's agenda. Leadership's personal commitments to stay healthy while in office (e.g., time for exercise or to go on retreats) are inevitably set aside due to the daily demands to get things done.

Chapters open and close with soaring rhetoric by incoming leaders. By the end of Chapter, new directions are forged, hopes are high, and newly elected leaders stand poised to take bold steps to further their mission. When the ballots are burned and the glow of Chapter begins to fade, the newly elected leaders sit down together for the first time and soon realize that their hopes for reinvigorating mission are overshadowed by the daily maintenance demands of community. Chapter acts, beautifully composed and promulgated, become one of many stacks of agenda on the desks of leadership.

Members and local communities, when in distress, require leadership's attention. The frail elderly and funerals draw upon leadership's pastoral attention. Vocation and formation teams and newer members need their support. Personnel need supervision. Buildings, land and healthcare issues need to be addressed. Complicated fiscal and legal matters won't wait for a delayed response. Sponsored ministries and boards require regular attendance. Assemblies must be planned, committees formed, and letters written, in order to involve the community in the ongoing work. The list is endless, the demands pile up, and there is never enough time for the agenda at hand.

This press results in teams moving quickly through the agenda, too often at the expense of their own relationships and needed in-depth dialogue. Misunderstandings, tensions and conflict are left unaddressed in order to get through the agenda. Important issues that require significant time, such as, genuine contemplation, reflection, discernment, searching out implications, in-depth sharing, creativity, exploring and working through differences, all take a back seat to getting tasks done.

Leaders are increasingly becoming ill, breaking down, or feeling inadequate for the job at hand. Yet, these are not inadequate or weak individuals. The system cannot adequately allow leaders to address the mounting maintenance needs of today, while simultaneously, thoughtfully and creatively plan for the future. The system is unsustainable.

Reflection: Crisis of Identity

---

1. *How would you describe your community's challenges related to identity (e.g., boundary confusion, mission drift or maintenance overshadowing mission)?*

2. *What impact are these having upon your mission and the lives of your members?*

3. *How are you addressing these as you plan your future?*

Crisis of Integrity

> *"To think is easy. To act is difficult. To act as one thinks is the most difficult of all." Goethe*

Integrity gap

Many communities experience an integrity gap, meaning the behavior of its members does not match their espoused values or beliefs. Mostly this is unspoken, but sometimes it is named aloud as, "We are not who we say we are." When this integrity gap has become pervasive and disturbing enough, some communities decide not to pursue new vocations believing that it would be "morally wrong" to invite people into their community "until we get our own house in order."

A stark example of an integrity gap came to light from the landmark study by David Nygren and Miriam Ukeritis. Their study of 9,999 religious men and women showed that while most speak of their commitment to the poor, 75% had little personal interest in working with the poor.[163] Barbara Fiand implored religious to face this challenge: "We can profess one thing and live quite another, refusing ever to face the inconsistencies in our lives and to embrace courageously the tensions between our present cultural situation and our call as religious to live creatively toward personal and societal transformation."[164]

The compromised integrity between the written word and lived reality undermines the morale among members. While these dynamics may not always be openly addressed, they persist in the subterranean life of many communities, eroding the core of what it means to be community, what it really means to be-in-it-together. Lawrence Cada and colleagues referred to this integrity gap as causing "doubt" among members, undermining members' basic belief in the integrity of community.[165] Challenges related to mutual interdependence, shared responsibilities, consumerism and scandals are frequently cited as examples of what chips away at the wellbeing of community causing a crisis of integrity.

Mutual interdependence

Figure 5: Continuum of Interdependence

Communities profess to live mutually interdependent lives by agreeing to pool their resources, share their gifts and talents, and sacrifice for the good of the whole. The vow of chastity speaks to this fundamental commitment to love and care unsparingly for one another and those they serve. An integrity gap exists to the degree in which commitment to mutual interdependence is not lived out behaviorally.

You can think of interdependence as a healthy mixture of independence and dependence. If we place these on a continuum, on one side you would have those people who are more co-dependent and on the other side you would have those who are more counter-dependent or individualistic. People on either extreme are fraught with insecurity, which prevents them from forming healthy relationships based upon mutual interdependence.

Co-dependent people focus upon the needs of others to the neglect of themselves. They are the proverbial "people-pleasers." Outwardly, they appear altruistic, which fits right in with the basic purpose of a religious community (i.e., to care for others). However, underneath, they are driven by their *need to be needed* and their dependency upon others for a sense of security.

On the other side of the continuum are those who are counter-dependent and overly focused on meeting their own needs. While they look outwardly stronger than co-dependents, they, too, are insecure. Underneath, they are afraid of depending upon others for fear of being abandoned. Thus, they counter their fear of dependency by keeping others emotionally at arm's length. They may happily serve the people of God, but on their own terms and in their own way.

Co-dependence

Early formation efforts not only encouraged excessive dependency on authority, it fostered co-dependency. Men and women became overly *other-oriented*. Many men and women did not complete the developmental task of separation and individuation. They remained deferential and subservient to others. They were taught not to identify and claim their needs and wants so as to focus upon the needs and wants of others. When asked, "What do you want?" it literally does not compute. They turn it back around and ask, "Well, what do you want?" The wires of self-assertion seem cut and they are incapable of asking for, let alone asserting, their own wants and needs – "Whatever you want is fine with me."

Many men and women joined Religious Life in order to help others, evangelize and save souls as well as advocate for the poor and marginalized. This care and concern for others, which is altruistic and admirable, in excess can become the sum total of one's identity. Those who become too focused upon others can lose themselves. Insecurity, low self-esteem and a poorly developed sense of self, feed their *need to be needed*.

Being needed becomes tantamount to one's self-worth. Meeting others' needs, and pleasing others, becomes such a driving force that they will give up anything (e.g., their needs, voice, power, identity) to hold on to the other. If push comes to shove in a relationship, and there is a conflict between meeting their own needs versus the needs of the other, they will give up the self, rather than risk losing the relationship.

Co-dependents end up disempowering the very people they are trying to help when they do for others what others can do for themselves. In their rush to be helpful, they speak for others who can speak for themselves, do for others who can do for themselves and, in so doing, they disempower the very people they are trying to help. The challenge for co-dependents is to claim their own voice and empower themselves.

Counter-dependence or individualism

Psychologists might use the term "counter-dependent," but most people speak of this dynamic as "individualism." Aside from its psychological underpinnings, individualism has deep roots in our culture that influenced its emergence in Religious Life. Individualism is as prevalent in Religious Life today as it is in our American culture with our pervasive use of iPhones, iPads, and other "I"-devices.

Patricia Wittberg once said, "Any community that de-emphasizes its group focus in favor of individual visions will have more difficulty explaining how they are different than laity."[166] Individualism is a systemic problem. In its extreme, it is a dynamic that works against the development of *community*. The determination to have "my voice heard," "my needs met," and the resources to pursue "my dreams," has superseded the collective voice, need and dreams of the community. It hampers a community's ability to make decisions based upon the good of the whole.

Individualism has its own unique history among religious and is deeply imbedded in our American culture. America was born through a revolution that claimed its independence from the royal authority of Britain. In the Broadway hit, *Alexander Hamilton*, Hamilton sings, "I am the one thing in life I can control. I am inimitable. I am an original." Add this to Roy Roger's, "Don't fence me in," or New Hampshire's state motto, "Live free or die," and you have a core theme describing what it means to be an American. We celebrate Independence Day, not Interdependence Day!

Despite our cultural craving for independence, prior to Vatican II, Religious Life fostered dependency, deference to authority, not a mature sense of independence or interdependence. Death to self was extolled as virtuous. Religious were told what to do, what to wear, what to say, and where to go. Ministries were assigned and "domestics" were sorted out from those tapped for higher education. Budgets were fixed and members could carry but a dime to their name when venturing out. Today psychologists might refer to such treatment as "infantilizing." When I ask members about these experiences, however, they laugh, call it "crazy," and shrug it off as the "good ol' days."

After those good old days, after Vatican II, the doors and windows to the world opened up and the pendulum swung the other way. No more meatless Fridays, Latin Masses, head coverings, pomp or pageantry. Religious were encouraged to think for themselves, choose their own clothes and ministries, do their own budgets, drive their own cars, and deal with their own issues. No longer was the superior the "keeper of the vows." Members were to discover for themselves what the vows were and how to keep them. They were given the freedom to individuate and reclaim their autonomy – a much needed developmental task. All of this took place, of course, in the context of the 1960s, during what Christopher Lasch famously called, the "culture of narcissism."[167]

The ordinary, yet delayed psychological task for religious, to develop a personal identity through a process of separation and individuation, was fueled by this cultural revolution. Once they had come to this freedom, community members also became increasingly resistant to leadership telling them what to do. As one leader put it, "Once you are in elected to leadership, you have the least amount of authority in community. No one listens to you." His members had become increasingly counter-dependent, accountability-avoidant and oppositional to anything that smacked of authority.

Challenge to reclaim community

The pendulum swing from dependence to independence was a needed developmental shift toward greater psychological health, allowing for the development of *self*. Members were encouraged to meet their own needs for personal growth and claim time for themselves and for family, leisure, education, and spiritual replenishment. However, the pent-up need and exaggerated expression of independence came increasingly at the expense of another important task – the development of *community*. The needs of the community took a back seat to the needs of individuals.

Individualism is draining the life out of communities. Senior members who lived through the pendulum swing, from hierarchical domination that fostered dependency and demanded compliance, are wary of losing their hard-earned independence. Younger members who carry none of this baggage are nonplussed by it all and, in many cases, tired of their elders' 50-year-old "authority issues."[168] Leaders struggle to blend their constitutionally ascribed, hierarchical authority with today's emphasis on mutuality, collaboration, shared power and inclusivity.

If community is to be more than a collection of individual vocations, more than an association of people who share a common set of values, then members need to learn to become *interdependent*. Ideally, community is intended to be a primary source of spiritual and emotional nourishment, mana for mission, a witness to the world of how to live the Gospel values of love, forgiveness, inclusivity, mercy and kindness. Such interdependence can offer a much-needed countercultural witness to our world that is fractionated by competition and tribal rivalries. The challenge today is to reclaim community.

Co-responsibility

Figure 6: Continuum of Responsibility

"Work is love made visible. And if you cannot work with love but only with distaste, it is better that you should leave your work and sit at the gate of the temple and take alms of those who work with joy." Kahlil Gibran

Members commit to being co-responsible for their life in community and their mission. Ideally, everyone chips in to the degree he or she is able. Ideally, the commitment to work in an external ministry is balanced by other commitments to care for, and participate in, the life of community. An integrity gap emerges when these dual commitments are imbalanced or unmet. On either extreme of a more balanced commitment are those who believe they have paid their dues and are complacent, and those who feel compelled to work all the time.

Complacency

If there is one chronic burr in the side of leadership that I hear most often, it is that too many able-bodied members are "complacent" or feel "entitled." There is a reciprocal dynamic between the over-functioning of some leaders and the under-functioning of some members. How does this happen?

Leaders regularly see the finances and worry about the disparity between revenues and expenses. Leaders hear daily of the troubles in local communities and are left to deal with "difficult" members when local community members can't or won't. Leaders are inundated with the present and future concerns regarding mission, community life, and the management of human, financial and material resources.

Meanwhile, most members are buffered from this daily dose of concerns. Members who serve on committees get a glimpse of this larger picture and share a piece of the felt responsibility. However, the members at large might only see and feel such things when and if they come to assemblies. Once the assembly is over, most members go back to own lives and personal concerns. They are not carrying home the communal concerns and felt responsibility that leaders carry on a regular basis.

While this might appear normal, some members seem especially free to exempt themselves from taking any responsibility for the good of the whole. Some see their ministry as the end-all-and- be-all of their responsibility. Meanwhile, the health and well-being of community is someone else's concern. They want to have the "right to vote" for leadership, or weigh in on matters of concern to them, but they don't feel obligated to show up for assemblies or discern matters that don't concern them personally. Some don't see planning for their community's future, the stewardship of community resources, or the quality of community life, as their concern. It's leadership's concern, "That's why we elected you!"

There are a certain number of members in every community who have emotionally "checked out" from their attachment to, and felt responsibility toward, community. Whether they feel entitled, thinking "I have paid my dues," or complacent, thinking "I'm fine, whatever," they are comfortable in their own lives and no longer feel responsible for the larger life of community. Perhaps they have been so wounded they have moved to the edges. Perhaps they have lobbied leadership, or community, to support their personal passion but, with repeated disappointments, they've lost hope and disengaged.

Workaholism

Americans work more and retire later than any other industrialized country in the world. Juliet Schor, who authored the best-selling book, *The Overworked American*, concluded that Americans worked an average of nearly one month more than other countries per year.[169] That was in the 1970s and the situation has only gotten worse. According to Dean Schabner of ABC News, "Studies have painted a grim picture of the American working world: Longer days, less vacation time, and later retirement."[170]

Europeans typically take six weeks off for vacation, while Americans barely take two. One-third of American's don't take any vacation and the one-third who do feel constantly preoccupied with work. Fifty-two percent of Americans fail to take the vacation time allotted to them and 68% regularly engage in work related emails while on vacation. The new term for working while on vacation is now part of our vocabulary – "work-cations."[171] We Americans wear our exhaustion as a badge of honor, showing others just how "busy" and "overworked" we are.

Religious are no exception. Leadership teams struggle to schedule a day of reflection because their schedules are so busy with work. Members struggle to come to one assembly per year, because their work is so "indispensable." Consequently, many communities still schedule meetings over holidays. Even so, the cardinal symptom of workaholism is not the hours worked. It is the nagging belief that "what I'm doing" (translated as "who I am"), "is not enough."

When I meet with leadership teams, we typically start with prayer and "check-in," inviting each person to share, "How are you coming to our time?" Invariably people speak of how "busy" and "tired" they are or, conversely, how "good" they feel because they "got a lot of work done." Politely, perhaps jealously, we smile in response to the people who confess to taking a day off. Though we encourage others to claim some personal time for "self-care," doing so is still seen by many as self-indulgent.

As religious (especially women) moved from the convent and into apostolic works, they kept their horarium from their monastic roots. Joan Chittister, in *The Way We Were*, described it this way:

> "In an atmosphere of rigidity, isolation, dependence, and the
> spiritualization of the mundane, work became the center of
> the life, and the schedule became the altar on which the sacri-
> fice of life was made. Sisters prayed, worked, prayed again,
> worked, prayed, ate, and 'recreated,' meaning talked to one
> another for forty-five minutes after supper, prayed again, and
> did school work or household tasks till 10:00. p.m. Every day.
> All days. With little or no possibility of diversion from that
> schedule for their entire lives." [172]

We give awards and praise for work achievements, not personal achievements. Success and self-worth are still measured according to what we do, not who we are. This is as much, or more, true for religious who continue to heap praise upon the most educated, the ones who bring in the most money, or the ones who founded a ministry and worked there for 25 years without a vacation. Meanwhile, the ones who have been quietly loving, kind, merciful, and present to others in their time of need, are eulogized at funerals, but seldom praised during their lifetime.

Moral beacons for societal change

The Church and Religious Life are looked to witness the Gospel and provide a moral beacon for societal change. Ideally, they are challenging the existing culture to live more fully a life of integrity. When this isn't the lived reality, many authors, even among the ranks of religious, have called this integrity gap a crisis.

Figure 7: Moral beacon vs. consumerism and scandal

Consumerism

Consumerism, which sits uncomfortably juxtaposed with the vow of poverty and the value of simplicity, is a challenge for communities. Once members were given the freedom to manage their own money and create their own budgets, there was finally room to take care of their own needs without "permissions." It was a liberating shift to give members control and choice over their personal finances. According to Sandra Schneiders, the financial immaturity that members had long experienced was finally being corrected during the time of renewal:

> "...early stages of adaptations took place when Religious were allowed to make some autonomous decisions about clothes, personal care, entertainment, travel, food and drink, revealed that the suspension of all financial responsibility from their late teens until they were forty or fifty years old economically infantilized many Religious who were mature, responsible adults in other areas of their lives." [173]

The pendulum swing from being infantilized to being autonomous, however, led to some problems. Sandra Schneiders described it this way:

> "Some solicited, received and kept gifts from family or friends without permission, manipulated superiors into allowing independent use of patrimony, persuaded secular friends and relatives to supply what they knew they should not ask of or would not obtain from the community, hoarded

all kinds of things against a 'rainy day,' or even engaged in business transactions that were in clear violation of the vow such as acquiring real estate, taking out personal insurance policies or appropriating retirement benefits for personal use." [174]

Adding to the challenges of managing money, members became conflicted about how they lived and what they witnessed to the world. Most communities have a middle-class standard of living: plenty of food, a comfortable abode, cars, cell phones, computers, healthcare provisions, etc. While it is true that most religious communities are "underfunded" for retirement, they are far more funded than most Americans who, on average, have $5,000 dollars socked away for retirement, and one-third have no retirement savings at all.

The type of safety net and security that most religious enjoy, is no where to be found among middle-America. Again, Schneiders:

"How could Religious talk about justice and the alleviation of poverty when they jetted around the world to attend the conferences discussing the problem of poverty, stayed in 'moderate' hotels where one room had more amenities than whole villages in Africa, worked on computers which cost more than the annual income of many third world families, and conducted ministerial business over dinners in restaurants that wasted more food in one night than some inner-city family ate in a month?" [175]

While religious communities ought not mimic the poor (it's not a virtue), or pretend that they are poor when they are not, their relative material comfort remains a source of discomfort for some whose families are living in poverty or others who serve people living in abject poverty. It raises their angst around consumerism and challenges them to clarify what the vow of poverty means and how to live simply. Such conversations on a theological level are hard enough, but when brought down to making common, concrete, collective agreements regarding personal budgets, vacations, gift-money, and the like, the dialogue quickly becomes contentious. It is hard for members to put their true cards on the table for fear of judgment or loss of personal freedoms.

Determining how much is too much for any member to have is for members and their communities to decide. What I know is that communities remain conflicted in trying to distinguish between *wants* and *needs*. Does everyone need a smart-phone, iPad, computer, car, and apartment? "It depends," is often the answer, but on what, and who decides? Absent any collective agreement, formal accountability is impossible. While every community has their Constitutions, policies and procedures, frequently these do not reflect the lived reality of how money and belongings are handled, marring a felt sense of integrity.

Scandals

Sexual abuse scandals in the Church and Religious Life have been going on for centuries, are world-wide and severely undermine the integrity of those involved. In 2009, the Archdiocese of Dublin reported a coverup of abuse of children by clerics from 1975 to 2004. In 2010, allegations of abuse surfaced from Austria, Germany, the Netherlands, Switzerland, and Brazil. In 2018, every bishop in Chile resigned after Pope Francis received a report of widespread sexual abuse.

Among the major sexual abuse scandals in United States, Louisiana was the first in 1985, then Boston in 2002 (dramatized in the movie, *Spotlight*). In August 2018, the Pittsburgh Post-Gazette reported the results of a statewide investigation. It revealed that over 300 priests had molested and raped over 1,000 children and they had a "playbook" for concealing the truth:

> "Most of the victims were boys; but there were girls, too. Some were teens; many were pre-pubescent. Some were manipulated with alcohol or pornography. Some were made to masturbate their assailants, or were groped by them. Some were raped orally, some vaginally, some anally. But all of them were brushed aside, in every part of the state, by church leaders who preferred to protect the abusers and their institution above all." [176]

In 2004, the John Jay Report tabulated a total of 4,392 priests and deacons in the U.S. against whom allegations of sexual abuse had been made. The numbers of reported abuse allegations and court cases has increased worldwide since then.[177] In 2018, Archbishop Theodore McCarrick of Washington, DC resigned as cardinal after revelations that he sexually abused boys and exploited adult seminarians. This followed countless other accusations, cover-ups and failed attempts to address these matters.

Sexual abuse of women religious has received much less exposure. Recent reports, however, have highlighted the sexual abuse and enslavement of women religious by priests. Women religious have also been abusers and criticized for covering up scandals. SNAP (Survivors Network of those Abused by Priests) has been particularly vocal in their criticism of women religious for failing to address these issues.

Such scandals have tarnished the reputation of the Church as a beacon of morality. Pope Francis has been criticized for failing to be more directly vocal in condemning these actions and for failing to take more direct action to address the sexual abuse by priests across the globe. In February 2019 he convened an unprecedented summit in Rome with over 200 Church leaders to confront the rampant clergy abuse. It remains to be seen what will come of it.

All of this is taking place within the context of the "me-too" movement which has highlighted the rampant abuse of women and children by men in positions of power. Alleged perpetrators of sexual abuse are in positions of power across America. Among the more notables are:

- Celebrities: Bill Cosby, Morgan Freeman, Kevin Spacey, and Garrison Keillor;

- News anchors: Bill O'Reilly, Tom Brokaw, Matt Lauer and Charlie Rose;

- Doctors: Larry Nassar and Richard Strauss;

- Business tycoons: Harvey Weinstein, Les Moonves, Steve Wynn, and Richard Branson;

- Politicians: Donald Trump, Brett Kavanaugh, Roy Moore and Al Franken.

Idia Delio has said: "We are at a crossroads in the Church, a decisive moment for the future of an institution that is sinking in corruption."[178] It remains to be seen if the Catholic Church can directly face and address these challenges, let alone provide moral leadership for the wider world. If the Church does not, it will surely continue to corrode its credibility and add to the exodus among the faithful.

Reflection: Crisis of Integrity

---

1. *How would you describe your community's challenges related to integrity (e.g., integrity gap, interdependence, co-responsibility, moral beacon for societal change)?*

2. *What impact are these having upon your mission and the lives of your members?*

3. *How are you addressing these as you plan your future?*

Crisis of Relevancy

> *"If you don't like change, you're going to like irrelevance even less." Erick Shinseki*

What is the unique role of Religious Life in our world today? Until this question is answered in cogent and tangible ways, Religious Life will very likely continue its decline. In an effort to address this question, Mary Johnson, Patricia Wittberg and Mary Gautier reviewed the literature and concluded: "If the Church is unable to articulate the Gospel message in a language that resonates with changing worldviews in the twenty-first century, it will become less and less relevant to the generations that inhabit it.[179] Schneiders adds to the chorus: "Until we can articulate *who* we are and *why* we are, and until we can do so in a way that is attractive to twenty-first century Christians…, we will not be able to refound our communities."[180]

Diarmuid O'Murchu conveys a similar message: "When the focus shifts from the world to the group's own power, success and survival… the group loses its bearings. The ideal they now serve is no longer God at the heart of the world, but an idol fashioned in their own image and likeness."[181] He goes on to say:

> "As the focus shifts inwards it is not uncommon to find wealth accumulating, material goods and possessions accreting, self-aggrandizement consuming time and energy, while the sense of prayer and contemplation deteriorates. Internal squabbles and conflicts may abound but are rarely addressed as in the case of a dysfunctional family where the discomfort of delusion is more tolerable than the pain of truth and honesty." [182]

Surveys attempting to understand the reasons for the exodus among our Catholics and mainline churches, converge upon a central theme: the Church and Religious Life are *out of touch* with the real world, science, the youth, sexual mores, and Gospel message today.

Out of touch, out of sync, out of date

Why is it that spirituality is on the rise in the United States while over 90% of mainline Churches are losing ground among the communities they serve? A five-year project headed by David Kinnaman sought to explore this very question, summarizing his research findings in a book entitled, *You Lost Me: Why Young Christians are Leaving Church and Rethinking Church.* The research project was comprised of eight national studies, including interviews with teenagers, young adults, parents, youth pastors, and senior pastors. The study of young adults focused on those who were regular Christian churchgoers during their teen years. They explored their reasons for subsequent disconnection and uncovered six significant themes:

1. Christianity, in general, is seen as shallow, boring, and irrelevant;

2. Christianity is seen as exclusive, close-minded, intolerant and unwelcoming;

3. Churches seem stifling, fear-based, risk-averse, ignoring the problems of the real world;

4. Churches come across as antagonistic to science and out of step with the real world;

5. Church experiences related to sexuality are simplistic, judgmental and out of date; and

6. Churches seem unfriendly toward those who doubt and are not a place for exploration. [183]

A recent review of the literature entitled, *Exodus: Why Americans are Leaving Religion—And Why They're Unlikely to Come Back,* found similar results. Among the primary reasons cited were: they stopped believing in the religion's teachings (60%). Those who were raised Catholic were more likely than those raised in any other religion to cite negative religious treatment of gay and lesbian people (39% vs. 29%, respectively) as well as the clergy sexual-abuse scandal (32% vs. 19%, respectively) as primary reasons they left the Church. [184]

A recent CARA study asked practicing Catholic women who had thought about leaving to share their reasons. The most common reason given pertained to disagreement with the Catholic Church's stance on a particular issue. [185] Another study found that two-thirds of unaffiliated Americans agree: "religion causes more problems in society than it solves." [186]

Desmond Murphy offered a laundry list of reasons for the decline in his book, *The Death and Rebirth of Religious Life.* For example, religious communities are: Too enmeshed with, and deferential toward, a paternalistic, hierarchical Church; too focused on survival; too out of touch with the original identity, purpose and myth and; the rules, laws and customs are seen as inviolable and take precedence over the Gospels, and they show a discrepancy between stated ideals and practices. [187]

Church teachings are out of sync with current times (e.g., pre-marital sex, birth control, abortion, homosexuality, infallibility of the Pope; role of women in the church). Traditional formation programs are viewed as infantilizing by newer members. Vows speak of deprivation, not enrichment. The Church does not foster mature faith development. Why is it that spirituality is on the rise in the United States and Churches are losing ground? One answer: *Churches are out of touch, out of sync, out of date and not responding to the spiritual hunger of our time.*

Lost prophetic edge and over institutionalization

*"The official church has evolved to a point where its char-
ismatic element has been crushed." Karl Rahner* _~30 yrs
ago + still_

Jesus' vision and mission were counter-cultural. He preached and modeled values that stood in tension with the prevailing norms of his day and he lost his life because of it. A key reason for the loss of relevance in our Church and Religious Life is the loss of its charismatic element, its prophetic edge. Sandra Schneiders says, "prophecy is a defining theological characteristic of Religious Life."[188] Yet, Michael Crosby acknowledges, "there is a sharp contrast between the way we articulate our lives as 'prophetic' and our everyday behaviors."[189]

Others share this same concern. Joan Chittister resonates, saying "The purpose of Religious Life is not survival; it is prophesy," and she wondered whether "there is still enough fire in these ashes to bring to flame the energy that is needed now to make Religious Life authentic."[190] Walter Brueggemann said, "It is the task of prophetic imagination and ministry to bring people to engage the promise of newness that is at work in our history with God."[191] But he, too, wonders if we, as Christians, can provide this witness as an alternative to the "royal consciousness" (i.e., dominant culture). Diarmuid O'Murchu wonders, as well, if religious orders can serve a "liminal purpose" because they are overly "identified with the institutional church, and, in some cases, with secular organizations."[192]

For many, the Church and Religious Life have become overly institutional-ized, domesticated, and so enmeshed with the culture that they have lost the capacity to self-critique. Crosby has been among the many voices hoping to change this, insisting that "without self-critique there can be no conversion."[193] Many have joined the chorus offering their own critique. Anthony Gittins warns that unless communities "undergo radical regeneration (in theological language, conversion or refounding), they slowly become sclerotic, and they too die."[194] He sees the Church as dysfunctional, paternalistic and fossilized, describing it as:

"highly centralized and authoritarian ecclesiastical institution that does not hesitate to lay down the law, while many
of its ministers are being exposed as hypocrites, professionally incompetent, or simply lacking credibility. They feel
cheated by a religion with a superabundance of doctrines
but a sad lack of compassion....Its reactionary authority
constantly adjudicates liturgical minutiae and private behavior but seems impervious to charges of authoritarianism,
high-handedness, and palpable lack of trust." [195]

Barbara Fiand does not mince words either, describing the Church as anachronistic and calcified.[196] She goes on to say: "We can either wither in the drought
and die of dehydration or face the challenge of 'our quiet little house' with all
the terror that this may initially bring."[197] Our "Theology is useless," says Fiand,
"unless it can be transmitted to the body of the faithful in language that clarifies rather than obfuscates, that speaks to present day reality rather than to a
worldview and reality no longer relevant."[198]

In fact, every author who has critiqued Religious Life from the "inside" has
offered his or her accounting of what is wrong and what can be done. Karl
Rahner, Sandra Schneiders, Walter Brueggemann, Patricia Wittberg, Richard
Rohr, Barbara Fiand, Michael Crosby, Diarmuid O'Murchu and many others
have said that Religious Life has lost its prophetic edge, merged with dominant culture and become irrelevant. Joan Chittister summed it up this way:

"In the name of the spiritual life we go to bed early and ignore
the poor; we get up early to pray and forget the exhausted;
we live in our warm convents and forget the people in the
tenements; we tell ourselves that we are too old, too young,
too small, too insignificant to do the things we used to do
and so we give ourselves permission to cease to be a presence, a prophetic voice. And we call it Religious Life. And
we wonder why it's dying." [199]

By the critique of its own constituents, the Catholic Church and religious
communities have become overly institutionalized and have lost the Gospel
message. Crosby warns: "No religious group that has been institutional-
ized into a monument phase can transform itself.[200] Members have grown

too enmeshed with the wider culture, rather than witnessing an alternative set of values. Instead of standing in tension with the dominant culture and witnessing a counter-cultural beacon of justice and compassion, Religious Life has merged with the prevailing culture and its norms of individual-ism, workaholism and consumerism. The spirit has become domesticated and its energy drained by the weight of outdated structures and the effects of institutionalization.

Do we ever have structures?

Reflection: Crisis of Relevancy

1. *How would you describe your community's challenges related to relevancy (e.g., out of touch, out of sync, out of date, lost prophetic edge, structures that no longer serve)?*

2. *What impact are these having upon your mission and the lives of your members?*

3. *How are you addressing these as you plan for the future?*

Structures that No Longer Serve

Beneath the crises of identity, integrity, and relevancy are structures that no longer serve. Many of the structures in Religious Life today are essentially ghost structures of the past that no longer serve the current and future needs of communities. They are not nourishing, flexible or nimble enough to meet the current needs of governance (to say nothing of transformation). They are not effective in addressing the tasks that need to get done or the relationships that need to be nourished. These structures typically do not provide the kind of environment that is conducive to interdependence, co-responsibility or mutual accountability.

For example, having one assembly per year, and Chapters very four to six years, does not work well for communities that are in the throes of planning. Such infrequent gatherings cannot respond to the rapid pace of change. The infrequency makes it impossible for the group assembled to develop the interpersonal safety needed for deeper conversations. Realtors, architects and potential partners cannot wait three years for Chapters to make certain decisions. Members forget what happened at the last assembly or Chapter.

Leadership structures, as discussed earlier, are challenged by the shrinking pool of willing, able, electable and compatible members. Reducing the number by one or two is not a solution. Just because a community has fewer members does not mean that the job of leadership is less burdensome. In fact, the ministry of leadership today is far more complex and demanding than in previous years when things were more smooth sailing and change was more incremental.

Each new Chapter cycle elects new leadership. The ending of one "regime," and beginning of another, too often results in a *disruption* of prior plans and a loss of momentum in the community's efforts. The community has to start over in a whole new way. Those who had been invested in the prior plans may lose funding, positions or support from the current leadership. These cyclical disruptions prevent communities from continuously building upon and integrating prior efforts.

Collision of Paradigms

For the most part, arguments over the habit, prayer styles and the "right way to live Religious Life" have subsided. In many instances, these differences were not necessarily resolved as much as set aside for the sake of getting along. The differences, and the pain associated with them, remain dormant among existing members unless, and until, a new prospective candidate comes along. When he or she arrives at the door, questions of "fit" surface these otherwise latent differences regarding the right way to live Religious Life.

Vocation and Formation programs, and their directors, are lightning rods that absorb the pain when an inability to resolve the "right way to live Religious Life" reemerges. This results in an impasse regarding the acceptance of a new member. For many, the recruitment of new members is tantamount to their only hope of new life. For others, it is the quality of life among existing members that holds this hope. These two hopes are embedded in two very different belief systems about what community ought to look like and how it ought to be lived. When these two paradigms collide, the pain strikes deep into the heart of community, especially vocation and formation directors and leaders.

Most communities have adopted a kind of *live and let live* attitude regarding the differences among existing members. However, these *live and let live attitudes* will not work when it comes to decisions around which members have a vested interest. If decisions are not addressed at these deeper levels, there will not be resolution. The viability of community and its future hinges upon its ability to reconcile these two paradigms.

Living in community today is the collision of paradigms.

Souls Misaligned with Life

"Unless religion leads us on a path to both depth and honesty, much religion is actually quite dangerous to the soul and to society." Richard Rohr

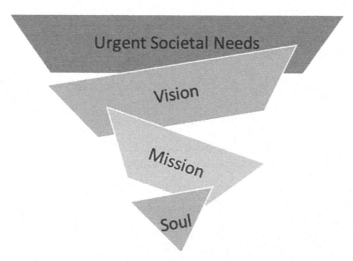

Figure 8: Souls misaligned with life

Below the tip of the iceberg and the cascading impact of demographic changes, beneath the crises and the collision of paradigms, lies a troubled soul. For many, the soul of their community is simply out of alignment with its mission;

its mission is not aligned with its vision for the future; and, its vision does not line up with how the community attempts to allocate its resources to meet the urgent needs of the world. Much like when the wheels of a car are out of alignment, when the soul of a community is out of alignment the life of a community becomes shaky. The mission becomes wobbly and starts to drift. When this malalignment happens, it shakes its members' confidence and eats away at their hope.

When members of a community are overwhelmed with their unrelenting losses, the rapid pace of change and endless maintenance responsibilities, it wears them down. When they are unsure of their identity, purpose, or relevancy, or when they profess one manner of living, but live another, it eats at them. When members themselves cannot agree on how they ought to live their lives, or what to ask of new members, it demoralizes them. All of this gnaws at the soul of members and at the soul community as a whole.

Joan Chittister said, "religious life is not a numbers game" or a "security blanket."[201] It's about the size, length and breadth of our soul, which "only grows as a result of the changes that tax and test our tolerance for the present, of the ability to find where God is rather than where we think God should be for us."[202] "The revitalization of religious life," said Chittister, "does not lie in the redefinition of its forms; it lies in the rekindling of its sense of purpose, its claim to meaning in the face of new concerns and present realities."[203] The metric for measuring a community's soul and the degree to which they are thriving has little to do with the number of members or new ministries; it has everything to do with the spirit among members and the meaning and purpose they ascribe to their lives.

Reflection: Collision of Paradigms and Misaligned Soul

---

1. *How would you describe your community's challenges related to the collision of paradigms and a misaligned soul?*

2. *What impact are these having upon your mission and the lives of your members?*

3.   *How are you addressing these as you plan for the future?*

Summary

While communities will be challenged to address the cascading layers of crises pertaining to survival, identity, integrity and relevancy, ultimately, it is at this level, the very soul of a community, that they must either transform or face extinction. I agree with Schneiders and others who believes that at the deepest layer, the greatest challenge for Religious Life is, "in the final analysis, spiritual…, something akin to what John of Cross called the 'Dark Night,' a dangerous and painful purificatory passage from a known and comfortable but somewhat immature spirituality to a radically new experience of God."[204]

PART II:
DISCERNING YOUR PATH
TO THE FUTURE

Assessment, Options, and Considerations

When I have presented the possibility of transformation to communities, I would sometimes ask a question like: "Do you have the means and motivation to engage in this work of transformation?" Invariably, no matter what part of the globe I was in, no matter how frail or vibrant the community, the answer was the same: a resounding "Yes!" I don't ask that question anymore because the answer means so very little: a quick response to a very large question. There are several questions that deserve more substantial consideration and discernment.

If it is a choice between life or death, everyone chooses life. The problem is that, early on in a community's discussion, most have little understanding regarding what choosing life really means when it comes to transformation. Many do not have a clear assessment of their own viability. Many do not know what options they might have, what these might require of them, and whether they have the resolve and capacity to pursue them. And, in many cases, communities have not reflected deeply on why they might choose a transformative journey and claim what they hope will come of it.

In order to make a wise decision about which options and direction to pursue, there are four questions I believe would be key to your discernment: 1) Where are you now regarding your current viability as a community? 2) What are your options for the future? 3) Do you have what it takes to pursue these? 4) What approaches to planning and visioning might yield the greatest transformative potential? Your reflection, dialogue and discerned responses to these questions will greatly enhance the collective wisdom and ownership from your members for any decision made. These are questions we will explore in the following four chapters.

Chapter 6:
Assessing Viability

Where are you in your lifecycle?

"You need only claim the events of your life to make yourself yours. When you truly possess all you have been and done... you are fierce with reality."
Florida Scott-Maxwell

Take a Long Loving Look at the Real

An important first step in discerning your options for shaping your future is to gain a realistic appraisal of your current state of viability as a community. In my experience, this involves a bit of *denial-busting* as communities tend to overestimate their viability and underestimate how close to death they might already be. They often fail to see how urgent it is to make decisions to take deliberate action *now*, before it's too late. Becoming "fierce with reality" is key to claiming your life and discerning your future.

Taking a hard look at your viability can be sobering, but it does not have to dampen your enthusiasm. To the contrary, it can to help you realistically assess your strengths and weaknesses and provide essential information for discerning your options. It will help you identify the types of attitudes, skills and resources you might need as you embark on shaping your future.

Many times, a portion of a community's membership is in denial about their current circumstance and the need for proactive planning. When these realities are placed before them, their response is often, "Trust in God," as if that is the only response needed. Hope in the future, faith in a provident God, and love of community and its mission, are essential to any successful journey, no matter which path is chosen. However, blind faith, wishful thinking and love expressed in words without action will not lend themselves to success. Communities need to break through these pockets of denial, ground themselves in reality, plan proactively for the future, and not wait passively for God to rescue them. This familiar parable says it well.

A fellow was stuck on his rooftop in a flood. He was praying to God for help. Soon a man in a rowboat came by and the fellow shouted to the man on the roof, "Jump in, I can save you." The stranded fellow shouted back, "No, it's OK, I'm praying to God and he is going to save me." So the rowboat went on. Then a motorboat came by. The fellow in the motorboat shouted, "Jump in, I can save you." To this the stranded man said, "No thanks, I'm praying to God and he is going to save me. I have faith." So the motorboat went on. Then a helicopter came by and the pilot shouted down, "Grab this rope and I will lift you to safety." To this the stranded man again replied, "No thanks, I'm praying to God and he is going to save me. I have faith." So the helicopter reluctantly flew away.

> Soon the water rose above the rooftop and the man drowned. He went to Heaven. He finally got his chance to discuss this whole situation with God, at which point he exclaimed, "I had faith in you but you didn't save me, you let me drown. I don't understand why!" To this God replied, "I sent you a rowboat and a motorboat and a helicopter, what more did you expect?"

This chapter offers three sets of criteria for assessing the viability of your community that you might want to consider. The first set of guidelines is from canon law and the Leadership Conference of Women Religious (LCWR). Although these guidelines are rather general, they provide a helpful overarching framework for consideration. The second set of criteria focuses upon ten cultural norms, those that favor life and those that favor death. The third set of criteria include nine broad dimensions of community and descriptive benchmarks positioned across a lifecycle continuum.

Criteria for viability

Canon law views *leadership, membership, mission,* and *money* as key elements of viability. Among the many requisites outlined by canonist Amy Herford for beginning a religious community are: a leader willing to radically live the gospel in dedication to mission, a growing membership (40 or more), and financial solvency.[205] For new communities, the Second Vatican Council (*Perfectae caritatis*) also reinforced the importance of a community's capacity to engage in mission.

On the flipside, it is noteworthy that there are no provisions in canon law for the ending of religious communities, other than suppression.[206] According to *Ecclesiae Sanctae*, the criteria for suppression are: "Taking all the circumstances into account, the following especially are to be considered together: the small number of Religious in proportion to the age of the institute or the monastery, the lack of candidates over a period of several years, the advanced age of the majority of its member."[207]

In 2000, the LCWR echoed these same four criteria for determining the viability of community: 1) adequate focus on mission; 2) adequate number of members; 3) adequate leadership; and, 4) adequate financial resources.[208] It will be important for you to define for yourselves what "adequate" means for your community. You may want to look to outside resources for additional definitions. For example, the National Religious Retirement Office (NRRO) has established criteria for what it means to be adequately funded for retirement and comparisons nationwide.

In 2000, the Collaborative Viability Project developed an instrument for assessing the viability of communities. It was a collaborative effort by the LCWR, NRRO and the National Association for Treasurers of Religious Institutes (NATRI). After two years of discussions these groups met to explore issues related to the viability of religious communities. The result of their culminating retreat led them to conclude that communities need the following in order to thrive:

1. Central focus upon mission;
2. Critical mass of members to maintain mission;
3. Pool of future leaders;
4. Financial resources for maintenance, mission, and enrichment;
5. Willingness to take risks;
6. Healthy relationships; and
7. Effective long-range planning.

They recommended that communities "step outside the boundaries of their past experience, think more creatively about collaborative efforts, create flexible structures, and explore new styles of community and ministry so that "new life could emerge."[209] Their emphasis on taking risks, healthy relationships and effective long-range planning is a refreshing addition to the general emphasis on mission, money, members and leadership.

Reflection: Keys to Viability

1. *To what degree is your community focused on your future mission (not just survival, administration, and the healthcare needs of senior members)?*

2. *Do you have a pool of willing and capable leaders who are trusted by your membership, and able to work together to radically live the gospel in dedication to mission?*

3. *Do you have a sufficient number of vibrant members to sustain your mission into the future and are you getting new members?*

4. *How healthy are your local communities and the interpersonal relationships among your members?*

5. *To what degree is your community taking risks, thinking and acting outside the box, to create a future that differs from the past?*

6. *How effective, and to what degree, is your community engaged in long-range planning in search of new life?*   *NONE.*

7. *To what degree are you financially solvent to live and provide for mission into the future?*   *OK.*

Cultural Norms Favoring Life or Death

> *"The past is alive in the Present Moment. The future is being shaped in the present moment; take good care of the present moment. Transform it. Live it...so that our earth, our children, will have a future."* Thich Nhat Hanh

The health of your members and mission, the strength of your human, financial and material resources, your community's capacity to plan, experiment and risk on behalf of the future, are all important criteria for discerning the viability of your community. Beyond these broad strokes and what you can observe on the surface, what else is there?

You have a *culture* of community that either nurtures a desire for life or seduces an inclination toward death. What are the cultural norms of your community and are these supporting the movement toward life or toward death among your members? Consider this now familiar, ancient Cherokee legend called, "Two Wolves."

> An old Cherokee is teaching his grandson about life. "A fight is going on inside me," he said to the boy. It is a terrible fight between two wolves. One is evil – he is anger, envy, sorrow, regret, greed, arrogance, self-pity, guilt, resentment, inferiority, lies, false pride, superiority and ego."
>
> He Continued, "The other is good – he is joy, peace, love, hope, serenity, humility, kindness, benevolence, empathy, generosity, truth, compassion, and faith. The same fight is going on inside of you – and inside every other person, too."

The grandson thought about it for a minute and then asked his grandfather, "Which wolf will win?" The old Cherokee simply replied, "The one you feed."

Which wolf is your community feeding by the culture it has created? Some communities, by the attitudes and behaviors that are normative, are nurturing life, while others are feeding the cause of death. Most likely, the culture you have created, and the wolf you are feeding, is not in your members' conscious awareness. With some reflection, however, you can raise your community's consciousness and assess whether you need to make more favorable choices.

I have put together ten dimensions to help assess the culture of communities: cultural norms favoring life or death. There are many elaborate and more scholarly definitions of "culture." However, for this exercise, let's use a simple and common vernacular for culture, defined as, "The way things are around here."[210] Use these descriptions, along with the table that follows (Table 1, *Cultural norms favoring life or death*), and the subsequent reflection questions, to help you explore and self-assess your community's viability.

Indicators of dying and thriving communities

Patricia Wittberg said, "even successful orders are fossilized by their own commitment mechanisms, lose their original fervor, and so become both unwilling and unable to meet the challenges of later environmental changes."[211] The size and age of a community's membership, even the number of new members, likely reveals less about its future viability, than the strength of its culture and the quality of life in community. In communities where death is near, when they have become "fossilized," there are telltale signs and symptoms. To what degree are these signs and symptoms present in your community?

1. **Dying communities have more memories than dreams.** Setting up the trophy room and spending more time reminiscing about the past than planning for the future is a sure sign of a dying community. Dying communities live life looking through the rearview mirror. They glorify the past. They spend more time and resources seeking beatification of their founders and foundresses

than they do on developing the current and future life among existing members. Meanwhile, life in community has become a museum of monuments, calcified and stuck in the past.

Thriving communities build upon their dreams. Communities that are thriving build upon the works, traditions, and inspirations of those who came before them. However, they lift up their own dreams and focus these upon the future. They listen to their deepest longings as the foundation for their planning. They listen to their wisdom figures and the dreams of their "newer" members. They listen to the needs of the world and align their mission accordingly.

2. **Dying communities are conflict-avoidant.** A dying community has a vast wasteland of unresolved conflicts that has poisoned the well of vitality and squandered the richness of diversity that is otherwise meant to nourish and strengthen community. While mostly avoided, intermittent eruptions of anger and hostilities occur. These are quickly swept back under the rug. Left unaddressed, the damage is done. If attempts to address conflicts are made at all, the lack of skill, discipline and practice make the odds of success highly unlikely. The history of failed attempts adds to the justification for avoiding such efforts ("Leave well enough alone."). A good meeting or assembly is defined as a "nice" one (i.e., without tension). Meanwhile, the baggage accumulates.

Thriving communities work through conflict and tensions. In a thriving community conflicts and tensions are addressed, not because of the joy of it (hardly), but because of the value seen in addressing them. They recognize the generative power of tensions as a source for creativity. They value the healing that comes from interpersonal reconciliation. They are able to reach across their differences and harvest the richness of diversity. They know that working through resistance is the heart-work of change. They have collectively acquired and continually practice the skills for handling interpersonal conflict and tension. These communities are successful more often than not because they have developed the skills and practice them repeatedly. Success builds on success leading to more confidence and a willingness to stay in the struggle.

3. **Dying communities avoid risks.** The more a group has accumulated things (e.g., buildings, ministries, reputations, resources and wealth), the more they are invested in keeping them, and the more they worry about losing them. An attitude of scarcity keeps them from taking risks that might jeopardize their security. Risking reputations by taking bold public stands, or risking finances on new ventures, are not the ways of dying communities. They would prefer to play it safe and not rock the boat. Their risk-avoidance leads them to make only small, safe changes that have little substantive impact.

   Thriving communities take risks. Every founder and every successful community, like every successful CEO or Fortune 500 company, has been successful because they have taken risks. They aimed high knowing they might fail. Failures, in thriving communities, are expected as a normal course of events. These are viewed as learning opportunities, not opportunities for blaming and shaming. Thriving communities have resiliency and can bounce back from failure. The only real failure is not to try, not to take risks, not to learn and not to bounce back.

4. **Dying communities are not a green space for growth.** In a dying community, there is no genuine community to nurture the growth of its members or mission. Members no longer grow inside community because it is too unsafe to try. Members, out of cumulative experiences of being hurt, no longer feel safe enough to be their authentic selves inside community. If they are fortunate, they have found green spaces elsewhere, in new local communities, new ministry settings, or in counseling and spiritual direction, where they can start afresh, free from any baggage or reputations. These new green spaces may allow for personal growth, but this by no means translates into *communal* growth.

Community remains an unsafe space until a community works as a whole toward changing its communal norms.

Thriving communities are a green space for growth. Thriving communities encourage growth in their members by offering each other a healthy dose of both affirmation and challenge. Breaches in trust, misunderstandings, and poorly handled conflicts, while inevitable, are redeemable. If someone flubs up, he or she may get a re-do, a chance to say it better and repair the damage. Members actively work at tending the garden of community: tilling the soil (building trust), planting seeds (new possibilities), watering (nourishing members), weeding (mending wounds) and repairing fences (shoring up boundaries).

5. **Dying communities use power for control.** In a dying community, those with *position power* (i.e., power that comes with position or title) use it to keep people in line. Tensions abound regarding who has the *right* to make certain decisions. Leaders hide behind their position power ("Do as I say because I'm the boss.") and the trust between leaders and members is low. Members who are resistant to the control and power of leadership attempt to garner power through numbers by forming *camps* of like-minded people. They jump the rails of *appropriate* channels and use back channels and closed-doors to caucus and build their case. Win-lose dynamics impede resolution of communal disputes and add fuel to the power struggles between we-they camps.

    Thriving communities use power primarily to empower others. Leaders and members share power according to their distinctive areas of responsibility. Position power is not used to hide behind, leverage or subvert members' *personal power* (e.g., the power to tell the truth, heal, forgive, create, love, challenge, support, etc.). Leaders use their power to empower others. Lines of authority are clear which makes their use of position power more effective. Those authorized with position power are not elevated to wield more power over others but to use their power in distinctive areas and share power more successfully. Personal power of members is robust regardless of the structure of governance (e.g., circular or hierarchical).

6. **Dying communities emphasize form over function.** A dying community suffocates from a proliferation of rules and the need to follow protocol. Rules are prescribed to keep things as they are and maintain the status quo. There is more emphasis on who does what and how, rather than on why and what works. Order and control take precedence over new possibilities. Hours are spent hammering out minutia, wordsmithing documents, approving minutes, taking rollcall, counting secret ballots, and chasing red herrings, while elephants sit prominently in the room. They ignore the deeper conversations about longing and desire. They are focused, instead, upon following the Constitutions, Robert's Rules, the handbook of policies and procedures, and the even larger handbook of unwritten norms (i.e., "The way we've always done things.").

   In thriving communities, why something might be done is more important than who might do it or how. Rules and norms are challenged, if necessary, in order to move beyond the status quo, get outside the box, and make room for change and transformation. They do not waste time changing the Constitutions, Directories or policy handbooks, but simply suspend them for the purpose of *experimenting*. In a thriving community, new agreements are not written in stone, but stamped as a "work in progress" and are subject to change. Thriving communities constantly keep their eye on the prize, stepping back periodically to ask themselves: "Why are we doing what we are doing? What is our definition of 'progress?' What are we doing well; where are we struggling; and what, therefore, do we need to do next?"

7. **Dying communities see opportunities as problems.** A dying community eschews opportunities for new ventures. New ways of doing things and new ideas, are seen as unwelcomed disruptions and an affront to tradition. Problems do not spur on innovation

We have sacrificed community for individual health care alternative — Executive House & Efficiency

or imagination as they did in the early years; rather, these are viewed as unfair interruptions to their best-laid plans. Not rocking the boat, avoiding new ways, and sticking with the "devil that you know" is the preferred mode of operating. They have stopped making down payments on the future and, instead, are in foreclosure.

Thriving communities see problems as opportunities for change. Problems signal a needed course correction. As with their attitude toward conflicts, problems are not enjoyable as much as valued for the change they can produce. Problems are addressed with an eye toward creative solutioning, an opportunity to reexamine issues and change people's perspectives. Problems necessitate that people change their approach, their patterned ways of behaving, their minds, their structures, or the system as a whole. Problems are seen as grist for genuine discernment, soul-searching conversations, and catalysts for personal and collective transformation.

8. **Dying communities attempt change by fiat.** In a dying community, change is decreed by legislation (e.g., changing the Constitutions, Directory or policy handbook) rather than through processes of dialogue and discernment. Change is mandated by leadership or brought to Chapter for a vote. The majority wins and those who lose feel disenfranchised. The ownership needed for implementation is also lost: "I didn't vote for this, so why should I support it?" The vote takes precedence over dialogue, creativity and working through differences. Robert's Rules, secret ballots, majority rule, the Constitutions, policies and procedures, along with traditions and existing norms, all support the way things have always been and inhibit any change.

Thriving communities view change as a collective endeavor. Thriving communities know that you cannot legislate conversion. They thrive on the collective emergence of newness and possibilities of change. It's not a matter of ignoring the Constitutions

Majority vote leaves the prophet crying in the wilderness.

or time-honored traditions. Rather than forbidding everything because *that's the way it's always been,* they opt for change, knowing the necessity of it. They engage in the messiness of open and honest discussions, creative solutioning, discernment, compromise and consensus, knowing that these produce the sweat-equity that yields ownership. Ownership, in turn, provides the personal investment needed for implementation.

9. **In dying communities maintenance overshadows mission.** Keeping things going *as is* sucks the life and energy out of any possibility for new growth and vision for the future. So much time, energy and resources are spent on maintaining and administering what presently exists that there is never enough remaining to address the future life and mission of the community. The daily press to get tasks done and keep things going, like a heavy wet blanket, smothers the life out of mission and its viability for the future.

   Thriving communities focus their energy, time, and resources on the future. The press of maintenance responsibilities urges them to try *different,* rather than continue to try harder. They understand that the system is broken. The maintenance-mission squeeze becomes an opportunity to look more broadly at the systemic structures and patterns of interacting that need to change. Leaders put members and the future of mission ahead of maintaining things as they are by handing over much of the maintenance responsibilities to laity (e.g., hiring outside management companies) or creating new structures that invite members to take on more responsibility for the life of community (e.g., circular models of governance).

10. **Dying communities are rife with complacency.** Members take little self-initiative and are reluctant to offer their time and talents to the community beyond their own ministry responsibilities. Many remark, "I've paid my dues." Other members are reluctant to offer because they expect to be *micromanaged* by leaders who aren't confident in their abilities. Indeed, leaders end up

micromanaging, or doing things themselves, because of what they perceive as members' minimal investment, self-initiative, capacity and follow through. A vicious cycle results where *leaders over-function* and *members under-function* in self-reinforcing patterns.

Thriving communities share the burden and privilege of caring for community and its future. Everyone pitches in as able. No one gets a pass. Self-initiative is encouraged. Subsidiarity is a lived experienced, not just a word written in documents. Members want to take initiative and leadership encourages and supports their efforts. Leadership does not micromanage. Instead, they provide mentoring, guidance, training and resources. There is a genuine partnership between leaders and members.

	Cultural Norms Favoring Life or Death	
	Attitudes and Behaviors Favoring Life and Growth	**Attitudes and Behaviors Favoring Death and Dying**
1.	Dreams are more important than memories	Memories are more important than dreams
2.	Conflicts are addressed constructively leading to reconciliation, deepening trust, creativity, change and healing	Conflicts are avoided and poorly addressed leading to inertia, mistrust, triangulation, more wounds, displaced hostility, and we/they camps
3.	Risk-taking is normative; success is measured by the degree of courage and creativity, regardless of the outcome; expectations often exceed results	Success is defined as achieved outcomes, smooth sailing, minimal risk-taking and maintenance of the status quo; results typically exceed the low expectations
4.	Community is a green space for growth; members feel safe enough to be authentic, to experiment and to take risks	Community is not a safe space for growth; members go elsewhere to be themselves, to risk and to grow
5.	Position power is used to empower and resource others; personal and position power are blended and shared	Position power is used to exert power over, micromanage and control others; position power preempts personal power
6.	The emphasis is why and what works, over form and past policies	The emphasis is on form over function, protocol over effectiveness, following rules instead of trying new things

7.	Problems are viewed as opportunities to create something new, a signal for needed change	Opportunities are seen as problems and obstacles to maintaining the status quo, order and control
8.	Change is the norm and continually emerges from leaders and members; everything is permitted, unless explicitly forbidden	Change is attempted by fiat and legislation; everything is forbidden, unless expressly permitted
9.	Future mission takes precedence over maintenance of the status quo; new means for attending to maintenance are sought	Maintenance overshadows mission, smothering the life out of mission and its future
10.	Mutual accountability (leader to member, member to leader, member to member), co-responsibility and self-initiative are normative	Complacency, entitlement and reluctance to serve drain the life out of community; there is little accountability, except for leadership who has to account to members

Table 1: Cultural norms favoring life or death

We look awful on this chart.

Reflection

1. *As you look at Table 1: Cultures Norms Favoring Life or Death, which cultural norms best represents your community today? In other words, which wolf are you feeding?*

2. *What stirs within you as you reflect upon the culture of your community?*

3. *What behavioral or attitudinal shifts might you want to consider, personally and communally, in light of your reflections?*

Continuum Across the Lifecycle

The third set of criteria is one I developed to help communities assess their current status along a lifecycle continuum. It offers descriptive benchmarks placed along different stages of the lifecycle. The benchmarks are categorized across nine broad dimensions of community. Table 2 that follows, Continuum of Lifecycle Viability Markers, provides an outline of these nine dimensions across the lifecycle. The complete assessment tool, with more comprehensive descriptions of these dimensions, can be found in Appendix A.

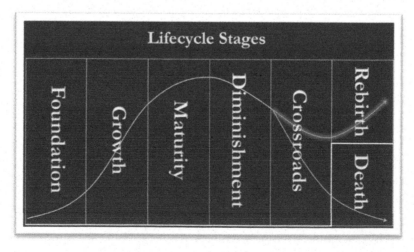

Figure 9: Lifecycle stages

Communities with whom I have worked have found this a helpful tool for reflecting upon and furthering their discussions regarding their current reality, viability and discernment of future options. It helps as a denial-busting tool and to assist communities to gain a common baseline and understanding from which to plan their next steps. The goal here would not be to pin down some kind of unanimous agreement, but to open up the conversation and share together what you see and why.

Reflection: Lifecycle Continuum

---

1. *Where do you see your community along this lifecycle continuum as you look across the benchmarks?*

2. *What is the impact upon you as you reflect on these dimensions and what insights emerge for you?*

3. *Where might there be convergence or divergence in the perception of your members, and how do you understand the divergences?*

4. *What are the most important implications of this assessment; and therefore, what ought to be your next steps?*

DIMENSIONS OF COMMUNITY	Continuum of Lifecycle Viability Markers Community Characteristics				NEW LIFE
	Strong Communities	Typical Communities	Marginal Communities	Near Death Communities	Transformative Communities
Mission and Charism	Leveraging resources mostly aligned with mission	Maintenance overshadows mission; resources misaligned	Maintenance grossly overshadows mission	Life is seen in the review mirror; maintaining what was in the past	Resources fully leveraged and aligned with mission
Ministries	A mixture of new ministries and succession plans for other ministries	Cautiously exploring new ministries and/or succession planning	"Founder's Syndrome," few new ministries	No new ministries, few active, external ministries	Embracing an abundance of future opportunities
Partnerships with Laity	Exploring affiliations, acquisitions and opportunities	Thinking more strategically about affiliations, but with ambivalence	Internally focused; reluctant to partner	Cultural lock and fear of outsiders; unwilling to collaborate	Creating new affiliations and partnerships in mission
Partnerships with Religious	Collaborating and creating new partnerships	Pursuing alliances, strategic collaborations, or mergers	Considering completion or covenants	No custodial arrangements made	Initiating new forms of life and collaborative efforts
Community Life	Meaningful, relational, real and healthy	Some meaningful relationships and some camps	Fragmented, camps, doing your own thing	Stifling, apathetic, disconnected, distant, lifeless	"See how they love one another" – and they do
Membership Departures/ Arrivals	Active and energetic vocation & formation efforts, averaging 1 new member/yr	Active vocation & formation efforts with much anxiety and tension, no new members	Vocation & formation efforts are mired in conflict and no new members	Inactive vocation/ formation efforts; no new members or hope for vocations	Active vocation & formation efforts, new forms of membership, > 1 new member/yr
Planning	Developing new directions for allocating resources and membership	Developing new goals to do better what's been done in the past	Crisis/survival mode; succession planning	Reactive, failure to plan; no hope for the future	Risking to birth new visions and being transformed by the journey
Leadership	Energizing and effective leadership team	Administrative focus on the status quo more than future visions	Maintenance oriented, focused on fixing problems, recycled leadership; little synergy	Suffocating under maintenance demands; ineffective; conflicted; low trust	Charismatic, courageous, innovative, and inspiring
Resources: Human, Financial and Spiritual	Adequate resources applied toward mission and community	There are enough resources if changes are made in how they are used	Resources are inadequate and viewed as "scarce;" they are driven by fear; periodic crises	Resources are grossly inadequate; they have frequent crises and are unable to resolve these	Resources are seen as "abundant" and well leveraged to plan for the future

Table 2: Continuum of Lifecycle Viability Markers

Chapter 7: Discerning Your Options

Pathways and options for change and transformation

"Two roads diverged in a wood, and I— I took the one less traveled by, and that has made all the difference."
Robert Frost

Pathways and Options

Now that you have a clearer picture of your community's current realities and viability, what are your options for change and transformation? What is the will and capacity of your members to engage in the work required of any of these? Knowing what each option might demand of you is an important part of your discernment. Too often communities underestimate the demands of each option and overestimate their capacity to do the work. They also tend to underestimate the pitfalls and overemphasize the desired outcomes of their choices. Ideally, your discernment will lead you to choices that are both desirable and realistic.

When communities reach a crossroads and are no longer able to function as they have in the past, a number of options can be considered. Some options could include variations on reconfiguring (e.g. merger), restructuring (e.g., new models of governance), refounding (e.g., renewed life). Some communities might choose to work toward completion and to "die with dignity." It is important to look at your options, consider the pros and cons, and carefully discern your path to the future.

It is important to note that while many of these options have the *potential for* transformation, none of them, as traditionally approached, are sufficient to bring about transformation. Why? Because most communities fail to incorporate the inner work of transformation (discussed in Chapter 9). They tend to focus primarily on external changes and neglect the internal work of transformation. Even so, these options ought not be discarded. They ought to be considered as part and parcel of the work of transformation. It is important that you have an understanding of what each option has to offer in and of itself, then consider the broader paths to the future you want to pursue.

As communities begin to implement their chosen options, they tend to go down one of three broad paths. These three paths diverge in very different directions and *the one less traveled makes all the difference*:

1. *The path of least resistance*, which is largely an unconscious decision not to act, to live in denial or perpetual conflict, and the result, predictably, is "death by default;"

2. *The path of completion*, a plan to "live with dignity" for the remainder of your days, which offers the possibility of hope, relief from practical burdens, and a measure of revitalization;

3. *The path of transformation*, the "Journey of Transformation," which is the topic taken up in Part III.

In this chapter, we will look at the specific options most familiar to you, namely, reconfiguring, restructuring and refounding. We will also look at some of the less familiar alternatives, such as covenants, commissaries, and new models of governance. We will then examine two of the three paths commonly taken, the *path of least resistance* and the *path of completion*, before turning our attention to one less traveled – Journey of Transformation (Part III).

Options for Change

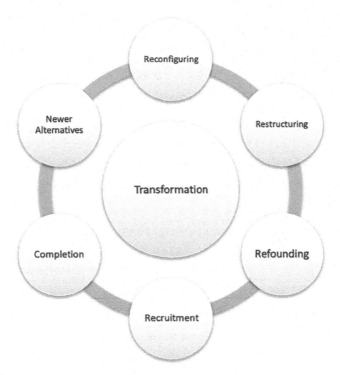

Reconfiguring

Reconfiguring is a change in structure that joins two or more congregations, typically of a similar charism, common ancestry or founder. These options are likely familiar to you and can include:

1. **Merger (or fusion)**: A smaller congregation is suppressed, and members are accepted into a larger one, usually of a similar charism.

2. **Union**: Two or more congregations give up their distinct juridic identity to form a new institute with its own name.

3. **Unification**: Congregations who had claimed the same founder or foundress, and over the years have been independent of one

another, decide to unite the independent congregations into one institute.

4. **Reunification**: Congregations that had been separated at one time and later decide to reunite with a new (or original) name.

5. **Federation or Alliance**: A loose association of congregations with a common charism or history.

The last option, federation or alliance, is less a matter of structural change and more a matter of formalizing collaborative efforts. There are other ways to partner less formally by simply making agreements between communities to share resources (e.g., personnel, ministry projects, finances, administration or healthcare).

These options, especially mergers, were common in the 1980s and 1990s but are less common today. The primary reason they are less common is because of the complexity, the length of time it takes and the costs they incur regarding human and financial resources. Mergers, for example, would involve a number of canonically required steps:

1. Conversations with membership among both institutes;

2. Preliminary request to each congregation (including consultation with bishop);

3. Chapter session with two-thirds approval;

4. Submitted request to Apostolic See;

5. Each member expresses willingness, strong majority (80% plus) preferred;

6. Those not wanting to merge can seek dispensation, transfer to another institute or pursue another form of Religious Life;

7. If two institutes agree, they petition Apostolic See;

8. Draft plans (e.g., new name, constitutions, interim leadership is selected, proposed chapter; civil and canonical affairs).[212]

In recent years, declining communities have been urged by Rome to join other more viable communities. However, as Amy Hereford and others observed, in light of the widespread decline among religious communities, "it is highly unlikely that many of the declining communities will be able to find flourishing communities with whom to merge."[213] Furthermore, mergers can take a decade or more to accomplish as a formality. It takes many more years, however, to merge two cultures (if this occurs at all). Because of aging and diminishment, few communities have the human and financial wherewithal anymore to go through processes of reconfiguration.

Restructuring

Restructuring is an effort made by a community to modify its existing organizational structure to better address its current and future needs. These arrangements could include downsizing or rightsizing, as well as reorganizing governance structures, administrative offices, and ministries.

Restructuring can provide relief for a failing system. Organizational structures these days are typically outdated. They are too bureaucratically unwieldly and inflexible to handle the rapid pace of change that is now occurring. Leadership is too burdened with the lion share of the load in caring for communities. Leadership teams are breaking down under the weight of it all. Assemblies held once-a-year and Chapters held every few years are too few and far between to sustain momentum and ensure continuity of efforts. Aging members are struggling to serve on boards and leadership positions. The system is broken.

Thus, many communities have sought to reorganize the way they are governing their lives and caring for community. They are transitioning off of boards, out of administration and handing the reins over to laity. They are hiring management corporations to administer their healthcare and ministry centers. Some are meeting more frequently in assemblies and working more closely with members and mission partners. "Extraordinary Chapters" are more common these days in order to extend the terms of leadership and change other Constitutional restrictions that are inhibiting change.

Caveats to reducing the number in leadership

Unfortunately, some communities continue to focus their restructuring efforts solely on the leadership structure. In light of the diminishing number of members in a community, and the smaller pool of willing and able members available for leadership, it is frequently proposed that the number elected into leadership should be reduced. The logic is obvious: a smaller community might seem to require fewer in leadership and, if electing fewer, the "shrinking pool" poses less of a dilemma (e.g., you might need to elect only three, instead of five).

What may be less obvious is that an older, smaller community facing a crossroads will have more demands of its newly elected leadership, not less. No matter what option a community chooses for its future, the road ahead presents enormous challenges that bring complexity and conflict. Organizationally, there will be complex legal and financial matters pertaining to buildings, land, ministries, boards, healthcare, and overall stewardship of both human and financial resources. Pastorally, there will be a host of delicate issues involving older members facing major losses (e.g., loss of cohorts, ministries, health and independence), and adjustments in their life (e.g., moving out of an existing residence into healthcare facilities and no longer driving).

Reducing the number in leadership at a time when the challenges facing a community are greater, might not, in fact, be the best idea. This option deserves just as much deliberation of its potential implications as any other option and ought not be short-circuited by what appears to be, on the face of it, a simple, logical solution. If a community has already chosen to "die with dignity," has worked through the pain of that decision, and has settled most of their affairs, then reducing the size of leadership might make good sense. However, if a community is still on the front end of these decisions, has yet to work through the pain and formulate and implement a plan, then burdening a smaller team with these complex and demanding tasks could be disastrous.

Refounding

Aside from reconfiguring and restructuring, communities have sought new life through processes of refounding, as well as renewal and revitalization. All of these efforts have a common theme: liberate new energy with the hope of generating new life. Gerald Arbuckle and others spoke of *refounding*, while Vatican II emphasized *renewal*, and Lawrence Cada and others preferred the term *revitalizing*. Sandra Schneiders, Diarmuid O'Murchu, Michael

Crosby and Patricia Wittberg, are among the other luminaries also advancing these themes.

The emphasis here is not so much related to structural change (e.g., reconfiguring or restructuring), but deep change in the spirit and vitality of a community. Whether this occurs in the existing community through renewal, or emerges in a new offshoot of a community through refounding, the focus is upon a new spirit infused with passion and liberated from the burden of existing structures and old paradigms. It is a return to the Gospel message seen through a new lens and lived in a new way.

Recruitment

As Arbuckle put it, "Refounding is not a search for an increase in vocations. That may happen, but it is primarily a question of the revitalization of Gospel quality living."[214] Even so, for the past 50 years, communities have worked hard to recruit new members. They have prayed fervently and spent millions on marketing. They have called upon all members to create a "culture of vocations" in order to assist in recruiting new members. They have researched what helps and what doesn't, and profiled those who are likely candidates and those who are not. They have offered "Come and See" gatherings, created hospitality and discernment houses, and established intentional communities with a mixture of laity and religious cohorts. They have sought to ease the financial and immigration barriers, offered new forms of membership, and more.

The results have not moved the needle. As we found, the average number of new members across the United States has remained around 150 per year and the vast majority of communities are receiving no new members. *Will you receive new members in the future?* No one can know for sure. But the odds are not good if your average age is over 75 and you have not received any new members (i.e., those that stayed) in over 10 years.

You might also wonder, *Is it right to recruit?* Some communities have put a moratorium on recruiting new members until, or unless, they can get their *house in order*. Some, because of internal strife, or unresolved differences regarding the *right* way to live Religious Life, have decided it is not right or good to recruit new vocations. They don't want to bring them into an unhealthy situation and have them caught in the middle of the community's unresolved differences. In many ways, recruiting new members as a way to address a fear of dying may be analogous to a couple who wants to have another child as a way to save a failing marriage. This new addition does not resolve the underlying issues. It compounds them.

Other communities do not believe it is morally right to bring in new members when they do not have a formative community in which to place them. It is one thing to recruit, it is another to provide the necessary formative experiences and supportive community for the duration of their life in community. For some communities, there are not enough newer members to provide peer support. For other communities, the average age may be such that after several years in formation, the new member might be immediately called upon to serve in an internal ministry because the community needs so much help, thus depriving them of ministry outside of community.

New vocations might be a byproduct of a thriving community but are not the solution for communities facing a crossroads. Too often communities are tunnel visioned in their prayers and recruitment efforts. Their only hope for new life in the future seems singularly focused on recruiting new members, and they are blind to the new life that could emerge from among existing members. They are looking outside themselves for the possibilities of new life and effectively sabotaging any possibility to revitalize or transform their own lives.

Completion

Some communities nearing the end of their time are fully aware and accepting of this reality. Many of these communities opt for the work of completion, meaning to map out and implement the strategies to eventually bring closure to the life of the community. This work can include legacy planning to ensure that the legacy of their presence and mission is honored beyond the life of the last member. It can include succession planning in order to gradually transition and hand over the reins of viable ministries to laity or other religious. It can include closing down ministries that they are unable to sustain or hand over to others. Ideally, it would also include rituals that allow for grieving and all the experiences of a gradual "letting go."

Completion work is not the official end of a community. Hopefully, it is not undertaken in the final year or two. Ideally, it is a proactive and discerned choice done well ahead of a community's final days. It is a way of preparing for the final years, even though a community may have members with many more years of life remaining. It is much the same as what many of our parents did to prepare for their late season in life and eventual final transition. They made arrangements in wills and trusts for dispensing their finances and belongings. They made arrangements for the care they might need when they could no longer care for themselves. Some made "ethical wills" and final testaments to ensure that their values and wishes would live on past their days on earth.

This option can be freeing for communities just as it is for many seniors outside of Religious Life. It can ease the worry and bring peace of mind for seniors and younger members alike. With worry and burdens lifted, it can also liberate energy in pursuit of new life. I have described this act of letting go as a "mature surrender" which can be a generative experience that gives meaning and purpose:

> "When the pain of letting go has meaning and purpose, it can become a more mature surrender, not a mere resignation by victims of circumstances. Mature surrender is an act of sacrificial love – a purposeful, proactive and generative choice to surrender what exists in the present in order to make way for something new in the future."[215]

Newer alternatives

In addition to the familiar options just named, newer options have emerged, especially in the last couple of decades. Among these options include covenants, commissaries and new models of governance.

Covenants

A relatively new way of addressing the dilemma of diminishing human and financial resources has been the development of covenants. Generally, these involve agreements made between two religious communities, one needing assistance and the other with the resources available to meet those needs. The set of agreements that are made form the basis of the covenant. These agreements vary widely in scope and timeline. Each one is uniquely crafted to meet the needs of a given institute and those who offer assistance.

The resources provided might include persons assuming leadership positions (e.g., superior or councilor), administrative positions (e.g., treasurer, secretary) or other key positions (e.g., formation director). One community might help another in arranging for the disposition of assets, or they might offer living space for senior members needing assisted or skilled care. Each covenant would be crafted according to the needs and resources of the communities involved.

The timeline and contingencies for covenants also vary according to need. This assistance can be planned and arranged so that an institute and its members are cared for until such time as it dissolves. Alternatively, covenants can be planned and implemented on a temporary basis. It may be, for example, that a community has a resurgence of members, or a financial windfall, such that it no longer requires the assistance from a donor institute. In other words, covenants are flexible, not fixed in stone, and can be modified to address changing circumstances.

An important advantage of covenants is in enabling a community needing help to hold onto its identity, its independence and, in many cases, its home for as long as is feasible and desirable. This is similar to the arrangements our parents made, permitting them to remain at home, or live in a continuum of care facility, getting the care they needed along the way. They remained in control of their lives and continued to function as independently as possible. The challenge, of course, is in finding a donor community with the resources available to provide the help needed. Given the diminishing number of communities with available resources, more and more are looking to lay persons and organizations for assistance.

Commissaries

The Resource Center for Religious Institutes (RCRI) describes a Commissary (sometimes called a Pontifical Commissary or Episcopal Commissary) as someone appointed by a Church authority (Holy See for pontifical institutes or the Diocesan Bishop), in consultation with the members, to act as "the canonical superior of another institute."[216] Commissaries are typically appointed when a community is unable to carry out the governmental functions (e.g., unable to elect a superior general and council), but still desires to continue living according to its own tradition and identity.

The Commissary is another religious, usually recommended by the institute as suitable. Lay persons cannot currently be appointed as a Commissary for a religious institute. Generally, a Commissary is given the canonical authority of the superior general for governance of the institute according to universal law, the constitutions of the institute he or she is serving, and the letter of appointment. The Commissary, as with every major superior, will need a council. This could be as small as three (sometimes two) and comprised of members from the institute or the Commissary's institute, although different arrangements can be made for the work of the treasurer."[217]

Circular models of leadership

The pyramidal structure of leadership is omnipresent in our world, as well as the Church and Religious Life. It is written into the universal and particular laws of the Church, as well as in the Constitutions and Directories of every religious community. But alternatives to hierarchical leadership can and have been created.

In 2006, I published, *Circular Models of Leadership: Birthing a New Way of Being*.[218] I put forth a new way of partnering among leaders and members. At a practical level this new partnership was an effort to solve the dilemma of having fewer members available to take on the complex and burdensome role of leadership. At a value level, though, it was an effort to shift the paradigm of a command-and-control, top-down, hierarchical structure of leadership and replace it we a *new way of being*.

The circular model of leadership is a structure which supports a value-base of *mutuality*: shared power, shared wisdom, co-responsibility, and mutual accountability. It is a structure that sees members as *good enough* (not inadequate); promotes being *equal partners* in terms of personal power (not hierarchically ranked in status); and provides a sense of being *in-it-together* (not fending for oneself). It is a structure that requires a new skill-set to make real what is in the minds and heart of its participants.

The birth of this model came while my wife, Dr. Beth Lipsmeyer and I were working with a community facing its crossroads and nearing its completion. They had no new members in over a decade and were down to 42 members. Their average age was over 80 and they had 18 members who were 75 and younger.

When planning for Chapter it soon became apparent that no one wanted to leave their name open for leadership. The reasons were obvious. They had a pattern of making Chapter decisions, but members later disowning these decisions and abandoning the work of implementation. When challenged by leadership to carry out the work, members resisted by either withdrawing (e.g., not showing up for meetings, ignoring emails), refusing to cooperate, or attacking leadership (e.g., complaining, badmouthing and triangulating).

In an effort to challenge these entrenched patterns, we arranged a meeting of the 18 youngest members (those 75 years of age and younger). It was an arbitrary age cutoff which we knew would cause the more senior members to feel excluded. Despite the anticipated fallout, we went ahead as planned believing it was necessary to break the deadly patterns of disengagement, triangulation and avoidance.

When we met with the 18 members and asked who might consider leadership, as expected, everyone had a reason why leadership was not for them. Some could not leave an important ministry. Some were facing a personal illness. Some were caring for a family member. And others acknowledged that they did not have the requisite skills of leadership. We remained in the conversation, holding them in the escalating tension, tears and anger.

Finally, in an act of desperation we chose a provocative intervention. We said, "If you don't want to take responsibility for your community, you are free to leave, no questions asked and with enough money to retire in comfort." In fact, they had plenty of money to support anyone you wished to retire in comfort (a tempting prospect). We explained that if no one was willing and able to take on the responsibility of leadership, they would be left with the prospect of suppressing the institute and individuals could either be dispensed from their vows or join another community.

As you might imagine, this provoked deep anguish. In response, they began to think outside of the box. Maybe each person could do a bit of leadership and not have such a burden? Maybe they could function part-time or rotate sharing the load? They splashed the walls with newsprint showing all the responsibilities that leadership was asked to do. They let go of some and divvied up the rest.

In the end, all 18 agreed to share the load. All of them were to become "leaders" in one capacity or another (according to ability). The canonically required offices (e.g., General Superior; Councilors) were elected and embedded within the circular model of leadership, requiring no change in their Constitutions. However, it was internally agreed that each person, while having distinctive areas of responsibility, had no greater power in major decisions than any other. It was an effort to support their desired mutuality and shared leadership.

There were plenty of challenges in creating the new circular model. Because it was new and untested, they had to invent new ways of gathering, making decisions, and implementing plans. The most challenging aspect was not so much the practical implementation, but the shift in *mind-sets, heart-sets* and *skill-sets*. However, because they created it, they owned it. They had the tears and anguish that went into birthing it, so they were committed to its implementation. Because it was new, it was also exciting. Because the load on any one person was eased, it was liberating. They birthed new life and created a *new way of being*, not by redrawing new circles, squares and lines on their organizational chart, but by the inner and interpersonal work that went into its creation. It was transformative!

Three Paths

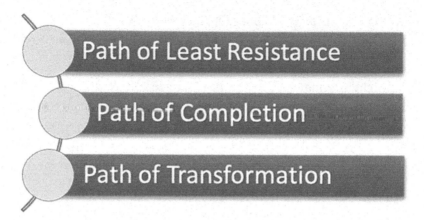

Figure 10: Three paths

Any of the specific options just reviewed hold the potential of transformation. However, the approach to these options or the paths that communities take in implementing them makes all the difference. Communities facing a crossroads tend to go down one of three divergent paths: 1) the path of least resistance; 2) the path of completion; or 3) the path of transformation.

Most communities will take the path of least resistance or the path of completion, while some take the road less traveled, the path of transformation. Before turning our attention to the path of transformation (Part III), let's look at each of the two more well-trodden paths in order to draw their distinctions and help you discern your own path to the future.

The path of least resistance: death by default

The path of least resistance essentially means allowing the future to happen to you, rather than proactively planning to shape it. Communities on this path are in high denial and too conflicted to make a deliberate and clear choice. They avoid, postpone, obfuscate, argue and equivocate about what to do. They end up making no definitive proactive decision.

While these communities are not overtly choosing to die, their actions lead them down this path. It is really a choice not to choose and, by default, not to change and to stay on the path they are already on. Absent their making any real decision, their default response to continue the status quo only guarantees the demise of community. Thus, this path results in *death by default* – the default response when making no decision.

This path of least resistance, sooner or later, will catch up with communities. Eventually, their denial will crumble in the face of realities that force their hand. Indecision will no longer be tolerable. Decisions will have to be made by the community (or someone else) about what to do with ministries, money and members, as well as land and buildings There is no escaping the work ahead. The greatest suffering will be wrought upon those who attempt to escape this work through denial, avoidance, postponement and indecision.

This well-worn path of least resistance is a path chosen primarily out of *fear*. It is a largely unconscious decision to not rock the boat or disturb the status quo. The choice is not typically voiced, or explicitly formulated as a decision to *die*. Rather, it is a failure to decide proactively to live and to definitively choose any substantive direction other than the status quo. Some members might be saying, "We need more information," while others might be saying, "We need to act now." With differing opinions left unresolved, in the absence of deliberately choosing a clear alternative, the default response is to remain *as is*. The result is a slow but predictable slide toward certain death.

It is tragic to see these communities slide down this slippery slope without making a more discerned and decisive choice. It is a failure of leaders and members alike to come to a resolute decision. They are, instead, stuck in a quagmire of conflicting opinions and too fragmented to cohere around one direction. Communities susceptible to this quagmire are those who have a history of unresolved and entrenched conflict and who have continually struggled in making major decisions as a community. Vulnerable communities may also be those who have succumbed to the *boiling frog* dilemma, too comfortable and complacent to move, not in the kind of pain felt acutely enough to push them beyond their status quo.

If they continue to wait, the challenges continue to grow and worsen. As time passes the community is older with waning energies and resources available to address these challenges. These communities are now more behind the eight-ball than before, but still have members, buildings, land, ministries and all the rest to address. Their odds of successfully addressing these issues grow slimmer as each day passes, as reality is continually denied, and decisions are left unanswered and delayed.

The ability to come together as a community to not only make decisions, but implement them, becomes increasingly improbable as each day passes and little is done. Eventually, leadership (or some outside authority) will intervene and settle the matter. Meanwhile, members have suffered from continued losses of cohorts, ministries, and homes. Whatever semblance of community they once had gradually disintegrates. Tragically, members have relinquished their collective meaning, purpose, right to be self-determining, and hopes for the future.

Themes and characteristics

The four primary characteristics of the path of least resistance are these:

1. The future happens to you;
2. The community collapses in on itself;
3. Mission and charism die; and
4. No hope for the future.

The future happens to these communities, when they don't make it happen on their own through deliberation and self-determination. Any changes that are made are too little, too late. They fail to plan proactively. Instead, they react with short-term, band-aid solutions. They try harder, instead of differently. As a result, they are increasingly forced by circumstances into fewer, less desirable options. They become increasingly fear-driven and crisis-laden. Their fear of losing their independence, privacy, finances, and familiar ways of being pushes them into making small, seemingly safe decisions.

The community ends up collapsing in on itself. They tighten their boundaries, individually and communally. Individualism takes precedence over communalism and privacy take precedence over partnership and transparency. Members disengage from one another and fend for themselves. The result is "culture lock." The community is locked in isolation, entropy, and decay. They disengage from parishes, ministries and networks of religious (e.g., LCWR, CMSM). They fragment, isolate and become more distant. They become apathetic and the familiar *chronic malaise* sets in.

As a result, the mission and charism die along with the members, who themselves are waiting to die. Fewer and fewer members are in active ministry. Hope for the future fades. Leadership is increasingly ineffective, stressed and overwhelmed with *busy work*. Members are increasingly apathetic, self-concerned, disconnected and lifeless. The future looks like more of the same. Failed promises, false starts, the lack of follow through and movement are demoralizing. Fear and anxiety over the loss of members, mission, community, and resources becomes a death spiral. The soul of the community withers away.

The path of completion: living with dignity

Nothing that lives, lives forever, and no community is meant to live forever either. It may well be that a community's best choice is to plan proactively and responsibly to "die with dignity," as it has come to be called. I prefer the term "living with dignity," not to deny the inevitability of death, but to emphasize the value of choosing life and living as fully as possible up to the very end.

Is this not what our parents and grandparents sought to do? Isn't this what we want in the late season of our own lives? If a community has reached the point where there are no new members in the pipeline, where its own members are becoming too few and frail to care for themselves, where the resources and capacity are dwindling quickly, perhaps it is time to plan for completion.

The recognition of a predictable end can lead to either resignation and despair or *mature surrender*. Those who choose completion because they do not see any other choice have essentially capitulated and "thrown in the towel." Their posture is one of desolation, victimhood and failure. There is no meaning, no hope for the future, and the results are predictably tragic. However, if the choice for completion is made out of a posture of mature surrender, it carries with it some transformative potential.

Mature surrender is one made from an attitude of gratitude for the life they have lived and a desire to hand over the gifts received to future generations. It is a posture of generativity. For communities that accept their impending death as a natural part of life's journey, they can plan proactively how to live out their days. The energy ahead of this decision is typically heavy and full of anxiety. But on the other side of it, there is new energy. Paradoxically, once the decision is made to bring a community to completion, energy is liberated that has the potential to bring new life to the community.

Once the decision is made, plans for the future can be made and there is excitement in the air. They can now plan for what to do with their land and buildings They can create succession plans for ministries, land trusts for their properties, and foundations for their mission. They can begin to hand over to others the future care of their mission and stewardship of their resources. They are freed from the burden of maintenance and able to spend more time being present to one other and ministries of their choosing.

Theme and characteristics

Let me focus here on the choice for completion emphasizing generativity and mature surrender, rather than despair and resignation. The four characteristics of this path of completion are:

1. Plan for life;

2. Plan for completion;

3. Nourished in the present; and

4. Hope for the future.

Living with dignity

Many communities facing a crossroads recognize the need for change. They set out to make plans for life, to choose life, not death. They want to plan for the care of their mission and members, and to be responsible stewards. The changes they make may be incremental. Nonetheless, these can help them live out their days with dignity.

For communities that choose to live out their days with dignity, change is proactive with an eye toward the long view. The community knows and accepts the fact that their days are numbered. They know the work in front of them will be increasingly challenged by advancing age, fewer members, and no prospects of new vocations. They have a realistic appraisal and acceptance of their circumstances. They enter willingly into mature surrender and proactively engage in planning.

These communities plan for completion by addressing five central areas: 1) transfer of the sponsorship of ministries; 2) plan for the care of aging members and buildings; 3) divestment of ownership and management of ministries, properties, healthcare and other facilities; 4) turnover of administration to non-members and of canonical leadership to another person or group; and, 5) engagement in legacy and succession planning. They look for the highest and best use of their resources. Generativity, not fear, is the principal value driving their decisions.

The community is nourished by its sense of being-in-it-together. The community is engaged in the meaningful work of grieving and planning. The boundaries of members, and the community as a whole, become more permeable and flexible. They are more open to collaborating and partnering with others. Members continue to have a sense of mission. They are bonded in a greater sense of belonging and home. There is hope for the future because they know they are planting seeds for it. They know they can live a life of meaning and purpose into the future. They are *living with dignity*, not despair.

Example

A community with whom I once worked was facing a decision to either *merge* or *split*. Five of the *youngest* members wanted to leave the community of predominately *older* members. The younger members wanted to pursue a life in mission, just as the older members once had the opportunity to do, and not be caregivers for the remainder of their lives. This was a women's community of 28 members with an average age of 85. They had no new members in over 15 years and the prospects for more were slim. Most of the members lived in the same convent their entire lives. The financial resources were adequate, but the human resources were fading fast.

We planned a discernment process, which began with individual interviews with each sister. I vividly recall interviewing one sister who was 97 years old and had entered the community when she was 12. She had lived in the same room for all of those 85 years! She had marked the years she had lived in community by collecting angels, one for each year. While interviewing her about her wishes, I could not help but look around at all the angels in the room. It was as if the angels were looking back at me, shaking their heads in chagrin and disbelief when I asked her, "Do you want to join another community?"

It was an utterly ridiculous question to ask in light of her age. Her entire life had been given to this community. She had lived in this same room with 85 angels now watching over her. It would be like transplanting a 97-year-old oak tree. It wouldn't survive and neither would she. She politely declined the invitation preferring, instead, to remain where she was and die there in peace. Nearly every member of the community expressed the same wish.

After much prayer and conversation, the community reached a peaceful decision. All but four of the members decided to remain in the convent and live out their days with dignity. One of the younger members felt called and chose to stay to care for the senior members. The other four members discerned their call and chose a different path. They joined another community.

While the discernment and dialogue had its conflicts, the result was not a "split." The decision for some to leave, and the rest to stay, was not about throwing in the towel. It was a plan for life, not death. It was a beautiful, peaceful, wholesome and holy decision that deepened the bonds of all members and liberated their energies for the future. The sisters who left to join another community stayed in contact with the elders who remained. While the good-byes were tearful and the losses were real, the decision was right and good for them.

The experience of this community illustrates that choosing to live out your days with dignity can be a choice for life, a choice not to give death the last word. It can be a choice to live fully, meaningfully and with purpose, into your remaining days. It can be a final gift to those left behind, an act of mature surrender. Should I have the awareness of death's arrival, and not be caught by surprise, I only hope that I have the courage, faith, and generosity of heart to gift others in the same manner as the religious I've seen who chose to live with dignity, gifted all those they loved and left behind.

Summary

There are a number of specific options that communities can consider. Some of these are familiar (e.g., reconfiguration), and some of these are less so (e.g., new models of governance).

None of these specific options are transformative in and of themselves. But all of them have the transformative potential, if they are integrated into a larger Journey of Transformation. Communities at the crossroads generally travel one of three paths:

1. The path of least resistance resulting in death by default;

2. The path of completion, which can be a choice to live out your days with dignity; and,

3. The path of transformation, which is the path less taken that makes all the difference.

Reflection: Options and Paths to the Future

Having looked at the options and two of three paths to the future:

1. *Do you believe your community will make (or has made) a discerned and decisive decision? Why or why not?*

2. *What further discernment might be needed regarding these options?*

The path of transformation

In this chapter, I am not going into the road less traveled by communities, transformation in the pursuit of new life. It is described in Part III of this book. Suffice it say that any of the options we discussed (e.g., reconfiguration, restructuring, refounding, etc.) have some degree of transformative potential. However, for these specific options to actualize this potential, they must incorporate the Journey of Transformation.

Chapter 8: What Does It Take?

Capacity and common questions

"Courage is not something that you already have that makes you brave when the tough times start. Courage is what you earn when you've been through the tough times and you discover they aren't so tough after all."
Malcolm Gladwell

"What does it take to transform our community and do we have the right stuff? What will we gain and what will it cost? How long will it take? Will it work? Is it worth it?" These are just a few of the questions I commonly hear voiced among those who are discerning their options. These are among the questions I have surveyed and explored with communities over the years and will share with you in this Chapter.

What Does It Take?

What does it take to transform a community? Everything you've got and then some. The work of transformation is exceptionally challenging. That is why so few communities are able to successfully go the distance. Based upon my research and experience, I have identified five requisites for what it takes to fully engage in the work of transformation. No community possesses all of these in their entirety. And no community scores high on these in the beginning. They are not *prerequisites*. But over time, these attitudes and skills can and must be developed, if the work of transformation is to succeed:

- Great motivation
- Total commitment
- Collective ownership
- New partnerships
- Trust your instruments

Great motivation

"How does one become a butterfly?... You must want to fly so much that you are willing to give up being a caterpillar." Anonymous

What motivates most communities to change, at least initially, is more desperation than aspiration. As a therapist, I can attest to the adage – "no pain, no gain." We simply do not change in any major way when we are comfortable with the way things are. We break through the status quo when the pain of bearing it becomes greater than pain involved in changing it. It is the same for communities as it is for individuals. If your community is not in significant pain, it simply will not change in any substantial way. High comfort, denial, apathy or complacency are poor prognostic indicators for communities endeavoring to transform their lives.

However, pain alone is not the only motivator. While the search for pain relief may be the initial impetus for change, it is not the lasting motivator or final determinant in shaping a great vision. Great visions are not built simply on pain reduction. They are built upon the noblest aspirations and sacrificial love. Think of John F. Kennedy mobilizing our country to go to the moon by asking us to think "not what our country can do for you, but what you can do for our country." Or recall the words of Nelson Mandela who sought to inspire a nation: "For to be free is not merely to cast off one's chains, but to live in a way that respects and enhances the freedom of others."[219]

In my research on communities seeking deep change, I found that what originally motivated them, was not the same as what kept them motivated over time. For most communities, their initial pain stemmed from the impact of aging and diminishment upon the lives of members and their mission (e.g., inability to sustain ministries, shrinking pool of leadership, financial and healthcare challenges). However, communities discovered that through the course of addressing these issues, when searching for the deeper meaning, more substantive and lasting motivators emerged.

For example, as they addressed the issues related to housing, it may have led to an exploration of what *home* means or how to strengthen a sense of *belonging*. Or they may have discovered their deeper *longings* or an awakened thirst for *new life*. Or they may have fallen in love again with community or engendered a deeper yearning to know what God desires for them. These are examples of what sustains and deepens the transformative efforts of communities over time.

Thus, a community must be in sufficient pain to initially break through the denial or complacency and choose to change. But if they are to successfully go down the path of transformation, they will need to have a motivation anchored in a longing for some kind of aspirational change, not just operational change. The articulation of these longings must be invited, nurtured and developed over time.

Total commitment

Communities can say that they want transformation, however, if their desire is not translated into a commitment evidenced behaviorally, then, their desire is but a dream. We might want to end an unhealthy habit, or learn a new language, but if that is not translated into a sustained discipline of behavior change, it matters not. Ninety percent of the people who lose weight while dieting, eventually gain it back. The same is true for New Year's resolutions and other skin-deep promises to change. Communal transformation takes a sustained and urgent commitment by members as evidenced in their behavior.

Commitment is typically strongest, at first, among leaders who experience the stress of systemic breakdown firsthand on a daily basis. Some members feel it, as well, especially those in key ministry positions. As members are called to the work of transformation, their commitment and buy-in, if they are succeeding, should grow over time. Still, they will not become committed all at once or equally. Over time, if successful, more and more members will buy into it. They will take ownership for the work as they experience the value of it. If that does not happen, if members do not experience progress, or do not grow in their commitment and ownership, something is not working.

Shared and sustained sense of urgency

Over time, members must attain a clear and common understanding of the community's current challenges, along with a shared sense of urgency. They need to know what they are up against and be called to embark upon the journey. The urgency to which I am speaking is not a sense of panic, but a sense of import that raises the commitment of this work to the community's number one priority. This priority is measured by the allotment of time in their calendars, finances in their budgets, and personal energies expended.

The work of transformation cannot be an add-on to the calendars, finances, and energies currently used to maintain life as it is. No one has extra days in their calendars, money in their budgets, or energy left at the end of the day. To attempt to add this work onto the work leaders and members are already doing will quickly lead to exhaustion, which will demoralize the community. The calendars, budgets and energies must shift in order to focus on this work. If this does not happen, something is not working.

Key people

I've seen all sorts of percentages reported regarding what constitutes a "critical mass" needed for systemic change, anywhere from 20% to 80%. I don't believe there is an exact percentage needed. In my experience it is less about a critical mass, than it is critical people. In other words, there must eventually be a commitment among key leaders, members and others, those who constitute both the formal and informal influencers. If these people become committed, then the base of commitment and ownership among all members will strengthen over time. If it does not happen, again, something is not working.

Uniform, all-out effort

What if some want to change and others don't? The truth is that some will be ready and others won't, some sooner and others later, and a few not at all. Typically, members' readiness and willingness build over time. But members will never commit in lock step or in totality. You simply need to start and not wait for everybody to be ready. If you are on the right track, most everyone will eventually commit. It eventually needs to become an all-out effort by the entire community.

However, even in the best of circumstances, a few will be left behind. No matter how hard you might try to encourage or cajole, not everyone will commit to the work. For a variety of reasons (e.g., they are too stuck, frightened, inflexible, committed to the past or, rightly, on their own path), they will not choose to join the community's new path to the future. In the end, every individual must choose his or her own path. That's a cost everyone must bear, the ones left behind and the ones who must leave them.

Collective ownership

If the work of transformation is owned only by a few, it will not succeed. Ownership provides the sweat-equity needed to implement and carry through on plans. When we own something, we invest in it. If we value it, we spend time, money and energy on it. If we invest in it, we feel responsible for seeing it through. How do members develop ownership? Easy, they are invited and become involved. Members must be invited by leaders to participate in the communal effort toward transformation.

Once they get engaged in the work of transformation, they must experience that their work makes a difference. It is not just involvement that counts, but *involvement that makes a difference.* They need to know that their voice makes a difference in the development of plans, deliberation of choices, formulation of processes and, ultimately, the progress that is made. The only way for them to know this is for them to experience it first-hand.

It also helps when they are told, by others who receive their input, the difference it makes in planning and decision-making. Work assignments given by leaders or planners to the members of community (e.g., readings, reflections, requests for feedback, etc.) need to have a purpose. The results of the members' efforts need to be collected, summarized and given back to them. It can be given back in writing, videos, or directly through face-to-face gatherings. One way or another, the work and input from the membership must be shown to have made a difference so members know, without any doubt, that they are *valued contributors.*

For example, no reading should be sent out to members just because it is a "good read." Sending out articles and hoping members will read them, and not knowing if they read them, or what difference it made, is not helpful. If readings are assigned, they need to have context and rationale directly connected to the work of transformation. They need to have an explicit goal and a viable process for accomplishing it. Their reflections or responses need to be collected and synthesized. The members' work needs to be fed back to them, so they know it didn't just drop down into a hole somewhere. Ownership is developed when members experience themselves as valued contributors and can see the difference their contributions make.

New partnerships

"Partnership is a commitment to a dialogue, not an act of concession." Peter Block

Leadership or committees cannot transform a community. Transformation cannot be done by fiat. It cannot be a Chapter mandate that is outsourced to a small group. Communal transformation takes place when a community, as a whole, takes up the charge with an all-hands-on-deck, all-out effort. In order for this to happen, leadership must build partnerships with members, and together they must build partnerships with others outside of community. If they cannot form a wider base made of partnerships, then efforts toward communal transformation will fail.

Leaders and members as partners

Because leadership cannot transform a community, leaders need to partner with and harness the full power of all members to do this collective work. Leaders and members alike must find their voice, participate fully and learn to share power. This does not mean flattening the hierarchy of leadership. Although circular structures are typically designed to promote more egalitarian partnerships, leaders in hierarchical structures can also learn to share power more fully. Sharing power, creating partnerships, and broadening the base of involvement is more a matter of mindset and practices than it is structures, per se. In whatever the structure that exists, leaders and members must partner together. It cannot be a top-down endeavor.

Ira Chaleff, in an excellent book, *The Courageous Follower,* flips around the usual follow-the-leader paradigm and emphasizes the need for partnership among leaders and members. He believes that the notion of leaders developing a vision, then handing it down to followers to implement is folly. Followers do not orbit around the leader. Rather, he suggests, "followers and leaders orbit around the purpose."[220] Courageous followers are those who fully embrace their power to use their knowledge and skills, speak the truth to power, believe in a common purpose and commitment, and make proactive choices. In this way leaders and members are co-creators with dynamic parity shaping a shared vision.

Partnership with laity

Additionally, communities will need to build stronger partnerships with laity and other religious. Their boundaries will need to become more flexible and permeable than in years past. Laity have been employees in the internal life of community, as well as collaborators in ministries, for years. But involving laity as genuine "partners," not just as advisors, helpers, consultants or collaborators is different and a big stretch for most.

Partnerships, according to Peter Block, have four requirements:

1. **Exchange of purpose**, meaning those involved co-create and mutually shape the purpose of their endeavor;

2. **The right to say no**, where neither party is boss over the other;

3. **Joint accountability**, where each party is accountable to one another for the outcomes; and,

4. **Absolute honesty**, such that not telling the truth is an act of betrayal.[221]

Some communities refer to the laity involved in their ministries as "mission partners." In most cases, using Block's definition, these are not genuine partners. These laity may be collaborators, co-ministers, employees, managers or board members, but they are not partners. They do not share the same power or right to say no. They are not mutually candid and honest, not in the same way members might be with one another. Most often laity are accountable to religious leaders and leaders can fire their lay collaborators, but the reverse is seldom true. In a partnership, there is no abnegation. No one simply walks away when the going gets tough.

Leaders and members committed to one another as partners, or laity and members committed to each other as partners, is a paradigm shift. It is a shift that is necessary in order to bolster the work of transformation. This is not just about increasing the labor force needed to carry out the organizational changes (e.g., deconstructing buildings, creating land trusts, transferring sponsored ministries, etc.). It is about creating new, healthy, interdependent partnerships. It is about forging a stronger mixture of energies, ideas and skills to co-create new opportunities and forms of life.

Trust your instruments

"An emergent work asks us to stand in a different place. We can no longer stand at the end of something we

visualize in detail and plan backwards from that future. Instead, we must stand at the beginning, clear in our intent, with a willingness to be involved in discovery. The world asks that we focus less on how we can coerce something to make it conform to our designs and focus more on how we can enter into the experience and then notice what comes forth. It asks that we participate more than plan."
Margaret Wheatley and Myron Kellner-Roger

The need for ambiguity

The ambiguity of transformation challenges even those with the highest "P" scores on the Myers-Briggs. There are no maps, quick fixes, easy answers or guarantees. It is the nature of transformation to not know what lies ahead. From the perspective of a baby in utero, its birth must seem like the end. The future is unpicturable and unpredictable. While you will have to make plans, you cannot plan your way through transformation. While you will have to establish goals, weigh potential options, assess risks, costs and benefits, you cannot engineer or control the outcome.

Transformation is an *emergent* process of making the path while walking. With each step taken, new information and circumstances are revealed which, in turn, inform your "next best step." Communities that are able to do this work, grow in their acceptance of the inherent ambiguity. Communities engaged successfully in this work value great questions over quick answers. They recognize and embrace this journey for what it is – a paschal mystery.

Ambiguity is not just an aspect of complex planning to be tolerated; rather, it is something to be embraced as a necessary condition for transformation to take place. I know that might sound strange, but it is true. Transformation cannot take place if we know the answers ahead of time, have a plan we have manufactured and know exactly how to implement it. Planned change around known and familiar matters is not the same as transformation. These are not the conditions that would transform us.

Navigating ambiguity

As an instrument rated pilot, I logged thousands of hours flying across the United States and Canada. It took only a short while to get my license (40 flying hours), but it took a long time (thousands of hours), and a lot of experience, to become proficient in flying, especially when flying through the clouds, at night, or through storms.

Without much training, a pilot can learn how to fly a plane on bright sunny days when you can see out the window. You can tell if you are "straight and level" just by your orientation to the horizon. You can tell where you are going by seeing the mountains, rivers, roads and other landmarks. You can see and avoid other planes, tall buildings and storms. You can see the landing strip, line up accordingly and know when you are about to touch down.

It is another matter to fly in the clouds, at night, or through storms. Absent any sight to orient yourself to a horizon, telling you when you are flying straight and level, our vestibular system and other sensory feedback sends our brain signals that are impossible to interpret. Not noticing any sensory change, our brain says we are flying straight and level, when we might actually be in a slow but steady decline, ascent, or turn. Feeling pressure on the buttocks, our brain says we are ascending, when, if fact, we might be turning. It is much like all of us have experienced when sitting still on a train or plane, when a train or plane rolls past us. We mistakenly believe we are moving, when it is the other train or plane that is moving.

Pilots have to rely on instruments, not their sight or seat-of-the-pants sensations, to fly through clouds. Instead of looking out the window, listening to the sound of the engine, feeling the pull of the yoke, or sensing the pressure on the seat of your pants, you have to look at a panel of instruments and learn to tune out your body. The instruments include such things as turn and bank indicators, power gauges, and airspeed indicators, as well as an artificial horizon (a round three-inch ball with horizontal and vertical lines that intersect).

Tuning out your bodily sensations, when you have relied upon these your entire life to navigate on *terra firma*, is a very difficult thing to do. It takes a long time to trust your instruments and not your own body. To develop this skill takes hundreds of hours of practice. To maintain proficiency takes regular practice. When flying through the clouds, your life, and the lives of all souls onboard, depends on a pilot's ability to trust the instruments and not his or her own sensory-perceptual interpretations.

The same is true for communities trying to navigate the ambiguity of transformation. You have to trust your instruments and not fly by sight or the seat of your pants. You cannot rely solely on reason, logic, and strategic plans. You will need to rely also on your intuitions, dreams and longings. You have to trust your instruments of prayer, reflection, dialogue, and contemplation, along with personal and communal discernment. This takes discipline, practice and patience.

For example, in discernment, it is only when we are truly "detached from the outcome" and "interiorly free" that we can hear God's voice over our own. Not insisting upon an outcome ahead of time, allows us to more fully listen to the emergent truth (i.e., truth discovered along the way). We can better listen to where God is leading us, rather than our own predetermined destination. If we are interiorly free from fear or "get-there-itis" we can appreciate better what might bring a smile to God's face. Embracing the ambiguity means listening for what might make God smile, rather than clinging to our own designs that prevent us from hearing that still small voice.

Reflection: Do you have what it takes?

The Journey of Transformation takes great motivation, total commitment, collective ownership, new partnerships and trust in your instruments. Of these requisites:

1. *Where are your strengths and weaknesses?*

2. *How can you build your overall capacity?*

Common Questions

I was recently invited to a leadership conference in Spain to present my work on communal transformation. Toward the end of the first presentation, one of the leaders asked, rather pointedly, "What are the deliverables?" Taken aback, I asked, "What do you mean?" She asked, now with a tone of skepticism, "What will we get out of it at the end of all this work?" Her question, though, is a good one that ought to be asked more often.

The question of deliverables opened up quite a conversation among everyone in the room. When I got back to the States, I included this question in a survey that I conducted among communities engaged in refounding and other transformative efforts. I asked questions you might ask: How long does it take? What were the costs and benefits? What are the learnings from those who went down this path? Let me address these questions and share some of what the survey responders said.

How long will it take?

How long does transformation take? Great question. As we now know, it takes nine months to make a baby no matter how many people are on the committee. The gestation period for elephants is 18 to 22 months, but it takes only days for a caterpillar to metamorphize into a butterfly. How long does it take to change a culture? It took decades for most of us to stop smoking and wear seatbelts. We have yet to eradicate racism or poverty. We can do our part, and do it well, but some things are on God's time, not ours.

Organizational change agents suggest that it takes three to five years to create the container for organizational change (i.e., a collective understanding and framework). When I first began accompanying communities in the work of deep change, I had hoped and thought it might take less, but this timeline matches my experience. It takes three to five years to get a community solidly engaged in the work of transformation, all pulling in the same direction with a common understanding of what "transformation" and "new life" means to them.

Many have asked, "How long will this take?" when they really mean, "How long will we have to meet like this until we can get back to *normal*?" There is no going back to normal, if normal means what you did in the past. Communal transformation is the new normal for groups that commit to it and it takes as long as it takes. Rather than trying to hurry up to get it done and over with, rather than focusing on fixed deadlines, it might be better to focus on the process, the journey, your inner work, and settle in for the long haul. You will need goals, but worry less about the destination and more about the quality of your efforts along the way.

It took the Israelites a long time to get to the Promised land, some forty years, but it wasn't the length of time that mattered. It was their journey with one another and God, and the transformation that took place along the way, that mattered most. Peter Block suggests, instead of asking, How long will it take? (as if faster is better), it is better to ask: "What commitment am I willing to make?"[222] I agree with Block who says, "speed is a defense against depth."[223] If expediency is your value, transformation will elude you.

After all of his hard work, Moses had barely a glimpse of the Promised Land. He never quite reached his destination. Transformation is not a location on a map or a project with a deadline. It is a pilgrimage toward God and set at the pace of God's timing. Although you will establish concrete goals and meet your deadlines along the way, the deeper work of transformation –healing, conversion, growing in love, – cannot be fixed on a calendar.

What are the benefits?

What are the benefits, gains or "deliverables" achieved through this work of transformation? What might you get out of it? For every community it is different, because for every community the circumstances, reasons for engaging it, and desired outcomes are different. Most communities, if they plan well, will accomplish the practical goals. Most are able to address and find solutions to the shrinking pool of leaders, needed ministry transitions, and healthcare challenges. These deliverables are easy to measure.

It is harder to measure progress when it comes to the deeper terrain, or *soft tissue*, of a community's heart and soul. Even so, reflecting on these matters helps a community to continually claim what they trying to achieve and assess their efforts. You have to go back to your goals, why you chose to do this work in the first place. As you move along, and new awakenings, insights and possibilities emerge, you can ask yourselves: "Are we getting from this what we had originally hoped?" The goals change over time requiring continual reassessments of what progress really means. When I have surveyed communities who are further into the journey, the most important benefits (deliverables) were not the concrete organizational changes, but these:

1. New Hope for the future;

2. New perspectives;

3. New sense of home and belonging;

4. Stronger partnerships;

5. Greater ownership;

6. Stronger identity;

7. A deepening faith.[224]

How much will it cost?

Some will ask "How much does it cost?" as if cheaper is somehow better. Peter Block suggests that it is better to ask: What is the price I am willing to pay?"[225] or "To what extent are you invested in the wellbeing of the whole?"[226] Transformation will cost more than most are willing to pay. The real cost is emotional not economical. It will cost you the emotional pain of letting go of things, ideologies, patterns, and structures that are safe, familiar and secure. You will pay for it with mistakes, setbacks and failures. You will pay for it in the loss of privilege, entitlement and unblemished reputations. It will tax your time, energy, human and finances resources. It will cost you the price of conversion.

When I surveyed communities engaged in this work, they noted the costs are time, energy, money. But the intangible costs, were perhaps more burdensome:

- An emotional toll of generalized fear and anxiety because of the ambiguity (not knowing where all this is leading) and having to take risks with no guarantees;

- The pain that members experienced as a result of divisions, conflict and disengagement by those who wanted to take different directions;

- The pain from facing the reality of "who we are" and "our own limitations;"

- A strong fear of *splitting* and *camps* being formed between "us and them;"

- The pain from *old wounds* that were unearthed in the process.

- The cost of letting go and grieving.[227]

The costs are never even. Some leaders, members, and laity will pay for it more than others. Some ministries will be let go, while others will be supported. Some members will have to move to new locations, others to new ideologies and traditions. The challenge is to learn how to trade off carrying each other. When some suffer because they have lost their ministry, can you carry them in their grief? When others feel inadequate because of a failed effort, can you hold them? Will you let others hold you, as well, when it is your turn to pay? The costs are never distributed simultaneously or evenly across all members. You will need to take turns supporting each other throughout the journey.

The German theologian, Dietrich Bonhoeffer, lamented the lure toward *cheap grace*.[228] Cheap grace for Bonhoeffer is an attempt to reap the benefits of Christianity without paying the price: to seek redemption without authentic conversion, or forgiveness without genuine repentance. The cost of genuine transformation is not a cheap grace, but the grace that comes with genuine discipleship, which, if all that it might cost was known ahead of time, many would never choose.

Will it work?

"I was given a thorn in my flesh, a messenger of Satan, to torment me. Three times I pleaded with the Lord to take it away from me. But he said to me, 'My grace is suffi-cient for you, for my power is made perfect in weakness.' Therefore I will boast all the more gladly about my weak-nesses, so that Christ's power may rest on me. That is why, for Christ's sake, I delight in weaknesses, in insults, in hardships, in persecutions, in difficulties. For when I am weak, then I am strong." 2 Corinthians 12:7-10

Malcolm Gladwell based his book, *David And Goliath*, on two premises: "The act of facing overwhelming odds produces greatness and beauty" and "Giants are not what we think they are."[229] Gladwell reinterprets the story of David and Goliath, explaining that what seemed like a miraculous outcome, is made possible because David didn't do what was expected. He didn't fight like the warrior everyone expected, using brute force and hand-to-hand combat. Instead he used the expectation others had of him to his advantage and surprised the giant with a slingshot stone's blow to Goliath's exposed forehead

Being an underdog, Gladwell asserts, can be a great advantage. It forces us to learn a different approach than the conventional one. It teaches us to study harder than most. We have to know our challenges more thoroughly and learn to compensate, deal with failure and innovate. He goes on to provide example after example of how being bigger, stronger, and the "best" at something, are not always an advantage.

Underdogs win more often than we imagine, on average a third of the time. More importantly, this percentage is doubled if they do not play by the rules, using conventional approaches. If it is true for basketball teams, companies, and biblical miracles, why not religious communities?

We have an outcome bias. We determine, in hindsight, whether something was good or bad depending upon how it turned out, rather than whether we made a sound decision. Then, in hindsight, we decide whether it was good idea. Then we adjust our memory and conclude, "I knew it all along." That's why we blame decision makers when things turn out badly and give them too little credit when things turn out well.

In a study by Philip Tetlock, he interviewed 2,854 people who made their living commenting and offering advice on political and economic trends. He asked them to predict trends within their field of expertise and the results were devastating, no better than chance.[230] Errors in prediction are inevitable because the world is unpredictable. It is especially poor in complex, far away predictions, like the stock market in 2030 or Religious Life.

Will a communal venture toward transformation work? I had been a therapist for years before I switched roles and sat on the other side. I was terrified as I sat on the client side of the room while waiting for my therapist to come into the room. I thought to myself, *I guess this is how my clients feel when they first sit down in my office. This sucks!* When he opened the door, before he even had a chance to sit down with his coffee, I glared at him and said, "My entire life is on the line. This had better work!" To which he replied, calmly and without missing a beat, "Well, that's entirely up to you."

I have since passed along that same advice to clients and communities alike. It is entirely up to you what "It had better work" means. What does transformation mean to you? What does progress mean to you? How hard are you willing to work? How do you define success? Keep asking yourselves these questions so you know if it is working, so you don't get too lost in the fog of ambiguity. And, one last caution, be careful what you wish for. Sometimes our prayers are answered in ways that are surprising!

Patricia Wittberg spoke of success this way:

> "The definition of success may be uncertain, but there is, however, one absolutely sure definition of failure. And that is never to begin at all – to mouth platitudes about 'dying with dignity' as we retreat into lethargy, to concoct alibis about 'the worldliness of society today' and 'young people's inability to make commitments,' to cover up the fact that we have never really tried to refound our congregations. The ultimate failure would be to stand idly by while the next generation of religious virtuosi seek their call elsewhere." [231]

Lessons learned and recommendations

The survey I conducted concluded by asking communities engaged in transformative efforts, what recommendations they could offer others who might be considering this type of work. Their top ten recommendations are worthy of your consideration:

1. Involve everyone, all members;
2. Be utterly honest and fully inform your members;
3. Do the soul work, the inner work of transformation;
4. Do the relationship work of healing and building stronger bonds;
5. Keep your eye on the prize, the big picture and ultimate goal;

6. Respect the differences and work through conflict;

7. Seek as much assistance as you need;

8. Be willing to pay the price;

9. Seek transformation, not simply change;

10. Be patient with the slow work of God.[232]

Reflection: Common Questions

Consider these common questions: How long will it take? What are the benefits and costs? Will it work? In light of these questions:

1. *What new insights emerge for you?*

2. *In what ways has your community grappled with these and what further conversations might be needed?*

Summary

Communal transformation takes great motivation and total commitment by a community. It cannot be relegated to leadership or delegated to a committee. It requires the collective ownership of all members. It requires partnerships among leaders and members and new partnerships with others beyond the community need to be developed. The nature of transformation is such that it also necessitates a great trust in your instruments – your personal and communal capacity to pray, reflect, contemplate and discern.

There are some common questions you might have regarding your own capacity to do this work, how long it takes, as well as its costs and benefits. These questions are important to reflect upon in the beginning and throughout the entire journey because your understanding of the journey and the answers you unearth will deepen over time.

CHAPTER 9:
CONVENTIONAL
APPROACHES TO PLANNING
AND VISIONING
Benefits, limitations and pitfalls

"People should think things out fresh and not just accept conventional terms and the conventional way of doing things."
Buckminster Fuller

Introduction

Most communities engaged in the work of planning and visioning use conventional methods. They might start by rewriting mission and vision statements, engage in strategic planning, then onboard the community and align their resources accordingly. While this is certainly a familiar and logical approach, it is not one that lends itself to communal transformation.

Some communities have explored other less conventional methods, such as, Appreciative Inquiry or Theory U. But these have limitations, too. As it turns out, while these conventional or unconventional methods are part of what you might use, by themselves, they will not transform your community. If used at all, they will need to be adapted and woven into a larger process aimed specifically at communal transformation.

In this Chapter I will focus primarily on the conventional methods as these are the ones most often used. We will examine the strengths and limitations of conventional methods and how to adapt and incorporate these. We will look at the use of mission and vision statements, strategic planning, and three different types of visions. We will then look at the pitfalls most commonly encountered when communities attempt transformation. I call these the "dirty dozen" and will invite your reflections on how to address these in your own community. We will gather the learnings and incorporate these into the overall Journey of Transformation.

Conventional Approaches: Necessary but Insufficient

In the corporate world, conventional approaches used for organizational change usually involve some combination of writing mission and vision statements and creating a strategic plan. Typically, the strategic plan flows from the vision statement, which, in turn, flows from the mission statement. The strategic plan includes goals, objectives, timelines, budgets and mechanisms of accountability. The mission and vision statements, along with the strategic plan, are what typically constitute a new plan and vision for an organization's future.

The leadership of an organization typically takes the primary responsibility for crafting the mission and vision statements and developing the strategic plan. The leadership might ask committees to help them and seek varying degrees of input from others. Once readied, the leadership will then *roll out* the vision in an effort to *sell* it to the members of their organization hoping to get their *buy in*.

Religious communities have approached planning their future in much the same way as the corporate world. Leadership (or a committee) coordinates the process using a mixture of local community and large group gatherings. Relevant materials and articles are sent out for personal study and community discussions. These flow into, and out from, the less frequent larger community gatherings. For religious communities, all of this culminates in Chapters wherein a new leadership is elected, and a new vision is ratified. The new vision is then summarized in Chapter acts or directional statements.

Religious communities are well versed in these approaches. Adopted largely from the corporate world, these approaches are tailored to a certain extent, then placed in a spiritual framework using prayer, discernment and language more befitting Religious Life. The processes are as familiar and predictable as the results.

These conventional methods have important benefits and will, to some extent, be used along with the Journey of Transformation processes described in Part III. However, these approaches also have a great many limitations and will not, if used alone or in a primary way, transform communities. While you will still need to create plans with goals, objectives, timelines, budgets and mechanisms of accountability, the transformative potential of these plans will be dependent upon how well these are interwoven into a larger process, the Journey of Transformation.

What got you to today, won't get you to tomorrow. There are four basic reasons why you cannot rely solely or primarily upon these conventional approaches in order to bring about communal transformation:

1. **It's insane to expect something different when you are doing what you've always done;**

2. **It's a different world requiring different approaches;**

3. **You are in a different stage of your lifecycle requiring a different approach; and,**

4. **Research indicates that conventional approaches don't work, especially in unconventional times.**

It's insane to expect something different

Many who express an interest in transformation simultaneously resist any suggested changes in the processes used for communal gatherings geared toward planning and visioning their future. They want to continue to meet, plan, dialogue, vote and implement decisions in much the same manner as they have done in the past. For example, even minor changes in the methods of electing leaders, who can participate in Chapters, or how agenda is surfaced, can be met with enormous resistance. If you want a different outcome than what you've achieved in the past, you'll need to engage in different processes.

Trying harder to do more of the same doesn't work. To expect that conventional approaches would bring about unconventional change and transformation, is expecting too much. Albert Einstein told us that this is the very definition of *insanity*: doing the same thing over and over again while expecting different results. How can you expect a novel result if you are using the same approach to planning and visioning as you have in the past?

Jason Jennings, author of the *Reinventors*, agrees: "'Conventional wisdom' is a phrase used to describe ideas or explanations that have been generally accepted as truths based on the past. Using conventional wisdom to predict likely future results in the new century is an innovation killer, because none of the old metrics and rules hold up anymore."[233] Conventional wisdom using conventional approaches result in conventional solutions, which are patently insufficient for unconventional times such as these. In order to create something other than the predictable future, you cannot do what you've always done.

It's a different world

Strategic planning has its roots in the 1950s and gained prominence in the 1960s when businesses began to see the benefits of this systematic way to forecast the future and plan accordingly. Conventional approaches, such as strategic planning, have been useful in the past, especially when our world was a bit more stable and predictable, and when change was more incremental and controllable. These approaches are not built for times of volatility, uncertainty, complexity and ambiguity. Conventional approaches, like strategic planning, are built upon the premise that the future is predictable and controllable.

As we saw in Chapter 2, the world today is quite different than it was even a decade ago. We are in a world that is changing more rapidly than ever before in history. For thousands of years the human species adapted at a pace that was on par with the changes around the globe. The current rate and depth of change in climate, technology, and globalization is outstripping our ability to adapt. Addressing the use of conventional methods, Thomas Chermack said, "the rate and depth of change have increased over time to the point that those methods are no longer useful."[234]

While these approaches may have worked well in ordinary times, they do not work in these extraordinary turbulent times of transition. Given the unprecedented changes in circumstances, and a future that is impossible to predict or control, it makes no sense to use approaches premised on the opposite. New approaches are needed.

You're at a different stage

Every new stage in the lifecycle requires a different approach to planning, organizing and pursuing its goals (refer to Chapter 10). The growth and mature phases are the most predictable, while the founding and crossroads phases are the most ambiguous and volatile.

Strategic planning, which is founded on the premise of predictability and control, works better in the growth and mature stages but not in times of chaos and uncertainty. A community in the mature stage is far more organized and systematized. They are drawn to the familiarity and logic of strategic planning. However, the crossroads phase, in which most religious communities find themselves today, requires a new and different approach if it aspires to transform and birth new life.

That is why communities at this transitional stage have turned to other methods like Scenario Planning, Theory U, World Café, Open Space Technology, Appreciative Inquiry and others. But even these are neither comprehensive enough nor tailored enough for religious communities to use as prescribed by their authors. However, along with strategic planning, these methods have much to offer and can be incorporated into the Journey of Transformation.

Research indicates that conventional approaches don't work

As the saying goes, "If you want to make God laugh, tell her your plans." Writing mission and vision statements and engaging in strategic planning continue to be used as the default planning methods for nearly every organization, from the government, to the military, and businesses, as well as parishes and religious communities. Strategic planning is likely the only known method of planning for most organizations and communities. Despite its ubiquitous use, the research does not support its reputation as a *best practice* for planning and visioning.

In a seminal meta-analysis, *The Rise and Fall of Strategic Planning*, Henry Mintzberg reviewed the prior studies and research that analyzed the successes and failures of conventional approaches. The results of his analysis revealed that up to 80% of the time, conventional approaches failed to accomplish their intended goals. In discussing the reasons for its failure, Mintzberg said:

> "Conventional planning tends to be a conservative process, sometimes encouraging behavior that undermines both creativity and strategic thinking. It can be inflexible, breeding resistance to major strategic change and discouraging truly novel ideas in favor of extrapolation of the status quo or marginal adaptation, ultimately, therefore, focusing attention on the short term rather than the long term."[235]

The research indicates that strategic planning is especially poor as a means for organizational transformation. When the world and organizations are stable, it works a bit better. But when the world and the future are as dynamic, unstable, and uncertain as they are today, it doesn't work. And when organizations are smaller, complex, have a strong culture steeped in history, are in a declining stage, as Religious Life is today, and need to adapt, it does not work. In these circumstances, Mintzberg says, the data is conclusive: this kind of planning "makes no sense."[236]

Kim Cameron and Robert Quinn came to many of the same conclusions in their review of the literature. They found that conventional approaches had failure rates up to 85%[237], and even downsizing failed 75% of the time.[238] They saw that these methods "failed entirely or have created problems serious enough that the survival of the organization was threatened."[239] They concluded that conventional methods simply do not result in systemic change or transformation. The reason, they concluded, is because even when procedures and strategies are altered, if the culture, values and traditions are not addressed, "organizations return quickly to the status quo."[240] Downsizing failed to produce the desired results so many times that it was sometimes referred to as "dumbsizing."[241]

While strategic planning has its limitations, it is not without its merits. Strategic planning does provide a known, easily understood and widely accepted way to plan. It is logical, rational and reasonable. It lends itself to situations wherein the problems can be defined and solutions are readily available. Mintzberg suggests building on the merits of strategic planning, saying: "if reconceived, made more flexible, and pitfalls are avoided, it can have an important role to play."[242] The same can be said for the more unconventional methods.

Learnings

What we have learned, thus far, is that conventional approaches simply cannot be used as the primary or only approach to planning and visioning, especially when an organization is in the transitional phase and desires deep change and transformation. These methods are useful only *if* they are revised to become more flexible, creative, open to novelty, and *if* they are incorporated into a more comprehensive approach aimed at deep change and transformation.

Reflection: Planning and Visioning

---

1. *What are the planning and visioning methods your community is using?*
2. *What is working well with these and what is not working well?*

Benefits and Limitations of Conventional Approaches

"The greatest danger for most of us is not that our aim is too high and we miss it, but that It is too low and we reach it." Michelangelo

Let's dig a bit deeper and learn what we can from the benefits and drawbacks of conventional approaches. We will look at the use of mission and vision statements, along with strategic planning, to determine how to integrate the best of what these have to offer.

Mission statements

Mission is commonly defined as the *WHY* of an organization's existence. An organization's mission is its essential purpose for existing or *raison d'être*. In order to articulate your organization's mission, you might ask: *What does it do for the world? If the world existed without our organization, what difference would it make?*

If you were to write a mission statement for your community, it should flow from your charism, capture the essential purpose of your community and speak to your core expertise, distinctive contributions and enduring values. It should be passionate and bold enough to inspire your community. Leonard Goodstein, Timothy Nolan and William Pfeiffer provide ten useful criteria for an effective mission statement:

1. Is clear and understandable

2. Is brief, less than 100 words

3. Specifies your purpose – who you serve; needs addressed and how; and why your organization exists

4. Identifies forces that drive your vision

5. Includes your distinctive competence

6. Is focused, yet flexible

7. Assists you in decision-making

8. Reflects your values and beliefs

9. Is realistic and achievable

10. Serves as a source of energy and rallying point for members.[243]

Vision statements

An organization's vision ideally flows from its mission and is the *WHAT* of its existence. It describes what the organization will do in order to accomplish its mission. While an organization's mission is more stable and tied to its core values, its vision needs to change over time according to changes within the organization and the world in which it exists. In other words, the vision must continually be adapted to evolving internal and external circumstances.

If you were to write a vision statement for your community it ought to be a succinct statement that identifies your goals. It should paint a picture of the scope of your community's endeavors. It should give you the basis for your own accountability, be concrete, specific and measurable, and preferably have no more than four or five goals.

Religious communities have spelled out their mission, charism, core values, guiding principles and other foundational dictums in their Constitutions that are intended to inform how they live their lives. However, most religious communities have also followed the corporate world in writing more specific mission and vision statements lending further clarity and a contemporary focus to their efforts. These are typically framed and placed on the walls of administration offices, posted on websites and added to an array of artifacts.

Unfortunately, most mission and vision statements have not lived up to the hype, either in the business world or within Religious Life. Too often they are framed and fixed in time, when most proponents, like Peter Senge, believe that visioning is a process that ought to be "ongoing and never ending."[244] Vision statements are often too broad and vague to establish a group's identity or give much focus to their efforts. "Group think" and a desire to be inclusive of all voices, lends itself to writing either all-inclusive, broad, general statements or a laundry list of small goals. As a result, these all-encompassing statements instill little passion and provide little practical use for planning. They become decorations on the wall, rather than living documents that continue to evolve and shape the life of a living organization or community.

If there is power in writing mission and vision statements, it is more often in the *process* of creating them, not in the statements themselves. In other words, what really affects people is what happens to them in the dialogue while creating the statements. It is in the power of exploration and the trust required for deep listening. It is the generative power that results from a dogged pursuit of the truth and the creative tension that results. It is the "ah-hah" moments of connections and the synergy that emerges in a group while engaged in the dialogue. All of these are very worthwhile. Those who craft these documents gain ownership, wisdom and passion for what they create together.

Unfortunately, it is only those who are in the dialogue that are affected in these ways. Those who are handed the documents to read, rubber stamp for approval, or are asked to follow through and implement, are not nearly as affected. They did not craft them, so they do not own them. They did not put the work into them, so they have no passion for implementing them. Ultimately, the commitment to a shared vision must be greater than the commitment to individual visions and fragmented pursuits. Shared visions, if they are attained, ought to be more than the sum of individual visions. Ideally, they become a synergistic product of the whole.

Strategic plans

Mission and vision statements together form the foundation from which strategic plans are developed. A strategic plan becomes the way in which an organization will accomplish its vision. It is the *HOW* of an organization's existence. It should include goals, objectives, benchmarks for progress, timelines, mechanisms of accountability and criteria for success. When these are done well, they can be a useful tool for mobilizing and aligning the human, financial and material resources.

Visioning processes and the visions they create

Visioning may involve as few as five, or as many as a dozen, steps. While every organization tailors its methods to their circumstances, the general approach is the same. A typical outline of the most common steps in visioning for a community would include the following:

Step 1   **Establish a Sense of Urgency**

- Stoke the fires by continuing to bring before the community the major opportunities, critical realities, potential crises and most compelling reasons for change

Step 2   **Form a leadership coalition**

- Assemble a group of leaders and members capable enough to lead the change process

Step 3   **Create a vision statement**

- Create an overarching statement and include measurable goals

Step 4   **Communicate the vision**

- Use every way possible to inculcate the vision into the minds and hearts of the community

Step 5   **Empower others to act on the vision**

- Tap the gifts and wisdom of the community, build upon their desires and work through their resistance as the heart-work of change

Step 6   **Produce short-term successes**

- Demonstrate success, improvement and progress and help the community recognize their contributions to this; connect these small successes to the big picture

Step 7 **Consolidate improvements and build on them**

- Use your increased credibility as leverage to further promote change

Step 8 **Connect and standardize new approaches**

- Articulate the connection between new personal influence and communal success and create new policies, procedures, and structures to support desired changes

This outline provides a useful roadmap for leaders and committees to follow for visioning. It has clearly defined steps and is useful as far as it goes. But, as we discussed earlier, by itself such a conventional approach is not enough if the goal is transformation. It must be used flexibly and integrated into a larger process aimed specifically at transformation.

Types of visions

The types of visions that come from these conventional approaches could be described as *restorative* or *directional.* They do not result in deep changes in the culture. They do not result in systemic change. The types of visions that are needed during transitional times are *transformative.* Let's look at each of the three types of visions.

Restorative visions

Most visions that emerge from traditional approaches are restorative. They are largely a continuation of prior visioning efforts, but with a new set of goals. These new and improved visions are a result of goals developed from an accumulation of learnings and a growing appreciation of current realities. These new iterations are basically an extension of preexisting projects updated to fit contemporary needs and circumstances. Such contemporized visions restore, build upon and extend into the future visions that were previously claimed. An example of this type of vision might be for a community to decide to renovate the motherhouse or bolster its support of an existing ministry.

Directional visions

Sometimes a vision is claimed that marks the beginning of an entirely new directional thrust for a community. A new set of goals and objectives from these visions will result in a major shift in the allocation of resources. Issues and events of the day may be described not only with new language, but also with new understandings as a result of new frames of reference. The challenges faced by the organization might be familiar, but their solutions are more innovative.

Such visions are *a breath of fresh air* that bring communities one step further along their developmental path. These visions become the cornerstone for developing new strategic plans, complete with new goals, objectives and timelines. Examples of directional vision might be when a community decides to: start a new mission in a developing country using the money from the sale of property; or put a moratorium on new vocations and start a house of discernment for people from all walks of life.

In summary, both restorative and directional visions lend themselves to an ease in planning. The terrain in which they are developed is familiar, the language for discussing things is largely the same and the vision can be easily broken down into a clear set of goals and objectives. With these in hand, both leaders and members know their assigned roles. The community knows its new set of priorities and can allocate resources accordingly. These goals can be easily translated into materials shared with others outside of community. Life can go on for most members with little disruption of the status quo. And therein lies their limitation: they do not substantially challenge or transform the existing culture or system.

Transformative visions

Occasionally a radical new vision may be pursued and, if successful, can usher in an entirely new era in the life of an organization. These rarefied visions not only reframe an organization's identity and context, but also shift the very assumptions, values and belief systems that undergird and give meaning to these. These are highly imaginative, out-of-the box, throw-out-the-maps kinds of visions that offer ground-breaking directions that were previously inconceivable or thought impossible. Such paradigm-changing visions unleash a pioneering spirit in an organization seeking to transform their lives. If an organization goes *all in* with such visions, it has the potential to set into motion the birthing of a new lifecycle in an organization's evolution.

These types of visioning efforts are most important during the transition or re-birthing phase of an organization. In other words, these are the visions needed at this stage in the current cycle of Religious Life. Transformative visions foster systemic change, spring from a new paradigm of understanding of the world and reshape the meaning and purpose of the organization itself. They involve deep change in the culture of an organization.

The most obvious example of a transformative vision for Religious Life was the sea change brought about by Vatican II. This birthing of a new vision had broad and irreversible consequences for all of Religious Life. It touched every religious community, Catholic institution and the people they served. It is still unfolding, being tested, resisted and reshaped.

Another example of such a transformative vision for a community might be if it decides to let go of the existing paradigm of membership and create a new paradigm. This new paradigm might reframe the nature of the vows and boundaries related to membership. Laity might join traditionally vowed members and form a new community through a different set of vows or commitments, with members living in or outside community, but each with equal rights of membership.

Transformative visions are not fixed or tied to one narrative. They are iterative and continually evolve to create new narratives. They involve reframing a community's identity in relationship with the wider world. They radically alter the assumptions and values that undergird the meaning and purpose of a community's existence. New structures, policies and practices must be adopted in support of the new vision. In these ways, transformative visions are intended to bring about not only organizational change, but deep change in the culture of community (i.e., systemic change). The impact is felt by the entire community, rekindling passion for mission and excitement about the future and, in some cases, birthing a new life cycle in a community's evolution.

The drawbacks, of course, are the flipside of the benefits. The disruption of the status quo brings conflict and resistance. Confusion results from the inherent ambiguity of a vision that is emerging but not yet clear. Chaos abounds because of the collision of paradigms (past and emerging) with no firm ground upon which to substantiate the nascent vision. The time and money that is spent in creating a future with no guarantees or clear pathway can bring forth doubt, impatience and fatigue.

In summary, restorative and directional approaches are certainly the most common, understandable and easiest to implement. This familiarity may be one of the primary reasons communities remain so wedded to them. They know how to create these visions and the cost in terms of disruption in their lives is minimal. And therein lies their limitation: transformative visions are the most challenging and also hold the most potential for promoting cultural change, systemic change, and the kind of deep change needed to transform a community.

Reflection: Types of Visions

---

1. What types of visions has your community developed in the last two chapters?

2. To what degree do you own your community's vision and believe you are a valued contributor for bringing it to life?

Pitfalls of Conventional Approaches

While the discouraging news is the high failure rate of conventional methods, the good news is that we know why. Because we know why, we can address the reasons and minimize or avert failure. If communities can identify, early on, their own potential pitfalls of conventional approaches, and where they might stumble in their own efforts, they have an opportunity to do something about it. They could address their own potential *Achilles' heel* and be proactive in finding solutions.

In reviewing the research regarding why conventional approaches fail, there were dozens of reasons cited. In working with communities over the years, I have repeatedly put these reasons in front of them and asked leaders and members to reflect upon the ways they might undermine their own efforts in planning I have surveyed communities in the United States, Canada, Mexico, Central America, Africa and Europe, and the results are amazingly consistent.

From these surveys I have winnowed down the list to what I call the "dirty dozen." These are the twelve most likely reasons that communities will fail in their efforts to transform and birth a new narrative for the future. These are listed in Table 3, Dirty Dozen, starting with the worst *Achilles' heel* of all: conflict avoidance.

Dirty Dozen	
Twelve of the most common ways communities undermine their efforts	
1. Conflict avoidance	7. Lack of integration and focus
2. Breadth over depth	
3. Failure to risk	8. Glorification of the past
4. Not enough urgency	9. Maintenance over mission
5. Less than an all-out effort	10. Moving too fast or too slow
6. Avoidance of ambiguity	11. Missing container
	12. Failure to partner

Table 3: Dirty Dozen

I would encourage your community to take a good hard look at these before embarking on any substantial change effort. These pitfalls, if they are not named and claimed by your community, and if measures are not taken to address these proactively, will very likely undermine your best intentions. If you reflect upon and claim your likely pitfalls, you can make deliberate choices to address them ahead of time.

Dirty dozen

1. Conflict avoidance and working around resistance

Conflict, chaos and tension are integral to the work of transformation and most people avoid it like the plague. Most people have a tremendous *fear of conflict* and are terrible at handling it because they have never been taught the skills or developed the courage and discipline to handle it. They shut down, act out, preach, judge, shout and *should* one another. Many just go silent if conflict erupts in their presence. Most try to circumvent it all together. Most groups would rather come to a meeting and have feel-good speeches, and *nice, polite* conversations, rather than go through the muck and mire of working through conflicts.

No sooner do communities claim a desire for change and transformation, than they seek to undermine these very claims by avoiding the conflicts and chaos required of it. Despite this well known change-resistance dynamic, members continue to collude in a dance of avoidance. While there are some who are brave enough to voice their disappointment, frustration and anger, most will see resistance as *out there*, in those *others* who give voice to it. Rarely do these people recognize their own collusion in the dance. Their resistance may be unconscious or, if they are aware of it, they choose to sit in silence. Either way, they allow the few vocal ones to take the heat, while they, themselves, take refuge in the camouflage of cooperation and appearance of propriety. Efforts at deep change and transformation are doomed to failure if a community does not learn how to handle conflict and resistance more directly.

2. Breadth over depth and fear of intimacy

Deep change and transformation require a choice for intimate conversations, a choice for depth over breadth. However, most groups continue to choose breadth over depth out of a basic *fear of intimacy*. They will insist that such intimate conversation ought to be "private" and addressed outside of a meeting. They might express a desire for depth, but most will not allocate the time or develop the trust to make that possible. Most groups are unwilling or unable to create the soul-space needed to work with in-depth processes. They will limit the face-time and have safe conversation.

Even if there are stirring calls to *push out into the deep*, rarely will communities stray far from the shore and, if they do, it is not for very long. Promises of *truth-telling* and *soul-searching* conversations are hard to keep. These promises, though sincere at the time, are immediately and continually assaulted by the natural resistance to personally disclosing in intimate conversations. The lack of trust and a backlog of old wounds leave people wearing masks and keeping their distance. Some will say, "We don't have the time," when really it is a rationalization for staying ashore and avoiding the risk of being vulnerable.

Without in-depth dialogue, communities risk building a house of cards. They will build a plan for the future based upon surface conversations. They will never get to the heart of the matter and, without the heart of the matter, they will never transform. They will have the real meeting outside of the meeting. They will value quick answers over great questions, use speed and getting tasks done as a defense against depth. The in-depth conversations needed for genuine transformation are easily negotiated away in favor of less costly, more expedient and familiar programs for change.

3. Failure to risk and innovate

Communities that are unable to innovate and be creative will fail to transform. A *fear of failure* will stymie most communities. Despite pledges of being *prophetic*, most communities are highly risk-averse. The daily grind of just keeping things going, and the need for consensus before making a move, whittles away at radicality. The gravitational pull toward the familiar, the melting pot of group think, and the challenge of placing their money, time and reputations at risk is just too great.

Most communities would rather have more study than dialogue, and more dialogue than action, for fear of making mistakes. They are too afraid to experiment out of a fear of failure. They prefer short-term fixes, rather than complex, long-term solutions. They'll go with the tried and true over the unknown and untested, the familiar over the novel, and a safe harbor with predictable outcomes over an adventure with unforeseen possibilities. It is hard for a group of accomplished, professional people, who are used to being the givers, to become receivers and learners. It is hard for people who are used to being in charge and having all the answers to let outsiders in as partners who would share power and help them think outside the box.

4. Not enough urgency

Undertakings to transform a community often wither and die because they were never made the priority they needed to be from the beginning. Transformation requires a sustained sense of urgency. It must be *priority one* on the list of priorities, not somewhere in the middle of a long list of priorities. Communities that fail are ones without urgency. If leaders do not make a clear, reality-based, compelling case for why this is a *do-or-die, now-or-never* moment, then members will easily return to their ordinary lives and business as usual.

The hard truth is that if a community is not in sufficient pain, it will not have the motivation to change, let alone transform. Providing members with the ten most logical reasons to change won't work. If the rationale is based upon diminishment, scarcity, fear, fault-finding, aging, and other depressing reasons for change, it won't work. If the motivation is based primarily upon fiscal determinants (e.g., cost cutting, belt tightening), it won't work. Members have to *feel* the pain and the only way for them to feel it, is if leadership lets them. Too often leaders protect members from their overwhelming sense of responsibility, their own fear and confusion on what to do next, and their own internal conflicts and stress.

The litmus test for whether or not transformative efforts become a priority is two-fold: calendar and budget. Time and money are the concrete resources that must be spent if this is truly a priority. Members must put their money and calendars where their mouth is. Most communities, sadly, will try to squeeze their change efforts into their already busy calendars and already swollen budgets. If you had a heart attack, you would immediately change your priorities with a great sense of urgency. Most communities succumb to the "boiling frog" syndrome and fail to see and *feel* the urgency. They don't know that their community has already had a systemic heart attack.

5. Less than an all-out effort

When life was in maintenance mode and there were plenty of people to go around, leadership and a handful of committees could suffice for shaping its future – not so for the work of transformation. Transformation requires an *all-hands-on-deck, no-holds-barred* effort. Leadership driven, top down approaches that attempt to sell a vision to members never work. It must be a total community endeavor where no one sits on the sidelines. Only those who do the hard work gain the passion needed when it comes time for implementation. Most communities, unfortunately, will leave it to a handful of overly responsible, already busy, stressed out people.

Sending out articles and meeting once a year as a community will not transform your community. Even if an assembly is inspiring, members will return home and back to business as usual, leaving the rest in the hands of a small group of people. Communal transformation requires a sustained effort by every member of the community, which means adjusting calendars and letting go of other commitments.

To sacrifice in this way, members must believe in what they are doing and be willing to see it through. Only *owners* feel that kind of responsibility and are willing to make such sacrifices. For ownership to occur, members must be involved in every step of the process, experience that leaders are listening to what they have to say, and that their voice matters in shaping the processes and outcomes. They must have real choices along the way and real power to say "yes" or "no" to these. Anything short of these measures will limit ownership and, as a consequence, any decisions that are made or visions that are claimed will be orphaned.

6. Avoidance of ambiguity

A *fear of the unknown* is a common experience of most people. The unknown frightens stock markets and it frightens communities. Communities want predictability, control, familiarity and security. Insisting upon a clear path with known answers, however, is the death knell of any transformative endeavor. Transformation is always a leap of faith, the same as getting married, starting a career, or joining a community. There is no way of knowing where it might lead, only that you are called. The work of transformation requires a huge tolerance of ambiguity. Communities that fail to transform are ones that want one clear vision for the future, to know ahead of time how much it will cost, when it will be done, what it will look like when it's finished, and that it will all be worth it in the end.

"Build the bridge while walking" is today's nearly hackneyed refrain because it is so true of transformation. The work of transformation requires taking one step at a time, discovering what you can, and then deciding upon the next best step. The process of transformation is *emergent, organic* and *iterative*. Creating a process that is rigidly followed like a script written for a play, defies the work of the Spirit who blows where she will. Fixing a timeline that does not bend to new discoveries and emerging circumstances will sabotage your efforts. Insisting upon certain outcomes and trying to engineer a process to guarantee these, also, will not work.

7. Lack of integration and focus

Communities are under siege right now just trying to maintain things as they are amid diminishing resources. Their challenge becomes one of integration, prioritization and focus. It is easy to lose sight of the forest for the trees. When communities commit to the work of transformation on top of all they are already doing, it can be the straw that breaks everyone's backs. There is too much agenda for too little time. Prioritizing agenda, when it is all so important and pressing, is easier said than done.

Integration means connecting the dots in a continual way and making sure everyone knows how one thing leads to another. It means letting members know how what they did in the last meeting influenced what is being done in the next. It means continually resetting the context, recapping what has happened, reiterating where you are now and how all this is leading to the next steps. It means never sending homework out to members without a specific purpose and without receiving feedback that is then summarized and returned to all members. It means never having a one-and-done assembly or assignment that does not build on what has been done before and is connected to what comes next. Most importantly, perhaps the most difficult of all, is integrating each member's head and heart throughout the process.

8. Glorification of the past and adherence to past methods

This is a tough one for a Church so steeped in ritual and tradition. Yet visioning processes that invite deep rather than incremental change are ones that require more time spent looking forward rather than in the rearview mirror. Processes that pit a loyalty to the past against a fidelity to the future are doomed. What are needed are visions that build upon the past with a bias toward the future. Planning for the future cannot be construed as an indictment of the past or past leaders.

Creative fidelity is key. Transformative processes require that any future claimed is one that includes and transcends the past, not severs it. If honoring the past means behaving strictly in accord with yesterday's interpretations of canon law, your Constitutions or the words of your founder, and that no new interpretations or changes are allowed, then transformation is preempted. Yes, the past must be honored, understood and appreciated and, simultaneously, it must be re-incorporated into new visions and understood in new ways. This newness carries with it a necessary departure from the past.

9. Maintenance over mission

The maintenance responsibilities of most communities (e.g., caring for aging members, facilities, and ministries), is smothering the life out of the responsibility to create a future. Groups are so heavily maintenance oriented that the time for contemplation and thinking strategically is sacrificed. Far more time, energy, money and personnel are spent on maintaining life as it is rather than on planning the mission and vision for the future. It is a huge challenge for leaders and members to let go of worthy calendared commitments in order to make room for the time needed to create a future.

I begin most meetings with prayer and "check-in." It might be something as simple as, "How are you coming to our time?" The check-in is meant to invite the participants to share the quality of *presence* they are bringing to the meeting. I would estimate that ninety percent of the time I hear something along the lines of: "I'm tired," "I feel pressed," or "I'm good because I got some things done," or "I hope this doesn't last long because I have a lot of things to do!" *Getting things done* is the press of the day. People are so busy getting things done, they are not only exhausted, they are losing sight of *WHY* they are doing things to begin with. They have little time and energy left to focus on the big picture, their mission and vision for the future, *unless they choose otherwise.*

10. Moving too fast or too slow

Transformation is a marathon, not a sprint. The speed at which leadership attempts to move the transformative efforts along is one of the very few things over which they have control. Leaders can push the throttle forward or pull it back. It is important to manage the pace of change. If it is too fast, people will become too overwhelmed and fragmented. If it is too slow, which is more often the case, people forget what happened in the last meeting and the process loses momentum. The challenge is to find the *sweet spot* that keeps members fully engaged over time.

Some communities move too fast in their press to *get things done*. Leadership wants to accomplish things before the next team is elected who might move things in a different direction. Members want a sense of *progress*, usually defined as making decision and implementing plans. The press to get things done too often sacrifices depth. On the flipside, some communities move too slow. They are either unwilling to commit to regular, more frequent gatherings, or are afflicted with *paralysis by analysis*. The paralysis and lack of progress causes members to feel frustrated and demoralized.

11. Missing container

A container is what holds the process together and the members in good stead throughout the journey. It is a holding environment in which members feel safe enough to engage the chaos and conflict, healing and conversion, depth and intimacy, and the creativity and experimentation needed for trans-formation. A container provides a common language and framework for understanding what they are doing and why. It gives everyone a solid sense of *we are all in this together*. Ideally, a container provides the sacred space needed to make transformation possible.

Communities that meet only occasionally cannot build a solid container. Communities that do not have their members on the same page regarding what they are doing and why, don't have a container. Communities that have not acquired the skills for handling intimate or conflictual conversations, or don't have a facilitator to help them swim in these waters, will not have the container needed to engage in the work of transformation. Without a container to hold everyone together in the messy work of transformation, it will fail.

12. Failure to partner

Communities are quick to say that they "collaborate" with others because they have lay staff and employees and others with whom they co-minister; all of which is true. However, the work of transformation requires not only collaboration with others but "partnership." Partnership means being-in-it-together, sharing power and control. It means opening your boundaries and inviting others in, not just to offer their advice and resources, but to co-create with you a mutually desired future.

Many communities balk at the prospect of having laity involved in vision-ing as partners. They might invite them in for an assembly to help and offer some new ideas, but to sit around the table and forge a future *together* is a big stretch. Many communities are frightened of losing control. It is essential to the work of transformation that communities learn to open their boundaries and partner with others, rather than insulate, isolate, and cling to their waning independence that only accelerates their decline.

In summary, the gravitational pull toward these "dirty dozen" cannot be underestimated. Each community has its own unique way of unwittingly undermining its efforts and returning to the status quo via the path of least resistance. If your community does not recognize and address its predictable ways of resisting change, you will fail. If you do address these, you will improve your odds of success.

Reflection: Dirty Dozen

---

1. What are the likely pitfalls for your community?

2. What might you want to do to constructively address these pitfalls and improve your odds of success?

Summary

> *"Masonry bonded with wooden beams is not loosened by an earthquake: neither is a resolve constructed with careful deliberation shaken in the moment of fear. A resolve that is backed by prudent understanding is like the polished surface of a smooth wall. Small stones lying on an open height will not remain when the wind blows; neither can a timid resolve based on foolish plans withstand fear of any kind." Sirach 22:16-18*

Conventional approaches are necessary but insufficient if your aim is communal transformation. They are necessary for planning purposes, but must be tailored, used flexibly and integrated into a more comprehensive process aimed at transformation. The same can be said for the more unconventional methods. Deep change processes aimed at systemic change, a change in the very culture of community, are necessary to bring about communal transformation.

If you have read carefully the "dirty dozen," you probably noticed a theme – *fear*. Fear is what undermines most groups, no matter how high their initial enthusiasm for transformation might be. Most are afraid of conflict, intimacy, failure, and ambiguity, as well as loss of power and control. Fear is ultimately the *Achilles' heel* that undermines the personal and collective efforts to let go of the past and transform our lives. Perhaps, that is why the bible has over 360 references to fear.[245] It is essential that communities endeavoring to transform their lives work with these pitfalls and the underlying fears.

PART III:
JOURNEY OF
TRANSFORMATION

What does this word "transformation" truly mean? The word is used frequently these days, often synonymously and erroneously with "change." Chapter 10, *The Nature of Transformation*, seeks to answer this question. We will look at what we know about transformation from a variety of different disciplines and will identify 10 essential learnings that will form the foundation for the Journey of Transformation: five key principles and five dynamic elements.

What is the Journey of Transformation and how does it work? How is transformation different from change? And how much can we truly know of the Divine Mystery of transformation? Chapter 11 addresses these questions and provides the overview of the Journey of Transformation. The Journey of Transformation is the framework, principles and processes used in communal transformation. The Journey of Transformation weaves together the five foundational principles and five dynamic elements identified in Chapter 10 into the inner work of transformation. It provides the means for cooperating with grace through the Divine Mystery of transformation.

The five dynamic elements of transformation, when braided together as processes, provide the method and means for communal transformation – the Journey of Transformation. Chapters, 12 through 16, will be devoted to each of these five dynamic elements.

Chapter 10: The Nature of Transformation

*Foundations for the Journey
of Transformation*

---

*"Life spirals laboriously upward to higher and even higher levels, paying
for every step. Death was the price of the multi-cellular condition; pain
the price of nervous integration; anxiety the price of consciousness."*
Ludwig von Bertalanffy

Growing through Stages, Cycles, and Spirals

*"All creation is eagerly expecting the transformation of
the People of God." Romans 8:19*

Life is an unending, spiraling journey, a long and circuitous road leading
toward greater union with the Divine. Individuals, communities and all life-
forms go through similar spiraling motions. We are pushed by circumstances

that require us to change and we are drawn by the lure and love of God toward the possibility of transformation and new life. Each ring around the spiral is a cycle and within each cycle are stages. We can see these spiraling movements in our own personal lives, in our communities, and in the universe unfolding.

In this chapter, we will examine the knowledge-base regarding personal, interpersonal and systemic change in order to help us understand the nature of transformation. We will look through the lenses of different disciplines, from psychological and spiritual, to social and organizational, to cultural and evolutionary perspectives. Looking through these distinctive lenses will lead us to glean important insights about the nature of transformation and the spiraling movements in which transformation takes place.

Admittedly, surveying such a broad terrain of theory and research does not permit a detailed description or analysis of any individual discipline. However, the goal here is not to drill down into the particulars of each discipline, but to look through all of these as lenses to understand the common threads regarding the nature of transformation. We will look for what each can uniquely reveal and we will search for convergence across all of these disciplines. These insights, in turn, will form the foundation for the *principles* and *processes* used in the Journey of Transformation.

Personal development

> *"The greatest and most important problems of life are fundamentally unsolvable. They can never be solved, but only outgrown." Carl Jung*

Theories of human development have changed over time, each one incorporating and building upon the insights of earlier theories. In medieval times, it was believed that a *homunculus* (a miniature man) could grow through a process of alchemy. In other words, this embryonic, yet fully formed *little man*, through some magical process, grows into a mature person. Voilà! Growth amounted to a human being, over time, becoming a larger version of its previously fully formed self. Time and alchemy provided the basis for understanding human development.

In the sixteenth century, St. Ignatius of Loyola advanced the theory of human development. He suggested that maturation was a matter of good mentoring and could be completed at a relatively young age, saying: "Give me a child for his first seven years, and I'll give you the man."[246] His belief was that an individual with the proper mentoring would mature into adulthood by age seven, whereupon little further development would take place.

A half millennium later, we advanced our understanding of human development and now know that our total being (body, mind, and spirit) continues to mature far beyond seven years. Sigmund Freud was among the first to theorize that we develop psychologically in *stages* past puberty into adulthood. Each stage, he theorized, is characterized by distinctive ways of perceiving and apprehending our world. While most theorists have not held onto the psychosexual aspects of his theory, those that followed him did reinforce the belief that we develop in stages well past the age of seven.

Cognitive development

Jean Piaget used stage theories in describing childhood cognitive development. He observed that we *assimilate* information and understand it according to our particular stage of cognitive development (e.g., *concrete operations*). Over time, occasional leaps in our cognitive development occur resulting in new and qualitatively different ways in which we understand and "accommodate" to our world. When this happens, it ushers in a new stage of cognitive development (e.g., *formal operations*), altering our pre-existing schemas of perception.

Moral development

Lawrence Kohlberg used stage theories to describe our moral development. He believed that each stage builds upon and transcends prior ones, with an increased capacity for handling complex moral dilemmas. As we develop, we move from being egocentric and directed by external rewards and punishments (*pre-conventional*) to being sociocentric and directed by an internalization of social standards and judgements about right and wrong (*conventional*). The last two stages (*post-conventional*) recognize ethics and principled behavior, the acceptance of diversity of all people, empathy, and the need for consensus and democracy. He also noted that not all people advance to the higher levels and, those that do, may vacillate between levels.

Spiritual development

While initial stage theorists focused upon development from infancy into early adulthood, Carl Jung, Erik Erikson, Jane Loevenger, Abraham Maslow and others began to extend the notions of stage development into later adulthood, focusing especially on spiritual development. Carl Jung, for example, believed that spiritual awakening typically occurs around midlife:

> "The afternoon of a human life must also have a significance of its own and cannot be merely a pitiful appendage of life's morning. The significance of the morning undoubtedly lies in the development of the individual, our entrenchment in the outer world, the propagation of our kind and the care of our children. This is the obvious purpose of nature. But… whoever carries over into the afternoon the law of the morning must pay for doing so with damage to his soul." [247]

James Fowler developed a six-stage theory of faith development, from primal or *undifferentiated* faith, up through *universalizing* faith developed in later life. If we progress in our faith, we grow in our tolerance of paradox and ambiguity; we rely more on intuition and imagination, we become more open to other religions and cultures; and, we are more able to let go of past disillusionments.

Harry Moody believes that all religions believe in progressive spiritual passages, which he described in his book, *The Five Stages of the Soul*:

1. *Call* to conversion;

2. *Search* for God;

3. *Struggle* to meet the obstacles and face depression, regret, disillusionment;

4. *Breakthrough* with an inner awakening connecting to God, the flow, the truth; and,

5. *Return* with new knowledge, wisdom and experience to bring back to the world.[248]

According to Moody, the stages of the soul are spiritual stages that shift the center of our being away from the external world and toward the inner life of the soul. Each stage increases our commitment to and development of *virtuous behaviors* (e.g., kindness, generosity, empathy, and love). Each new stage raises our consciousness to a higher level that "awakens new and extraordinary faculties within us."[249] Increasingly, we desire to give back to the world what we have gained spiritually, and we desire to devote ourselves to the service of others.

Joseph Campbell researched cultures throughout history and across the globe describing our spiritual journey as "heroic." In his seminal book, *The Hero with a Thousand Faces*, he spoke of it this way:

> "We have not even to risk the adventure alone, for the heroes of all time have gone before us; the labyrinth is thoroughly known; we have only to follow the thread of the hero-path. And where we had thought to find an abomination, we shall find a god; where we had thought to slay another, we shall slay ourselves; where we had thought to travel outwards, we shall come to the center of our own existence; and where we had thought to be alone, we shall be with all the world." [250]

Spiritual development and aging

Robert Atchley, in his book, *Spirituality of Aging*, reviews the works of James Fowler, Erik Erikson, Ken Wilber and others. He sees the path to spiritual maturity as one that develops our capacity for wisdom, generativity, and transcendence. We develop more intimate connections with the larger web of life and direct experiences of the sacred (i.e., mystical experiences). We move beyond self-absorption to empathy and concern for others, from religious codes and creeds to seeking. We cycle through spiritually transformative experiences requiring "not just incremental improvement", but a "fundamental restructuring of the way we see things."[251]

George Vaillant, in his book, *Aging Well*, provides a meta-analysis of contemporary research, proving convincingly how we can grow and mature in later life, *if we choose*. Among his many conclusions, "Adult development is neither a footrace or moral imperative."[252] In other words, maturation is a slow process, and is not an inevitable consequence of aging. While there is no roadmap, there are factors that greatly improve our odds for successful aging: adaptive coping mechanisms, lifelong learning, creative outlets, and caring social networks.

Gail Sheehy's book, *Passages*,[253] Daniel Levinson's book, *The Seasons of a Man's Life*,[254] and Judith Viorst's book, *Necessary Losses*,[255] popularized the idea that human emotional-spiritual development occurs in stages unto death. *Gerotranscendence*, according to Lars Tornstam, is the final stage of late life, where we are invited through a spirit of generativity to mentor and empower the next generation.[256] Contemporary spiritual luminaries have followed suit in describing our lifelong, developmental spiritual journey toward God. For example:

- Richard Rohr's, *Falling Upward: A Spirituality for the Two Halves of Life*;[257]

- Parker Palmer's, *A Hidden Wholeness: The Journey Toward an Undivided Life*; [258]

- Joan Chittister's, *Gift of Years: Growing Older gracefully*;[259]

- Ronald Rolheiser's, *Sacred Fire: A Vision for a Deeper Human and Christian Maturity*;[260] and,

- Diarmuid O'Murchu's, *Adult Faith: Growing in Wisdom and Understanding*.[261]

Key learnings

What do all of these contemporary theories of emotional, cognitive, moral, and spiritual development tell us? In essence, life is a continuous spiral of growth and transformation. We grow and transform through stages, each one characterized by unique ways of apprehending and responding to our world. A stage lasts for some time wherein we grow incrementally, accumulating knowledge, honing our skills and gaining mastery. Periodically, however, we grow in leaps and bounds, transforming the fundamental way we understand ourselves, our world, and the meaning and purpose of our lives.

Our emotional-spiritual maturation is an arduous, if not heroic, journey that not everyone is equipped to handle. Emotional-spiritual maturation is not guaranteed as a function of age. Spiritual awakening, if it occurs, typically begins in midlife and can continue throughout our lifetime. We can get stuck along the way, regress to earlier stages, and our relative success or failure at any stage has implications for how well, or if, we will succeed in reaching a new maturational stage.

Each successive stage in our emotional-spiritual development moves us further from egoic self-concerns and worldly attachments, toward greater care, compassion, empathy and concern for others. Each successive stage brings us: *inward* toward greater union with the Divine (God, Truth, Love, Wisdom, or Bliss), *outward* with more care and compassion toward our world, and *upward* to a new level of consciousness with a wider, more inclusive and morally nuanced level of understanding.

Social and Organizational Development

Though many theorists speak of human development as occurring in stages, others, like Erik Erikson, describe personal development as *cyclical*.[262] The notion of cycles, along with the introduction of systems theory, worked its way into the theories and practices of individual and family therapy, as well as organizational and social change.

What is common to these theories about cycles is that organizations (businesses and communities) move through *phases* within a given cycle, and the cycle itself is recurring. With each recurrence of the cycle the phases are repeated but in a qualitatively different manner. For example, as businesses repeat a business cycle, they will go through the same phases as before (e.g., product development, marketing roll-out, rapid growth and diminishment of sales). However, they are not simply recycling old products. A new cycle is begun with new products aimed at meeting new market demands.

Furthermore, there is no guarantee that an organization will make it from one cycle to the next. Radical adjustments must be made in order to accommodate to new circumstances if a new cycle is to be birthed. Otherwise, an organization will plateau, diminish over time and, eventually, die out. Those that radically transform are rare. Apple computer, for example, has been through several business cycles, each time re-inventing itself and its products.

Systems theory and systemic change

In 1962, Thomas Kuhn published his groundbreaking book, *The Structure of Scientific Revolutions.*[263] He challenged the prevailing view that progress within the scientific community followed an incremental accumulation of new discoveries. Instead, he posited that periods of gradual accumulation of new information and conceptual continuity were intermittently disrupted by anomalies. These anomalies, which, by definition, did not fit an existing paradigm, caused revolutionary new paradigms to emerge. In other words, periods of incremental change within an existing paradigm are periodically disrupted by new and unfamiliar occurrences that require paradigmatic shifts to accommodate and make sense of them.

Ludwig von Bertalanffy later published *Perspectives on General System Theory*[264] and provided a framework for understanding the dynamics of change in complex social systems. Family and social systems theorists adopted this approach as well, looking at the stages in life that repeated themselves in cyclical fashion. Elizabeth Carter and Monica McGoldrick, for instance, were among the first to describe this for families in their book, *The Family Lifecycle.*[265]

In addition to helping us see cycles and patterns, systems theory introduced the concepts of *open and closed systems.* Open (healthy) systems have flexible and permeable boundaries. These systems have solid enough boundaries to foster a secure sense of *identity*, yet are flexible and permeable enough to allow for an exchange of people, ideas, and energy in order to foster continued growth. For example, many countries allow people in and out while still holding on to certain restrictions, preserving a sense of what it means to be a citizen. Clear and permeable boundaries are what ensures the core of national identity, personal freedom and growth, and the continued evolution of a nation with new energies, talents and ideas. The same is true for families, organizations and religious communities.

What constitutes *normal* boundaries varies greatly from one culture to the next. What is normal in an Asian culture is very different than what is normal in an Italian, German or Irish culture. As a rule, though, the extremes for any culture or organization will begin to manifest problems. At the extremes of the continuum, identity and relationships break down and the system becomes dysfunctional.

An extremely closed system with rigid boundaries would not permit the exchange of people, information, energy or ideas. For example, a community with rigid boundaries, whose members share little among themselves or with the wider civic community, will end up siloing themselves and failing to adapt to changing circumstances. They will also lose a sense of identity as a community because they have few significant relationships around which an identity could be formed. Communities that have inflexible and closed boundaries fade away more quickly because they have closed themselves off from the world, a phenomenon called *culture lock*. Without permeable boundaries allowing for the exchange of energy, they turn in on themselves, entropy takes over, and they die out.

At the opposite end of the continuum are enmeshed systems. These organizations have highly porous or no boundaries, and they have unclear rules regarding who is in and who is out. For example, communities with blurred and porous boundaries are highly chaotic. Each person's business becomes every person's business, and there is no sense of privacy or autonomy. Consequently, emotions and gossip reverberate throughout the system, and one person's crisis becomes a crisis for all. Blurred boundaries make it impossible to form clear relationships and, in turn, a solid and distinct identity (e.g., vowed religious and associates). Enmeshed systems, like closed systems, are compromised in their ability to meet successive organizational challenges and are also prone to breaking down.

Learning organizations

Systems theory was popularized in the business world by Peter Senge in his landmark book, *The Fifth Discipline*. Senge proposed that for organizations to learn, grow, and create a viable vision for the future they need to acquire five disciplines.

1. **Systems Thinking**: See patterns, rather than snapshots; recognize the whole from its parts; spot the structures, patterns, and parts that offer the best leverage points for change.

2. **Personal Mastery**: Develop the communication skills among individuals to speak and listen to the truth; work through resistance and hold creative tensions; integrate reason and intuition; grow stronger in empathy for one another and commitment to the whole.

3. **Mental Models**: Break out of the prison of current understandings, and open up new ways of understanding the organization, its mission and markets through skills of inquiry and reflection.

4. **Shared Visions**: Unearth shared pictures of the future that foster commitment and connections (rather than compliance); move from personal to shared visions (rather than top-down).

5. **Team Learning**: Strengthen the capacities for dialogue, deep listening, exploration, suspended judgments, and shared learning among teams representing core units of learning organizations.[266]

These five disciplines allow an organization, in Senge's words, to "learn how to learn," to move beyond the prison of an organization's own thinking, and to "continually expand its capacity to create its future."[267] You are probably familiar with Otto Scharmer (*Theory U*[268]), Margaret Wheatley (*Leadership and the New Science*[269]), Peter Block (*Stewardship: Choosing Service Over Self-Interest*[270]), and others who have built upon Senge's work and translated his insights into a language more amenable to religious communities.

Business cycles

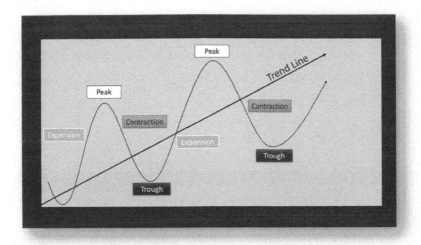

Figure 11: Business Cycle

Continual expansion of an organization's capacity to create its future is an enticing notion explored by countless authors. Many have looked at this from the perspective of a cyclical progression of stages or phases. The business cycle is often used to explain the cyclical expansion and contraction of the economy and businesses. It is used by businesses to forecast and plan their future. It is used by investors to understand the cycles in the stock market and know when to invest, divest, or sit on the sidelines.

Business cycles generally involve four phases, classified in their most modern sense by American economists Arthur Burns and Wesley Mitchell. The four primary phases of the business cycle include:

1. **Expansion**: A speedup in the pace of economic activity defined by high growth, low unemployment, and increasing prices. It is the period marked from trough to peak.

2. **Peak**: The upper turning point of a business cycle and the point at which expansion turns into contraction.

3. **Contraction**: A slowdown in the pace of economic activity defined by low or stagnant growth, high unemployment, and declining prices. It is the period from peak to trough.

4. **Trough**: The lowest turning point of a business cycle in which a contraction turns into an expansion. This turning point is also called recovery.[271]

Lifecycles

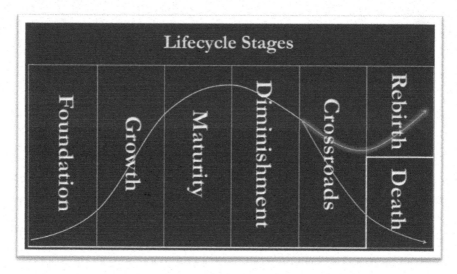

Figure 12: Lifecycle Stages

Just as individuals grow through stages in life so, too, do organizations. The life of an organization progresses through stages, each with its own characteristic risks, challenges and opportunities. The degree to which an organization successfully transitions from one stage to the next will determine its overall health as it moves forward to the next stage. In other words, if an organization is able to learn from, integrate, and transcend the efforts made in the earlier stage, its health will be stronger going forward.

Each stage in the lifecycle of an organization brings its own set of developmental tasks that must be accomplished in order to progress to the next level. And each set of development tasks has its own risks and rewards, demanding uniquely different skill-sets and mind-sets from its leaders and members. The number and description of stages in a given lifecycle are described differently by different authors (Adizes,[272] Arbuckle,[273] Cada,[274] Dunn[275]). However, they tend to include the following.

Phase I: Foundation

The birthing of a new vision is the cornerstone for any new organization. Typically, a charismatic leader (or a small group of pioneers) gives birth to a new vision with a burst of inspiration and energy. The passion and dogged determination of the leader to actualize the vision evokes the same response in others who are attracted to the cause. Undaunted by obstacles, there is unwavering pursuit of the vision as the excitement of a new venture mobilizes those involved. *Inspiration* and *innovation* for carrying out the vision mark the early stages of any organization.

New beginnings are a leap of faith. The spirit, at inception, is greatest when structure is at a minimum. There is flexibility in meeting the needs in service of the mission (i.e., whatever works). Problems are seen as opportunities and action outweighs planning. Those involved have fire in their belly, and a sense of ownership and urgency to see the dream become a reality. While the spirit is highest at this stage so, too, are the risks for organizations. Startups make it by a wing and a prayer.

There is a huge difference between having a dream and creating an enterprise that harnesses the energies of others toward that same dream. With few rules and many inconsistencies, mistakes and conflicts abound. At this stage, an organization needs leaders who inspire and followers with a can-do spirit to overcome the chaos. Unfortunately, the vast majority of startups, upwards of 90%, never make it past the first year.

Phase II: Growth

As the vision begins to take hold and others are drawn to it, there is a period of rapid growth and development. There is an exponentially accelerated rate of expansion of ideas, people, resources and projects. The system can barely keep up with the influx of new members, new ideas and new projects. Structures, organizational charts and plans are considered a work in progress, and are constantly being created anew as the venture builds momentum. *Rapid growth, experimentation,* as well as *trial and error* learning, are the hallmarks of this time in an organization's development.

This is the stage where more is better. More members come, more jobs are started, and more problems create more possibilities. The spirit is high as people flock to the excitement of the founder's dream and it becomes their dream too. There is excitement in seeing their dream become a vision, their vision become a reality, and being a part of something that is full of life and vitality. Because there is so much to do and barely enough people to get it all done, the tasks are organized around persons, not an organizational chart. In other words, tasks are done by whoever can take the ball and run with it, regardless of who has the qualifications or what their title might be.

The risks at this stage are great as well. *Founder's syndrome* is a well-known risk that can bring premature death to an organization. Founder's syndrome is that experience of a founder who is incapable of *letting go* of his or her dream so that it can become the organization's dream. It is like possessive parents who are so tied into their *baby*, they can't let go so the baby can grow on its own. In addition to Founder's syndrome, this stage is characterized by loyalty conflicts and inconsistencies between old timers and newcomers.

If the leader can successfully let go of what was originally just his or her dream so that it becomes the organization's dream, then the organization will flourish. If they can make the transition from founder to leader, they can succeed. If not, it will fail. The *ownership* for the dream must become shared by everyone in the organization for it to continue on to the next stage. The type of leaders needed in this stage are those who can share power and the type of followers needed are those who can self-initiate and take hold of the dream.

Phase III: Maturity

The cumulative effect of multiple mistakes, power struggles, and growing pains takes a toll on a growing organization. The response is to bring order to the tensions and conflicts inherent with growth. Jobs are assigned to people who are qualified, rather than to whomever is willing. Endeavors are more predictable, planned, controlled and organized. The chaos is managed and the risks are reduced and, so too, is the spirit. *Order, control,* and *security* are characteristics of this stage.

In order to find its stride and the means for carrying out its vision, an organization begins to standardize, departmentalize, organize and stabilize. It seeks to maintain its successes by institutionalizing its methods. As explosive growth slows and steadies, the organization has time to systematize its efforts, preferring sanity, security and predictability over chaos, instability and risk. Offices and titles are stamped into the organizational chart and behavioral expectations are written into handbooks of policies and procedures. *Institutionalization* and *maintenance* of the status quo are hallmarks of this period.

The organization is becoming more formalized, risk avoidant and conflict avoidant. They are focused more on smooth sailing, self-preservation and financial security, rather than new initiatives, development and growth. They are slow to move and adapt to new possibilities, preferring instead to protect their turf, wealth, old ideas, and past accomplishments ("If it ain't broke don't fix it"). The revolutionaries are becoming bureaucratic conformists, and their spirits are being tamed and domesticated. They are looking more often in the rearview mirror, rather than forward into the future

The organization is functional, results-oriented, stable, predictable, and controlled. They are well organized and more mellowed. However, they are becoming complacent, and lethargy is setting in. People are getting tired of meetings. There is more time spent in the office than in the market. They are increasingly rule-centric, boss-centric and bureaucratic ("Do what you're told and don't rock the boat"). The system is losing spirit, energy, flexibility, creativity, and the capacity to innovate. They are turning in on themselves, rather than outward and onward.

Phase IV: Diminishment

The next stage of an organization's lifecycle is destabilization and decline. The original vision has lost its luster and participants have lost their zeal.

Inspiration and innovation are in short supply, and what is predictable, controllable, and manageable takes precedence over what is not. Those who offer a new way of thinking and possibilities for growth are judged and labeled as disobedient, disloyal or crazy. The tried and true takes precedence over trial and error, and the organization stops learning, adapting and growing. *Stagnation* and *despair* are hallmarks of this stage.

During this phase, the system is struggling to survive. It seeks reassurance by writing well-polished mission statements, carving statues, and giving awards to honor its past champions. While it takes pride in past achievements and reminisces over the glory days, it is, all the while, calcifying, fossilizing and decaying. Having lost its root energy, and divorced itself from contemporary relevance, new people are no longer attracted to join. New blood trickles to a halt, cutting off supplies of new energy, ideas and people.

Ironically, the system begins to die by its own narrow focus on survival and its efforts to forestall the inevitable. It has come to value, and has been designed to maintain, what has already been accomplished. It no longer values new ventures. It places controls over innovation and experimentation such that adaptation to a changing world is prevented. Those who built and believe in the system are promoted, appointed, elected, and re-elected in order to preserve an illusion of security through familiarity. They serve and protect the system which they created and supported. By preventing radical change they unwittingly collude in its demise. Fidelity to the past takes precedence over an allegiance to the future.

The heaviness of structure and loss of hope for the future weighs on the system like a wet blanket, smothering the life out of the organization's spirit and mission. It becomes too rigid, too encumbered with structures, policies, proce-dures, and bureaucratic red tape to adapt any longer. People speak more of their memories than of their dreams for the future. The organization's spirit is dying and, conscious of this or not, spoken of or not, deep inside they know it.

Phase V: Crossroads

In general, there is an inverse relationship between the spirit of an organization and its degree of structure. Albert Einstein said that when there is maximum entropy, there is minimum useful energy, and the reverse is true as well. In other words, the spirit is highest at the foundation stage, when the passion of a charismatic leader ignites a synergistic response to a new vision and structures are yet to be put in place. The spirit is lowest when ghost structures of the past have all but vanquished the future. The original flame is dying out. The hallmark of this crossroads, where the pathways of life and death cross over, is the point at which the organization's *spirit has reached its nadir*.

At this point, Elisabeth Kübler-Ross' stages of grief are all present simultaneously, permeating the system with a surreal admixture of emotions. *Denial* is present among those who don rose colored glasses, insist that *all is well*, and continue to cheerlead for the future. There are others who are *angry* and bitter, festering in the toxic waste of unreconciled pain from old disappointments and wounds. Some are *bargaining*, looking for quick fixes and brokering new deals, while others pray in quiet desperation for divine intervention. Others are *depressed* and have checked out, thrown in the towel, and resigned themselves to the end. Finally, there are those who have *accepted* and come to terms with the current realities. They are the ones aware of the crossroads at which they now stand and are asking, "Now what?" They are the ones discerning real options.

The system has hit bottom. If enough people are consciously aware of this, and dare to speak it aloud, then the system has a choice. They can consciously, deliberately attempt to restructure, reorganize, rekindle or rebirth a new life. If these choices are discerned well and resolved peacefully, any one choice can liberate the spirit. Even a discerned choice for *completion* can release the spirit from its quagmire and the endings can be grace-filled. Likewise, if the choice to create life anew is discerned well, it too can liberate the spirit and bring new energy to the task.

Tragedies happen at the crossroads when choices are not made at all or are not made well. Choices that are made out of fear, capitulation or coercion are disastrous. Choices that are made out of unrealistic, wishful thinking are equally disastrous. Some believe that they have to choose life (After all, who would say "No" to this Deuteronomy invitation?), but have not discerned what that truly means for them. Some groups think they are choosing life, when all they are doing by their minimal, incremental efforts is guaranteeing their own demise. Some choosing life, no longer have the capacity, will, or forbearance to take the journey.

Cultural and Evolutionary Spirals

Beyond stages and cycles, futurists talk of *spirals*. They posit that as individuals or organizations develop through life, there are *phases* within each larger spiraling movement. Unlike cycles with discrete stages, phases within a spiral are typically seen as less definitively circumscribed, more interwoven and overlapping. As individuals or organizations loop through the spiral, they return to what looks like similar phases. However, in looping through these similar phases, their external circumstances are different. More importantly, the individuals or groups themselves are internally different. They are transformed and more mature for having reached a new level in the spiral. Their perspective transcends earlier ones; meaning, it includes the earlier understanding and goes beyond it as well.

Clare Groves, Don Beck and Chris Cowan used the image of spirals to describe the nature of cultural evolution in their book, *Spiral Dynamics*. They believe that cultures progress in a spiraling manner to construct increasingly complex networks that are more favorable toward the development of humanity as a whole. They have identified a model of eight archetypal cultures and describe the unique set of *memes* for each. Memes are essentially cultural worldviews, paradigms, or a set of values that determine how we interpret and interact with our world. They reflect our core beliefs and guide our decisions and behaviors.

They describe eight levels of memes, from the lowest level of the spiral (i.e., cultures of bands and tribes), to intermediate levels (i.e., authoritative and pyramidal cultures), to the highest level in the spiral (i.e., cultures that are egalitarian, holistic, flowing and integrative). As a given culture progresses through the spiral of development, it *includes* and *transcends* the previous set of memes. While there are eight archetypal cultures, the permutations are endless and no one culture is presumed to be "best" (i.e., they each have pros and cons in how they serve the people and are right for their given time and place).

The eight levels of memes move up the spiral in a pendulum-like fashion, alternating between *self-focused* and *we-focused* anchored motivations. In other words, sometimes we are focused on personal growth and other times we are more focused on the good of the whole. We swing back and forth from *me* to *we* in our motivation and focus for change.

Each meme level emerges without eliminating prior levels. We may surge, regress, fade or stabilize along the way. In other words, progress is not linear, neat and tidy, or guaranteed. Memes have phases of development, each with characteristic tensions and ways of coping. Memes increase in complexity and integration as we move up the spiral. Beck and Cowen poignantly describe the current global status of these memes:

> "We inhabit a polyglot, diverse, but not yet interdependent world. All of the stratified human life forms, from tribal societies to info-techies, are in daily conflict over niches and resources. The end of the bipolar world dominated by super-powers brought a resurgence of old mindsets, surprising intruders from the dark and violent history of our kind. At the same time, fresh approaches to living on Earth are being liberated. We are going back to the future and forward to the past, engaging all of history's villains and saints in quick time." [276]

The unfolding universe

Barbara Marx Hubbard, Brian Swimme, Carter Phipps, John Haught and other evolutionary futurists, rely heavily upon the notion of spirals to describe the manner in which our universe is unfolding. Brian Swimme and Thomas Berry, in their pioneering book, *The Universe Story*, introduced the principles of cosmogenesis as key to the spiral: "The evolution of the universe will be characterized by *differentiation* (i.e., diversity, multiple forms, complexity), *autopoiesis* (i.e., self-organizing, presence, identity, inner voice) and *communion* (i.e., relationship, interdependence, mutuality) throughout time and space and at every level of reality." [277] These are the governing themes representing the intentionality of all existence.

Barbara Marx Hubbard gazed upon the unfolding universe and immersed herself in scripture as well as the writings of Teilhard de Chardin's, *The Phenomenon of Man*.[278] She envisioned a spiraling evolution of consciousness moving toward increasing complexity, wholeness, beauty, communion and compassion. She described how each turn of the evolutionary spiral is preceded and provoked by crisis and is drawing the universe into new, qualitatively distinct forms of life. She held that "through our unprecedented scientific, technological, social, and spiritual capacities, we can evolve consciously and co-creatively with nature and the deeper patterns of creation (traditionally called God), thus enabling us to manifest a future commensurate with our unlimited species and planetary potential."[279]

In 2012, in her keynote address to the Leadership Conference of Women Religious (LCWR), Hubbard began her remarks by saying, "The system is not sustainable as it is." She, like other futurists, believes that we have reached a tipping point, a new threshold in the spiral of humanity, wherein we will either become extinct or we will evolve. She invited those present to consider the power they have to build upon the story of Christ, "to evolve by choice, not by chance," and help birth a new cycle in the spiraling journey of humanity ascending.[280]

Ilia Delio, like Teilhard de Chardin, seeks to combine Christianity (Catholicity, in particular) with evolution. She describes an evolutionary ontology of *becoming* wherein evolution's energy, its dynamic impulse of love, is coming from the God ahead (not God above). Delio sees God as pulling us toward an unpredictable and ever-expanding future. God becoming increasingly incarnate in the world through the body of Christ (i.e., the whole cosmos), and she believes that each one of us contributes to this incarnation through our search for unity.[281]

Elizabeth Johnson also ties Christianity to evolution. She asks a provocative question: What can the beasts teach us? Her answer astounds:

> "Scientifically, they have come into being, grown into their complex beautiful forms, and fit into their diverse ecological niches through a powerful unscripted evolutionary process that has lasted hundreds of millions of years. Theologically, they are the work of the Spirit of God who vivifies the

community of creation from which we humans have also emerged. The ineffable holy mystery of Love creates, indwells, and empowers plants and animals, delights in their beautiful, wise and funny ways and grieves their sufferings. In the unexpected Christian view, the living God even chooses to become part of their story in Jesus Christ… whose death and resurrection pledges a hopeful future for all." [282]

What these "spiral" theories have in common is that we are on a journey toward the ever-alluring God ahead, a journey toward an ever-increasing capacity to individuate, cooperate and love one another. Each new movement of the spiral is preceded and provoked by a crisis, and opens up new choices. We grow in life through particular phases of a cycle and, with each new cycle, we move *inwardly*, more deeply into the spiral gaining more wisdom and maturity along the way. We move *outwardly*, caring for others and our world, with a greater capacity for mutual, interdependent relationships. We move *upwardly* toward a more transcendent, morally sophisticated, and all-encompassing appreciation of ourselves and the world around us.

Ten Foundational Learnings

Taken together, what do these different disciplines of human, social and cultural development tell us about the nature of transformation? Let me offer a synthesis: ten essential lessons upon which the Journey of Transformation is predicated. Five lessons form the *principles*, and five lessons inform the *dynamic elements*, which are concepts and processes we will incorporate into the Journey of Transformation.

Foundations for Journey of Transformation	
Guiding Principles	**Dynamic Elements**
1. Maturation is a life-long journey	1. Shifts in consciousness
2. Maturation moves in spirals	2. Reclaim our inner voice
3. We plateau for a time, then transform	3. Reconciliation and conversion
4. We breakdown to breakthrough	4. Experimentation and learning
5. Pain brings us to the cross-roads, but Love pulls us through	5. Transformative visioning

Table 4: Foundations for the Journey of Transformation

Guiding principles of transformation

"To exist is to change, to change is to mature, to mature is to go on creating oneself endlessly." Henri Bergson

1. Maturation is a lifelong journey

Maturation is a lifelong journey with endless opportunities to become more of who we are called to become. We are neither pre-formed at birth, nor do we stop growing at the end of puberty, at twenty-one, or ninety-one. Life is growth and growth is lifelong, *if* we choose it to be. Neither are we preprogramed at birth, nor is our growth a given. Our maturation, our transformation and, ultimately, our destiny are the result of *choices* we make throughout our lifetime. The longer we live, the more opportunities we have to choose, but the choices are ours to make and there are no guarantees of success. Every crossroads is a leap of faith, an opportunity to grow, transform and become more of who God intends for us to be.

Carl Jung once said, "The privilege of a lifetime is to become who you truly are." In other words, aging is not the same as maturation. Your age only tells us how long you've lasted, but it says nothing about how much you've risked to grow, love, stumble, forgive, grieve, create or to care for others. How many times you've failed in these efforts matters less than how many times you've gotten back up and what you've learned. In the end, it matters less how long you've lived but how fully you've lived, and how faithful you have been to who you were called to become.

2. Growth and transformation move in spirals

"One of the chief beauties of the spiral as an imaginative concept is that it is always growing, yet never covering the same ground, so that it is not merely an explanation of the past, but it is also a prophecy of the future; and while it defines and illuminates what has already happened, it is also leading constantly to new discoveries."
Theodore Andrea Cook

We grow and transform in an inward, outward and *upward spiraling manner.* Each transformative turn of the spiral is a movement of growth that brings us to another developmental plateau and new possibilities. Life can be smooth sailing for a time, but it doesn't remain that way for long. The river of life is always changing and unfolding. It never stands still, repeats or goes backward. Our seasons in life may appear to repeat themselves, but only in general. No one season is a carbon copy of the last.

We have stages, phases and cycles, all moving along a spiral. We descend inwardly toward greater depth and wisdom. We grow outwardly, caring more about others and the world in which we live with greater capacity for empathy, love and appreciation of beauty. We ascend upwardly, subsuming and transcending prior developmental phases, thus enlarging our capacity for a more nuanced morality and fullness of life. Our spiraling growth is dynamic. It is an inside-out, soul-to-surface, future-oriented and open-ended movement, a teleological trajectory toward a greater union with the God ahead.

We must honor each stage, phase or movement throughout the journey. As we move up the spiral, with each new level of maturity, it is important to honor the prior levels. Each level is necessary and right for its time. We need to honor each level for what it is and not judge one as *better* or *worse* than another, any more than we would judge a 7-year-old as better than a 3-year-old, or one season of life as better than another. There is wisdom, constraints, gifts and challenges at every level and all are a part of the ongoing spiral of growth and transformation.

3. We plateau for a time, then transform

"We must be willing to let go of the life we have planned, so as to have the life that is waiting for us." E.M. Forster

The spiraling movement is continuous overall, but it is not linear or stepwise. We plateau for a period of time, then periodically transform and leap to new levels. When we plateau, we gather knowledge, hone skills, integrate and consolidate our gains, and develop confidence. These periods of relative stability and consolidation are punctuated by periodic transformative leaps wherein our fundamental schemas for understanding ourselves and our world shifts. It is a paradigm shift, a shift in worldviews, memes or mind-sets. In computer terms, we have gained a new and different operating system. Both our software, and the information gathered, are processed in a fundamentally different way.

We grow in fits and starts. Phases might awaken, surge, fade, merge, regress or transcend, but are never eliminated. Though we might be predominantly in one phase, we are never purely in one phase. Often, we exist in a blurred mixture of overlapping phases. We can regress a phase or two, but we can never skip a phase or two. Regression takes us back to old ways. Ideally, it would be a roundtrip, giving us a chance to loop back and reintegrate what was not integrated successfully before. For example, a current loss might trigger prior losses, ones which were not grieved successfully in the past. This gives us a chance to revisit our grief in a new way. With greater maturity, we can grieve our losses, old and new, with greater integration and resolution.

4. We breakdown to breakthrough

"Whoever finds their life will lose it, and whoever loses their life for my sake will find it." Matthew 10:39

It is nature's way, one of life's most agonizing paradoxes, that we breakdown to breakthrough. We have to fall down to grow up. We have to die in some way, let go of some treasured person, place, thing, belief, or way of life, in order to make the turn. Life and death, light and darkness, yin and yang, are artificial and illusory bifurcations of an unpartitionable whole. Death paves the way for resurrection, a transformation that is as messy and painful to personally experience as it is beautiful and exciting to witness in others and in creation. We fret and agonize through the dying on the front end of transformation, yet we find liberation and new life on the other side.

Life is not a game of perfect, but a game of recovery. We are all fragile. We all fall and fail and make mistakes. And all of these are necessary for us to grow. Crisis and breakdown precede and provoke transformation. There is no way around it: "No pain, no gain." It is nature's way. If there is no death, there will be no metamorphosis, no new life, and no future. We must lose our self in order to find our self once more (Matthew 10:39).

The degree of success to which an individual passes from one phase to the next influences how well he or she might move through subsequent phases. Successful breakthroughs to each new phase strengthen our capacity and bolster our confidence to make the passage through to the next developmental hurdle. However, phases and passages that are incomplete or unsuccessful carry the residual doubts and unfinished business into subsequent ones. Failures or fixations encumber us, but we are not doomed as damaged goods. Healing, repair work, recovery, and redemption can take place anytime throughout our entire lifetime. It's never too late!

5. Pain brings us to the crossroads, but Love pulls us through

*"Therefore, I am now going to allure her; I will lead her
into the wilderness and speak tenderly to her." Hosea 2:14*

It is pain that brings us to the crossroads, but it is Love that pulls us through.
Mounting internal and external pressures in life provoke and, eventually, force
us to change. Pain and suffering bring us to the threshold of transformation,
but it is Love that impels us through to the other side. God lures us into the
wilderness. And it is both through our efforts and our cooperation with grace,
that we are truly transformed. Transformation requires both the *stick* (suffering) to push us to the crossroads, and the *carrot* (Love) to pull us through to
the other side. Pain gnaws at us to relinquish our complacency and move,
and Love points us to where we long to go. Suffering holds our feet to the fire
until we finally let go, and let die what needs to die, in order to allow Love to
awaken us, compassion to carry us, and grace to transform us.

At a graced crossroads, we are lured by God into the crucible of transformation. The pain that we want so badly to go away cracks open the shell of our
psychological armor, hardened hearts and hubris. The shell that has protected
us has also prevented us from experiencing God's grace. These painful *come-
to-Jesus* moments are a necessary suffering because it breaks the shell open,
allowing God's grace to break through. The pain that we so desperately want to
escape, the pain that got us into this mess to begin with, and for which we want
answers, is never answered in the way we expect. What we receive, instead, is
grace and answers we could not have previously understood or conceived. It
is, ultimately, through Love that we can withstand the pain of letting go, make
meaning of the pain, and transform our suffering, so that new life can emerge.

Dynamic elements of transformation

1. Shifts in Consciousness: Creating a new narrative

> *"With every move we make... we're dictating the next few*
> *lines of the text called our lives, composing it as we go."*
> *Mary Catherine Bateson*

Each developmental leap constitutes a shift or transformation of consciousness and opens the door for a new narrative in our lives. Each new turn creates in us a new consciousness and a new way of being. This transformation of consciousness vaults us higher into the spiral, and we grow into greater sophistication. Intellectually, we can grasp more complex ideas, irony and paradox. We gain greater empathy and appreciation for more socially complex situations and moral nuances.

Gradually, we mature through an accumulation of knowledge and with each transformative leap we grow in wisdom. In each turn of the spiral we move beyond the confines of outdated paradigms. We move the boundaries of our own mental fences to encompass a wider landscape and a new worldview. The evolution of the brain gave us the cerebral cortex, capable of leaping us from prose to poetry, from basic math to quantum physics, from playing scales on the piano to playing Brahms.

Include and *transcend* is the constant refrain in every turn of the spiral. Each new turn gathers up and carries with it all that preceded it, including, transforming and transcending all that was. The law of the universe assures us that nothing is lost. No prior memories and none of life's existence or energies are lost. They are subsumed and transcended, re-organized and re-integrated, transformed and made new, but never lost or left behind. All that ever was, still is. All that ever was, is now and not yet. We, and our universe, are works in progress, constantly transforming, transcending and including what was before into something even greater, the eternal story always unfolding.

2. Reclaim our Inner Voice: The seat and source of everything that lives

"There is in all visible things ... a hidden wholeness."
Thomas Merton

In every turn of the spiral, every maturational leap, we shed worn out vestiges of ourselves and claim anew our own inner voice, the seat and source of everything that lives. With every turn, layers of our false self are sloughed off. We turn inward again to the soul-truth of who we are, until our true self emerges anew. Every turn is our soul's homecoming, a return to our hidden wholeness. We return to the hidden source of life becoming more fully who we are meant to be, more fully who God beckons us to be. We are drawn to *the more*, to that primordial ache to come home. And we can come home, more alive, more whole, more fully ourselves than before.

As we mature, we grow in our uniqueness and complexity. We individuate, differentiate, and distinguish ourselves from the herd. We grow in our truth and in our capacity to speak it. We grow more comfortable in our own skin, more secure and grounded in ourselves, helping us to better hear and be influenced by the truth of others. When we are younger, we want to try it all. We want the sampler plate. But, as my 100-year-old step-father likes to say, "At my age, I know what I like and don't like." We grow in knowing our likes, in claiming our wants and needs, and in discovering our gifts and talents. In so doing, the universe grows with us. The universe seeks diversity over sameness and creativity over conformity. It grows in and through the panoply of diversity brought forth by each lifeform claiming its uniqueness and maturing into fullness.

3. Reconciliation and Conversion: The womb of our becoming

"Wholeness does not mean perfection – it means embracing brokenness as an integral part of life." Parker Palmer

We spiral toward greater wholeness and connection through reconciliation and conversion, the womb of our becoming. The universe has an appetite for wholeness. Call it autopoiesis, if you like, but we have a built-in self-organizing drive and an innate capacity to move toward unity and wholeness. We don't like missing pieces in our jigsaw puzzles, things left hanging, or tensions unresolved. We want things whole, resolved, connected and completed. Hence, each turn of the spiral is a process of reconciling, reconnecting and reintegrating what has otherwise been broken or disconnected. The process of reconciliation and conversion is the very crucible of transformation where we are forged anew.

All forms of life, each in their uniqueness, are strands in the fragile web of life, parts of a whole, not siloed and separate but braided together. It is only in our illusion of separateness, and in the brokenness we create, that this gossamer web seems to fracture. We are interdependent with all that exists. No life lives alone – not a cell, a person, a nation or a planet. When we are transformed into a new level on the spiral, we can see that more clearly. We move from self-centeredness to empathy, compassion, generativity and altruistic concern for others. We grow in concern for the web of life, our common home. We become more desirous and capable of intimacy, more aware that we are all in this together.

As we move up the spiral, we can see more clearly and poignantly that we are called to deeper conversion and healing. Each transformative leap is an exercise in reconciliation, restoring wholeness, and healing wounds that have kept us apart and damaged the web of life. The more we mature, the more we can embrace diversity and build bridges of understanding. We become more capable of mutually exchanging ideas, energies and talents with others, without losing our own identity. We are transformed in and through our reconciled relationships with others and, in so doing, we restore the fragile web of life.

4. Experimentation and Learning: Acting our way into a new way of being

"First there is the fall, and then we recover from the fall. Both are the mercy of God!" Lady Julian of Norwich

Each new turn of the spiral demands experimentation and learning, requiring us to act our way into a new way of being. We have no clear picture, no clear path and no guarantees of success as we grope and intuit our way forward. We live our lives forward but understand them backward. Once we climb to a higher vista, we can look back and see where we have been. When we go through a new passage, it is always a leap of faith, and it always involves risk. If we try to reduce the risk by insisting upon an ending of our own design, we only bring more suffering. We cannot predict, engineer or control the outcome of transformative experiences. That is what makes it all so terribly unnerving. That is why it is an heroic journey.

When we are first growing into a new phase, groping and clamoring to reach the other side, we stand on spindly legs. We do not yet fully understand nor are we fully equipped for this new phase of development. We have to become learners again by adopting a beginner's mind. We have to experiment with and acquire new mind-sets, skill-sets and heart-sets. We have to fail and fumble. Gradually, we accumulate knowledge, refine and master our skills, and gain more solid footing in this new phase. It is evolution in action.

5. Transformative Visioning: Gather the wisdom, weave a dream

"I would love to live like a river flows, carried by the surprise of its own unfolding." John O'Donohue

Each new turn in the spiral is a process of transformative visioning where we gather the wisdom and weave a new dream. Each new turn in the spiral twists the kaleidoscope and brings into view an entirely new picture. The elements inside the kaleidoscope are the same – a mixture of our realities and our deepest longings – but when newly transformed and arranged, they create a new vision. When we reach a crossroads, we cannot see the vision of the future unfolding ahead of time. We can't know ahead of time what life will be like with all of its twists and turns. We are, instead, carried along by our hopes and dreams, carried by the surprise of its own unfolding.

Figure 13: Rose glass window of Notre Dame

The vision of the future is not one we can manufacture to our exact specifications. It is organic, emergent and iterative. It is *organic*, derived from life, not artificially engineered. It is *emergent*, showing only a glimpse of itself as we move along, each step taken revealing the *next best step* to take. We can't know ahead of time, what will be on the other side any more than a caterpillar knows that it will become a butterfly. It is *iterative*, in that we articulate one version, then another, each time adding clarity, texture, wholeness and depth. It is as if we begin a turn along the spiral, holding only a few small pieces of stained-glass window. Over time, we gather more pieces. More is revealed until an entire mosaic, like the rose glass of Notre Dame, comes into full view.

Conclusion

*"We shall not cease from exploration, and the end of all
our exploring will be to arrive where we started and know
the place for the first time." T. S. Eliot*

It seems to me that Abraham and Sarah, Moses and Mohammed, Jesus and John of the Cross, along with Freud, Fowler, Senge, Wheatley, Delio, Rohr and Chittister all understood the nature of transformation. Scientists and seekers, alike, are discovering what ancient traditions have always known: life is an unending, spiraling journey toward the Divine.

Chapter 11: The Journey of Transformation

A method and means for cooperating with grace

"Very truly I tell you, unless a kernel of wheat falls to the ground and dies, it remains only a single seed. But if it dies, it produces many seeds."
John 12:24

Overview

The Journey of Transformation is an approach to communal transformation that integrates the pragmatics of planning and visioning along with processes aimed at deep change. These processes, taken as a whole, provide communities with a framework for collectively understanding their work of transformation and a container that holds communities together while encountering the necessary chaos. It is a multidimensional, multilayered and integrative approach. In essence, it is a communal faith journey aimed at helping communities discern God's call to new life and transform the meaning, purpose and lived expression of their community and its mission.

The Journey of Transformation provides a method and means to cooperate with grace through the Divine Mystery of transformation. While the inner workings of grace upon our soul will remain forever inscrutable, the human mystery of transformation is made more fathomable if we take into account: 1) the recent accumulation of knowledge through science and the humanities; 2) the insights gained from countless experiences of transformation that we have all had personally and witnessed in creation; and, 3) the paths of transformation we know from ancient and contemporary faith traditions. It is on the basis of these three foundations that this Journey of Transformation is predicated and developed.

Communal transformation takes place through our proactive cooperation with grace. We cooperate with grace by doing our part, by doing the inner work of transformation. This inner work of transformation involves five *dynamic elements* (key processes) that, when woven together, constitute the Journey of Transformation. They are the method and means for cooperating with grace that I will outline in this chapter and elaborate upon in remaining chapters.

Framework and container

The Journey of Transformation is, first of all, a framework for understanding communal transformation. Every member of your community likely has a different understanding of your current situation and opinions about the needed approach for change or transformation. Without a common frame of reference, leaders and members will end up pulling in different directions. The Journey of Transformation provides a common framework for understanding what is at stake, the options before you, and how to engage in the work of communal transformation, should that be the choice you make.

This framework for understanding also establishes a container, or holding environment, wherein members can journey together in their collective inner work of transformation. It provides a way for everyone to be on the same page as to what they are doing and why. This gives the community a way of orienting themselves and hanging together when the going gets tough and chaos ensues. They are more willing to stay in the struggle when the intimacy, ambiguity, conflict, and overall messiness of transformation evokes fear, anger, confusion and other uncomfortable, albeit necessary, emotions. The inner work and its messiness are more manageable when everyone has a common understanding as to why it is so necessary to go through the chaos and how they can go through it together.

Figure 14: Multidimensional

Multidimensional

The Journey of Transformation is multidimensional and holistic. It combines and integrates *personal* (i.e., emotional and spiritual), *interpersonal* (i.e., relational and communal), and *organizational* (i.e., structural and systemic) processes. If any one of these three components is missing, then communal transformation will fail. If every member of your community sought spiritual direction or therapy, but collectively avoided the interpersonal or organizational dimensions, communal transformation would not occur. Similarly, if you sought to address the interpersonal dynamics in community, but avoided the personal or organizational dimensions, communal transformation would fail. And if you simply focused on organizational changes, but neglected the personal and interpersonal work, your efforts would fail. The vast majority of communities attend to the organizational changes but fail to address the personal and interpersonal dimensions.

Multilayered

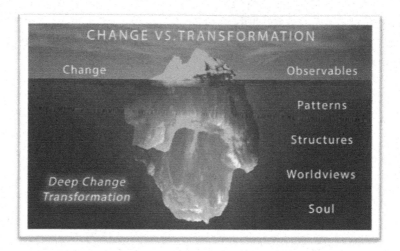

Figure 15: Change vs. Transformation

The Journey of Transformation is also multilayered. It addresses the visible realties and **observable** challenges facing communities that are evident on the surface of community life. These include, for example, land, buildings, finances, healthcare, ministries and demographics. These are the tangible dimensions of life that are typically addressed through conventional change processes (discussed in Chapter 10). These external aspects of community must change in order to adapt to internal and external pressures. However, focusing only upon these external changes will not bring about transformation. Communal transformation also involves the less visible challenges related to patterns, structures, worldviews and the soul of communities:

- The **patterns** and practices within communities are less tangible and obvious than the observables, yet these shape how members understand who they are and what they are about. These are the normative ways in which a particular community orchestrates life (e.g., gathers, prays, makes decisions, forms members, builds trust, handles conflict, celebrates, grieves, shares information, manages boundaries, exerts power, uses authority, creates budgets, etc.). These practices include what is written in Constitutions and other governing documents, as well as what is established by unwritten norms and traditions. Shifting patterns is much harder than making surface changes, yet this kind of deep change is key to transforming the culture of community.

- **Structures** include those gatherings and groups that support a community's life as it is in the present or has been in the past. These are the forums for gathering (e.g., local communities, assemblies, clusters, regions, provinces, etc.) and all of the offices in the organizational chart (e.g., leadership, finance, health care, vocation, formation, maintenance, development, communications, boards, etc.). In order for a community to transform itself, it must *destructure* to make room for the spirit and, simultaneously, create new, more flexible structures that are aligned with the future a community hopes to create.

- **Worldviews** and mindsets include all of the prevailing ways of understanding life as it is in the present or has been in the past. It is expressed in the narratives of a community, in other words, how a community understands and tells its story. These stories are revealed through the myths, truths, untruths, assumptions and events that shape and explain life as it is today. Worldviews and mindsets create the paradigm that shapes meaning and purpose for members, along with their core ideology, values, and vows that support the paradigm.

- The **soul** of a community is similar to the soul of an individual. The soul is the essence or inner voice that is reflected in a community's charism. The soul is the place where the divine dwells deep within a community and it is the seat and source of life for a community. Transforming the soul of a community is a journey through the dark night where members confront the gap between who they say they are and how they live their lives. The essence of a Journey of Transformation is a faith journey, a pilgrimage through the paschal mystery of life, death, resurrection and new life.

If the external, pragmatic changes are made without integrating and addressing the internal, underlying elements in which these are embedded, there will be no transformation. For example, you can change where you live but, as they say in Alcoholics Anonymous, "you will take your patterns with you." In other words, you can change the size of your buildings, the number of people you have on a leadership team, how you provide healthcare for your members, but you take your patterns, structures, and worldview with you. Unless you do the inner work, your soul remains untouched and unchanged.

The Journey of Transformation to which I am referring not only seeks to change what is on the surface of your lives, but to transform what lies beneath. The deeper patterns, structures, worldviews and, indeed, the very culture and soul of a community must be transformed in order to bring forth greater wholeness and fullness of life. It is not the surface changes that will transform you, but the deeper work that ultimately transforms a community.

Integration and alignment

The Journey of Transformation *integrates* organizational planning and visioning with the inner work of transformation. It integrates the strategic planning processes related to organizational change with the processes related to deep change and transformation. These processes are woven together and combined to provide the method and means for communal transformation.

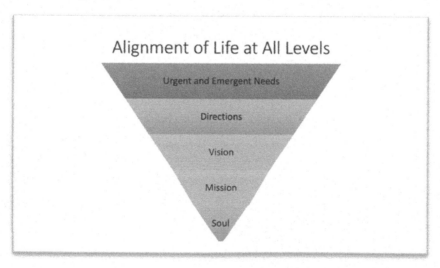

Figure 16: Alignment of Life at All Levels

The Journey of Transformation aims to realign life at all levels (see Appendix B, *Alignment and Misalignment of Life*). The goals here are: to better align the soul of community with its mission so that the two are more connected and integrated; to forge a vision that flows more directly from a community's mission; and in turn create directions that are more integrally linked to the vision. The overall purpose then is to align life at all levels so that a community becomes more relevant and responsive to the urgent and emergent needs of the world.

The essence of this journey is the core of our creed – the Paschal Mystery of life, death, resurrection and new life. It is a journey that builds upon the virtues of faith, hope and love. In this sense, it is more a pilgrimage than a plan, more about the sort of people you are becoming, rather than an effort to create some kind of grand vision. It is about coming home to God and one another. It is a journey in which Christ is formed in us and through our own lives, so that we become agents of transformation for others and our world.

In summary, the Journey of Transformation is a multidimensional, multi-layered and integrative approach. At a pragmatic level, it helps communities create a plan and vision for their future. At a deeper level, it helps communities listen and respond to the lure and love of God to make manifest their deepest longings. It is a journey that invites greater wholeness and authenticity among members, while embracing such values as mutuality, shared power and collective wisdom. It demands great courage, creativity and forbearance, asking nothing less than a no-holds-barred, all-out effort of every member of community.

Difference between Change and Transformation

"When we are no longer able to change a situation, we are challenged to change ourselves." Victor Frankl

The journey I am describing is aimed at *transformation*, not simply *change*. These two terms, although often used synonymously, are qualitatively distinct phenomena. Among the most important distinctions are these:

1. Transformation is an internal process, while change is an external event;

2. Crisis inevitably leads to change but merely invites the possibility of transformation;

3. Transformation involves deep, not incremental change; and,

4. Transformation is a life-long, spiraling, maturational movement.

1. Transformation is an internal process

Change is an *external event,* a new arrangement of things that we can see and touch on the surface of our lives. Transformation, on the other hand, is an *internal process* that brings about new patterns and perspectives in response to change. It is a process that takes place over time and not as a result of a one-and-done event. While transformation always involves change, the reverse is not necessarily true. Transformation is not a concept or idea out there, it is an inside-out, soul-to-surface, highly visceral experience.

You might change where you live, your ministry, your attire, your relationships, but you take your patterns and perspectives with you. Communities might change administrative structures or merge with another community, but they take their culture with them. Communities might downsize, sell property, hire lay management for their healthcare, but they take their existing language, assumptions and worldviews with them. Communities might change every conceivable aspect of their lives, but their soul remains untouched and unchanged *unless* they do the inner work of transformation.

Organizational change is not the same as organizational transformation. Changing the bricks and mortar of your lives is not enough to transform a community. Transformation involves inner work that engages members in deep change processes aimed at shifting the meaning and purpose of community and its mission, patterns, practices, structures, mind-sets, skill-sets and heart-sets, down to its very soul.

2. Crisis offers a deeper invitation

Crisis insists upon change and offers an opportunity to listen for a *deeper invitation*. A crisis by definition is an experience wherein our ability to cope is overwhelmed by challenging circumstances. The status quo no longer works. Our coping skills are maxed out and we are in such acute or enduring pain that we fall apart. We have what is euphemistically called a *breakdown*. This breakdown is a necessary antecedent to transformation. We must break down before we break though. However, transformation only occurs in the breakdown if we listen for a deeper invitation and make a conscious choice to pursue it.

When we break down we have an opportunity to break through, but it is not automatic and there are no guarantees. We have choices to make and work to do. We could simply change things by removing ourselves from the stressors, reducing the them, or learning new and more effective ways of coping with the them. Alternatively, we might choose to listen to a deeper invitation. A crisis requires that we change and provides an invitation to transform, but the choice is always ours. Communities could choose simply to adapt, or they might choose to also discern what God is asking of them. The former leads inevitably to change, while the latter leads to the possibility of transformation.

3. Transformation involves deep change

Transformation is an experience of *deep* versus *incremental* change. Throughout most of our life we change gradually and incrementally, accumulating and honing our skills, gathering knowledge and understanding. However, these periods of relative stability and incremental change are periodically punctuated by deep change. Piaget called this episodic leap *accommodation*, Gregory Batson referred to it as the *difference that makes a difference*, communication theorists call it second order change. When referring to organizations or cultures it is typically called *systemic* or *paradigmatic* change. In the language of faith, it is called *conversion*.

According to Robert Quinn, "incremental change" is rational, predictable and occurs in small linear steps. It is gradual, narrow in scope and reversible. It makes new and improved versions of the past, extending the past into the future. It is much more about holding on than letting go, and typically leads to entropy and slow death (unless countered in some way). "Deep change," on the other hand, is intuitive. It occurs in sudden leaps and the results are unpredictable. It requires new thinking, is broad in scope and irreversible. It transcends and is discontinuous from the past. It is more about letting go and taking risks with a leap of faith.[283]

4. Transformation is a life-long, spiraling, maturational movement

We grow in a spiraling motion with periodic leaps of maturation, self-transcendence and expanding consciousness. We grow incrementally for extended periods of time and periodically go through a transformative process resulting in qualitative shifts in consciousness. These transformative leaps result in new levels of consciousness wherein we gain a wider, more inclusive perspective and see ourselves and our world in an entirely new way. These spiraling cycles of maturation and growth occur throughout our lifetime for as long as we choose to embrace their possibilities.

Our review of systems theory and Spiral Dynamics showed us how organizations and cultures change in a similar cyclical, spiraling fashion. The same transformative movements are observed in communities and Religious Life as a whole. David Nygren and Miriam Ukeritis, in their studies of Religious Life, said that transformation refers to "qualitative discontinuous shifts in the members' shared understandings of the organization, accompanied by changes in the organization's mission, strategy, and formal and informal structures."[284] This spiraling cycle continues throughout a community's lifetime for as long as they choose to embrace these possibilities.

Connecting change with the inner work of transformation

"Groups made ornamental changes.... They changed their habits but not their hearts, their language but not their ideas." Joan Chittister

One of the most important lessons from what we know of personal change is that symptom relief is not the same as the in-depth work of personal transformation. Even Weight Watchers has come to realize that weight loss by itself will not be sustained unless there is a change in lifestyle. Their new app no longer just counts calories for food intake. It teaches coping skills for stress reduction and even mindfulness. Personal transformation is an in-depth, holistic change process that promotes a new integration of our inner emotional and spiritual being, our values and beliefs, along with their outward behavioral expressions.

Lessons from our review of organizational change tell a similar story. Pragmatic surface changes, even structural changes, do not by themselves bring about transformation. Organizational change efforts fail to transform organizations if these efforts neglect the inner work, which most do. For example, a community might merge with another community, reduce the number in leadership, downsize buildings, or consolidate administrative offices, hoping to bring about some kind of transformation. Many communities attempt to frame these efforts in a spiritual context hoping their members will make a deeper connection and embrace it. But it doesn't work.

Simply overlaying spiritual language on top of what is essentially an organizational change process, without providing processes that explicitly integrate the two, has little substantive impact. Members aren't fooled. Rhetoric that is not backed up with processes that clearly link the concrete changes to the personal, interpersonal and organizational work of transformation has no lasting impact. Members have heard these speeches before and, having experienced no lasting change, no real transformation or signs of new life, they become skeptical. They are no longer convinced or motivated by rhetoric to commit their time or energy to shallow, organizational changes.

Transformation does not take place as a result of a great speech, a great article or one-and-done assemblies. It does not fit neatly into artificial timelines, such as, Chapter-to-Chapter cycles. It is an ongoing process of conversion that takes place over time as a result of a community's unwavering commitment, courage and creativity. *A key to communal transformation is to continually integrate the inner work of transformation that engages the hearts and souls of members with the outer work of change that addresses the community's concrete adaptations and plans for the future.*

Keys to The Mystery

"What the caterpillar calls the end, the rest of the world calls a butterfly." Lao Tzu

If transformation is ultimately a Divine Mystery, how can we possibly understand it, let alone create processes to make it happen? How do we know our part to play, or are we left only to pray?

In a 1939 radio broadcast, Winston Churchill said, "I cannot forecast to you the action of Russia. It is a riddle, wrapped in a mystery, inside an enigma; but perhaps there is a key." The same might be said of transformation. Its outcome cannot be forecasted. We never know ahead of time where it might lead. Transformation is a riddle wrapped in mystery. While the innermost workings of grace upon our soul will always remain mysterious, transformation itself is not completely obscured from our understanding. There are some keys to unraveling this mystery.

I believe there are these three keys: *knowledge, experience* and *faith*. We have partially unraveled this riddle through a vast accumulation of knowledge. We saw in the last chapter the ways in which modern science has shed light on the nature of transformation. There is more to it than alchemy and time. We also know of transformation through our own experience of it. We witness it daily and live through it throughout our lifetime. We can draw upon our experience to know of its ways. Beyond our knowledge and experience, the rest of this mystery is left to faith, not a passive-dependent faith that hands everything over to God but a mature faith in which we do our part.

Let us unravel this human mystery of transformation as much as we can, because without some way of understanding it, we cannot intentionally plan for how to engage in the work of it. We cannot do our part if we do not know what is our part to play. Let us consolidate our knowledge-based learnings from the last chapter, and add to these our reflections upon what personal experience and faith have taught us regarding how we might proactively cooperate with grace.

A riddle unraveled by cumulative knowledge

We have developed as a species over our 250,000 years of existence. In the last century and a half, through advances in science and humanities, we have learned a great deal about human development. We have unearthed new understandings of deep change processes in humans and in organizations, communities and cultures we create. Our knowledge of human development, understandings of systemic change, and what we now know of evolution, has shed a great deal of light on this mystery of transformation.

We reviewed this knowledge-base in the last chapter and gleaned ten essential learnings. The mystery of transformation is made more understandable in the light of what science and the humanities have taught us. We now know these from our review in the last chapter:

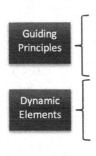

Guiding Principles
1. Maturation is a lifelong opportunity
2. Growth and transformation move in spirals
3. We plateau for a time, then transform
4. We breakdown to breakthrough
5. Pain impels us, but love pulls us through

Dynamic Elements
1. Shifts in consciousness: creating a new narrative
2. Reclaim our inner voice: the seat and soul of everything that lives
3. Reconciliation and conversion: the womb of our becoming
4. Experimentation and learning: acting our way into a new way of being
5. Transformative visioning: listening to our deepest longings

An enigma unwrapped by experience

Adding to our knowledge base is our own lived experience of transformation. Transformation of life, through death and the birthing of new life, is so common an experience that we can fail to notice, or know our part in, this astonishing mystery. It is a mystery hidden in plain sight. Death has never had the last word. It is *always* a new beginning. Every new beginning is always some other beginning's end. This mystery is so ubiquitous, though, we can lose sight of the miracle it truly is: the diurnal movement from dusk into darkness, and from darkness to dawn; seeds that bud, bloom, die and return to life again next spring; the metamorphosis of the caterpillar into a butterfly or an embryo into an infant; the loss of someone or something we loved, opening a doorway to someone or something new.

We have lived through transformative experiences repeatedly over the course of our lives. We know of this mystery, and we know of the inner work of transformation when we move through our own dark night experiences. We know of it when we suffered an emotional or spiritual crisis, lost who or what we could never imagine losing, only to emerge again as new, more compassionate, wiser and more alive than before. We know it when we have been called by a deep love that lures us out of our dull existence into one with meaning, purpose and passion. Throughout our lifetime we have countless experiences of endings (large and small) leading to new life.

Reflect for a moment upon your own experiences of transformation. The most obvious example of this for religious men and women is your vocational call to Religious Life. When you joined a community, you did not simply change your address, your garb or your title. You changed your rhythm and patterns in life, the ways in which you celebrate, grieve, pray and make decisions. You changed your primary relationships in life. You changed your relationship with God and the very meaning and purpose of your life. Your identity shifted profoundly. You were completely, radically and forever transformed, your soul enlivened in an entirely new way.

Reflection: Your Experience of Transforming while entering Religious Life

Reflect upon your experience of transformation upon entering Religious Life. You had a hand in this transformation. It didn't just happen to you. You actively participated in transforming your life. Take a moment and jot down your reflections.

1. *What was the inner work you chose to do?*

2. *How did you get through it? Who helped you through it and how?*

3. *What did your experience teach you about the nature of transformation, about your role and the role of grace?*

Now reflect for a moment on other types of crossroads, the more common and painful ones: the loss of someone you loved, a serious illness, a betrayal by a friend, an experience of abuse, a spiritual or emotional crisis of some kind that brought you to your knees. At some of these crossroads you may have chosen to make changes, alleviating the distress and coping better, but not really doing the inner work. At other crossroads you may have listened for a deeper invitation and engaged in the inner work of transformation. Reflect upon these transformative experiences.

Reflection: Your Experience of Transforming through a Painful Crossroads

Take a moment and jot down your reflections. Explore what your own personal experiences of transformation taught you about the inner work required and your active participation in the mystery of transformation.

1. *What was the inner work you chose to do?*

2. *How did you get through it? Who helped you through it and how?*

3. *What did your experience teach you about the nature of transformation, about your role and the role of grace?*

Reflect back upon your own transformative experiences and see if these resonate with the following insights gained from thousands of men and women I've surveyed across different cultures. These surveys validate what the knowledge-base of modern science has taught us, that if we are to grow and transform, it does not occur by happenstance. It is not the result of alchemy or time. Rather, it is a consequence of the choices we make and the work we do to cooperate with grace. Experience tell us that we are transformed when we:

1. experience a shift in consciousness and rewrite the narrative for our lives;

2. dig deep to shed our false images and come home to our true selves;

3. reconcile with those who matter to us, and reckon with our own pain that we previously tucked behind our psychological firewalls and neglected out of fear or shame;

4. become learners again, experimenting and risking new behaviors, possibilities and approaches to life; and,

5. transform our vision of the future based upon our deepest longings impelling us toward new life.

If we reflect upon our own past experiences, we can see how we had to deliberately let go of the old to make room for the new. We can see how we grew and transformed in ways that were transcendent. We can see how we preserved the core of our identity, while shedding old mind-sets, heart-sets and skill-sets in favor of new ones. We can see with each developmental leap in our lives that we moved to a new level of consciousness that was wider in its acceptance of diversity, more capable of empathy and interdependence, more nuanced in its morality. The mystery of transformation is made more understandable in the light of our own lived experiences and the insights these provide.

A Divine Mystery known by faith

"The great heresy has been to turn faith's darkness into certitude. There is no wonder, no astonishment, no awe, no humility. There is no Mystery." Richard Rohr

Transformation is a mystery understood partially from our own experience and further enlightened by the knowledge we have gained through modern science. But at the end of all our experience and knowledge, transformation is *a mystery we know by faith*. Where knowledge and experience leave off, faith helps us walk the pilgrimage of transformation. Just when we thought we had all the answers; somebody changes the questions. When we are brought to a crossroads, the life we have known begins to break down. The breakdown serves a purpose. We are stripped of all pretense, emptied of all hubris and hollowed out for a reason. This hollowing out (*kenosis*) makes us more amenable to the workings of grace and the inbreaking of God's covenant love.

Once again, think back to a crisis you experienced in life, the kind of crisis that brought you to your knees. These kinds of come-to-Jesus moments bring us to a crossroads in which going back to where we were is no longer an option, and the way forward seems impossible to fathom. This is where we step out into faith. Edward Teller describes it well: "When you come to the end of all the light you know, and it's time to step into the darkness of the unknown, faith is knowing that one of two things shall happen: Either you will be given something solid to stand on or you will be taught to fly."[285]

Reflection: The Role of Faith in Transformation

Take a moment and jot down your reflections. Explore the role your faith has played in your transformative experiences.

1. *In what ways did your faith carry you through when reason no longer could?*

2. *What did you're your faith teach you about the nature of transformation, about your role and the role of grace?*

Stepping out into faith does not occur without our own volition, and we are not transformed without our own arduous inner work. These experiences do not just happen to us. We do not move through these crossroads as passive bystanders being carried along by grace or as marionettes whose strings are pulled by some puppeteer god. Good intentions are not enough to transform us. Prayers alone will not transform us. We have to act. We have our part to do and we pray that our actions are in accord with grace and that God is companioning us along the way. We have to learn how to act in cooperation with grace, the very praxis of faith.

Cooperating with Grace through the Inner Work of Transformation

> *"And I said to the man who stood at the gate of the year: 'Give me a light that I may tread safely into the unknown.' And he replied: 'Go out into the darkness and put your hand into the Hand of God. That shall be to you better than light and safer than a known way.'" Minnie Haskins*

Thus, transformation is partly a Divine Mystery, forever inscrutable and dependent upon grace. And it is partly a human mystery that we increasingly understand through an accumulation of scientific knowledge, insights from our own transformative experiences and what we know of faith. It is this human part that depends upon our active participation, our own hard work, our willingness and ability to cooperate with grace. But how do we cooperate with grace? We cooperate with grace by engaging the inner work of transformation.

Dynamic elements of transformation

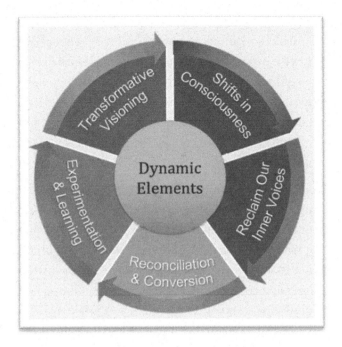

Figure 17: Dynamic Elements of Transformation

There are five dynamic elements that are key to the inner work of transformation. These five essential processes, when combined, provide the method and the means for cooperating with grace. These are the dynamic elements, or essential processes, involved in the Journey of Transformation:

1. Shifts in Consciousness: creating a new narrative

2. Reclaim our inner voice: the seat and source of everything that lives

3. Reconciliation and conversion: the womb of our becoming

4. Experimentation and learning: acting our way into a new way of being

5. Transformative visioning: gather the wisdom, weave a dream

Here is a brief outline of these essential processes. The remaining chapters are dedicated to each of these elements.

1. **Shifts in consciousness: creating a new narrative**
   Einstein famously taught us that we cannot solve today's problems with the same level of consciousness that gave rise to them. Healers have always known this as they emphasize the need to shift the perspectives, patterns, emotions and beliefs in which our wounds are otherwise embedded. Ultimately, a shift in perspective or transformation of consciousness enables us to write new narratives for our lives, ones that are authentic, liberating and life-enhancing. Pouring new wine into new wineskins enables new life to emerge.

   For your community, this involves a shift in perspective regarding the meaning and purpose of your lives, reframing what mission and community mean to you and rewriting the narrative of your communal faith journey. Beyond this shift in perspective, though, there is the deeper work of growing toward higher levels of consciousness. For communities this requires practicing mindfulness and other approaches to awaken and expand your personal and collective consciousness. Without this collective shift, or transformation of consciousness, communities would see and, therefore, shape the future much as they have in the past. A new consciousness helps you to recognize the stories you are telling yourselves that are no longer true and to open up new narratives more fitting with who you are becoming.

2. **Reclaim our inner voice: the seat and source of everything that lives**
   When we are broken and brought to our knees and have drifted from our own soul's desires, we eventually reach a point where this is no longer tenable. Our false self crumbles in the face of hypocrisy and we know our lives to be inauthentic. We start the long road back to reclaiming our true selves, reclaiming and re-authenticating our inner voice, renewing our soul and claiming our life in a whole new way. It is an heroic journey that brings us home to our true selves, to those we love, and to God.

   For communities this means taking off your masks and laying down your defensive armor in order to engage in highly intimate conversations about your deepest longings. It requires rebuilding trust and restoring the green space for growth to occur inside community. It means going through your own dark night as a community to become more real, to come home to your true selves and reclaim your inner voice. It is a journey for heroic communities to reclaim their soul, the seat and source of their existence. Without this soulwork communities will merely make changes on the surface and build a house of cards as their vision for the future.

3. **Reconciliation and conversion: the womb or our becoming**

   Reconciliation and conversion are at the very heart of transformation. There can be no transformation without healing our unhealed wounds and no one can do this for us. Healing our personal wounds, reconciling our relationships, and restoring wholeness to what has become separated and torn apart, comprise the ongoing work of conversion and the pathway to new life. This inner work is the crucible of transformation, the womb of our becoming.

   Religious are not immune to brokenness. Communities have accumulated baggage, years of unresolved wounds and conflicts. Working through these conflicts, reconciling relationships, and healing the wounds of community is the heart-work of transformation. It is also the Achilles' heel for communities as none will succeed without proper training and assistance. It is painful personal and interpersonal work which most communities avoid. Without this work of reconciliation and conversion, though, there will be no transformation. Members will become more emotionally distanced and the collective whole will become increasingly fragmented.

4. **Experimentation and learning: acting our way into a new way of being**

   Transforming old ways into new ways means experimenting and learning. This requires risking failure and getting more comfortable with being uncomfortable. It means acting our way into a new way of being. It means fumbling without perfection before we have it all figured out. It means learning from our mistakes rather than shaming and blaming others.

For a religious community, it means becoming a *learning community*. Being a learning community requires letting go of the need to prove how much you already know. This involves breaking entrenched communal norms, parting from tradition and behaving in novel ways that are outside your comfort zone. It involves trying things differently rather than just trying harder. It means making mistakes and learning from them. It requires acting your way into a new way of being, instead of succumbing to paralysis by analysis. Without experimenting, incubating new and creative possibilities, risking new ventures, and partnering in new ways, there will be no transformation.

5. **Transformative visioning: gather the wisdom, weave a dream**
   Transformation involves listening to our deepest longings and greatest aspirations to create a new vision for the future. It requires letting go of what is no longer true, real or life-giving and listening to God's call to new life. It is an organic, emergent and continually iterative process of visioning the future. It involves taking steps without having the full picture, seeing what emerges and taking the next best step in light of new understandings.

   For your communities this requires using more than just the conventional approaches to planning and visioning. When the problems are clear and the solutions are known, conventional approaches may be adequate. However, when engaged in deep change in search of new life, known maps and traditional ways of planning are inadequate. Your communities need new approaches for planning and visioning, ones that will aid in the work of transformation, tap your deepest longings and create opportunities for new life to emerge.

These five dynamic elements are universally involved in both personal and communal transformation. Your community can shift its resources, but it will not be transformed without a *shift in consciousness*. You can write your mission and visions statements, but without *reclaiming your inner voice*, these words will not hold the authenticity, passion and ownership needed among your members to make them real. Your community can try to avoid the tensions and conflicts that are a part of any human organization, but it will not become whole without doing the heart-work of *reconciliation and conversion*. You will not give birth to new life unless you become a learning community willing to *risk, experiment with and learn* new mind-sets, heart-sets and skill-sets to support it. You will not *transform your vision* for the future unless you listen to the lure and love of God and give voice to your deepest longings.

These dynamic elements represent the inner work of transformation, the type of work communities must do in order to cooperate with grace and participate in the Divine Mystery of life, death and resurrection to new life. None of these elements stand alone. They need to be translated into processes to be interwoven and connected. The combined, dynamic movement of all five of these processes is what gives rise to a new life and a new way of being in the world. Your success will depend heavily upon the courage, commitment and creativity you bring to this journey. The rest is grace.

Disposed to Grace through the Virtues of Faith, Hope and Love

> *"Love is the true goal, but faith is the process of getting there, and hope is the willingness to live without resolution or closure." Richard Rohr*

We can do our part to cooperate with grace but how do we dispose ourselves to the workings of grace? How can we carry ourselves throughout the Journey of Transformation in a manner that we become more amenable to grace, so that grace can enter in? According to John of the Cross, the best way to carry ourselves the through dark night is in a manner that deepens the virtues of faith, hope and love. In other words, we dispose ourselves to grace by nourishing the virtues of faith, hope and love, "but the greatest of these is love" (1 Corinthians 13:13).

Disposed to grace through faith

"Reason is in fact the path to faith, and faith takes over when reason can say no more." Thomas Merton

We make ourselves more amenable to grace when we walk in faith. We dispose ourselves to grace by listening to God, counting on God's covenant to be with us and by doing what makes sense. "Faith is the assurance of things hoped for, the conviction of things not seen" (Hebrews 11.1.) With the eyesight of faith, what might God be saying to you? What do your current demands for change say to you about a deeper invitation? Are you listening, discerning and doing what makes sense, doing what might bring a smile to God's face?

Thomas Merton asked the same kinds of questions you are asking and they brought him to this now familiar and most fitting prayer:

> "My Lord God, I have no idea where I am going. I do not see the road ahead of me. I cannot know for certain where it will end. Nor do I really know myself, and the fact that I think that I am following your will does not mean that I am actually doing so. But I believe that the desire to please you does in fact please you. And I hope I have that desire in all that I am doing. I hope that I will never do anything apart from that desire. And I know that if I do this you will lead me by the right road, though I may know nothing about it. Therefore will I trust you always, though I may seem to be lost and in the shadow of death. I will not fear, for you are ever with me, and you will never leave me to face my perils alone."[286]

You might not ever see the results of your labor, but I know, as people of faith, you have the desire to please God. This journey is led more by faith and a desire to please God, than by strategic plans and reasoned agendas. There is no off-the-shelf plan, seven-point program or sure path to success. The path you'll need to take is one you make as you go. It is made by taking one step at time, pausing, discerning and choosing the next best step. We cooperate with grace through our faith, through our listening and discerning: "By day the LORD went ahead of them in a pillar of cloud to guide them on their way and by night in a pillar of fire to give them light, so that they could travel by day or night" (Exodus 13:21).

We have heard it time and again that the journey itself is the destination, or how you get there is where you arrive. It is about how we journey together and who we are becoming along the way. It is about becoming more authentic, reconciled, grace-filled and passionately engaged in the fullness and joy of life. It is about becoming more of who we are meant to become, images of God, Love incarnate. That's the end game!

Moses never made it to the promised land, although, while sitting beside God, from across the way, he had a glimpse of it. We may never make it to the promised land in our lifetime either; although we too have had glimpses. And it is these glimpses, though fleeting, that renew our faith. It is in these fleeting moments, when we are sitting with God sharing our deepest longings that we are comforted by God's love, assured of the path we are on, and strengthened in our faith to keep going.

When we dispose ourselves to grace in this way, we are assured of God's covenant and promise of new life. *God's covenant is unwavering*: "When you pass through the waters, I will be with you; and when you pass through the rivers, they will not sweep over you. When you walk through the fire, you will not be burned; the flames will not set you ablaze." (Isaiah 43:2). *God's promise is unequivocal*. God's promise to Moses, the Israelites and their descendants, and to those of us who follow God in faith, is that we will be saved (Exodus 19-34). Persons and communities who cooperate with grace by being resolute in their faith will be accompanied by God and assured of new life, perhaps not within our preferred timetable, perhaps not in the ways we imagined, but surely within God's.

Disposed to grace through hope

"Hope begins where optimism ends." Sandra Schneiders

We open ourselves to the ways of grace through a *hope that knows of a future just beyond our grasp, but well within our reach*. While you will have your goals and desired outcomes, the Journey of Transformation does not rest on these alone. It rests also and especially in a hope that relies upon God's promise of new life.

This type of hope is not an over-spiritualized wishful thinking or an attempt to look at life through rose-colored glasses. It is about taking a long, loving look at the real, seeing its challenges and opportunities, and knowing that in the hardship we are not alone. It is experiencing, even in the seeming impossibility of it all, a complete trust in God's providence. This is not a passive-dependent reliance upon God, or a release from personal responsibility. It is an active hope that requires our responsible participation and partnership with God and one another to make it real.

Marcia Allen's outgoing presidential address at LCWR was entitled *Transformation – An Experiment in Hope*. She said, "We are wrapped in a sense of futility, doing more of the same in a most tiresome and enervating way…the status quo prevails…. After all the rational has been tried; after the solutions have been articulated and failed; when old language turns to ashes in our mouths, then we are reduced to silence. That is when hope is activated."[287] That is when we are most amenable to God's grace and responsive to the alluring love of God.

This work of transformation and your fidelity to your life as vowed religious cannot be tied to the hope for results. Thomas Merton knew that when he prayed only to please God. In the now famous prayer written to commemorate Oscar Romero, *A Future Not our Own*, we are encouraged to take the long view: "We may never see the end results, but that is the difference between the master builder and the worker."[288] Václav Havel grasped its essence when he said that hope "is not the conviction that something will turn out well but the certainty that something makes sense, regardless of how it turns out."[289]

Joan Chittister, in her book *Scarred by Struggle, Transformed by Hope*, tells us, "There is no one who does not go down into the darkness where the waters do not flow and we starve for want of hope."[290] Yet in the starvation, in the struggle itself, lies the seedbed for hope. Hope emerges through the process of conversion. We are transformed and our transformation, she says, "brings total metamorphosis of soul."[291] We all know this place, the place where we are forged in this darkness and transformed by hope emerging through the struggle. Hope enables us to endure the darkness, prevail in the struggle and transform our soul.

Is there hope for your community and the future of Religious Life? There is hope for the future as long as your hope is an active hope, not just a passive hope made of prayers alone. In their book, *Active Hope*,[292] Joanna Macy and Chris Johnstone draw the distinction between hope as something we *have* as distinct from hope as something we *do*. They stress the need to not only have hope but to do our part to bring it to fruition. Acting in hope on behalf of your community will dispose you to the workings of grace.

Disposed to grace through love

"No eye has seen, no ear has heard, and no mind has imagined what God has prepared for those who love him."
1 Corinthians 2:9

Tina Turner asks, "What's love got to do with it?" After all, it's a "second-hand emotion," a "sweet old fashioned notion." "Who needs a heart when a heart can be broken?"[293] Love and heartbreak have a great deal to do with transformation. Love and heartbreak both make us amenable to the workings of grace.

Richard Rohr believes there are two great forces that aid in our transformation: "great love and great suffering."[294] I couldn't agree more. It is great suffering that compels, pushes and forces us to change and transform our lives. Great suffering breaks us down and hollows us out. It brings us to our knees and eventually to a crossroads, the threshold of transformation. But it is love that pulls us through. It is love that impels, lures, entices us to transform our lives. It sustains us in the struggle and obliges us to reach beyond. It is the combined effect of this push-me, pull-me dynamic of heartbreak and love that transforms us.

It is not love that brings people to therapy. It is pain. It is pain that gets us in the door, but it is love that heals and pulls us through. The studies on the effectiveness of psychotherapy, comparing one approach to another, all end up with the same conclusion. While certain techniques are more or less effective for specific disorders, the healing agent for all approaches is *compassion*. In other words, if there is genuine regard and compassion for the client by the therapist, and if the client believes in the therapist's belief in him or her, then healing can occur. Some call it unconditional positive regard, others call it presence. Some just call it love (that second-hand emotion).

The same is true for communities. *It is pain that brings you to the crossroads, but it is Love that pulls you through.* What else is there? It is the reason we endure the costs and stomach the sacrifices, so we can give to the people we love the values and things that we cherish. It is the reason we stay in the struggle when the going gets tough, rather than bail on the people we love. Knowing that we have been loved by God and by those in our life who have sacrificed for us, gives us the gratitude and obligation to love others and sacrifice for them in return.

To cooperate with grace means to risk loving again, and allowing ourselves to be loved again, when doubts and pain from old wounds would urge us to hold back. Cooperating with grace means learning to love, not in general, but specifically your community's members and its mission, as well as your God. The Journey of Transformation is not a concept or idea, it is an inside-out, soul-to-surface, wholly spiritual and concretely literal experience. It is love incarnate, love in action (John 15:12).

Never Go Ahead of Grace

"Our real journey in life is interior: it is a matter of growth, deepening, and of an ever greater surrender to the creative action of love and grace in our hearts."
Thomas Merton

Who will you be when all of your organizational changes are completed? Who are you becoming while you are making all your plans and getting things done? The Journey of Transformation takes seriously these questions. It invites you to explore the deeper invitations amid the multitude of changes communities are now facing. It invites you to discern God's call to new life.

The Sisters of St. Joseph have a maxim that says: "Never go ahead of grace by an impudent eagerness, but quietly await its movements, and, when it comes to you, go along with it with great gentleness, humility, fidelity, and courage."[295] We ought not run ahead of grace, linger too long, or fall behind from where grace would want us to go or have us become. The Spirit moves in real time and blows where She will (John 3:8). We cannot engineer Her ways or control where She leads us. Only if we are attentive, courageous, nimble and disciplined enough, can we can learn to cooperate with grace.

Chapter 12: Shifts in Consciousness
Creating a new narrative

"And no one pours new wine into old wineskins. Otherwise, the wine will burst the skins, and both the wine and the wineskins will be ruined. No, they pour new wine into new wineskins"
Mark 2:22

Introduction

In order to transform our life, we need to see our life differently than the way we have viewed it up until now. A shift in consciousness involves a transformation in how we see and understand ourselves and our world. This not only brings forth new insights but frees us to create *new narratives* for our lives, ones that liberate our true calling to live into the future. When combined with the other four dynamic elements, a shift in consciousness brings about a *new way of being*; our lives become increasingly attuned to the flow of grace.

A shift in consciousness can occur at two levels. The first is a *shift in perspective*, which shifts *what* we see. It is akin to putting on a new lens, or twisting a kaleidoscope, enabling us to see realities and ourselves differently than the way they were seen before. The second involves a deeper transformation in the very *nature of consciousness* by removing the distractions and distortions of worldly preoccupations and self-concern. This shift is akin to acquiring a new operating system which transforms *how* we understand what we see. Arriving at a shift in perspective is a bit easier, while the deeper transformation takes a great deal of patience, discipline and practice to acquire. Both contribute to a shift in consciousness, making available greater wisdom and new possibilities previously outside of our awareness and understanding.

Einstein famously said, "No problem can be solved from the same level of consciousness that created it." We need, as Jesus said, a *new wineskin* (new consciousness) in order to hold the *new wine* (new narrative). Such a transformation of consciousness moves our mental fences, widens our perspectives, invites creative alternatives, elevates our morality and deepens our spiritual journey. It allows us to breathe new life into the ongoing and ever-evolving narrative of our life. It does not invalidate our prior perspectives, rather, it incorporates and transcends them. In this way, shifts in consciousness become *soul-shifts* that liberate us to grow more fully into who we are called to become.

We cannot bootstrap ourselves into a shift in consciousness. However, we can do certain things that can either help or hinder its possible development. In this chapter, we will first look at what inhibits us from seeing a different perspective, then explore ways to enable us to shift our perspective. This will be an important step toward a more profound transformation of consciousness and the creation of new narratives, which we will discuss in the second half of this chapter.

Windows on the World

Friedrich Nietzsche once said, "We look at the world through different windows." Pope Francis and Donald Trump, for example, must be looking at the world through very different windows as their worldviews are so radically different. A ten-year-old girl trying to survive amid the rubble of Syria sees a different world than a ten-year-old girl on a rural farm in Kansas. A beggar dying on the streets of Nairobi sees a different world than a CEO sitting high above Wall Street. Your perspective on life and the world will vary greatly depending upon your window on the world. Peering through a different window can transform your entire worldview.

Thomas Merton discovered a new worldview on Fourth and Walnut: "Then it was as if I suddenly saw the secret beauty of their hearts, the depths of their hearts, where neither sin nor desire nor self-knowledge can reach, the core of their reality, the person that each one is in God's eyes. If only they could all see themselves as they really are. If only we could see each other that way all the time."[296] If only we could see ourselves as we really are. If only we could see others, the people we serve, our community, as they really are. If only we could see, as God sees, the depth and beauty that we and others hold in our hearts. If only we could see each other that way all the time!

What blocks our view

Windows on the World was a restaurant located at the top of the North Tower of the World Trade Center in lower Manhattan, which was destroyed during the attacks on September 11, 2001. Out of the blue, on that beautiful September day in New York City, our window on the world was forever changed. The impact upon us in the United States and across the globe was seismic. The ripple effects continue to this day. A new window on our world emerged that was as dark and foreboding as the December 7, 1941 attack on Pearl Harbor.

Both events, in 1941 and 2001, were literally inconceivable. How could we not see these coming? By all accounts we had the information but were unable to imagine these horrific possibilities becoming a reality. Although the intelligence agencies had all of the information required to forecast these events, and warnings were given by those collecting the data, those making the decisions could not think outside the box of their own expectations. Their expectations conformed to what had been, not what could be.

One of the most challenging aspects of any transformative journey is the constraints we place upon ourselves, others, and our possible futures, by our own existing worldviews. Our worldview tells us what is possible and what is not. It is our internal operating system that organizes and interprets what we see, hear, touch, taste and smell. Our worldview shapes our mind-sets, creates our heart-sets and determines the skill-sets we believe we need to exist in the world we created. It is what determines whether we are cynical about our future or hopeful. It governs our choices on a daily basis and what we do when we reach a particular crossroads.

Remember why groups fail to transform? They make new improved versions of the past, try harder rather than try differently and download the same information using the same operating system. Unless your thinking shifts in a way that offers you a new window on the world, your efforts to solve today's problems will fail. What prevents us from looking out through a new window? Here are four of the most common barriers:

1. Inability to think outside the box;

2. Tunnel vision;

3. Future blindness;

4. Imprisoned by reputations.

I will describe these for you so that you might reflect upon whether you and your community are prone to any of these barriers. If so, perhaps you can choose a window with a better view.

1. Inability to think outside the box

"The difficulty lies not so much in developing new ideas as in escaping from the old ones." John Maynard Keynes

I am sure you have seen this diagram (Figure 19: Nine Dots) and tried this exercise before, but indulge me and try it again. I have given this challenge to thousands of people across different cultures and very few could solve it. The challenge is this: first, draw these nine parallel dots on a blank piece of paper, then connect all nine dots with four, contiguous, straight lines. In other words, once you put your pen or pencil on the paper, you may not lift it off the paper while drawing the four lines. All four lines must be straight and contiguous. Good luck! You can check your answer at the end of this chapter.

Although there are several possible solutions, I found that only a handful of people per hundred could solve this puzzle. Among those who did solve it, many were successful because they saw it done before and they remembered (rather than discovered) the solution. This illustrates just how hard it is to think outside the box and see reality in a new way. More often than not we connect the dots in the same way we always have, even when we know it doesn't work. Einstein's statement that we need to solve problems with a different mindset than the one that created them is easier said than done.

Figure 18: Nine Dots

To illustrate this point further, tell me what you see in this picture (Figure 19: Two women). You may have seen this picture in an introductory psychology class. Although you may have seen it before, you may still be challenged to see more than one woman, an old and a young woman. Can you see both? It is hard to think outside of the box, to shift perspectives away from the one with which we are used to seeing.

This is a major barrier for communities seeking to create a new vision for the future. They will need help in connecting the dots of their reality in a new, fresh and liberating way. They will need others outside the system to help them think outside of the box.

Figure 19: Two women

2. Tunnel vision

On December 28, 1978 United Airlines flight 173 left the Denver airport bound for Portland, Oregon with 189 souls on board. All three pilots were experienced having accrued over 36,000 combined hours of piloting. Upon descent into Portland they lowered the landing gear and noticed that one of the three indicator lights had not turned green, indicating that the landing gear was not completely extended and locked into place. This would be unsettling for new pilots. But for seasoned pilots, this was an event for which they train many times during recurrent flight training.

The crew requested a holding pattern to give them time to investigate. All three pilots became preoccupied with trouble-shooting the failed indicator light. All three pilots failed to scan their other instruments and navigate the plane. As a result, the DC-8 ran out of fuel and crashed some six miles from the runway, on a perfectly clear day with three seasoned pilots. The NTSB report listed the cause of the crash as fuel exhaustion resulting from the pilots' "preoccupation with a landing gear malfunction."[297] Without question, the pilots needed to trouble-shoot the light. However, they had tunnel vision when they became so focused on the indicator light that they failed to see the big picture.

An example of tunnel vision occurring in communities is when its members become completely preoccupied with *recruiting new vocations*. Understandably, this can be a priority for communities that might have the means to form new members. However, some communities become so focused upon new members as their only hope for the future, they fail to see the big picture. They fail to see hope residing in the current members and emerging opportunities. This tunnel vision blocks their view and their ability to look through new windows on the world that might otherwise offer hope for new life.

3. Future blindness

> *"What makes this world so hard to see clearly is not its strangeness but its usualness. Familiarity can blind you too." Robert M. Pirsig*

Yogi Berra once said, "It is tough to make predictions, especially about the future." Nassim Nicholas Taleb builds upon Yogi's pithy statement in his fascinating book, *The Black Swan: The Impact of the Highly Improbable*. The black swan, according to Taleb, has three attributes:

1. "It is an outlier, as it lies outside the realm of regular expectations because nothing in the past can convincingly point to its possibility;

2. It carries an extreme impact;

3. In spite of its outlier status, human nature makes us concoct explanations for its occurrence after the fact, making it explainable and predictable."[298]

Taleb notes that most of history is written by rare unexpected events in life (i.e., black swans), not the expected ones (i.e., white swans). History is made from low probability, high impact events, such as the rise of Nazism, the rise of Islamic fundamentalism, the market crash of 1987 and the 9/11 attacks. The status quo, or more of the same, does not make history. Our future does not arrive on our schedule, nor does it come from our planning. The wheel, the computer, the laser and the internet did not come from a strategic plan.

Taleb argues that we expect to see what we've always seen before, but it is what we don't know and can't predict or see that will likely have the greatest impact upon our narrative for the future. "History is a museum," says Taleb, "where one can go to see the repository of the past and the charm of the olden days. It does not help to forecast the future."[299] The black swan logic makes what you don't know far more relevant than what you do know. Thus, we need to open ourselves to see what others see, to serendipity and God's providence.

Taleb suggest that we are all prone to a "narrative fallacy" or our mistaken interpretation and filtering of facts based upon history, rather than seeing the facts for what they are now. We remember the facts of the past that fit and confirm our existing narrative, while neglecting others. We don't remember the truth, but our reconstructed truth. In this way we are all prone to "future blindness." In order to avoid these tendencies and write a new narrative, we have to see the facts as they are today.

Communities need to trust their experience, stay close to the data and invite others to help them see new possibilities. They will need to intentionally look closely for what is emerging, rather than quickly conclude it is more of the same based on history. Getting the perspective of others who have not been part of their history helps communities see with new eyes and avoid the narrative fallacy.

4. Imprisoned by reputations

"If you think you are so enlightened, go and spend a week with your parents." Ram Dass

Maybe you have had the experience of returning home to your family of origin only to be placed back in the box of a reputation you had received some 10, 25 or 50 years ago. Our reputations get frozen in time. For example, because you were the oldest of four growing up, perhaps you had more responsibility than your younger siblings and were expected to help out by doing laundry, dishes or yard work. Even though 25 years have passed, your siblings remain lingering over Thanksgiving dinner, waiting for you to clear the table and do the dishes, just as you had in the past. Although you have moved away, grown well past these moments in time, it is hard to shake a reputation. Thanksgiving dinner revives them on a yearly basis.

The "Pygmalion effect" is well known among educators as to its damaging effects upon students' reputations. The Pygmalion effect tells us that a teacher's expectation becomes a self-fulfilling prophecy. For example, if a teacher thinks Mary is not a very smart student, the teacher will set the bar of expectations low and challenge her less. As a result, Mary adapts her performance to meet the expectations of her teacher. Indeed, Mary gets lower grades. Our reputations, deserved or not, shape how others see us and, in turn, how we respond.

Members have reputations that imprison them for years in communities. Not only can the perception of members be frozen in time but so, too, can their collective contributions to the communal narrative. The communal narrative – stories members tell themselves about their community – can likewise be stuck in time. Reputations, and the stories you tell yourselves about one another and your lives, can continue well past their basis in reality, remaining unchallenged as self-fulfilling prophesies.

The point is this: *The inability to think outside the box, see the big picture, notice the black swans, and free ourselves from outdated reputations and stories, greatly limits communities from transforming their lives and creating a new future.* What can be done about it?

Enabling Shifts in Perspective

> *"If you don't like something change it; if you can't change it, change the way you think about it." Mary Engelbreit*

What helps us gain a new perspective? What is it that shifts our thinking, opens our hearts and helps us see with new eyes a world that otherwise *appears* much the same as it did yesterday? It is not so much our eyes and ears that need to change, but our *perspective* that needs to shift in order to interpret differently what we see and hear. We need to attend to and process what we hear and see differently, from a different vantage point. We need to try on a different lens or twist the kaleidoscope. Here are three ways to shift our perspective:

1. Listen to the prophets;

2. Welcome the stranger; and

3. Expand or shrink the system.

Listen to the prophets

"What is familiar is what we are used to; and what we are used to is most difficult to 'Know' - that is, to see as a problem; that is, to see as strange, as distant, as 'outside us'." Friedrich Nietzsche

If your community is searching for a new perspective and is primed and ready to listen, then listen to the prophets. Prophets are those who can see beyond the horizon that most of us see and challenge our current vision of reality in ways that bring us closer to the future. They reframe reality in ways that both disturb and resonate with us at a deeper level. It is this combination of disturbance and resonance that impels us to search for a deeper, more liberating truth. They speak a language that is counter to conventional wisdom and pushes us to think and act counter to prevailing norms. They are not disturbers who obfuscate the truth and bring chaos to our world, but agents of transformation calling us to see the familiar in a new, more hope-filled way.

There are many prophets among us, both lay and religious, who seek to reframe our customary worldviews and offer refreshing perspectives on Religious Life. They call us to a deeper, more liberating truth about emerging new paradigms. The religious prophets of our day are reframing the vows, offering ideas about new forms of Religious Life, and advancing perspectives on the meaning, purpose and future of Religious Life. Their prescient words can provide stepping stones toward the future, if we let them. Here is a small sampling.

Joan Chittister, in her trailblazing book, *The Fire in the Ashes*, said this: "The fact is that religious life was never meant simply to be a labor force in the church; it was meant to be a searing presence, a paradigm of search, a mark of human soul and a catalyst to conscience in the society in which it emerged."[300]

Diarmuid O'Murchu, in his recent book, *Religious Life in the 21st Century*, speaks of a paradigm shift from the "ideology of the hero" to the "archetype of the lover." He believes this shift is an effort to "reclaim a deep, ancient wisdom inscribed in both monastic and apostolic forms of the vowed life – but largely subverted by the ideology of the patriarchal hero."[301] O'Murchu uses the term "paradigmatic visioning" and describes this as one that favors relational webs over isolated parts, connections over distinctions, collaboration over competition; it celebrates commonalities rather than differences.[302]

Barbara Fiand, in her book, *From Religion Back to Faith*, asserts that the emerging worldview is one that is moving away from a dogmatic and fossilized religion and is returning to an emphasis on spirituality and faith. "Theology is useless," she says, "unless it can be transmitted to the body of the faithful in language that clarifies rather than obfuscates, that speaks to present-day reality rather than to a worldview and reality no longer relevant. The power of Christianity is tested in the hearts it reaches and the transformation it effects."[303]

Michael Crosby, in his book, *Repair My House*, agreed with Pope Benedict XVI that the Church in the western world has a "crisis of faith," but turned this around saying that the crisis is not a loss of faith in the Spirit, but a "lack of faith in the institutional church itself." He goes on to say: "At the core of every refounding lies a power in the refounding person or persons that offers something beyond simple repair of cosmetic cracks in the façade. There is a rebirth that springs from the way that person or persons grasp the power of the original mystery"[304]

Sandra Schneiders re-frames Religious Life as "a charismatic lifeform, called into existence by the Holy Spirit, to live corporately the prophetic charism in the Church. It is not a workforce gathering recruits for ecclesiastical projects and it does not receive its mission nor the particular ministries of its members from the hierarchy."[305]

John Dear offers a new lens for the Gospel call to peace-making.[306] David Courturier suggests that the vow of poverty should be based upon a "theology of abundance" and "compassionate collaboration."[307] Elaine Prevallet offers a new lens for the vows.[308] The list could go on: Richard Rohr, Ilia Delio, Peter Senge, Margaret Wheatley, Robert Putnam, Elizabeth Johnson, Peter Block, Barbara Marx Hubbard, Anthony Gittens, and many others. All of these scholars, theologians and futurists are offering new lenses for understanding the evolving nature of Religious Life within the context of our evolving world. They reframe our theology and worldviews, pouring new wine into new wineskins.

You have your own prophets, too. In every community there are those on the edge of change, instruments of transformation who march to the beat of a different drummer. They go about their ministries with tremendous zeal making a profound difference in the lives of those they serve. Sadly, they are often pariahs in their own community, dismissed as disloyal or crazy. Though they may not have been proclaimed *prophets*, they are prophets. Famous or not, they offer new perspectives and visions of the future. They are agents of transformation.

Whether or not these particular prophets resonate for you, the invitation here is to search for those that do. Explore and reflect upon these possibilities in order to discover how they might shift the perspective you presently have for understanding your lives. Invite those who can help you see over the horizon and look anew at Religious Life. Invite those who will stretch your thinking, not simply reinforce your current way of thinking. Listen to the visions that resonate, disturb and bring new meaning and hope to your life and mission. There are prophets among us who can broaden our perspectives, if only we choose to listen.

Welcome the stranger

"The alien who resides with you shall be to you as the citizen among you; you shall love the alien as yourself, for you were aliens in the land of Egypt: I am the Lord your God." Leviticus 19:34

Communities can alter their perspectives by welcoming the stranger and strange ideas. Sometimes I find communities stewing in their own juices, having the same conversations, using the same language, looking through the same lenses, going about things in the same way and ending up in the same place (Einstein's definition of insanity). It helps to bring *outsiders* into the conversation. Welcome the stranger into your conversation, someone who is outside of your ordinary circle and who looks at life through a different lens. Strangers can help us see things from a new perspective and open up new possibilities.

An example of this happened in a recent consultation I had with a leadership team. A problem arose because they had allowed a number of senior members who were fairly independent to live in a Motherhouse community originally intended for members needing assisted living. This worked fine for a time because there were plenty of rooms to go around, but soon they were running out of space for more members needing assisted living. Unfortunately, the members now living there considered it their *home* and were highly resistant to moving out. The team was stuck. What to do?

It was midafternoon during our discussion and there was no creative energy left in the room. I said, "Just for the fun of it, let's invite some other folks into the conversation." I asked them, "Go and find the first person you see in the hallway, whomever it happens to be, and bring them in here." They got up from the table and came back a few minutes later with whomever happened to have been around at the time: the Communication Director, a kitchen helper, a housekeeper, and the Director of Maintenance.

When they came into the room, we explained the dilemma we had been wrestling with then asked for their thoughts. Reticent at first (more likely shocked), they slowly began offering their thoughts, then with their increasing comfort, their candid advice. The energy in the room began to shift from the dead air we had before they came in, to nervous laughter, then to an exciting back and forth. New possibilities were tossed around until an idea with some potential emerged. A house nearby, partially occupied by members, offered great space for assisted living. They began to strategize on how this might work and made a tentative plan.

The newcomers left saying "thanks" for the conversation. It not only gave them a reprieve from their afternoon doldrums, it was fun. They seemed to enjoy being *included* in a closed-door session with the leadership and being *dignified* by having been asked to help. I asked the team what they noticed about the exchange. They described it as being filled with "energy," "possibilities," "laughter," "fun," a "breakthrough."

Communities are used to bringing in realtors to help with real estate, lawyers to help with legal matters, theologians to add to their theology, and all of this makes good sense. I would not suggest otherwise. But when you are stuck, going in circles, out of creative ideas and energy, think of adding new people to the conversation. Add ones you have not ordinarily had in the conversation. Bring in outsiders, especially those from other disciplines, life circumstances and perspectives. Welcome the stranger and their strange ideas.

Expand or shrink the system

"The real voyage of discovery consists not in seeking new lands, but in seeing with new eyes." Marcel Proust

Often, when reaching a roadblock as a therapist with a client, I would bring other family members in or out of the conversation. If I was seeing an individual client who was stuck, I might bring in the family. If I was seeing a couple or family who were stuck, I might ask for an individual session with one of them. If I was seeing a religious in individual therapy, I might meet with his or her superior or local community. I would expand or shrink the system to open up a new perspective.

I once treated a priest who was severely depressed and suicidal. Michael was referred by his superior following a stint at an inpatient treatment facility. I learned that this was his third inpatient stay, each one occurring on the heels of a suicide attempt. He had been clinically depressed and in treatment for many years. Given his condition, he was not your ideal community member. Consequently, he had been moved from one local community to the next. Eventually each community would reach the point where they could no longer tolerate his heavy presence and their walking on eggshells in fear of his potential suicide. Each time, the superior would intervene, move him to another community and on it went.

After a few individual sessions with Michael having little to say, I decided to visit him in his local community to shed more light on the situation. I met with all six of the local community members in the community room. While I oriented the group, Michael sat mute in his corner chair staring at the floor. Everyone was a bit uncomfortable (including me). The other five men talked *about* Michael like he was a package in the room, not a person. They were treating him as if he were a fragile piece of glass that might break into pieces if not handled with kid gloves. I told the them, "If you treat someone like a cripple, you cripple them. If you treat him as fragile, you 'fragilize' him. Talk with him directly about how you experience him."

It took a bit to get them going, but they began to talk with Michael directly about how they experienced him and how they were affected by his behavior. The tension in the room grew. Michael became angry hearing how they perceived him ("moody," "not much fun," "a loner," "scary to be around"). But the anger was better than the apathy and isolation that preceded it. Rather than remaining mute and disengaged as he had been, he looked directly at them and became engaged in the conversation!

Engaging Michael and his local community opened up the possibilities of a new way forward. Having a larger reality in the room allowed us to forge new behavioral agreements between the local community members and Michael aimed at improving their relationships and challenging his isolation. I made monthly visits with the local community while continuing weekly visits with Michael, who then had plenty to talk about. The new perspectives added greatly to the focus of individual therapy and this was supported by a home situation which now reinforced healthy behaviors, rather than walking on eggshells and reinforcing his withdrawal and isolation. Enlarging or shrinking the system, alters the perspective and opens up new possibilities.

A shift in *perspective* is a necessary step in the transformation of consciousness and the creation of new narratives. Tunnel vision, future blindness and other barriers prevent communities from seeing beyond their own view of reality. Most communities remain stuck, unable to imagine possibilities outside of their own awareness and habitual ways of thinking. But there are things they can do to help them move their mental fences and open up new perspectives and possibilities: Listen to the prophets, welcome the stranger, and expand or shrink the system.

Reflection: Shifts in Perspective

Recall your own experience in community:

1. *When have you experienced your community's barriers to new perspectives (inability to think outside the box, tunnel vision, future blindness or imprisoned by reputations)?*

2. *When has your community been liberated by listening to the prophets or strangers and their strange ideas, or when have they expanded or shrunk the system?*

Cultivating a Transformation of Consciousness

"The devout Christian of the future will either be a mystic...
or he will cease to be anything at all." Karl Rahner

While a shift in perspectives is a good start, a deeper and more enduring transformation of consciousness requires more than a cognitive shift in perspective. A deeper transformation of consciousness involves altering the very source and quality of our consciousness. It is a change in the operating system, a soul-shift that aligns oneself more fully with the movement of grace. For Eckhart Tolle, such a transformation is a "burning up of the ego."[309] Burning up the ego enables a deeper cooperation with grace that moves us, ultimately, toward what the Hindus call *enlightenment*, the Buddhists call *nirvana* or what the Christians call *salvation*.

At the zenith of Christian salvation, we might arrive at what Jesus referred to as heaven. Eckhart Tolle invites us to participate in co-creating this heaven on earth – a new earth – in the same manner as Jesus spoke of it, not as a location up in the sky, but as an inner realm of consciousness: "Then I saw 'a new heaven and a new earth,' for the first heaven and the first earth had passed away, and there was no longer any sea" (Revelation 21:1.) For Tolle, then, "A new heaven is the emergence of a transformed state of human consciousness, and 'a new earth' is its reflection in the physical realm."[310]

Everything in the universe is evolving, even our consciousness. How can we cultivate this transformation of consciousness and participate in its evolution? To understand what might cultivate a transformation of consciousness, we first need to more fully understand what is meant by "consciousness." Ken Wilber has written extensively on the subject and draws a helpful distinction between "states" and "structures" of consciousness.

States of consciousness

States of consciousness are temporary and broadly categorized into two types. The first category includes the *natural* states of consciousness, such as wakefulness, dreaming and deep sleep, which everyone experiences. The second category includes *altered* states of consciousness, such as meditative, drug induced or peak experiences, sometimes referred to as "spiritual experiences."[311] Peak experiences are the most common of these altered states. Let's explore peak experiences to illustrate what these types of altered states might involve.

Peak experiences

Peak experiences are powerful emotional and spiritual experiences that jolt us out of our ordinary consciousness and into altered states. Most people have had one of these as a result of falling in love, a brush with death, or standing on the edge of the Grand Canyon. Sometimes, as in Merton's case on Fourth and Walnut, we are simply walking down the street when a heightened awareness happens upon us and an epiphany emerges that changes everything. All of these peak experiences can dramatically impact the way we see ourselves and our world, though their impact might only be fleeting.

But even fleeting ones leave a residual mark. We are different for having had the experience. They help us to know that there is, in fact, another realm of consciousness. They help us to wonder that if we had this profound experience once, maybe there could be another. Perhaps there is a doorway to something more in our life than what we ordinarily experience. One example of a peak spiritual experience from my own life was the death of my sister-in-law, Norma Lipsmeyer.

> "When Beth's sister, Norma, was nearing her final days, she called her family to come join her for what she referred to as her 'come to Jesus party.' Everyone came from our busy lives to share in the celebration of her life at this party co-hosted by Norma and Jesus. Upon receiving the invitation my wife and I immediately made arrangements to leave a Chapter we were facilitating in Oregon. We arrived at the Mercy health care facility in Fort Smith, Arkansas the next day.
>
> When we walked into Norma's room her eyes immediately met ours as she smiled saying, 'Thanks for coming.' She welcomed each person in much the same way, her inviting eyes, a smile radiating love and her arms as open as her heart in total welcome. She embraced us as she did each person with her entire being, seemingly oblivious to her own pain or impending death. Because her clothes had become such a bother, she lay unabashedly naked as the day she was born welcoming each person to her 'party' in gratitude. Both Jesus and she were glad to have us come.

Norma spent time with each one of us. Regardless of others who may have been in the room at the time, when she spoke with you it was as if no one else was there. She told each one of us why she loved us and how we had been a 'gift' to her. She shared her hopes for us while promising to pray for us as she journeyed on. She was entirely present to us in her loving way, so much so that we could not help but be drawn to her in the same way. The clocks and calendars that ordinarily prodded us through life mattered not. Phones, food, to-do lists and the everyday chores of life were lost on us as each one of us, Jesus and Norma met on hallowed ground.

Everything seemed to coexist without argument, as if held in a cosmic embrace and a great Amen. It was surreal and entirely real at the same time. Pain and laughter, tears and smiles, grief and gratitude, stillness and conversation, were all comfortably juxtaposed. And in it all, Jesus kept saying, 'Of course!' Life and death sat side by side and all was acceptable. We prayed and sang, talked and sat in silence, hugged and held each other with no sense of urgency. We were on God's time and in God's home and that's all that mattered.

Norma didn't want to die. She didn't want to leave us. She was as frightened of death as the rest of us. Being a Sister of Mercy did not make her immune to being human and she wasn't shy about expressing her anguish. And when she did, we felt it as if it were ours. Along with her anguish we witnessed Norma's total acceptance of the truth, her love that knew no bounds and her faith that was stronger than most. We were transfixed and transformed by her astonishing presence while she and Jesus loved us through it all."[312]

Her presence to us and ours to her was one of the most loving, human and sacred experiences I've ever had. I am sure that you have had these kinds of peak experiences, as well. It is unfortunate that it often takes death to shock us into this kind of presence, however, these kinds of experiences remind us that this profound gift of presence is always available to us. All we have to do is awaken this gift.

One peak experience, fleeting though it may be, is enough to give us a *contrast experience*. Although temporary, such an altered state of consciousness helps us distinguish the temporal from Eternal, truth from Truth, and love from great Love. It helps us know there is a nondual existence where the sublime and humor, life and death, grief and gratitude can comingle without prejudice. Peak experiences are indelible touchstones we can return to over and over again when discerning what God, Jesus or Love would ask of us, the path we ought to take and with whom.

Structures of consciousness

Structures of consciousness are stable and enduring holistic patterns. They are more flowing and overlapping than static and rigidly separated, analogous to "waves," a "spiral" or "colors of the rainbow."[313] Wilber studied and documented dozens of versions of these structures across different cultures and traditions. He found that some ascribe to only two levels of consciousness (matter and spirit); others three (matter, mind, and spirt); still others name four or five (matter, body, mind, soul, and spirit) or more.[314]

As we ascend through new structural levels of consciousness, we attain not only a new sense of identity, but a "new and higher view of the world, with a wider and more encompassing set of morals and perspectives."[315] In other words, we move from egocentric, to sociocentric, to worldcentric. The higher-level structures are not givens, but potentials some of us can attain.

But how do we intentionally evolve to new structural levels of consciousness? Aside from peak experiences, which are largely outside of our control, what can we do to intentionally transform our consciousness? It takes training and practice. Temporary *states of consciousness* can become increasingly permanent *structures of consciousness* with practice, as with meditation and contemplation. In other words, according to Wilber, "The more you experience meditative or contemplative states of consciousness, the faster you develop through the stages."[316]

However, Wilber is also quick to point out that the higher levels of consciousness are particularly challenging to reach and are not possible for all adults. "Only those who rigorously train," he says, can move toward these higher levels.[317] With that caveat in mind, let's turn to some of the kinds of training and practice that might assist in the personal and communal transformation of consciousness.

Mindfulness

"The ultimate purpose of human existence is to bring
'presence' into the world. Being in the flow with Christ."
Eckhart Tolle

Mindfulness exercises are ones that open wide our field of awareness. According to Wilber, mindfulness is "bare awareness" or "choiceless awareness," an awareness without preference, comment, judgement analysis or interpretation."[318] Referring to centering prayer as a mindfulness exercise, Cynthia Bourgeault says, "every time the mind is released from engagement with a specific idea or impression, we move from a smaller and more constricted state of consciousness into that open, diffuse awareness in which our presence to divine reality makes itself known along a whole different pathway of perception."[319]

According to Wilber, the aim of these mindfulness exercises is threefold: to come to know one's own mental processes; to gain the power to control them; and to free ourselves from psychic conditions that are otherwise unconscious and uncontrolled.[320] Richard Rohr would say that the aim is to "live with ambiguity, mystery, and uncertainty, and where I can balance knowing with unknowing…. the heart of the mystery of biblical faith."[321]

Such a transformation of consciousness, according to Eckhart Tolle, requires that people let go of their "identification with form, dogma, and rigid belief systems and discover the original depth that is hidden within their own spiritual tradition… and themselves." He sees these methods of mindfulness as a means for transforming our consciousness beyond the preoccupations of our ego and into an experience of a heaven that is always in our midst.[322] Mindfulness, then, has more to do with the quality of the field, than what is grown in the field; more to do with the quality of the sea, than the waves that ripple, rise and recede in it.

Once again, temporary states can become more permanent structures of consciousness with assiduous practice of mindfulness exercises, such as, prayer, meditation, and contemplation. These particular practices have been with us for thousands of years and religious communities are well versed in many of these. Therefore, let me highlight three other methods of mindfulness that are a bit more contemporary. These have an *interpersonal* emphasis and are practiced among some religious communities. They involve knitting together an inward contemplative focus of individuals with an outward focus and dialogue with others in community:

1. Presence;

2. Communal discernment; and

3. Contemplative engagement.

These methods, like prayer and meditation, are *skills* that can only be developed through a great deal of patience, practice and discipline. When done well, these methods create a rhythmic flow of listening and responding to the Spirit moving within and among participants. When done well, over time, these methods can transform both the personal and collective consciousness of those involved. When done poorly, without patience, practice and discipline, these methods amount to little more than "fluff." Unfortunately, most communities fail to train in and practice these skills routinely, and with the same degree of rigor as they have practiced personal prayer, meditation or contemplation. Consequently, they are often discarded as just another fad.

1. Presence

Presence is a skill, not simply an attitude. It is more than being physically present. It is a skill that is foundational to communal discernment and contemplative engagement. In my experience, however, the skill of presence is often absent, even among groups who claim its importance. Something is getting lost in the translation from theory to practice. I'd like to be a bit more specific here, because without presence, attempts at communal discernment or contemplative engagement will bear little fruit.

When teaching the skill of presence, I often begin by asking a community, "When we started prayer this morning by saying, 'Let us bring ourselves to the presence of the Lord,' what did that mean to you? What does the word 'presence' mean to you in that context.?" What I typically hear back are comments such as: "focus," "attention," "grounded," "searching" "clarity," "listening to God." The kind of presence we bring to prayer is the same kind of presence we can offer to others, if we choose. It is a skill that needs to be developed in much the same way as learning to pray or to play a new instrument. It takes training and practice.

To be present means to show up, pay attention, and to *bathe another in your full attention*. This means turning off your cell phone, closing the door and being with another person as if there were nothing more important than just that person. It means refraining from reacting, judging, advising, analyzing, fixing and problem-solving. What's left if you can't do all these things we ordinarily do?

We can come to the conversation with utter curiosity, wondering not so much about the literal facts of what another might be saying, but listening for the *deeper story* unfolding. Presence means coming to the conversation with humility, recognizing the privilege it is to be invited into the intimacies of another person's life, honoring the sacredness of life. It means coming to the conversation trusting that whatever struggles the other person might share, they also have the wisdom and resources within to discover the answers they need. It does not mean sitting beside them presuming that we know what is best and right for them. We have only to be present to help them discover from within what they need.

Being present to another takes patience, practice and discipline. Much like learning *sitting prayer*, wherein beginners might last ten minutes before becoming distracted and impatient, the same is true for beginners in learning to be present in conversations. Ten minutes is what most of us want to give another on any given topic, before we want to have our *airtime*, jump to another topic, check our smartphones or get back to work so we can get our *to-do* list done and over with.

Presence, bathing one another in your full attention, is a skill that can be learned and developed. When applied with discipline, it can transform our consciousness from the kind of surface awareness we have of ourselves and others to a deeper level. It calls forth our natural empathy and compassion for others once we hear the deeper story underneath the literalness with which we otherwise interpret, analyze and judge others. We see the other with new eyes.

2. Contemplative engagement

Every faith tradition has emphasized contemplation of some kind as a means for exploring mysteries both human and divine. It is as ancient as humanity itself. Contemporary expressions of this ancient practice give it new names. Some call it *contemplative engagement*, while others call it *contemplative listening*, or *contemplative dialogue*. And, when it is not done well, or the group is not well prepared, some call it "fluff."[323] When it is done well, it is a means to listen to the movement of the Spirit unfolding within individuals and the community gathered.

Every community I am privileged to visit engages in some form of shared prayer and reflection. What makes contemplative engagement different is that it deliberately weaves together the "I" and the "We" into a collective understanding. It is not simply a group of people in a room each praying aloud, or in contemplative silence, in a siloed or parallel fashion. Nor is it simply faith sharing wherein each person shares while others listen silently (i.e., without verbally responding). Rather, it is an effort to integrate personal contemplation with active listening and dialogue in order to unearth collective insights.

Principles of contemplative engagement

Every community is different in their approach to, and reasons for using, contemplative engagement. The practice of contemplative engagement must be tailored to a particular community and their specific goal. However, as an orientation to the process, I usually offer these general guidelines.

1. *Embrace deeply your truest self* and unbind one another from the reputations that otherwise keep you hidden. Instead, seek to know one another as ever-awakening, yearning to be understood for who you are becoming.

2. *Tend to the garden of* your once treasured relationships by weeding out sources of mistrust or confusion and engage in skilled conversations that seek compassionate understanding.

3. *Listen, as if for the first time*, and not for what you expect to hear, are afraid to hear, wish to hear, or think you've already heard a hundred times before.

4. *Prepare your heart* to listen for the grain of truth among those hard-to-hear differences or pearls disguised as resistance or disagreement.

5. *Become captivated* by the heart of the matter and by the deeper story that is unfolding before us, rather than on superficial distractions and unrefined comments.

6. *Discover the themes* underneath the soundbites, as well as the universal struggles that all of us share by virtue of being human.

7. *Surrender* your need for quick fixes or pain-free answers and relish the gift of revelation in these soul-searching conversations.

8. *Savor the silence* and resist the urge to fill it with empty words and reactive comments.

9. *Listen to your inter-connectedness* with one another as companions on a shared journey.

10. *Trust the wisdom of the community* to call forth and glean the fruits of the Spirit moving within and among everyone gathered.

3. Communal discernment

*"The reason two antelopes walk together is so that
one can blow the dust out of the other one's eyes."*
African Proverb

Discernment has been practiced in one form or another since humans first began pondering, "What would God say about this situation?" Prior to the 1970s there were few publications using the word *discernment*, however, it has always been the intention of religious to bring their lives more fully in alignment with *God's will*. Every faith tradition, ancient or modern day, has had its own means for listening more deeply to, and discerning, what might please God.

Within the Catholic tradition, St. Ignatius of Loyola is credited with formalizing a method of discernment he called the *Examen*. St. Ignatius (1491- 1556) was also the founder of the Society of Jesus (Jesuits). Since the development of Ignatius' Examen, the Jesuits have kept this practice alive and shared it widely among other religious and laity.

Discernment is an in-depth process of prayer and reflection aimed at making choices that would more closely reflect God's desires. In other words, it is an effort to align our will with God's, to see as God sees, and make our decisions accordingly. It requires us to sift, sort and distinguish what might be urgings from God versus urgings from our own egos. It is used as a means for making major life decisions born of wisdom and in the service of furthering God's mission.

Today, communal discernment is commonly used among religious, especially women religious, for electing new leadership and making other important community decisions. While there is no one methodology for communal discernment, most efforts draw upon the pillars of Ignatian discernment, namely *interior freedom* and *detachment from the outcome*. To be interiorly free means to rid ourselves as much as possible, or to hold more lightly, our fears, anxieties, wants and desires that might drive our decision, so that we can be more disposed to God's desires. Detachment from the outcome means to hold at bay our preoccupations or conclusions about a specific outcome and to stay focused on the here and now. Both of these efforts help us to listen to the movement of the Spirit and the truth that is actually emerging, rather than our predetermined, self-imposed ideas.

Communal discernment, when done well, can be among the most sacred experiences of a community rapt in God's loving presence. When it is not done well it, too, might be seen as "fluff." Communal discernment for many communities has, in practice, been little more than personal discernment done in parallel fashion. Each person in the community, in other words, may be engaged in personal discernment while together in the same room, so they call it communal discernment. Parallel personal discernment is not the same as communal discernment. This is much like Piaget's notion of *parallel play* wherein several children may be playing in the same sandbox, but they are each doing their own thing, not playing *together*.

Having accompanied many communities through processes of communal discernment, I can attest to the fact that the more communities practice it, the more adept they become at weaving together the interplay of *my will*, *our will* and *God's will*. The more they practice, the more they mature in their capacity to engage in communal discernment. Each effort is an opportunity to learn the skills and discipline required of communal discernment that go beyond parallel personal discernment.[324]

When communities become more able to engage in genuine communal discernment, their experience becomes increasingly transformative. Their consciousness shifts back and forth from "I" to "We" as the collective wisdom is braided together. If they can hold the tension of their diverse understandings, remain interiorly free and detached from the outcome, and not collapse into *group think*, then they can experience a kind of *group grace*. This group grace, the fruit of genuine communal discernment, brings forth a powerful personal and communal transformation of consciousness.

Thus, altered states of consciousness are temporary but can evolve into higher structures of consciousness using mindfulness exercises. We can learn to quiet the endless stream of egoic preoccupations (*monkey mind*). We can learn to transform and elevate the quality of our own consciousness. Mindfulness exercises, whether intrapersonal (e.g., prayer and meditation) or interpersonal (e.g., presence, communal discernment and contemplative engagement) all have the potential to bring about a transformation of consciousness. There is no guarantee, of course. But if these methods are practiced regularly by communities (not every few years at Chapter), then they can create the conditions for a transformation of consciousness to occur both personally and communally.

Reflection: Transformation of Consciousness

Recall your own experience in community:

1. *When have you experienced a personal or communal transformation of consciousness?*

2. *What is your experience of your community's ability, when gathered, to be genuinely present to one another, or to participate in authentic communal discernment or contemplative engagement?*

Writing New Narratives

A shift in perspective or transformation of consciousness enables us to see with new eyes. This, in turn, enables us to write new narratives for our lives and bring forth new life. We each have narratives, stories we have told ourselves about ourselves and our lives. We have stories about God, ourselves, and the meaning and purpose of our lives. These narratives are ones we have internalized from the stories our elders and others have told of us. These stories are but dim reflections of our true selves and the deeper story of our lives. Rewriting these false or outdated narratives into ones that more clearly reflect the inner truth of who we are *becoming* is integral to a transformation of consciousness: "For now we see only a reflection as in a mirror; then we shall see face to face. Now I know in part; then I shall know fully, even as I am fully known" (1 Corinthians 13:12).

In order for your community to birth a new way of being, you will need to search out fundamentally new ways of seeing your lives and writing new narratives for your future. These new narratives are ideally more authentic and aligned with who you are *becoming*, rather than who you have been in the past. A new, more fully aligned narrative, according to Tolle, brings acceptance, joy and new life.[325]

What do Jesus' *Sermon on the Mount*, Martin Luther King's *I Have a Dream* speech, and Kennedy's *Moonshot* speech all have in common? These were all paradigm-changing orations that inspired and transformed those who were ready to listen. These narratives opened the minds of people to believe in things they either could not previously imagine or have thought possible. They opened the hearts of people, infusing them with hope and excitement for a future toward which they previously felt numb, helpless or lost. They liberated people from a status quo anchored in place by the constraints of existing worldviews. They inspired people to act in ways that enabled dreams to become reality.

But even the most inspiring orators cannot craft *your* narrative. New narratives are not taught or given to us. Rather, they emerge through us. Others can inspire, plant seeds and offer alternatives, but you have to craft and claim your own narrative. Furthermore, your narrative will not turn on a dime and arrive in one "Ah-ha" moment. Even if you have an epiphany, or if someone suggests an alternative perspective on your life that deeply resonates, it will take time for you to assimilate its meaning and adjust to its possibilities. A new narrative requires a continual testing of its authenticity and resonance with the truth of your experience as a community.

Listening to the prophets, welcoming the stranger, reframing and changing patterns are all helpful methods and can open up the possibility of new narratives. It also helps to reverse this process and focus directly on the narratives as a means to help you shift your perspective and aid in the transformation of consciousness. Let me give you two exercises as a way to begin creating new narratives. These exercises are not intended to be one-and-done conversations in community, but ones that are built upon and continually woven into an emerging narrative by the community over time.

Example 1: Back to the future

An exercise I frequently use and have found helpful is one I call "Back To The Future." I invite members to engage in deep prayer and reflection with a spiritual companion (living or deceased). I ask them to imagine with them what the future of their community might be (five or ten years hence), based upon their deepest longings and the fruits of their prayer. They are then asked to write a letter to the community sharing the fruits of their prayer and reflection, looking back from the future. It is an exercise that not only taps their fears of mortality and hopes for their legacy, but their yearnings for new life and generative aspirations for the future. See Appendix C, *Back To the Future*, for an example of instructions that might be given.

The power of the exercise is not only in the depth of reflection that is asked of them, and what it evokes in them individually, but in the sharing of the letters and what happens to the community when this is done. The sharing is intimate, sacred and brings a community to a deeper level of awareness about what is at stake for them and how they might journey together. Conversations like these provide rich material to further the emergence of new narratives.

Example 2: Unfolding new narratives

When communities reflect deeply upon the stories they keep telling themselves, those that are no longer true and those that are emerging, it is an eye-opener. Sharing the threads they hope to preserve and what they see emerging on the horizon is key. For example, I often invite communities to reflect upon the narrative of their lives, using these questions:

1. What are the stories you still tell yourselves about your lives that no longer fit your emerging reality?

2. What are the threads or parts of your story that are still true and would be wise to preserve?

3. As you gaze upon the horizon with the eyesight of faith, what do you see unfolding that might be part of your new narrative?

Summary

Shifts in consciousness involves shifts in perspective, how we see and understand ourselves and our world. These shifts in perspective are akin to putting on a new lens or twisting the kaleidoscope. A more profound transformation of consciousness, though, is one that brings about new states and potentially new structures of consciousness. These can be cultivated by practicing mindfulness exercises such as presence, communal discernment and contemplative engagement.

A shift in perspective or transformation of consciousness enables us not only to see with new eyes and elevate our quality of consciousness, but liberates us to create new narratives for our lives, ones that liberate our true calling. When combined with the other four dynamic elements, these soul-shifting processes foster *a new way of being*. Such transformations involve your entire being, a soul-shift wherein you become more attuned to the flow of grace.

Answer to Nine-Dot exercise

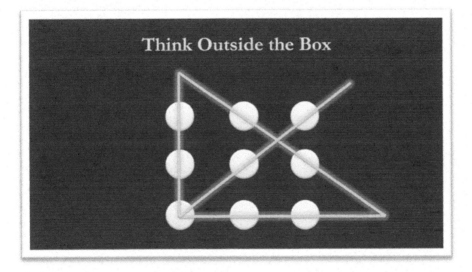

Figure 20: Nine Dots solution

Chapter 13: Reclaim Our Inner Voice

The seat and source of everything that lives

---

*"There's a thread you follow. It goes among
things that change. But it doesn't change.
People wonder about what you are pursuing.
You have to explain about the thread.
But it is hard for others to see.
While you hold it you can't get lost.
Tragedies happen; people get hurt
or die; and you suffer and get old.
Nothing you do can stop time's unfolding.
You don't ever let go of the thread."*[326]

The Way it Is, by William Stafford

Introduction

If we pretend to be something we are not, and violate our own soul, we will pay a terrible price. If communities make choices about the future disconnected from the seat and source of their life, from what is real and honest and what matters most, they will build a house of cards. There will be no transformation. For some communities, sadly, their inner voice has gone silent. For communal transformation to occur in your community, you will need to reclaim your inner voice both individually and collectively. If you can honor your soul in this way, you will honor the sanctity of life.

In his book, *Care of the Soul*, Thomas Moore tell us: "There is nothing neutral about the soul. It is the seat and the source of life. Either we respond to what the soul presents in its fantasies and desires, or we suffer from this neglect of ourselves."[327] What good is it to have planned well for the bricks and mortar of your lives, arranged your finances to be more fully funded for retirement, or to have solved your community's leadership crisis, only to have neglected the soul of your community? Is there a price you wouldn't pay to reclaim your inner voice and restore the soul of your community? Jesus' message is clear: Do the soulwork because nothing else matters.

Transformation is an inside-out, soul-to-surface movement. Reclaiming the inner voice of the community requires that communities create a space hospitable for its own soul to thrive. This is the work of rebuilding the kind of trust among members that allows for intimate exchanges about their longings, heartaches and vulnerabilities. Such intimacy requires that members remove the masks and armor that have been built up over the course of time. Creating this kind of soul-dwelling space is key to the inner work of transformation.

What is the soul, the inner voice of a community, and what is the soulwork communities must do in order to transform their lives? While there will always be much about the soul that is left to *mystery*, it is Mystery itself that beckons us to wonder and search for answers. In this chapter, we will first look at the individual soul and then at the soul of community. We will explore the challenge of living soulfully, the role of the ego and how easy it is for our inner voice to be silenced. We will then look at the soulwork you can do, both individually and as a community, to reclaim your inner voice.

The Unknowable, Unnamable, Unsayable Soul

"But the Unnamable was not in the wind. And after the wind, an earthquake; but the Unnamable was not in the earthquake. And after the earthquake, a fire; but the Unnamable was not in the fire. And after the fire, a still, small voice." 1 Kings 19:11-12

The unknowable soul

What do we know of this unknowable soul? As a child, I recall once asking my mother, "What is a soul?" Straining for an answer, and placing her hand over her heart, she replied, "It is inside you, like your heart, only it's invisible. It's where God talks to you." *Hmm*, I pondered. As I reflect on my mother's explanation, I'm not sure I could explain it any better to my own grandchildren. I'm still pondering this unknowable, mysterious soul.

If you have ever sat vigil with someone who is dying, you know when the person's soul is present and when the soul has left the body behind. A soul with a body is a person, a human being, breathing and alive. At the moment of death, you can sense, and almost see, the soul separating from the body. It is no longer a person. It is a *corpse*, lifeless, breathless and decaying. In that final moment, with our soul no longer tethered to form, it is trans*formed*, its energy freed.

The soul is the seat and source, the very essence and wellspring of everything that lives. And, according to Plato, it is immortal and imperishable. The soul is not so much a thing made of matter, not a physical organ, but an energy or lifeforce. Every living thing gives off some kind of vibrational energy, a lifeforce, unique unto itself. When a lifeform stops living, this immortal, imperishable energy is liberated from form.

You may not know of the soul in the same manner you know of tangible things, but you can know of its presence. You can feel the energy, the *vibes* that people give off, when you walk into a room. Sometimes you feel a warm, welcoming presence and other times it is something foreboding that makes your skin crawl. Like a tuning fork, we resonate with the energy of some and are repelled by others.

The unnamable soul

How have we named the unnamable? There are many names for the soul or inner voice: the Buddhist's *original nature*, the Quaker's *inner light*, or the Hasidic Jew's *spark of the divine*. Eckhart Tolle refers to it as the *non-egoic* self. St. Teresa of Ávila spoke of it as our *interior castle* and Thomas Merton as our *hidden wholeness*. Richard Rohr is fond of referring to the soul as our *true self*. Described in his book, *The Immortal Diamond*, the true self, says Rohr, is "the part of you who knows who you are and whose you are."[328] "It is that absolute reference point that is both utterly within you and utterly beyond you at the very same time."[329]

Ruth Haley Barton provides a more gritty description:

> "When I refer to the soul, I am not talking about some ill-defined amorphous, soft-around-the-edges sort of thing. I am talking about the part of you that is most real – the very essence of you that God knew before he brought you forth in physical form, the part that will exist after your body goes into the ground. This is the 'you' that exists beyond any role you play, any job you perform, any relationship that seems to define you, or any notoriety or success you may have achieved. It is the part of you that longs for more of God than you have right now, the part that may, even now, be aware of 'missing' God amid the challenges of life in ministry."[330]

One of the most beautiful descriptions of the soul is from Parker Palmer in his book, *A Hidden Wholeness*:

> "Like a wild animal, the soul is tough, resilient, resourceful, savvy, and self-sufficient. It knows how to survive in hard places…. Yet despite its toughness, the soul is also shy. Just like a wild animal, it seeks safety in the dense underbrush,

especially when other people are around. If we want to see a wild animal, we know that the last thing we should do is go crashing through the woods yelling for it to come out."[331]

The soul, or whatever name you give it, is the ground and wellspring of life within each of us that intersects with the source of all life throughout the universe.

The unsayable soul

What is your unsayable soul trying to say? Ralph Waldo Emerson once said, "Who you are speaks so loudly I can't hear what you're saying." What do people feel in your presence? Words may fail us when trying to describe exactly what it is, but we recognize our own inner voice when it speaks. We know what it wants and is trying to say to us. Once more, Parker Palmer describes it well:

- "The soul wants to keep us rooted in the ground of our own being, resisting the tendency of other faculties, like the intellect and ego, to uproot us from who we are;

- The soul wants to keep us connected to the community in which we find life, for it understands that relationships are necessary if we are to thrive;

- The soul wants to tell us the truth about ourselves, our world, and the relations between the two, whether that truth is easy or hard to hear;

- The soul wants to give us life and wants us to pass the gift along, to become life-givers in a world that deals with too much death."[332]

Palmer's words resonate for me greatly. We long to be *grounded* and able to live more fully out of our inner truth. We yearn to be in relationships that are *life-giving* and to give life in return. Although we play hide and seek with the truth, we know our own inner voice and long to hear its *deeper truths*. If we cultivate our inner life, we grow in familiarity with this inner voice. We get better at discriminating the voice that comes from our true self versus our false self. We know what it feels like when our soul is thriving and when it is kept from speaking.

We all have some intuitive understanding of what our soul wants. There is a certain kind of beauty, art or literature that speaks uniquely to each one of us. When our soul is roused, tears well up and words elude us. When we are awestruck by nature's beauty, a poem, music, or piece of art, goosebumps and all, the only words left are, "Wow!" or "Amazing!" We may not have words at all, but we know our soul has been stirred when we are made to tremble.

The labyrinth of our inner life is revealed to us in paradox and dreams. Our inner voice has a language all its own. Our soul resonates more through emotions, intuition and imagery, more than it does through intellect, reason or analysis. It awakens more through poetry than prose. It craves depth, beauty, truth and freedom. In our solitude, it tells of our deepest longings.

It also speaks to us in the ordinary, unspectacular flow of everyday life. It wants to be connected to the nitty-gritty of life and our world. David G. Benner describes it this way:

> "Soul thrives in reality but withers when we choose to live in places of illusion or denial. Soul calls us to be so grounded in the ordinary reality of our life that the meaning of our life can be found in these mundane events. Soul finds the extraordinary in the midst of the ordinary because soul is always tethered to life in the world."[333]

The unknowable, unnamable, unsayable soul is much as my mother described. It is where God talks to us, listens to our deepest longings and forever calls us home. It is the anchor that grounds us yet urges us ever on to new adventures. It has its own tranquility and contentment, yet is always searching for more – more depth, wisdom, connection, integrity, beauty and peace. It is playful, sublime and charged with passion. There is a rightness we recognize when we are centered within our soul and acting out of its urgings. It is a unifying force but ever-changing and flowing like a river or the wind. This still small voice has an energy many simply call Love, the seat and source of all life.

The Soul of Community

"You exist more truly where you love than where you merely live." Bonaventure

The Ancients believed that a soul exists in all manner of things, not just humans. A wolf, a flower, an insect, each has its own inner energy, as does a river, a mountain range or a valley. The Rocky Mountains in Colorado hold a different energy than the Green Mountains of Vermont. The Redwood forests in California feel different than the forests of New England. Every living thing has its own authentic, inimitable, essential nature. Echoes of this belief are heard in Teilhard de Chardin's *Divine Milieu*,[334] Brian Swimme's *Universe Story*,[335] and St. Francis', *Canticle of the Creatures*.

Communities have their own soul, too. You can recognize the difference when you walk into a community. Each has its own unique energy and vibration. Each has its own inner voice, some more audible than others. Those who have immersed themselves in understanding the nature of organizations speak of an organization's soul or spirit: Harrison Owen, for example, speaks of transforming the soul of organizations in his book, *Riding the Tiger*: "Every organization has a Spirit"[336] and its transformation requires breakthroughs that "reach the level of Soul."[337] Peter Senge, Peter Block and Otto Scharmer, and others who plumb the depths of organizations speak this language too.

Charism as a reflection of soul

The closest communities have come to describing their own inner voice has been when speaking of their *charism*. According to the Catholic Church, charisms are "graces" imparted by the Holy Spirit, entrusted to the "founders,"[338] and distributed among the faithful to "every rank."[339] The second Vatican Council urged communities to go back to their roots in order to reclaim these charisms in the hope of revitalizing Religious Life. Communities were urged to return to their founding documents and the original inspiration of their founders and foundresses.

Studying and writing were an important part of a community's efforts to reclaim their roots and renew their lives. For many, this was the first time they reflected upon their founder's original writings and the word *charism* became part of their vernacular.[340] It helped them identify their core theology, founding inspiration and unique heritage. It helped them, in other words, claim their identity. There was a new energy brought forth by the collective exercise of studying their history and crafting new documents.

Unfortunately, their efforts to describe this expression of their inner voice too often led them to focus on their deceased founders, rather than the collective inner voice of their living members ("every rank"). They turned to the history books, rather than toward one another to learn how to be soulfully present. It became a focus on writing "charism statements" for websites and brochures, rather than a focus on living community as an authentic, here-and-now expression of their living charism.

Furthermore, the charism statements of most communities are so general and vague that they are hardly distinguishable from one community to the next. A charism cannot be fixed in an abstract, verbal definition any more than a soul can. John Futrell addressed this saying, "To attempt to do so is to attempt to identify living, individual communities on the level of theoretical 'natures.'"[341] Anthony Gittins went further in his criticism, referring to charism as "a lazy and an irritating word, a catch-all term which hardly bears scrutiny."[342]

The Church was on the right track encouraging communities to restore a sense of identity and purpose in the hope of renewing their spirit. However, studying and writing about your charism can only take you so far. Communities have traditionally held their founder or foundress with great reverence. While a founder's charismatic inspiration is an important reference point, you cannot locate your charism in the history books. In order to locate and lift up the charism of your community, you will need to listen to and lift up the authentic inner voice of your members who are alive today, and hold this voice with the same measure of reverence as you have the words of your founders.

Care of the soul through care of community

A charism is but one expression of a community's soul. In *Care of the Soul,* Thomas Moore tells us, "When you look closely at the image of soulfulness, you see that it is tied to life in all its particulars – good food, satisfying conversation, genuine friends, and experiences that stay in the memory and touch the heart. Soul is revealed in attachment, love, and community, as well as in retreat on behalf of inner communing and intimacy."[343] The soul of a community is the energy flowing through, and emanating from, its physical and cultural existence, its land and all the particulars in the lives of its members.

The soul of your community is alive today to the degree that your members can express the intimate depths of their being in both their words and in the manner in which they live their lives. Francis Weller, in *The Wild Edge of Sorrow,* tells us, "A healthy village requires healthy individuals and to become a healthy individual, you need a healthy village."[344] To authenticate this inner voice means to bring this healthy soulfulness of individuals to the village, the community as a whole.

These kinds of genuine, healthy, loving and intimate exchanges are exactly what Jesus modeled for us. This is what Jesus wants from us: imitation, not admiration. Ronald Rolheiser brings it down to earth for communities, "In essence, Jesus is saying: You cannot deal with a perfect, all-loving, all-forgiving, all-understanding God in heaven, if you cannot deal with a less-than-perfect, less-than-forgiving, and less-than-understanding community here on earth."[345]

The Challenge of Living Soulfully

"To be nobody–but–yourself in a world which is doing its best, night and day, to make you everybody but yourself – means to fight the hardest battle which any human being can fight – and never stop fighting." E.E. Cummings

Are you winning or losing the battle to live more soulfully? For many, our ego is more in charge of our lives than our soul. The world we created for ourselves is doing its best to stifle our inner voice. Americans now spend over 8 ½ hours a day working and 11 hours per day listening, watching, reading and interacting on media. I don't know what is left for sleeping, to say nothing of our soul! The role of ego in navigating the material world seems to have usurped the soul's role in directing our lives.

The Dalai Lama captured the foolishness of our ego-driven lives: "Man sacrifices his health in order to make money. Then he sacrifices money to recuperate his health. And then he is so anxious about the future that he does not enjoy the present, the result being that he does not live in the present or the future; he lives as if he is never going to die, and then he dies having never really lived." It is a vicious cycle.

Thomas Merton warned of the same folly: "If I had a message to my contemporaries it is surely this: Be anything you like, be madmen, drunks, and bastards of every shape and form, but at all costs avoid one thing: success. If you are too obsessed with success, you will forget to live. If you have learned only to be a success, your life has probably been wasted."[346] Who is running this show, our ego in search of success or our soul in search of God?

Ego and soul: parts of a whole

"What good will it be for someone to gain the whole world, yet forfeit their soul? Or what can anyone give in exchange for their soul?" Matthew 16:26

One of the central challenges to living more soulfully lies in strengthening the partnership between our soul and ego. Many believe that the ego is an enemy of the soul, and that to live more soulfully, you must vanquish the ego. However, the ego is not the nemesis of the soul. The ego is integral to the soul's capacity to navigate our world. The task is not to destroy the ego, but to strengthen its capacity to cooperate and exist in harmony with the soul.

The ego is the navigator, but the soul is the pilot. The ego helps us know how to get from point A to point B, but the soul knows where to go and why (i.e., to live in union with God). Our soul exerts its longings and desires, but our ego has to find our way to these. Our soul wants adventure, passion, love, fulfillment of purpose, and to thrive in the flow of grace. The ego wants safety, security, familiarity, comfort, control, and to protect our survival. When these parts of our being are in sync, and aligned with one another toward the same end, we are at peace. When in perfect harmony, some might say we are in heaven. When at war with one another, some might call this hell.

Too often, the ego has gotten a bad rap. For example, Richard Rohr uses the terms ego and false self interchangeably. He sees the ego as "good and necessary as far as it goes…, bogus more than bad, and bogus only when it pretends to be more than it is." It is our "launching pad" into the world, but it has its "trappings" too. Once we are launched, and move beyond our false self or ego, says Rohr, there is "freedom and liberation."[347]

Yet the ego is not bogus or bad; it is simply different than the soul. Without an ego we would be defenseless and adrift. We would have no way for our soul to navigate the world. Psychologists will tell you that the critical functions of the ego are to help us organize a solid sense of identity, distinguish reality from fantasy, cope with life's challenges and enjoy life's pleasures. In fact, when psychologists are working with clients whose ego capacities are underdeveloped (e.g., those with personality disorders or psychoses), the task is to help strengthen their ego, foster a more solid sense of identity and improve their capacity to cope.

Jansenism, a theological movement in the 17th century, epitomized the split between the so-called depravity of the body and purity of the soul. By extension, there was a split between worldly things and spiritual things, the terrain of the ego and of the soul, respectively. Centuries later, some still see the ego as the nemesis of the soul. Today, many think of the ego as narcissistic and something to overcome or defeat.

We erroneously label people with a big ego as *narcissists*. We tend to think of politicians, for example, as narcissistic and all about their big egos. Narcissists do not have big egos. They have dysfunctional egos. Their egos are, in fact, poorly developed and weak. They like to see themselves as superior and special

("God's gift to mankind"). They exaggerate their achievements and talents and are in constant need of praise and recognition. They are arrogant and self-centered, monopolizing the stage and belittling others.

All of this grandiosity and bravado is a way to compensate for the narcissist's fragile and brittle ego. The slightest slight can puncture their veneer of self-importance and send them into a rage. Those with healthier egos can manage criticisms and setbacks, learn from mistakes, distinguish fact from fiction, treat others as equals and are capable of empathy. A healthy ego is a good thing, not a bad, bogus or narcissistic thing.

The ego's focus on external reality is not the problem, unless this focus upon the world becomes magnified. It then dims our awareness of our inner being and vies for control over our lives. We need our ego to function in the world and to make manifest our soul's desires. We need to harmonize these two, not eradicate one in favor of the other. The movement toward higher levels of consciousness requires that we *transcend* the ego, not destroy it, and thus allow for more spacious access to our innermost being. Our maturational task then is not to liberate ourselves from the ego, but to achieve balance, integration and harmony between the ego and the soul.

Madness of the soul

"What's madness but nobility of soul at odds with circumstance?" Theodore Roethke

Let's face it. After hitting enough potholes and the usual wear and tear in life, we can grow out of alignment with our true selves. We can drift from what we once cherished, what once gave us meaning and purpose, and begin to behave in ways that no longer reflect the soul of who we truly are. Out of a fear of rejection, we begin to conform to the expectations of others. Out of a fear of abandonment, we push others away to mitigate an anticipated blow. We don our masks and armor and hide out in our psychological foxholes. We pursue worldly things as a substitute for genuine happiness. As a result, we begin to lose ourselves and the people we profess to love.

It's a slippery slope. We have a hard time knowing if we are living out of truth, denial or rationalizations. Yet deep inside we know it; our hypocrisy and self-evasion eat away at our soul. With our soul no longer tethered to our worldly existence, we lose energy, interest, creativity and power. The joy in life eludes us and life becomes a chore. We stay in relationships that have long since died and work in settings that violate our values. When we have been told we aren't "good enough," "loveable enough," "smart enough," we start to believe it and go into hiding. When we move against the soul, disavow who we are or what and who we love, it is madness. It can happen to anyone.

When we have been wounded and unable to heal those wounds, we disown them. We take those parts of ourselves we think are the cause of our wounds, both our brokenness and our gifts, and we bury them beneath the floorboards of our consciousness. We project them onto others, rationalize them away, drown them out with work, numb them with all kinds of addictions and anesthetize our pain in a thousand other ways. We stay clear of the shadowlands of these discarded wounds and do the best we can to pretend all is well.

Sound familiar? Those who live in community are no exception. When members wear masks, and sacrifice authenticity for safety, the community itself loses its inner voice. It is madness.

Reflection: Your Personal and Communal Soul

The reasons and ways in which we have silenced our souls are unique to each one of us, but the story is timeless and universal.

1. *As an individual, in what ways is your life aligned with the soul of who you are, or have you drifted unknowingly from the life you were meant to live? Are you living a life that is safe and comfortable, or are you still risking in order to grow and become the person God is calling you to be?*

2. *As a community, in what ways is your communal life aligned with the soul of who you are, or have you drifted unknowingly from the life you were meant to live? Is your community living a life that is safe and comfortable,*

or is your community still risking in order to grow and become the community God is calling it to be?

Soulwork We Do Alone

"Deep within the heart there is a primal pain of longing, the cry of the soul separated from its source. The pain comes from the memory of when we were together with God. This process allows us special moments in our life when we can taste of this union, a taste of the divine remembrance." Judy Schroeder

Reclaiming our inner voice, or soul, is key to the soulwork of transformation. It is the work of redemption and returning home to our true self. It is an effort to reclaim our silenced souls by freeing ourselves from the illusions of control and the hubris of "I-alone" am in charge. It is about taking off the masks and listening for that still small voice beyond the cacophony of worldly distractions. It means taking ourselves off the anesthesia and allowing ourselves to return to our treasured hidden wholeness.

All spiritual traditions tell us there is a self that has to be found and one that has to be renounced in some way: "For whoever wants to save their life will lose it, but whoever loses their life for me and for the gospel will save it" (Mark 8:35). Parts of our self must die if we are to claim that "treasure in the field" (Matthew. 12:44) or capture that "pearl of great price" (Matthew 13:46). But how? What do we mean by coming home to our true self and reclaiming our inner voice?

An Heroic journey

"We have only to follow the thread of the hero path. Where we had thought to find an abomination, we shall find a god; where we had thought to slay another, we

shall slay ourselves; where we had thought to travel outwards, we shall come to the center of our own existence; where we had thought to be alone, we shall be with all the world." Joseph Campbell

Joseph Campbell spent a lifetime examining the universal themes of transformation across different cultures throughout history and detailed these in his classic book, *The Hero with a Thousand Faces*.[348] While there is no surefire method for reclaiming our inner voice, his studies revealed patterns that are helpful for understanding the nature of this soulwork. What Campbell found common to all transformative experiences was the same heroic drama involving these ten universal steps.

Step 1: The world as we know it. Before a would-be hero can enter the special world, he or she must first live in the ordinary world. The ordinary world is the community and culture in which the hero now lives.

Step 2: The call to adventure. The adventure often begins with a blunder resulting from suppressed desires and conflicts. The misstep is a gateway from the known world to a new world. The hero is ultimately forced to make a critical decision at this crossroads: respond courageously to the summons to choose life and embark on an adventure, or respond in fear and remain in the ordinary world with its illusion of security and certain death.

Step 3: Cross the first threshold. This is the point of no return when the hero lets go of the trapeze and takes that leap of faith. There is no turning back. Crossing the first threshold is a breakthrough, however it is only the first of many hurdles.

Step 4: Trials, friends and foes. Along the journey the hero encounters many obstacles. Some people may try to stop the hero, saying, "You're crazy" or "unrealistic." The naysayers are often well-meaning friends or family, nonetheless they hinder the hero's development. The hero's ability to identify those who would thwart him or her, and align more fully with supporters, is key to success.

Step 5: Wise sage. Generally, at an early stage in the adventure, the hero is graced by the presence of a wise sage who guides the hero. Sometimes cloaked in mystery, hidden in a secret disguise or language, the mentor appears when the hero is ready.

Step 6: Dragon's lair. Entering a villain's castle or evil mansion, this second decision usually puts the hero in significant physical, spiritual and psychological peril. Within the walls of the innermost cave though, lies the treasure of the special world where the hero pursues his or her objective.

Step 7: Moment of despair. As obstacles confront the hero the future begins to look grim. In these moments of despair the hero must access hidden parts of himself or herself. The hero must dig deep for one more scrap of energy, strength, creativity or faith to find a way out of the belly of the whale, calling upon inner powers previously unknown.

Step 8: Ultimate treasure. Having slain the dragon the hero accomplishes the mission and receives the treasure. Whether the reward is monetary, physical, romantic or spiritual, the hero is transformed. The prize, however, is secondary to the hero's transformation and greater satisfaction in serving others.

Step 9: Homecoming. Now the hero must return to the ordinary world with the sacred elixir (newfound wisdom and power). Challenges still lie ahead in the form of villains, roadblocks and inner demons. The hero must deal with whatever issues were left unresolved. However, the newfound insights help the hero identify weaknesses that will have to be addressed along the way.

Step 10: Rebirth. Before returning home there's often one more unforeseen ordeal. It provides one last test to solidify the growth of the hero. Returning with the treasure, the hero's experience of reality is different. The hero has evolved and is now capable of handling even greater challenges.

Campbell ominously warns that a "refusal of the summons," a refusal to let go of the present system, results in boredom, drudgery, a perpetuation of problems and a loss of power. The individual becomes a "victim to be saved." The once flowering world becomes a "wasteland of dry stones and his life feels meaningless." Whatever house the hero builds becomes a "house of death." The victim seeks to "perfume, whitewash and reinterpret" reality and his or her own darkness and ends up projecting these struggles onto others.[349]

The journey, or its refusal, is the same for communities. There is a call to leave the known and familiar world. A crossroads decision must be faced to either remain as is, die a sure death or journey on to an uncertain adventure. There is resistance from friends and foes alike. There is an emergence of new mentors. There are obstacles to face requiring communities to dig deep and discover a courage, creativity and faith they never knew. Therein lies the hidden treasure, though secondary to the journey itself. With newfound power and wisdom, a heroic community evolves to serve the world with even more daunting challenges. For communities refusing the summons, Campbell's warnings are indeed ominous– a wasteland of dry stones.

The net effect of a successful transformative journey according to Campbell "is the unlocking and release again of the flow of life into the body of the world" represented "spiritually as a manifestation of grace."[350] The energy of a transformed community, in other words, is released again to flow into the world. The destination for communities is the same as it is for individuals: to align the community more fully in union with the flow of Grace, the spirit of Love, the eternal Truth, to be in union with the Divine.

Soulwork We Do Together

"The shell must be cracked apart if what is in it is to come out, for if you want the kernel you must break the shell. And therefore, if you want to discover nature's nakedness, you must destroy its symbols, and the farther you get in

> *the nearer you come to its essence. When you come to the One that gathers all things up into itself, there our soul must stay." Meister Eckhart*

Alignment of life at all levels

Communities silence their inner voice in much the same way that we do as individuals and for many of the same reasons – unhealed wounds and too many worldly distractions. It may be madness, but it is not a mystery or out of the ordinary. Many members do not feel safe enough to be open, honest and vulnerable, especially in *public* (e.g., community gatherings). They refrain from sharing more intimately for fear of being judged and hurt. They put on their social personas and reserve sharing more candidly for *private* spaces, such as with close friends or in spiritual direction or counseling.

With their inner voice on mute, a community's plans for the future are built upon safe conversations, not upon what they passionately believe. Their future is built as a house of cards, not on a foundation of their souls' deepest longings and wisdom. The Journey of Transformation is one that seeks to reclaim and realign the inner voices of individual members with the community as a whole. It seeks to realign the life of community at all levels: Soul with mission, mission with vision, and vision with the gifts of its members responding to the needs of today.

Individual and communal soulwork

The soul of a community is alive today to the degree that its members are living authentic, communal lives rooted in God and offering their unique gifts in serving the world. In order for communities to transform and become new again they need to reclaim and re-authenticate their inner voice, not in written statements but by how they communicate, live their lives and carry out their mission. If your community's desire is to come home to your true selves, you will need to engage in personal and communal soulwork.

The more individuals are engaged in this soulwork, the better the odds of communal transformation. Many members go to spiritual direction or counseling to aid in this work. While this individual soulwork is important, if the community is not also engaged in this work collectively, there will be no communal transformation. You could have every member of a community go off to spiritual direction and still the community would not be transformed. The community is a lifeform unto itself with its own norms, patterns, structures and soul. No matter how enlightened the individuals who comprise a community may be, the community itself requires its own soulwork to change the cultural norms to touch and transform its soul.

Creating a Space Hospitable to the Soul

"Afraid that our inner light will be extinguished or our inner darkness exposed, we hide our true identities from each other. In the process, we become separated from our own souls. We end up living divided lives, so far removed from the truth we hold within that we cannot know the 'integrity that comes from being what you are.'"
Parker Palmer

Reclaiming the inner voice of community requires that communities create a space wherein members can relate in ways that are more real, honest and loving. It is an effort to create a space in which your members grow in trusting one another enough to share honestly and vulnerably. The soulwork of community involves creating a space hospitable for the soul to emerge. While there are many ways to approach this work, I have found these four guiding principles particularly helpful: 1) build a strong container; 2) restore and tend to the trust; 3) encourage mature surrender; and 4) come home to one another.

1. Build a strong container

*"Your sacred space is where you can find yourself over
and over again." Joseph Campbell*

Communities need to build a strong container, a type of holding environment, that sustains them throughout the challenging soulwork. Without this, they can easily fragment and fall apart. They need a space that allows their inner voice to emerge. Such a container consists of three things:

1. a framework that provides a common understanding and language as to the compelling reasons *why* members are engaged in these efforts, *what* they hope to accomplish, and *how* they will go about it;

2. a green space wherein people commit to engaging more intimately so as to risk, grow and learn together as a community; and,

3. a sacred space where the soul feels safe enough to share, listen, and cooperate with the Spirit moving within and among the group in real time.

A strong container is a space free from judgement, harshness or the arrogance of absolutes. It is a space that emphasizes personal presence, positive regard, truthfulness, deep listening and understanding. No fixing, advising, or rescuing is allowed. It is a place where the urges to fight or flee, evade or invade, persuade or dissuade, are held in check. Building a strong container ideally creates a soul-honoring *sacred space* that fosters growth, intimacy and the possibility of transformation.

Creating a strong container ensures that a community can withstand the chaos that is required of transformation, including the unnerving ambiguity of where the Spirit might lead. In this space, risks and mistakes are seen as necessary for learning. Conflicts and resistance are valued as necessary creative tensions. Creativity is understood as an acceptable challenge to tradition. Vulnerability is required for being honest and real. And breakdowns and breakthroughs, dying and letting go, are understood as the doorway to new life.

The very process of creating this kind of space is itself transformative because it challenges the existing norms that have kept communities masked and armored. Each community is unique in its normative patterns for interacting at local community gatherings, committee meetings and assemblies. Table 5, lists twelve of the more common normative patterns I see across communities that serve to silence the soul of a community.

Norms that Silence Our Communal Soul	
1. Talking about one another, instead of with one another.	7. Judging, "shoulding" the group, instead of claiming passions as personal.
2. Having the meeting outside of the meeting, instead of in the meeting.	8. Experiencing conflict and tension, but not addressing and resolving it.
3. Sharing thoughts and ideas, but not feelings;	
4. Having enmeshed or ridged boundaries regarding who is involved and what is shared, instead of clear and permeable boundaries that promote mutuality.	9. Speaking for anonymous "others," instead of speaking for oneself.
	10. Keeping the elephants silently on the sidelines, instead of out in open and dealt with directly.
5. Allowing members to be spectators who expect never to be "put on the spot," instead of participants who expect to speak openly.	11. Sharing a series of opinions, monologues, and pontifications, instead of engaging in mutual dialogue.
6. "Naming" struggles, but not working them through.	12. Focusing only on tasks and getting things done, instead of focusing on both the agenda and the relationships among those participating.

Table 5: Norms that silence our communal soul

These kinds of norms reinforce an environment where tasks might get done but there is no container for the soulwork. Wounds go unattended, intuition, imagination and emotions are treated as second class citizens, intimate conversations are avoided, and the inner voice of the community remains on mute. Members need a clear and effective way to work with both the tasks they need to accomplish and the relationships that need tending. If they do one without the other, both the tasks and the relationships will suffer. Most groups work hard to get the tasks done and avoid the interpersonal dynamics. However, without tending to these dynamics, and creating a space that invites it, members feel too unsafe to share their vulnerability, express their feelings, address any tensions or speak from any depth.

How do you build a strong container? There is no formula, but here are four elements that consistently help to create a soul-honoring space: a) put a premium on presence; b) invite all voices; c) encourage depth; and, d) train a pool of facilitators.

A. Put a premium on presence.

"When we sit with a dying person," says Parker Palmer, "we understand that what is before us in not a problem to be solved but a mystery to be honored."[351] Think of the people who helped you grow, those with whom you felt comfortable in sharing your vulnerability. Likely these were people who offered their *presence* with no agenda other than to listen to what your soul had to say. During your community gatherings accompany one another not with judgement, but with curiosity, compassion and hopeful expectancy. Safeguard and encourage the freedom to speak, listen, and understand the truth. Touch into what brings you joy as well as suffering. Encourage risks and learn from your mistakes. Bear witness to each other's journey by being present in these ways.

B. Invite all voices

Members do not want to be fans of leadership or spectators at community gatherings. They want to be participants and partners. A simple and helpful logistic is to make sure every table at community gatherings has its own microphone. It is easier and less intimidating for an individual to grab a microphone from his or her own table, than it is to walk up to a microphone and speak before the community. The easy access helps the more reserved members have their voice and it helps to promote dialogue between members in the open forum. Having just one or two microphones in a room only encourages the usual suspects to line up and wait for their *airtime* to opine, rather than dialogue directly with others. Other technologies are available to invite all voices among those who cannot be physically present (e.g., videoconference).

C. Encourage depth

Following prayer, before jumping into the agenda, start with a *check-in* that asks each person to speak to how they are coming to the meeting. This sets the expectation that everyone speaks and sets the tone for personal sharing. During the meeting give ample time for in-depth personal reflection and sharing at tables, breakout groups and in the assembly as a whole. Invite members to talk with (not about) one another and encourage them to express their feelings (not just their thoughts). End a meeting with a *check-out* that invites everyone to speak again regarding how they are leaving their time (e.g., how they feel about how they participated or what might have been an important learning).

D. Train a pool of facilitators

I typically ask communities to put together a pool of facilitators who can become an ongoing resource for the community. I offer training to bolster their skills and help them function as table facilitators in large assemblies and committee meetings. They also can then facilitate local community meetings or dyads who might want their help. I typically brief and debrief with table facilitators before and after each large assembly. We share our learnings, trouble-shoot any difficulties and call upon one another to improve our skills.

The types of skills I help facilitators develop address both *tasks* and *relationships* aimed at promoting a space hospitable for the soul. Examples of these are outlined on Table 6, Facilitating a Space Hospitable for the Soul.

Facilitating a Space Hospitable for the Soul	
Tend to the Tasks	**Tend to the Relationships**
1. Provide the context	1. Help build safety, trust and hope
2. State the goals	2. Foster a sense of being-in-it-together
3. Explain the process	
4. Share responsibilities (e.g., scribe)	3. Encourage balanced participation
5. Check for clarity and clarify as needed	4. Invite, engage & explore emotions
	5. Invite, engage & explore resistance
6. Focus upon the task at hand	6. Invite, engage & explore tensions
7. Use active listening (e.g., paraphrase)	7. Reframe judgments and loaded words
8. Search for the "new" (e.g., surprises)	8. Affirm and challenge each participant
9. Intervene when group is stuck	9. Seek and offer understanding
10. Manage your time and direct the process	10. Share power with the group
	11. Admit mistakes and work with them
11. Summarize the outcomes	
12. Bring closure	12. Offer observations and reflections on the group

Table 6: Facilitating a space hospitable to the soul

2. Restore and tend to the trust

"We can't change the human experience, but we can turn toward, not away from, those struggling."
Margaret Wheatley

Communities shy away from having more intimate conversations for good reason. Members have long histories of living together and have accumulated a great deal of *baggage*. Wounds that have been left unhealed for years, sometimes decades, have left many members unwilling to risk again. Along the way, members have been judged, labeled, dismissed, put down or betrayed by other members. As a result, members learn to avoid the risk of putting their honest truth into conversations at community gatherings. They come guarded, feeling too unsafe to trust one another with what they believe deep down inside for fear it will be judged unacceptable.

Those who dare to speak more honestly and openly in these low-trust settings are often those who have grown a "thicker skin." They try to steel themselves against any anticipated criticisms in the name of truth-telling or some other virtue. However, can you imagine Jesus saying to his disciples, "You just need a thicker skin!" The answer to feeling unsafe can't be more armor. Souls will not flourish by growing thicker skin. We speak and listen from the core of our being when we feel safe enough to let down our guard and choose willingly to open up. The challenge is to restore the trust and build the safety.

When I am with communities exploring their difficulties with one another, after a painful experience has been named, I often hear the plea, "We just need to trust one another!" as if that will resolve it. However, this plea, while well-intentioned, will do absolutely nothing to restore trust. First of all, trust is never fixed or permanently established. Like the stock market, it goes up and down. It goes up if we feel safe, understood and cared about by others. And it goes down when we have a misunderstanding, been hurt, or when conflicts arise that are left unresolved. The vicissitudes are normal, so pleas for trust never to plummet are futile.

Second, trust ought to be thought of as more a verb than a noun. Trust is something we actively and continually work at building or restoring, not something we somehow possess just because we like someone and want to gift them with our trust. *Trust-tending* is an ordinary and ongoing maintenance chore in any relationship. Just as caring for our home requires constant upkeep, time and attention, so too does caring for one another. Trust-tending is never finished or fixed once and for all.

It won't do any good to plea, "We just need to trust one another." That is like saying, "We just need to weed the garden!" Well, how do you suppose that will happen? We have to go and weed the garden and we have to do it together. We do this by turning toward one another in our mistrust, in the pain of our separateness, in our fear of making things worse, or hurting one another. We can't promise to always trust one another, but we can promise that when our trust is in jeopardy, we will *turn toward one another* and do the work of restoring it.

Turn toward one another

What does the behavior of restoring trust look like? Members need to re-engage one another and risk again, even with all their fears. It is often said that fear is contagious, but courage is as contagious as fear. If one person takes a risk, others are more likely to do the same. Restoring trust when trust has been broken means risking the possibility of being hurt again. The risk needs to be taken but in a new way. Here are some specific examples of ways to restore trust:

1. Those involved need to turn toward one another in their vulnerability and address the waning trust, rather than avoid the tension or wait the other out.

2. It helps if the one starting the conversation acknowledges his or her fears for taking the risk. Sharing your vulnerability will encourage others to share theirs.

3. Mutually share the perception of what happened that led to the hurt, anger, shame, guilt or other feelings related to the broken trust.

4. Describe the experiences without using labels or casting judgment.

5. Speak only for yourself and avoid piling on by dragging others into the conversation (e.g., "Other people think so too").

6. Each person needs to take ownership for his or her contributions to the difficulty and invite the other person to do the same.

7. Move beyond the misunderstanding by searching for new understandings through mutual exploration.

8. Stay in the struggle and do not abort the exploration by moving too quickly to say, "I'm sorry" or start problem-solving, which only serves to shut down conversations.

9. Offer an olive branch (e.g., an admission of regret or a way to bridge a new way forward) and acknowledge it when others offer you an olive branch.

10. Make new agreements to restore the trust and revisit the conversation in a few days or weeks later to determine how well these are working.

These are only examples of ways to dialogue that can help restore trust. In reality, it is always scary and unpleasant. However, these are the kinds of steps it takes to restore the trust between people. For communities to reclaim their inner voice, to create a space hospitable to the soul, they will need to restore and tend to the trust in an ongoing way.

3. Engage in mature surrender

"And even in our sleep pain that cannot forget falls drop by drop upon the heart, and in our own despair, against our will, comes wisdom to us by the awful grace of God." Aeschylus

Viktor Frankl once said, "Everything can be taken from man but one thing: the last of the human freedoms – to choose one's attitude in any given set of circumstances, to choose one's own way."[352] In order to choose your own way, I have urged communities to: make a free choice to let go of things for reasons that you value (do not capitulate in resentment or despair); listen to what life is asking of you (not what you are asking of life); search for meaning in ministry, beauty, and especially suffering; and live purposefully in the present with a hopeful expectancy toward the future.[353]

The soul of communities these days is filled with grief from the unrelenting loss of treasured people and places. Absent any meaning these losses hold only despair. For what good reason are you letting go of all your treasured people and places? Surely, all of this letting go cannot be just about "aging and diminishment" and a continual "downsizing" unto death. What, through all of the letting go, might be the *deeper invitation* and possibilities for *new life*? When the pain of letting go has meaning and purpose, it can become a more mature surrender, not a mere resignation by victims of circumstances.

The aching soul of communities needs to be heard, embraced and treated with compassion. Your letting go needs to have meaning beyond the numbing narrative of "death" and "diminishment," beyond emptiness and despair. In order to achieve what I call a "mature surrender," communities need to grieve together and make meaning of the suffering they must endure.

Mature surrender is an act of *sacrificial love* – a purposeful, proactive and generative choice to surrender what exists in the present in order to make way for something new in the future, not a capitulation in despair. It takes a certain maturity to reckon with an ending we prefer not to face and accept knowing it is necessary for a new beginning to emerge. Mature surrender is a *generative* choice, a choice that favors a life larger than the one we've known for the sake of future generations. It is an act of sacrificial love, no strings attached, a gift freely given to others and a future not our own.

Mature surrender requires that we do the soulwork of grieving our losses. We need to go through the *process* of letting go, of expressing the ache, so that grace can open a path for a new way. Each person's process or manner of grieving is different and needs to be respected. And for a community, there must be a way to grieve *together*. The soul of a community emerges when this collective grieving occurs.

There is an alarming statistic that I heard many years ago about couples who divorce. Ninety percent of couples that had a spouse who had lost a parent, or together they had lost a child, divorced within one year of the loss. The primary reason for the high divorce rate is because they did not grieve *together*. They grieved separately. As a result, their grief became an emotional wedge, rather than a bridge for deeper understanding. The couples fragmented and fell apart, instead of growing closer.

The same risk is true for communities. If you do not grieve together, you will grieve separately and risk fragmenting and growing apart. The losses are enormous and unrelenting. Each member must find his or her own way of grieving, but there must also be opportunities for members to grieve together.

Workshops and rituals are not enough

Beyond funeral services, many communities have offered workshops on grief and engaged in grieving rituals. Workshops are helpful in understanding the experience. And rituals help groups move through their grieving when words are not enough. However, these have their limits too. Grief does not fit neatly into a timetable for scheduled workshops and rituals. Grieving is ongoing, and everyone's timing and manner of grieving is different.

Elizabeth Kübler Ross popularized the notion that grieving is a process that occurs in stages: denial, anger, bargaining, depression, and acceptance. Individual grief experiences, however, are never this linear or definitively sequenced. Communities, even more so, are an amalgam of all of these stages having different members experiencing different aspects of grief at any point in time. Workshops and rituals are not enough.

Communities need to offer continuous and ongoing opportunities for grief-work. It is important to seize opportunities as they arise, for example, at local community meetings, during committee or board meetings, while sharing a meal, or during an assembly or Chapter. This does not necessarily mean tossing aside a planned agenda. It merely means incorporating this *emergent* grief-work into the planned agenda to the degree that it is possible.

Grieving is a process, not an event. It emerges often when we least expect or wish it to, not when we schedule it. Something we read, a comment, look or touch of another person may spark it. Our dreams might evoke it. It might come in the form of anger or apathy, wrenching sadness, a fond remembrance, guilt or unspeakable shame. The point here is to seize the opportunities when they occur to walk more deeply and gently with one another. Be on the lookout for the grief that might be underneath the surface conversations and invite one another to share what is in their aching soul.

4. Come home to one another

"In everyone's heart stirs a great homesickness."
Seymour Siegel

John O'Donohue once said: "The awakening of the human spirit is a home-coming. Yet ironically our sense of familiarity often militates against our homecoming."[354] Members might think they know one another because they have lived together for years. Like a couple who has been married for years, members start finishing each other's sentences, believing they know one another. Yet there is so much more to the story, if we are willing to listen. Come home to one another and listen for the inner voice that yearns for understanding.

When I return to my birthplace, a small town in Connecticut, I know it as home by the hue of the sunlight against the trees, the grass that carpets the land, and the stone walls and streams that carve its labyrinth. I hear the crow's soulful echo during the day and the peepers' chorus at night. I can still drive the winding roads and walk through the woods from memories etched in my soul from over 50 years ago. As I approach a familiar beach and the salt air wafts its familiar fragrance, I can almost taste it. I know I am *home*.

Thomas Wolfe famously said, "You can't go home again," which is true if this means returning to the home of our past. While we cannot go back, our soul still yearns for a place where we know we *belong*, a place where we are *at home* in our own skin. I can recognize the land of my childhood home by what I see, hear and smell, but my soul remembers home as more than a geographical location, more than a waypoint on Google Maps.

I have lived in fifteen geographical locations during my lifetime, but only a few of these became *home* for me. There have been only a few places wherein I felt like I belonged and was comfortable in my own skin. These are places I felt free enough to grow, to fumble and stretch into a new way of being without a fear of looking foolish or being judged a failure. These are places where I thrived in *becoming* more fully who I was meant to be at the time. These are places I hated to leave for fear I would never find another. These are places I found with other people who accepted me for the person I was.

In order to reclaim your inner voice, members need to come home to one another. Reflecting together on what would help you feel more at home is a helpful exercise. Think about your entire life in community. Recall a time when you experienced your greatest sense of home or belonging. Recall with whom you lived or ministered and the ways in which you found yourself growing. Remember how you experienced each place and where your felt at home. As you reflect about your experiences of belonging and feeling at home, what contributed to these?

I find this kind of reflection and sharing among community members very poignant. I know you did not join community because of the members as much as the mission. However, I also find that members, like every human being, yearn for a place of home and belonging. Just above Maslow's needs of basic safety, food and shelter is a universal need of belonging, to know you are cared about and feel at home. Thomas Moore tells us that community is a group of people "held together by feelings of belonging."[355] Peter Block goes further saying, "Community exists for the sake of belonging."[356] Community's emphasis on mission needs a counterweight, a renewed emphasis on community as a place of home and belonging, a place to be nourished for mission.

Reflection: Reclaiming Your Inner Voice

Reflect upon the ways in which you might reclaim the inner voice of your community (e.g., build a strong container, restore and tend to the trust, turn toward one another and engage in mature surrender).

1.   What might it be like for your community to engage in these kinds of efforts?

Summary

The unknowable, unnamable, unsayable soul of community needs to be reclaimed if communities wish to transform their lives and birth possibilities for new life. The call to reclaim your soul involves both peril and promise. To avoid the call conjures up ominous consequences. To respond courageously to the call and transform your lives is nothing less than an heroic journey. Build a strong container, tend to the trust among members, engage in mature surrender and come home to one another. These measures will help you reclaim your community's inner voice.

Chapter 14: Reconciliation and Conversion

The womb of our becoming

"A new heart I will give you, and a new spirit I will put within you; and I will remove from your body the heart of stone and give you a heart of flesh."
Ezekiel 36:26

Living in a World of Hurt

"There is a world of hurt out there and to heal the past requires apologies, reconciliation, reparation and forgiveness.... By receiving sorrow, hearing admissions, allowing reparation, and participating in reconciliation, people and tribes whose ancestors were abused give new life to all of us. We are the transgressors and the forgivers."
Paul Hawken

We are living in a world of hurt. Pick any day to glance at the headlines in the news and you will immediately be reminded of our political vitriol and the violence that flows from it. What are the mindsets undergirding this violence? Hegemony (domination by authority or "Might makes right"), solipsism (egocentric individualism or "I alone matter"), and jingoism (bellicose nationalism or "The hell with you") are among the most pernicious. These are the mindsets embedded in the leaders who run a large percentage of our governmental institutions and the followers who put them there.

The world spends over a trillion dollars each year on weapons of death, while a billion people are chronically malnourished. There are over 50,000 nuclear weapons across six nations. Estimates of the number of people killed through armed conflict world-wide throughout recorded history are as high as one billion. According to Chris Hedges, in the last 3,400 years, our world has been at peace (i.e., fewer than 1,000 deaths from armed conflict annually) only 268 years or 8% of the time.[357] The United States has been at peace for only 18 years since 1776, or 7.5% of the time. In other words, if you pick any day in our history, you would have over a 90% chance of finding the United States in a military battle somewhere in the world. Perhaps that is why much of the world sees the United States as the number one threat to world peace.

Regarding global violence, in 2017 Nicholas Kristof declared that it was the "very best year in the long history of humanity"[358]. Apparently, in the long arc of history we are more enlightened and less warring than in past centuries. However, if we are to continue this evolutionary path toward enlightenment and away from violence, then we must learn how to resolve our conflicts nonviolently and alleviate the suffering we experience in our lives. In order to evolve, we must learn to reach across our differences in age, gender, sexual orientation, race, ethnicity, politics and culture. We need to be able to hold the tension in the differences we encounter if we are ever to harness the richness of our diversity. "The choice is no longer between violence and nonviolence," said Martin Luther King Jr. the night before he was assassinated, "it is between nonviolence or nonexistence."[359]

Our future rests on our ability to harness the generative potential that exists with our differences and the tensions they produce. We need to learn more than what NOT to do when we are in tension or conflict. We need to know what to do: to make wise *choices*; work with our better *intentions;* and apply the *skills* and *discipline* needed to address conflicts constructively. And when we stumble and fail and wound one another, which is inevitable, we need to know how to heal our wounds, reconcile our brokenness and become whole again.

We know that wounded people wound other people, *if* they have not done the soulwork to address their own wounds. To the degree that individuals do this inner work, they unburden the community in which they live from the pain they would otherwise inflict upon them. Without doing their soulwork, they are more likely to judge, shame and blame others for those parts of themselves they have suppressed and projected onto others. They are likely to disown and act out the pain from their unredeemed wounds and fail to recognize their own contributions to the interpersonal struggles within their own community.

The work of reconciliation and conversion is the crucible of transformation. When we reconcile with others, when we heal our own brokenness, our lives are transformed. When we do this in community, we transform community. The world cries out for communities that can show us how to reach across our differences, resolve conflicts, offer and receive forgiveness, and help us transform a world of hurt into a world where peace and love can flourish. Our hearts of stone can be made of flesh again, but not without a great deal of courage, discipline and skill to face the painful tensions, conflicts and chaos of transformation. This Chapter will address reasons why reconciliation and conversion need to be done as an entire community and provide examples of how to approach it.

The Womb of Our Becoming

"Growth is the boundary between the darkness of unknowing and the light of new wisdom, new insight, new vision of who and what we ourselves have become."
Joan Chittister

Who we are today always holds the tension between who we have been and who we are growing to become. For those on a faith journey, this tension invites us to enter the privileged place of reconciliation and conversion, setting before us choices for life anew. This is where we are invited to reckon with our hidden payoffs for denying our own goodness. This is where we can ask ourselves questions, like, "What does grace enable me to be?" and "What on earth is holding me back from claiming this?" This is where our loyalties to the way things have always been come face-to-face with our fidelity to truths we are growing to embrace and current realities that insist upon new wineskins. This is where our growing edges encroach upon the status quo of relationships, causing us to look anew at what we have hidden from one another and kept from the people we love. *This is the womb of our becoming.*

Transformation all boils down to this: for new life to emerge, you must grow in your capacity to reconcile the wounds of the past, reach across your differences, and work through the conflicts and tensions that are part and parcel of transformation. Communal transformation is painful, conflict-laden work. There is no way around it. Patricia Wittberg suggests that refounding, for instance, is always "fraught with schism and controversy."[360] The irony here may be that a community that is not in sufficient pain already will not choose to engage in this painful work of transformation. Pain, unfortunately, is the catalyst and impetus that pushes communities to take a good hard look at themselves and search for what needs to change. Without it, they are not sufficiently motivated.

Reconciliation and conversion are undoubtably the most challenging of all the transformative elements, just as they are the most redemptive. This work is not only the most anguishing, it is the one we are least equipped to do. Most of us are terribly conflict avoidant and have never learned effective ways to work with tension, resolve conflicts and heal our wounds. Thus, communities suffer from the cumulative effects of unhealed wounds and unresolved conflicts. Though individuals might go elsewhere for healing, the community, as a system, will be left unhealed and unredeemed, unless and until they are addressed by the community as a whole.

Conversion

"Return to the LORD your God, for he is merciful and compassionate, slow to get angry and filled with unfailing love." Joel 2:13

"Conversion," says Richard Rohr, "is a journey of transformation."[361] To choose to grow is to choose conversion, to transform and become more than we have been in the past. Norman Mailer once said, "Every moment of one's existence, one is growing into more or retreating into less. One is always living a little more or dying a little bit."[362] We always have the choice to grow or retreat from our struggles. And hidden in every struggle is the possibility to become new again, the possibility of conversion.

Throughout our lives, each one of us has been crucified in one way or another and each one of us has risen again. The seedbed of hope is the memory we have of these death-resurrection experiences. Our hope rests on the decision to count on these memories, to believe that once again God will wait for us in the darkness and companion us through our struggle to grow. For Joan Chittister, "The essence of struggle is neither endurance nor denial. The essence of struggle is the decision to become new rather than simply to become older. It is the opportunity to grow either smaller or larger in the process. There is, then, a gift hidden in the travails of a graced crossroads, a gift of beginning again – *conversion*."[363]

Jesus' very first message in the Gospels is to call forth this gift of conversion, to repent and reform (Matthew 4:17; Mark 1:15). It is a call that is ongoing and lifelong. Conversion (metanoia) means to turn around and to go back to God. It means to turn back from our deceitful, blaming and shaming ways and instead become more honest, loving and merciful. This U-turn is neither swift nor simple. It is agonizingly slow and toilsome. We want it to come simply by uttering the words, "I'm sorry." But the heart-work of conversion takes more than uttering these worn out words. Our hardened hearts don't turn easily, "but the one who endures to the end will be saved" (Matthew 24:13).

Gerald Arbuckle recognized conversion as key to communal transformation and refounding: "We must enter into our own darkness or wilderness to confront our sinfulness and our utter need for God who is Light, for that darkness would not be dark to you; night would be as light as day."[364] Raymond Fitz and Lawrence Cada, thought so too: "Personal transformation and conversion is central to revitalization."[365] We have to sit awhile with those painful and rejected parts of ourselves and choose again between being right and being human, between our false self and our true self. We have to expand our awareness, own the parts of ourselves that have been disowned, let go of the pain and take our learnings forward. This is where our bitterness is transformed into peace, hate into love, and hurt into healing. If we can endure this kind of work, the reward is peace, wisdom, freedom and new life.

Reconciliation

"What had been severed for the sake of our preserva-
tion must now be rejoined for the sake of our healing."
Carl Jung

Reconciliation means to put back together what once had been whole but then became severed. The caveat is that it can't be put back to what it was before. It must be put together in a new way, one that is stronger, more integrated, more whole than before. It takes more than putting a salve over a wound by saying, "I'm sorry." It is more than stitching things back together by problem-solving and calling it "fixed." It is personal and interpersonal healing combined. The personal work of conversion involves owning the less than honest and loving parts of ourselves that contributed to the wounding. The interpersonal work of reconciliation is in acknowledging this to those we have injured, connecting with compassion and empathy, searching out deeper understandings, and mutually working toward forgiveness.

Reconciliation is a two-way street requiring both parties to do their own work in acknowledging their contribution to the rift in the relationship. This kind of work leaves neither party innocent or exempt from responsibility. Neither one can just sit back and let the other person do all the work. Both may not have contributed equally to the problem or be in the same amount of pain, but both have to work at repairing what is broken. Both must bear the hardship of being vulnerable, honest, and own up to whatever has been their respective contributions. Both must offer olive branches (e.g., expressing a desire for healing, acknowledging regrets and extending compassion toward the other) and accept those offered by the other (saying "thanks", or "that means a lot to me"). If it is not mutual, then one person will feel righteous, the other blamed. One will win, one will lose, and reconciliation will fail.

Communal healing

You might be wondering: *Does everyone need to go through a process of reconciliation and conversion for our community to be transformed?* No. I don't believe every member has to go through a process of reconciliation and conversion. However, I believe that everyone needs to be invited to do so, and the more people that take up the challenge, the more possible it becomes for a community to transform as a whole.

Still, you might ask, *Why is this work so necessary for communities to do as a whole? Why not send those who need it to a therapist or spiritual director to do their own inner work?* Because healing individually does not heal a community. The system itself is not healed. The web of relationships in community as a whole remains broken unless and until the community itself choses to repair it. The struggles, conflicts and wounds that happen in the community need to be healed by the community.

To illustrate this need for systemic healing, imagine a table conversation during an assembly. Imagine that Sheri, during the table conversation, gets upset with another member, Sally, and lashes out with a judgmental remark. Sally then shuts down and now everyone is on eggshells. During a break, Sheri and Sally go to separate corners to commiserate with others. Now, feeling consoled, Sheri and Sally both return to the table after the break.

However, the table participants as a whole are still where they left off, on eggshells and feeling unsafe. Even if they all went off on a break to shake it off individually, they might return less personally upset, but the safety among them as a table group, if left unaddressed by the group, has not been restored. They are less trusting that anyone will deal with things effectively if another spark of anger occurs. Until or unless they talk as a group and ease the tensions directly with one another, the group remains unsafe. Furthermore, this table's lack of safety will impact the entire assembly as they are part of the whole. The system, as a whole, is affected.

How many times have you been at a local community or committee meeting when some kind of emotional eruption occurred and it was ignored? Perhaps someone teared as a result of sharing vulnerably, someone felt hurt by another's curt remark, or the group went silent following someone's sarcastic, cutting comment. Or, perhaps you have experienced someone attempting to address these situations, but their lack of success left everyone at the meeting feeling unsafe? People might go off to their separate corners and talk on a break, but upon returning to the group the lack of safety sits like an elephant in the room. The hurt feelings and the awareness of feeling unsafe may subside over time, but any hint of a similar tension will bring it all back.

Tending The Garden

"Let us cultivate our garden." Voltaire

Conflicts arise in community just as they do in every relationship or organization. However, when communities are at a crossroads their conflicts are steeper and more consequential if not successfully reconciled. The situation is compounded by *lack of ownership, conflict-avoidance* and *boundary confusion.* My image for many communities is a garden that once flourished, but has since been abandoned, has become overgrown with weeds, and the fences are in disrepair. Let me explain.

Whose garden is it?

When a group of people first meet and find a resonant connection, they create a garden of sorts that nourishes their lives. They till the soil, plant the seeds, water it and God does the rest. Right? But whose garden is it? Who owns it, weeds it, mends the fences and keeps it nourished? If a garden is planted, then left unattended, it dies. Right? The same is true for communities. Who is tending the garden, the life in the community, the wellbeing of its members and the fragile web of relationships? When tensions emerge and boundaries are breached, who mends these?

When the garden needs weeding

Imagine this scenario. Sr. Sara was hard to live with. She had her rough edges. Maybe she never volunteered to do the chores. Maybe she was gruff in her manner or unkempt. Maybe she talked too much, was always late for prayers, or was too picky about what she ate. Sara's irksome behaviors became a "problem" for her community. The community started to distance from her. Sara felt the distance, felt unwelcomed and, when all of this was left unaddressed, the difficulties worsened.

As things progressed, the community no longer wanted Sara to live with them, so they asked leadership for help. Leadership stepped in to "fix" the identified problem – Sara. They tried to talk with Sara about her behavior, citing what "some sisters" had said, but she denied the problem and demanded to know who went behind her back. They refused to share who those "some sisters" were in the name of "confidentiality." Sara didn't trust the anonymous second-hand feedback and leadership didn't know whom to believe, so they agreed to find her another local community.

Lo and behold, the same kinds of problems emerged in her new local community, so she was moved to yet another local community. Again, the pattern emerged, but her behavior worsened. Sara became depressed and eventually suicidal. Consequently, leadership sent Sara to inpatient treatment. Upon her return, no local community wanted to live with her, so she now lives at the Motherhouse, the last stop in an endless cycle of failed relationships in community. Sound familiar?

Maybe, if others in community had been able to give Sara constructive feedback years ago, they might have been able to work out their struggles and learned to live together. Maybe, if they had talked with her early on, they would have known about her diagnosis with cancer that led to her irksome behaviors. Maybe, someone could have helped the community work through their struggles as a community and things would have been different. Maybe not. All we know for sure is that Sara was never given *direct, constructive feedback* by her sisters, nor did Sara do her part in raising these conversations. She never directly heard from others who were brave enough, skilled enough, and cared enough to tell her how her behavior was affecting them. She became the problem, eventually a "patient," when she might have become a viable member of community.

Whose responsibility is it when a member of community is struggling? Everyone's. When individuals in local community begin to exhibit difficult behavior, too often local community members do not address it openly. Individuals in community, like anyone else, get in trouble, withdraw into depression, have angry outbursts, act out sexually, drink too much, gamble too much, hoard too much and on it goes. Everyone might be talking *about* the person behind closed doors, but seldom are they talking *with* the person. The situation is either ignored or left to leadership. Whose garden is it and who is weeding the garden?

Who will mend the fences?

Imagine this scenario of boundaries in disrepair. In one community, Brother Tom was drinking so much that the local community became alarmed and asked leadership to help. After some lengthy conversation, he was sent to inpatient treatment despite his protestations. He came home from treatment seemingly contrite but confided with his friends how leadership had *forced* him to go to treatment. They felt sorry for him and asked to speak to leadership on his behalf. Leadership refused to talk with them citing "confidentiality."

Tom's friends were angry at leadership for how they had unfairly treated Tom and for refusing to talk with them. They began talking with others who were also sympathetic to Tom's plight. Meanwhile, friends of the leadership team caught wind of it and began defending leadership. Camps were formed of like-minded people: those defending Tom, others defending leadership, and leadership who was publicly silent in the name of confidentiality. Soon the entire community was swept into the conflict. It spilled over into Chapter when, during an open forum session, someone demanded that leadership speak to why they had treated Tom so poorly. Again, leadership refused to talk citing confidentiality. Chapter proceedings came to a grinding halt.

There are two boundary problems here. The first is the "triangulation" that began to emerge with individuals, then in groups (camps), adopting the roles of *victim, villain* and *rescuers*. Tom was the victim. Leadership was the villain. And Tom's friends were the rescuers. You might see leadership as the rescuers trying to help Tom, or as victims being unfairly blamed by the community. It is all in your perspective. Everybody has a part to play and all of these roles are interchangeable. Triangulation is a systemic problem and "the root cause of triangulation is conflict avoidance."[366]

The second boundary issue in this scenario is a misappropriation of what constitutes confidentiality. Confidentiality is a term that is misused and abused so often it has become meaningless, if not mystifying and dysfunctional. Too many people tag too many conversations as confidential, meanwhile everyone is talking to everyone behind closed doors about whatever it is that is supposed to be confidential (e.g., "I was told this 'confidentially,' but I think you should know...."). Additionally, too many things that ought to be community business are kept secret causing unnecessary confusion and dysfunction.

More often than not, when sharing a personal matter, most people simply want privacy. They want their confidences and boundaries respected, not some formal agreement of confidentiality. The overuse of confidentially may be, in part, a carryover from years past when such sensitive conversations were left unspoken or shared only with the superior. Too many conversations that ought to be more transparent and shared with the entire community are shared only with leadership and expected to go no further.

Additionally, when there is an appropriate need for a confidential conversation, it is typically assumed to be a one-way street. What ends up happening is that leadership, for example, keeps their end of the bargain, while the member with whom the agreement has been made is free to talk to whomever, and frequently they do. Often a member may be badmouthing leadership or another member while leadership remains gagged. This is a lopsided, one-way, dysfunctional arrangement. I have encouraged leadership teams to make confidentiality agreements a two-way agreement with contingences. There are no HIPPA laws that apply to community leaders. Not every private conversation with leadership ought to be assumed to be, or excitedly tagged, as "confidential."

For example, leadership could say, "We will agree to hold this confidential if you do as well. However, if we learn you have shared it with others, we will feel free to likewise share what we deem necessary in order to address any confusion or difficulties that might emerge." Without such two-way agreements, leadership's hands are tied while others are free to share, and too often this freedom is abused without recourse.

Whose garden is it and whose responsibility is it to mend the fences in community? Everyone's. The garden of community is everyone's responsibility to heal, restore, and maintain. Too often it is abandoned and left to leadership to fix. Trust-tending, boundary maintenance and nourishing relationships are activities of daily living. In community, it is not someone's job, it is the job of every member. It is a labor of love.

Reflection: A Labor of Love

---

1. Whose responsibility is it to care for the garden, the quality of life in community?

2. Who weeds the garden (tends to the trust) and mends the fences (repairs the boundaries)?

3. What are your learnings from these experiences and how might you apply them?

Learning to Work Through Conflict

"Let no one hope to find in contemplation an escape from conflict, from anguish or from doubt." Thomas Merton

Bridging the tragic gap

Parker Palmer calls our universal tendency to avoid conflict our "tragic gap." It is our fatal flaw that prevents us from bridging our differences, reconciling our relationships and becoming whole in community. When this happens, says Palmer, "humility, compassion, forgiveness, and the vision of a beloved community do not stand a chance."[367] The cause of this tragic gap, he believes, is our innate fear of the "alien other" – those who look, act and think differently than ourselves. He believes that our instinctual response to fight or flee needs to be, and can be, overcome with the development of skills and the discipline of dialogue.

This is one reason why my wife and I have devoted our career to training communities to bridge this tragic gap. We know that, with training, communities can grow in their ability to bridge this tragic gap. Communities can grow in their willingness and capacity to reach across their differences, learn to hold the tension and harness its generative, creative power. Communities can learn to reconcile conflicts and transform their pain, rather than transmit it. When they do, they are transformed.

Communities have tried a number of methods for dealing with their conflicts and collective pain. Some communities might *name* their pain, but then fail to take the necessary steps to *work through* it. Members become demoralized and frustrated from the repetitious naming of issues without resolution. Consequently, some communities attempt to put a *moratorium* on further discussion of painful issues hoping to put an end to their anguish. Other communities attempt healing rituals or offer workshops. Many make renewed promises to "trust" one another. I have not yet seen or heard of any such moratoriums, rituals, participation in voluntary workshops, or pleas to *trust one another*, transform a community steeped in pain. What then will work?

"Oh no, not another workshop!"

We have all "been there, done that" and no one wants to go to another *communication workshop*. I don't blame you. If the goal is to train people in a complex set of skills, workshops don't work. Workshops can impart ideas, plant some seeds, and pique some interest. They can help people network, search out resources and brush up on training they have already received. But workshops are not the same as *training* and they don't bring about communal transformation.

Many communities have had workshops on communication, along with the Myers-Briggs and Enneagram. Even having had these workshops, communication challenges persist. I have surveyed communities who have had these workshops and their challenges remain:

1. We fail to speak using even the most basic skills (e.g., "I" statements);

2. We gossip and talk about one another behind one another's backs, instead of speaking directly with one another when we are upset;

3. We "should," judge and label one another;

4. We blame, complain and criticize;

5. We live mainly in our heads (mostly on the left side) and are divorced from any affect;

6. We have meetings outside the meeting; and,

7. We avoid confrontations like the plague, intermittently explode with hit-and-runs, obfuscate our anger with veiled remarks and passive-aggressive behavior, or we suppress and internalize our pain.

Weekend workshops will not put a dent in these kinds of patterns. Training a few individuals in your community with skills to help your community will not transform your community. But training an entire community in more effective ways to dialogue and relate can be transformative. Let me share one example of the kind of training that can be transformative.

Bridging the tragic gap with CARE

*"Transformation is about altering the nature of our relat-
edness and changing the nature of our conversation."*
Peter Block

Beth and I developed and direct a training program called, "Conversational Approach to Relational Effectiveness," or CARE.[368] It is a program intended to bring about systemic change and transformation. We have trained couples, schools, hospitals and other systems. In the last 30 years we have focused our efforts primarily among religious communities. We train communities who wish to acquire new mind-sets, heart-sets and skill-sets to strengthen their relationships through methods of non-violent communication. We believe that communities, whose members have committed their lives to Gospel living, can embrace the principles of CARE which are based upon the Gospel call to "love one another" (John 13:34-35).

The training we provide communities takes one to two years to complete (depending upon the size of the community) and covers eight skill areas, the last of which involves reconciling conflicts with the skills of "confrontation." For the purposes of this discussion, I will focus on the skills of confrontation.

Reframing Confrontation

Sigmund Freud came to the United States only once, lecturing at Clark University in 1909. While some aspects of his theories have not lasted the test of time, he is still considered the "father of modern psychiatry." He set forth a solid foundation for our understanding of human development and introduced a viable approach to healing, namely psychoanalysis. He brought the understanding of human development and approaches to healing into the modern era, which Alfred Adler, Carl Jung, Karen Horney and others further developed.

One of the many psychoanalytic techniques he introduced was *word association*. He believed that if you could get patients to relax their defenses (ego), and bypass the ordinary social censuring (superego), then you might gain access to their unconscious (id), thereby gleaning insights into the nature of their neuroses. For example, he might invite a patient to verbalize associations to the word "mother," to better understand his unconscious experiences, thoughts and feelings related to his mother.

With a bit of tongue-and-cheek, I've used the same technique with communities in the CARE training. I'll instruct the group as follows: "Please close your eyes. When I tell you to open them, look at the word you'll see on the screen and, without thinking or censoring, just blurt out your associations to the word." Then I display the word, "CONFRONTATION." They open their eyes and pandemonium ensues with the words shouted aloud (some of them unrepeatable here): fight, hurt, run, slap, scream, anger, win, lose, tension, pain, hit, etc. If there is any credence to Freud's technique, these words represent to be our uncensored experiences, our genuine thoughts and feelings of confrontation (conscious or not).

We then probe early learnings from our families about anger, conflict and confrontation. I'll ask, "What were the messages your parents taught you, directly or indirectly about conflict and anger?" We also explore the early messages received by our teachers and in our religious formation. The responses are the same across cultures. We learned to: "Offer it up;" "Turn the other cheek;" "Take it outside;" "It's not nice to be angry;" "Don't talk back;" "Children should be seen and not heard;" etc.

In sum, with very rare exceptions, we have learned from our parents, teachers, formators and from our own experiences that confrontation is "bad," "wrong," "ugly," "hurtful," and "sinful." Furthermore, we have learned to "avoid it at all costs" and "keep the peace at any price." As children, we were never directly taught how to lovingly confront, constructively express anger, or effectively resolve interpersonal conflicts. We were taught what *not* to do, but never what *to do*.

Most of us are simply afraid of conflict, avoid it as much as possible, and remain woefully ill-equipped to handle it. We live the best we can in avoidance, until it boils over and we erupt with anger. Because we have avoided it and therefore haven't practiced how to work with conflict, when it does erupt, we do not know how to handle it. Consequently, we end up acting out the "bad," "wrong," and "sinful" behaviors that we were trying to avoid in the first place. Feeling worse about the situation, we redouble our efforts to keep the peace through avoidance. We shove it back down, periodically blow up and act out, and the same self-reinforcing vicious cycle continues. It is self-defeating and universal.

After the training group has acknowledged just how bad, wrong and sinful conflict has been for them, I then ask them to dig deep and reflect upon an experience they've had wherein a confrontation led to something "good." I ask them to identify, "What was the *good* that came from it?" and "How do you suppose that happened?" In other words, what made it turn out to be something *good*, rather than something *bad* or *destructive*. Nearly everyone can find at least one of these experiences. Again, across cultures, here is a sampling of responses.

What was the good that came from it?	*What made it turn out that way?*
• We cleared the air	• We listened
• We resolved the issue	• We knew the other cared
• We became friends	• I apologized
• We had a greater understanding	• She didn't argue
• We had compassion	• He didn't judge me
• Our trust deepened	• We were patient
• He forgave me	• We stayed in the struggle

From our own experience then, we can acknowledge that confrontation is not *always* bad, wrong, ugly and sinful. There can be "good" confrontations that bring about "good" results. What we know for sure is that confrontation is powerful, and this power can be used for good or bad. A confrontation has the power to heal or to damage, bring intimacy or alienation, understanding or confusion, violence or peace, wholeness or fragmentation. It can go either way. It depends upon how we approach it.

What makes the difference?

> *"Violence is what happens when we don't know what else*
> *to do with our suffering." Parker Palmer*

I will never like conflict. It is not fun for me. But I have grown to see the *value* in it, the necessity of it, and the expression of fidelity and love it can be. It can be transformative, *if* certain conditions are met. If we are to become more adept at reconciling conflicts and tilt the odds more in our favor, there are five things that help:

1. *Make wise choices and own the choices you make;*
2. *Prepare your heart, not your case;*
3. *Acquire and apply the skills;*
4. *Develop discipline to manage your reactions;*
5. *Put the rest in God's hands.*

1. Make wise choices and own the choices you make

What are the good reasons to confront another person and what are the good reasons not to confront? Have you ever thought about it? I've asked many groups this same question. They work diligently to come up with their "A-list" of reasons, most of which you might consider valid, as well. For example, it is good to confront someone as a matter of integrity, when speaking truth to power, or if they are harming themselves or others, etc. It is not good to confront someone if they have dementia, if they might physically retaliate, or while you are driving a car, etc.

Here is the point. There is no "A-list," per se. The exercise is meant to have you think through your decision and own the decisions you make. Meaning, it works best if you take a good hard look at your decision to confront or not confront, otherwise you could make a reactive decision (fight or flee) and not a well thought through, deliberate choice. If you react rather than deliberately choose, things are likely to go south. You will be less likely to accept and own the consequences, especially if the results do not turn out so good. Here are a few common ways we tend to fool ourselves, things you might want to consider in making a deliberate choice to confront or not confront.

Rationalizations: What many of us do is make a choice not to confront someone because, bottom line, we are afraid. We are afraid of making things worse, hurting them or being hurt in the process. It's fear, plain and simple. But we pretty-it-up, justify and rationalize our fear, thinking to ourselves: *They are too busy, too tired,* or *now is not a good time.* I'm not saying every choice not to confront is really determined by fear. I'm saying take a good look under the hood because often it is fear, and the rest is rationalization.

The flipside can also be true but is less frequently the case. Sometimes we choose to confront another person for reasons other than what we say to ourselves. Sometimes, we really just want to win, be right, score a point, or get back at them, but we rationalize these intentions by saying it is a matter of integrity, or it's what is good for them. Check under the hood.

Fragilizing: Sometimes we avoid a confrontation and excuse ourselves because we think the other person is not up for it. We think they are too fragile. However, *if you treat someone like a cripple, you cripple them.* You make them more helpless by treating them as if they are helpless. You might call this enabling, misplaced compassion or co-dependency. Call it what you will, but don't call it loving, because it is not.

I had a client whose husband was on his deathbed after a long battle with Aids. She was boiling over with anger because he had contracted the disease from a relationship outside of the marriage. Some people might avoid this conversation, thinking *the poor guy is dying, leave him alone.* After a great deal of soul-searching she decided to go to the hospital where he was in hospice care and confront him. It was one of the most powerful experiences of reconciliation I have ever witnessed. It released her from what could well have been a lifetime of bitterness and enabled him to let go in peace. If you think it is not a good time, or that the other person is not in good place for a difficult conversation, ask them. *Do not assume and unilaterally decide what is good and right for another person.* Ask them.

It's not worth it: *It's not worth rocking the boat. It's really no big deal.* Ever say or think these kinds of things? This could very well be fear talking. While there is a place for not sweating the small stuff and learning tolerance, be careful. It is a slippery slope of choosing to remain silent when you are upset. In isolation, any small incident may be no big deal. But if it becomes a *pattern* of yours to sluff off one thing after another as not worth it, or no big deal, then you are gradually giving away your power and taking a bit of worth out of the relationship as well.

If you have repeatedly given away your voice, wants, needs, opinions and power, eventually you will lose yourself and, consequently, the relationship. That's a big deal! The next time you think to yourself, *It's not worth it,* before you speak out loud, translate that into, *He's not worth it,* or *She's not worth it.* Because that is what, in effect, you are doing. You are withdrawing a little bit of investment in your relationship with each withdraw from conflict. Each time, you have divested and distanced a little more until eventually, over time, nothing is worth it. He or she is no longer worth it.

2. *Prepare your heart, not your case*

My wife is fond of saying to groups, "No one has the God given right to confront another person. You have to earn that right." It is Beth's way of stressing the necessity of doing your personal work in preparation for the interpersonal work of confrontation. Given the potential harm that can come from confrontations that go awry, we need to prepare well. It would be irresponsible to do otherwise. In order to earn the right to confront another person we have to *prepare our hearts, not our case.*

Most of us, when thinking about a troubling conflict and anticipating our conversation with the other person, run scenarios though our head about what he or she might say and how we might respond in return. Often, we are simply going in circles, ruminating about what was said and done to us, deepening our hurt and adding fuel to our anger. We search for ways to justify or excuse our behavior and reasons why the fault lies more with the other person. We *prepare our case* against the other and search for evidence to support our claims.

Prepare your heart, not your case, means readying yourself for reconciliation by making your heart more supple and open to being influenced by what the other might say. Preparing your heart means clearing your heart as much as possible of motives to win or punish the other and, instead, claim motives that might bring healing (e.g., "I may be hurt and angry, yet I want healing even more than vengeance"). Granted, you may not be able rid yourself entirely of rancor and replace it with compassion just by thinking about it, but you can work toward it. You can claim the intention and set your heart in the right direction as you move into the conversation.

Other ways to prepare your heart and earn the right to confront someone might include taking time to reflect upon the following:

- What do I really want as an outcome of the conversation? What is my goal?

- Do I want to win, get back at them, score points, or convince them I'm right? Do I really want to understand them? Do I want to reconcile or do I want revenge? Am I willing to be vulnerable enough to acknowledge ALL of my motivations to the other person?

- How do I intend to use my *personal power* (to listen, be truthful, express my feelings) and my *position power* (my authority and right to make decisions because of my role)?

- What do I need to challenge in myself that may have contributed to the conflict? For what might I need to apologize, express regret or make amends?

- What might be their contribution to the conflict that I may want address? How can I invite them to explore this with me, rather than judge, blame or insist that they change?

- What are the judgments I am making toward the other person or myself? How can I translate the judgements into behavioral descriptions, rather than using pejorative labels?

- What is the heart of the matter for me and what do I imagine is the heart of the matter for them? Walk around for awhile in their shoes.

You don't always have time to prepare in this way, but the more you practice this kind of heart preparation, the more self-knowledge you gain and the more prepared you will be for spontaneous confrontations.

3. Acquire and apply the skills

The skills of confrontation are among the last set of skills we teach in CARE because these build upon the prior skillsets. At this point in the training the group has been immersed in the model of mutuality as the foundation. They have learned the skills of *presence, giving and receiving feedback, self-disclosure, empathic listening* and *intuitive listening* and more. We then teach a number of new skills related specifically to confrontation. Most of us have only been taught what *not* to do. We help the group acquire a new set of skills they can use in order to deal effectively with confrontation.

A sampling of these skills is shown on Table 7, Do's and Taboos of Confrontation. We teach and then brave volunteers demonstrate these skills with real confrontations (not role-playing). The group then practices, practices and practices some more. With practice, coaching and feedback, they grow in their capacity to apply these skills.

DO'S AND TABOOS OF CONFRONTATION	
Do's	*Taboos*
1. **Speak face-to-face**	1. Avoid emails or phone calls
2. **Slow down, take your time**	2. Don't rush to a quick apology
3. **Build bridges, not walls**	3. Don't negate or try to win
4. **Partner with them**	4. Don't be so self-protective and defensive
5. **Respond deliberately**	5. Don't react without thinking
6. **Listen thematically**	6. Don't get stuck in the literal
7. **Think invitation**	7. Not accusation

8. Give them choice and chance to change	8. Don't insist they change; focus on your changing
9. Free yourself of the need to be right	9. Stop convincing them why you're right
10. Free yourself of the need to be totally safe	10. Don't avoid the truths that may hurt
11. Free yourself from insisting upon only the outcome you want	11. Let their perspective, their desires, and the dialogue, reshape the outcomes
12. Deal with the little things along the way	12. Don't let them pile up until you have a gunnysack full of anger
13. Take responsibility for and own your anger	13. Don't blame or make it their fault ("You *made* me feel angry")
14. Speak concretely and focus on a couple of specific examples	14. Avoid bringing in the kitchen sink
15. Speak directly: me and you	15. Don't triangulate by dragging in family, friends, or anonymous others
16. Stay open to possibilities and willing to be flexible	16. Avoid ultimatums, bottom lines and too many non-negotiables
17. Engage, engage, engage	17. The truth hurts, but silence kills
18. Challenge distortions or misinformation	18. But don't argue because it's not about the facts
19. Speak to them ASAP	19. Don't avoid or procrastinate
20. Stay in the struggle and explore, explore, explore.	20. Don't start a conversation you are unwilling to finish

Table 7: Do's and taboos of confrontation

4. *Develop discipline to manage your reactions*

If you *choose* to engage in a conversation, *prepare your heart* and bring along your *skills*; you are off to a good start. However, if it is a serious conflict, things will definitely heat up. Somewhere along the way in the conversation, your *buttons* will be pushed. You will begin to feel hurt, angry, guilty, ashamed or some other unpleasant emotion. You will naturally want to defend yourself. What will you do?

When conflicts erupt, most of us run from them and a few will stand and fight. The ones who run for the hills find cover in their defenses: sublimation, repression, suppression, denial, rationalization, intellectualization or compartmentalization. Some fight directly or indirectly with their defenses: projection, blame, verbal or physical assault, sarcastic remarks or passive-aggressive behavior.

The Four Horsemen of the Apocalypse was the metaphor used by David Gottman to describe the four worst ways couples deal with conflict. Gottman found that couples who resorted to *criticism* (fault-finding and blaming), *defensiveness* (justifying with excuses), *stonewalling* (withdrawing and shutting down) and, worst of all, *contempt* (name-calling and mocking) while in conflict, were highly likely to divorce. In contrast, couples that did well in addressing conflict and had successful marriages, were able to listen to one another while in conflict. They approached their conflicts with exploration ("Tell me more.") and curiosity ("Isn't that fascinating!"). They did not enjoy the conflict, but they saw the value in respecting and engaging their partners in exploring and resolving their conflicts.[369]

The Four Horsemen behaviors are just as commonplace and destructive in communities as they are in marriages. In order to develop the discipline needed to handle the heat of a confrontation, you need to know your defenses, catch yourself when you are reacting defensively, and work with them in a disciplined manner. The simplest way is to acknowledge your reaction and your desire to engage otherwise. For example, "When you said I was 'lazy' I had an urge to argue and I don't want to do that. I wonder if you could describe what you meant by 'lazy' instead of using that label?" This will help you take the edge off of your reaction and help the listener know how to engage more constructively.

5. Put the rest in God's hands

You might make good choices, prepare well, bring the best skills and use them with discipline, and still not succeed in having a successful conversation. Why not? First of all, there is another person in the equation, and he or she will have some say-so regarding how well things will go. You cannot unilaterally determine the outcome for the two of you.

But even if both of you bring your very best intentions, skills and discipline to the dialogue, it still might not succeed. Why not? Because your timing may not be God's timing. Call it providence, serendipity, or whatever you like, there is something more at play than just what two people bring to a conversation. This is not an excuse to over spiritualize things, let go of your responsibility and leave it all in God's hands. It is simply a recognition that we can't engineer healing, reconciliation or conversion of hearts. We can't control or guarantee the outcome. We can do our part, as much as we humanly can, and the rest is grace.

I had a ten-year rift with my son. During that very painful period of time for both of us, he and I both tried to address it. After many unsuccessful attempts, he eventually withdrew and refused to talk, so I wrote him a letter. Along with the letter I gave him a gold pocket watch that had been my grandfather's, then my father's, who passed it down to me. I gave it to him as a symbol of my everlasting fidelity. The message at the end of the letter said, "I'll wait for you." I said that I'd wait for whatever time it might take, and for whenever he might be ready to talk. I waited ten long years before we talked and began our healing.

He is every bit my prodigal son and I cared about nothing more than to have him back in my life. Despite our deep desire for healing, despite whatever skill and discipline we both might have brought to a conversation, we could not have done it ten years earlier. Only in retrospect could we see that we weren't ready at that time. We couldn't have known, understood or accepted certain things ten years earlier. Call it providence or serendipity. I think grace worked its way through our lives. It took a while until we, by our own free will and readiness to cooperate with grace, were finally able to reconcile, heal and come home to one another.

Common pathways to healing

Learning effective ways to reach across your differences, handle conflictual conversations, use tensions creatively, and reconcile and heal relationships, are among the hardest skills to learn. In contrast to workshops, *training* that involves an entire community is far more effective in transforming the way communities relate. CARE is only one example of an approach that I know works. Communities who wish to heal their brokenness, reconcile their woundedness and experience genuine conversion must go through the same arduous processes as any other individual, couple or group seeking wholeness and healing:

- Turn inward and engage in utterly honest and very painful introspection in order to reclaim truths that have been left ignored or unintegrated;

- Strip away the layers of defenses that keep our wounds, and the painful truths they conceal, from our awareness;

- Risk further injury by courageously turning toward others from whom we have long since turned away either because of the pain we caused them or the injuries we experienced due to their behavior toward us;

- Cease blaming others for our pain and take responsibility for our own healing and for companioning others in theirs;

- Let go of our need to justify our actions and admit the naked truth of our failures;

- Only after honest searching, shared exploration, mutual empathy and compassionate understanding;

- Do the work of self-challenge, as well as the work of challenging others in order to stretch and grow into a new way of being;

- Offer and receive expressions of forgiveness, atonement, or restitution;

- Only after such direct conversations, try out new behaviors, and allow others to do the same in order to create new patterns, new growth opportunities and new foundations of trust.

Reflection: Working with Conflict and Tension

---

1. *To what degree is your community effective in dealing with conflict, handling tensions and healing wounds?*

2. *When was the last time you avoided having a direct conversation with another member with whom you experienced tension? When was the last time you sat as a bystander in a community meeting when conflict emerged, and you did nothing to help? When was the last time you engaged in a successful confrontation in community?*

3. *What are your learnings from these experiences and how might you apply them?*

The Narrow Gate of Forgiveness

"Enter by the narrow gate. For the gate is wide and the way is easy that leads to destruction, and those who enter by it are many. For the gate is narrow and the way is hard that leads to life, and those who find it are few."
Matthew 7:13

Transformation through forgiveness

Forgiveness is more than saying, "I'm sorry." Forgiveness does not excuse or absolve the offender from the consequences of their actions; rather, it places them squarely in their lap. Forgiveness does not require that we resume the relationship, though it may open the door for that possibility. It does not change the past, or mean that we forget the past; rather, it can keep us from being stuck in the past and help us open up to the future. Forgiveness does not mean relinquishing our right to feel hurt or angry; rather, it invites the expression of painful feelings that helps us to let go. Forgiveness is not an event; it is a process. It is a gift. It is a grace that transforms our hardened hearts.

There is *No Future Without Forgiveness*,[370] wrote Desmond Tutu. We all have betrayed others and been betrayed. We have abandoned others and been abandoned. We all have been silently complicit when our friends have been maligned, even though we know what it is like to have been slandered and abused. We all have withheld a kind gesture, a word of encouragement, a tender embrace, our vulnerability and forgiveness, though we know what it is like to have been unloved and unforgiven in these same ways. We have badmouthed leaders behind their backs, even though we know what that felt like when we were leaders. There will be no future until we learn to forgive and transform our pain, rather than transmit it.

There will be no future if we cannot turn around and reconcile, as well as offer and receive forgiveness. When will we learn that we are all the same, less than perfect, in need of forgiveness and needing to forgive others just the same? We want mercy and forgiveness when we have injured others, but when we are the injured one, we want the other punished in the name of justice. We seek vengeance and call it an *eye for an eye*. We call the other an *evildoer* and claim God to be on our side. We fail to see the speck in our own eye but are quick to condemn others for their faults. "Let any one of you who is without sin be the first to throw a stone at her" (John 8:7). We have a long way to go.

An eye for an eye remains the dominant paradigm for dealing with our wounds, despite what Jesus taught us. He taught and modeled for us how to break the cycle of violence by not retaliating or running away when in conflict, but by being willing to stay in the struggle (Matthew 5:38-42). He taught and modeled for us how to break the cycle with acts of love, even toward our enemies (Matthew 5:43-45). He said, to forgive is to forgive your brother at least 490 times (seventy times seven), meaning never stop (Matthew 18:21-22).

Forgiveness is key to breaking the cycle of violence. It is both *gift* and *grace*. It is a gift we have been freely given and can give to others just the same. Beatrice Brutreau says, "Forgiveness is the gift of goodness given in abundance to another when love has been distorted or annihilated. The paradigm of forgiveness is the creative act of Jesus on the cross."[371] Richard Rohr speaks of forgiveness as a grace that transforms:

> "I think forgiveness is the only event in which you simulta-
> neously experience the three great graces: God's unmerited
> goodness, the deeper goodness of the one you have forgiven
> and then you experience your own gratuitous goodness
> too. That's the payoff. This makes the mystery of forgiveness
> an incomparable tool of salvation. There is really nothing
> else quite like it for inner transformation, which is why all
> spiritual teachers insist upon it, both in the giving and the
> receiving."[372]

To the degree we accept the gift and grace of forgiveness and learn to share it with others, we unbind and unburden others, the community and our world. "When you forgive others, they are unbound; and those you don't forgive, you keep them bound up" (John 20:22-23). When we forgive, we also unbind and unburden ourselves. We cease transmitting our own unredeemed pain to others. We break the cycle of violence begetting more violence. Forgiveness is a creative force that breaks the cycle of repeating the past. Forgiveness literally transforms the past and allows the new to emerge.

We know that the suffering inside us contains the suffering of our ances-tors, our fathers and mothers, and their fathers and mothers. They may not have had a chance, or known how, to heal their wounds, so they may have passed it along to us. If we can transform rather than transmit our suffering, conflicts and wounds, we are healing our parents and our ancestors, along with ourselves. We are healing the suffering in the world, the suffering of those with whom we minister, the suffering here among ourselves.

The *Trail of Tears* represents the forced relocation of Native Americans from their homelands carried out by government in the 1800's. The relocated peoples suffered from exposure, disease and starvation while en route, and many died before reaching their destinations. At the end of the Trail of Tears, located in Oklahoma, Francis Jansen's Monument of Forgiveness stands. Jansen spoke of it saying:

> "It is my belief that wherever violence has been perpetrated
> upon our environment, the Earth, and its inhabitants, there
> is a lingering vibrational imprint of that violence, still held
> in the energy field or information field of that place and in

the human beings there. It is a kind of embedded traumatic memory that continues to resonate and negatively impact the collective consciousness until it is fully acknowledged, honored, and reconciled. If it is not addressed, then over time, there is a tendency for a kind of hardening to occur in the psyche of humankind that can perpetuate a loss of sensitivity or emotional numbing, as well as the tendency to continue the pattern of violence against self and others."[373]

Summary

"The rabbi asked his students: "How can we determine the hour of dawn, when the night ends and the day begins? One of the rabbi's students suggested: "When from a distance you can distinguish between a dog and a sheep?" "No," was the answer of the rabbi. "Is it when one can distinguish between a fig tree and a grapevine? Asked a second student. "No," the rabbi said. "Please tell us the answer then," said the student. "It is then," said the wise teacher, "when you can look into the face of another human being and you have enough light in you to recognize your brother or your sister. Until then it is night, and darkness is still with us." Hasidic Tale

Reconciliation and conversion are the third dynamic element woven into the larger Journey of Transformation. This personal and interpersonal work is the very crucible of transformation where new life is conceived and forged in the womb of our becoming. This dynamic element of transformation is the Achille's heel for most communities, indeed our world, which remains largely untrained and ill-equipped to handle tensions and conflict. Too often, this work is avoided, relegated to leadership or some other well-meaning rescuer. The world has no shortage of victims, villains and martyrs of our own making. Yet, tending the garden is all of ours to do. It is a labor of love for every member of a community, everyone who has cast their lot together.

If we forgive and transform our own suffering, we are better able to transform the suffering of others. We can turn our suffering into compassion and love, *if*, we acknowledge it, embrace it, understand it, and allow God's grace to transform it. Reconciliation and conversion involve the gift and grace of forgiveness. Communities that receive and offer this gift, can help heal and transform their collective body. They can help heal and transform our broken world. They can bring dawn to a new day.

Chapter 15: Experimentation and Learning

Acting our way into a new way of being

"We make the road by walking"
Antonio Machado

Introduction

"The whole globe is shook up, so what are you going to do when things are falling apart? You're either going to become more fundamentalist and try to hold things together, or you're going to forsake the old ambitions and goals and live life as an experiment, making it up as you go along." Pema Chödrön

Recall, once again, a crossroads in your own life. When you faced your own crossroads, recall how you needed to *act your way into a new way of being* without having all answers ahead of time and without controlling every step of the process. Recall the perseverance and sheer will it required for you to push on, the courage it took to risk potential failure and the learnings it took to become new again. Remember how your community, facing one of its crossroads, had to make room to reinvent itself by letting go of old buildings and ministries, as well as old ways of doing things and outdated worldviews. Remember the courage it took for your community to risk experimenting with new relationships, new ministries, new approaches to life, and all of it with no guarantees of success.

Your founders and foundresses did not launch communities with a strategic plan. They had no roadmaps, insurance policies or fully funded retirement plans. They had only a passionate belief in what they were doing and the courage to make their dreams a reality. They faced setbacks, hardships, resistance from others and odds that were stacked against them. They experimented with different approaches, succeeded with some, failed with others, and learned from all of these experiences as their dreams unfolded. They had the audacity to act upon their dreams, where most people might have dreamt but never acted at all.

By and large communities these days are far more risk-averse than their ancestors. The older we get, the more we value security over adventure. Our financial advisors, doctors, lawyers and insurance agents all reinforce this: "Don't risk it. At your age, you won't have the time, wealth, health, or stamina to recover." We are afraid to fall because we might break a hip. We are afraid to chance new investments because we want to hold onto the security we've gained. We get set in our ways and entropy sets in.

When facing the crossroads, most communities will succumb to fear, rather than muster the courage to risk any unguaranteed pursuits. Those who transform have the courage to experiment and become learners again. How much time has your community spent in the last five years creating new ministries, acquiring new skills, or developing new partners? What radical letting go, bold new experiments and innovative steps have you taken? Patricia Wittberg, asserts: "It is unlikely that a community that fails to innovate when returning to a purely traditional model will be able to meet the needs of a society which has radically diverged from the situation which had given birth to that model."[374] Gerald Arbuckle agreed: "Innovation is at the heart of survival and growth. Without innovation in response to rapidly changing conditions, human groups stagnate and die."[375]

The fourth dynamic element of transformation is *Experimentation and Learning*. Communities that transform themselves are learning communities. They are open to experimentation, willing to fumble in faith as they take on new ventures. Learning communities innovate new processes, practices, ministries and mind-sets, and refuse to cling to the "way we've always done things." They are not paralyzed by needing guarantees or having all the answers beforehand. They see the value of mistakes as a source of learning, not a cause for blame or justification for leaving well enough alone.

In this chapter, we will explore what it means for you to become a learning community and act your way into a new way of being. We will look at how your community can better harness the power of creativity and imagination. And we will explore ways that you might gather greater courage to risk, experiment and take bold new actions. We will look at what it means to enlarge your soul by becoming lifelong learners with an insatiable will to live.

Acting our way into a new way of being

"To avoid criticism, do nothing, say nothing, be nothing."
Elbert Hubbard

It may be an occupational hazard, but I value the kind of work that unearths insight and opens doors to new learnings. I know that gaining insight into our patterned ways of thinking, feeling and behaving can be liberating. Such depth work can release us from the unnecessary suffering we experience as a result of unconscious and faulty mindsets that neither fit reality nor bring us joy. We can be relieved of these self-defeating scripts if we can first name and claim them. If we can become conscious of them and own them as ours, then at least we have a choice to either hold onto them or create something new.

However, I also recognize that insight alone does not result in, or necessarily precede, change or transformation. Oftentimes, insight emerges only after taking a step, after experimenting with a new behavior and coming to a new place. The new place offers us a new perspective. Sometimes you have to act your way into a new way of being (rather than think your way). Sometimes you just have to throw your hat over the fence, thereby forcing yourself to get it, lest you stay mired in your own ambivalence and fail to act.

This is where I have great empathy for the *doers* in community who are tired of all the talk, the "navel gazing" and want to "get something done!" When all of the talking produces very little movement, the diagnosis reads, *paralysis by analysis*: a chronic, highly contagious and debilitating disease plaguing a great many communities. When no action steps are taken, members, especially the doers, become demoralized and disengaged. The cure for this disease is not more insight, but more courage to act, to act even in the face of limited clarity, control, or consensus, to act even in the face of fear. It means to adopt that same *pioneering spirit* that your founders and foundresses had and not let perfect be the enemy of the good.

Unfortunately, communities are prone to caution, wanting consensus, clarity and guaranteed outcomes before making a move. Such caution leads them down the well-worn path toward the default future, the predictable decline and death of communities. In a transformative journey you cannot possibly have the answers ahead of time. You cannot control the entire process. At times, you need to act your way into a new way of being without having the kinds of assurances you would ordinarily want. Sometimes you have to jump the rails and act in ways that defy logic or reason. Such transformative leaps are not ones that spring from strategic plans. Acting your way into a new way of being is another way of saying, as so many say of transformation, you must build the bridge while walking.

You can plan what to do with your buildings or finances, but *you cannot plan your way through transformation*. Psychologists are fond of saying, "Fake it till you make it." They say this because too many people want the answers ahead of taking action. They want perfection before they have practiced. They want guarantees and are frightened of failure. Unfortunately, in order to become new again we must act in the face of fear, ambiguity, and the possibility of failure. Mother Teresa once said, "The first step to becoming is to will it. After you will it, you need to act on it."

If we are to be *evolution in action*, as Teilhard de Chardin asserts, then we must act. If communities are to transform and become new again, they must act upon their evolving consciousness and lift the dreams of the next generations toward greater fulfillment of God's dream. Members who are educated, seasoned and accomplished professionals, who have themselves educated nations, need now to become the learners. For communities to transform themselves, they must experiment with and acquire new skills and act without promises of safety or success. In order to transform, your community will need to:

1. Become a *learning community*, and reclaim community as a *green space* wherein members can walk with one another in their learning, grieving, growing and transforming;

2. Summon the *courage to risk* failure and disappointment and become free enough to experiment; make mistakes and learn from them without resorting to blame and judgment;

3. Harness the *creativity and imagination* of your members and invite others to add theirs; and,

4. Become *lifelong learners* and bear down with a tenacious will to live, in order to persevere through the inevitable challenges and setbacks, override any inertia and patiently endure the slow work of God.

Become a Learning Community

According to Peter Senge, a learning community is one "where people continually expand their capacity to create the results they truly desire, where new and expansive patterns of thinking are nurtured, where collective aspiration is set free, and where people are continually learning how to learn together."[376] Have you ever been in this kind of learning community?

Recall for a moment the communities, teams or living situations in which you were able to learn and grow personally or professionally. My hunch is, when you reflect on these, you might have experienced that everyone in the group participated and was respected as a valued contributor. There were probably not bystanders excused from the work and allowed to sit back in judgement. Participants likely felt safe enough to take risks, to make mistakes without the fear of judgement or reprisal. Mistakes were learning opportunities, not occasions for blame or excuses to no longer try. There was likely a balance of support and encouragement, along with challenges to stretch and grow.

These are the types of settings, learning communities, in which we grow and transform. For your community to become a learning community it will need to help its members adopt a beginner's mind and learn how to learn together.

Adopt a beginner's mind

"The most beautiful thing we can experience is the mysterious. It is the source of all true art and all science. He to whom this emotion is a stranger, who can no longer pause to wonder and stand rapt in awe, is as good as dead: his eyes are closed." Albert Einstein

Adopting a beginner's mind means owning the fact that who you are and what you have are enough to learn and create all that you need for the future. It requires that you rekindle your passion. You'll need to be free to make mistakes, be vulnerable, and learn whatever is yours to learn. Adopting a beginner's mind means opening your eyes and letting yourselves remember what it was to be curious and wonder. Remember?

Who you are is enough!

What I see holding communities back from creating a future of their own choosing is a false belief that somehow they don't have enough of what it takes. They don't think they are smart enough, healthy enough, wealthy enough, or have enough time or members to do and become what they might wish. A beginner's mind never questions this basic premise: *Who you are is enough!* A beginner's mind is free from fear or felt inadequacy. Focus on what you do have now and who you are today, and work from there.

You have enough time, money, people and smarts to deal with the hand you have been dealt and find your way. It is a matter of *accepting* the hand you have been dealt and going from there. Success in life does not always come from holding a good hand. More often it comes from knowing how to play a poor hand well. You can bemoan the fact that you only have a certain amount of money, people or time, or you can say: "This is what we have. Now what do we want to do with it?" You could look around and compare yourselves to other communities and grumble about their better circumstances, or you could say: "This is who we are. Now who do we want to become?"

Take the advice from Thomas Moore in *Care of the Soul* and be good at what you are good at, otherwise you move against the soul.[377] I don't deny the fact that many individuals have had shaming experiences in life. Many have been told by parents, teachers, and formators of all kinds that who they are is not good enough. Working with this faulty perception and residual shame is part of the inner work of transformation. You were made in God's image (Genesis 1:26-27). You have an abundance of resources. You have limits, but you also have gifts and talents and the capacity to learn more. Don't try to be someone you're not. Claim the gifts that are yours to claim, own your limitations and your life, build upon these and count on grace.

Passion, wonder and resilience

To engage in the work of transformation you will need to adopt a beginner's mind, full of imagination, free to explore and wonder. A teacher observing her students in class, looked over at a little girl drawing and asked, "What are you drawing?" "I'm drawing a picture of God," said the little girl. The teacher smiled wryly and replied, "But nobody knows what God looks like." The girl said, "They will in a minute." Children have little need to draw within the lines, fact-check their assertions, or inhibit their ever-present outpouring of imagination. We only learn these limitations as adults.

Picasso once said, "All children are artists." Before we learned of competing and our ranking on report cards we were all artists. We were, as children, creative, full of wonder and with no hint of performance anxiety. We were free to draw, sing, dance and create whatever was stirring in our imagination. If I ask my four-year-old granddaughter to dance, she'll gladly display her talents wearing her treasured purple tutu. Give a group of educated adults a drawing task, or ask them to dance, and very quickly you will unearth some anxiety.

Walter Isaacson authored books on Leonardo de Vinci, Benjamin Franklin, Albert Einstein, Steve Jobs and others, in an attempt to uncover what makes a genius such a genius. What he discovered is not their brain power but their playful and insatiable curiosity, their efforts to integrate knowledge across disciplines, their resilience to bounce back from setbacks, and their ability to see patterns and themes amid the clutter and chaos. Malcom Gladwell reported a similar finding in his book *Outliers: The Story of Success.* He found that successful people were intensely curious and passionately obsessed with their areas of interest. He noted that successful people had mastered their trade having practiced it for over 10,000 hours.[378] Passion, persistence, wonder, and resilience are all part of a beginner's mind.

Freedom to make "mustakes"

*"First there is the fall, and then we recover from the fall.
Both are the mercy of God." Julian of Norwich*

It is widely recognized that we learn more from our mistakes than our successes. Consequently, in order to maximize learning and create alternative futures, communities need to be free to make mistakes. What makes us terribly unfree to make mistakes is our fear of failure. Too often our mistakes bring judgement and blame. We are shamed into never trying again. In order to retrieve a beginner's mind, communities need to become free to make mistakes in order to optimize their capacity to learn, grow and transform.

A story is told of a student who traveled a long distance to meet with a famous rabbi. The student humbly asks, "Rebbe, how do I become wise?" The rabbi looks carefully at the student and answers, "From making good choices." "But Rebbe, how will I know how to make good choices?" The rabbi responds, "From experience." "But," the student continues, "How do I get that experience?" The rabbi smiles and answers, "From bad choices."

In order to retrieve these capacities communities need to give their members permission to say, "I don't know" (rather than pretend that they do), to color outside the lines (rather than insist upon dogma and tradition), and to experiment with new possibilities and make "mustakes" (without blame and shame). We need to see our mistakes as Richard Rohr sees them: "What looks like falling can largely be experienced as falling upward and onward, into a broad and deeper world, where the soul has found its fullness, is finally connected to the whole, and lives inside the Big Picture."[379]

While working with a community and discussing this need to experiment I met an elementary school principal. When students were sent to her office for their *bad* behavior, she'd start the conversation by saying, "Isn't that fascinating!" She meant it. She adopted a posture of curiosity, rather than judgment, and joined the child in exploring what might have happened so they could both learn from whatever mishaps had occurred. She didn't exempt the child from taking responsibility or making amends, if need be, but the goal was learning to do better. I wish she had been my principal when I was in elementary school!

My years between kindergarten and graduate school were not what most would describe as academically stellar. Most of the time I felt bored, not because it was all too easy, but because I felt intellectually inferior and too unsure of myself to try and risk failing, so I tuned out. I recall the shame I felt for being in the "slow reading group" in second grade and for my first F I received in fifth grade spelling. What I recall most from these instances was the disappointment from my father and mother. They were both highly educated and expected more. I felt ashamed and had a tremendous fear of failure that held me back from trying. It took years to ease this internalized shame, this belief that "I'm not good enough," and to learn to love learning.

No one who has become successful in life has become so without having the courage to take risks and having failed many times. We have to fail in order to learn. It's the only way to succeed. Michael Jordan acknowledged this saying, "I've missed more than 9,000 shots in my career. I've lost almost 300 games. Twenty-six times, I've been trusted to take the game-winning shot and missed. I've failed over and over and over again in my life. And that is why I succeed."[380]

Thomas Edison made one thousand lightbulbs before inventing the lightbulb we have today. We have to make mistakes to learn.

Still, who doesn't love the feeling of being right and hate being wrong? Kathryn Schultz, understands this and wrote a book about it, called, *Being Wrong: Adventures in the Margin of Error*. She begins by confessing just how much all of us love being right: it's better than chocolate, surfing, or kissing. Even though our efforts to constantly prove how right we are rubs others the wrong way and prevents us from learning, we persist in this self-defeating behavior. Schultz offers a theory of "wrongology," encouraging us to learn to love being wrong for the learning, wisdom, growth and transformation it produces.[381]

Richard Rohr tells us: "The Crucified and Risen Christ uses the mistakes of the past to create a positive future, a future of redemption instead of retribution. He does not eliminate or punish the mistakes. He uses them for transformative purposes."[382] If you are not prepared to be wrong, you'll never be creative or original. Help your community become a safe place to make mistakes. Instead of casting blame when someone makes a mistake, gather the learnings and offer them a redo ("Try again."). Stop the judgements, groaning and eyerolling, and help each other recover and move on. It is a beginner's mindset to learn to succeed by learning from our *fascinating failures*.

Freedom to be vulnerable

Probably the hardest part for adults in regaining a beginner's mind is to rid ourselves of the need to feel entirely safe so that we can be free enough to be vulnerable. When I went off to my internship at Rutgers Medical School I knew I had one year to soak up as much as I could in a fantastic learning environment. I had nothing to lose and everything to gain by taking risks. There were professors at Rutgers whose books I had studied during graduate school and I was excited to learn from them firsthand. I was like a kid in a candy store and wanted to grab as much learning as I could from this once-in-a-lifetime learning opportunity.

The first week I was there, Monica McGoldrick asked for volunteers to be a guinea pig, of sorts, for a symposium on family and group therapy. I shot up my hand and jumped at the chance. *Great*, I thought, *I'll learn from the best*. It sounded great in September but come February, two weeks before the symposium, I was getting cold feet.

I went to Monica and said, "I don't know if I should do this symposium." "Why?" she asked. "I just, uhm, don't know. If they start probing my family, and ask about my sister who has schizophrenia and all, this could get really uncomfortable." "So?" she queried nonchalantly. "Well", searching for a bit more compassion, "I might start crying." "So?", she inquired, still with no empathy. "So, I could fall apart in front of everyone!" I exclaimed, with one last plea for pity. "So what." She replied, this time with a tinge of irritation. "We all have issues. They don't care. They're not focused on you. Everyone is just there to learn about family and group therapy."

They might not care, but I do, I thought. I could tell my pleas for mercy were of no use. She was not going to let me off the hook. With no escape, two weeks later, I did go, and promptly fell apart. I survived though, and learned a great deal about myself, my family and about family and group therapy. I also learned that I could fall apart (in other words, cry), even in front of a large audience, and could live to tell about it. My mini-breakdown was a mini-breakthrough. I claimed a newfound freedom to be vulnerable and cry without the terror of judgment. *Isn't that fascinating!*

Brené Brown offered a Ted Talk entitled the *Power of Vulnerability*. She summed it up this way:

> "To let ourselves be seen, deeply seen, vulnerably seen ... to love with our whole hearts, even though there's no guarantee…to practice gratitude and joy in those moments of terror… is to believe that we're enough. Because when we work from a place, I believe, that says, 'I'm enough' then we stop screaming and start listening. We're kinder and gentler to the people around us, and we're kinder and gentler to ourselves."[383]

Learn as a community

Peter Block tells us: "To create an alternative future, we need to advance our understanding of the nature of communal transformation.[384] Personal growth does not translate into systemic change for a community. For example, if a small group of individuals in a community went off to receive some kind of training, such as, conflict resolution, anti-racism, or discernment using Theory U, they would return to a community who has not had that same training. If they tried to engage the community using their newly acquired insights and skills, they would quickly encounter resistance. There would be a collision of paradigms regarding the *right* way to resolve conflicts, dismantle racism or engage in discernment. However, when an entire community goes through a substantial training experience *together* it impacts the community's collective growth.

Attending a workshop is not the same as *training*. You could take a three-day workshop to learn to fly an airplane, but I wouldn't fly with you. Acquiring new skills, whether it is playing the piano, learning a new language or how to engage in communal discernment, takes training and lots of practice over time. Workshops don't transform communities, collective training does.

In summary, communities that grow and transform have adopted a beginner's mind. They have come to accept that who they are and what they have are enough. They make room for passion and wonder. They learn from mistakes and feel safe enough to be vulnerable. The have learned to become learning communities.

Harness Creativity and Imagination

> *"The future of the church cannot be planned and built up merely by the application of generally recognized Christian principles: it needs the courage of an ultimately charismatically inspired, creative imagination."*
> *Karl Rahner*

When people think of being creative or having a good imagination, they usually think of artists and musicians. But anyone who has sufficiently mastered the skills in their chosen profession can be creative, imaginative and visionary. Architects see the art in numbers and angles. Scientists appreciate the beauty in creation. Chefs know the soul in food. When athletes are in the *zone*, or in the *flow*, they ski, skate and play basketball with grace. Every one of us can imagine and create, if only we let ourselves *go with the flow*.

Sir Ken Robinson, a highly regarded educator, believes that education is killing our creativity and disenfranchising our children. His main thesis is that creativity is now as important in education as literacy and that we are squandering the talents of our children. He suggests that our education systems are too focused on intellect over affect and empathy. They focus too much on rationality over intuition and imagination, as well as the outer world over the inner world of mindfulness and consciousness. In other words, our educational systems do not educate our whole being, just our heads (mostly the left side), nor does it take into account the diversity of talents and passions of our children.[385] The same could be said of most communities.

Everyone (not just artists) has the hardwiring for creativity. We simply need to reclaim it as important and provide the necessary training and curriculums to harness its power. For a community to transform itself, it will need to harness the creativity and imagination of all its members, not just the artists. It will need to start by raising its collective intelligence.

Learn to hold the tension

There are two types of thinking that take place when a group comes together to innovate or decide upon a new endeavor: *divergent* thinking and *convergent* thinking. Divergent thinking is the fun part, when the diversity of ideas is invited into the room. Convergent thinking is harder because it involves winnowing down the options and ultimately making a decision. Between these two ends of the process is what we could affectionately call the *groan zone*. This is the space wherein people are searching to make sense of the diversity of ideas, feelings, and possible solutions or directions. This is where groups sit in the tension of diversity and the muck and mire of confusion in an effort to unearth the integrative wisdom of the group.

The groan zone gets its name because participants usually groan when sitting in the muck and the mire. People grow increasingly tense and impatient. They start moaning and groaning: "I can't believe we are still taking about this!" "We are going in circles." "This is taking us nowhere!" The frustration, tension, defensiveness, and impatience often build to a crescendo until some-body puts a stop to it: "Let's take break" or "Let's just vote and get it over with." Sound familiar?

The groan zone is no fun at all, especially for those who value expediency, clar-ity and closure over creativity, integration and in-depth dialogue. It is full of frustration and confusion. As a result, most groups shortcut this groan zone and make decisions that end up aborting the creative process. They would rather have a quick, sanitized, feel-good process. Consequently, they forfeit the richness of diversity, lose out on the collective wisdom and are deprived of the all-important ownership for decisions that are made. The ownership that gives members incentive and commitment to carry out a decision is lost when groups avoid the groan zone.

Creativity is, by its very nature, a messy process. Even when choosing it, most will moan and groan because of the discipline it requires to stay in the strug-gle. However, if you value things like innovation, depth, integration, wisdom, and ownership for decisions over speedy processes, frustration-free and "nice" conversations, then you will have to enter the groan zone. You would choose this not because it is fun but because of the value it holds for the group. If you choose it, your community will need to acquire the skills to hold the tension and harness the diversity.

Raise your communal IQ

The average individual IQ is 100. For college students the average IQ is around 115 and for graduate students it is upwards of 125. Let's say your community is made up of geniuses, with individual average IQ's around 145. If you bring all these smart people into an assembly to create possibilities for the future, would they innovate? Would your communal IQ be higher, lower, or the same as the average of its individual IQ's?

I have seen a great many communities whose members are smart and well educated but, as a group, their collective IQ is, well, let's just say below aver-age. I have seen other communities who have no Harvard professors or MIT engineers but whose collective creativity is phenomenal. Their synergy is great and their communal IQ is genius. Why is this the case?

A community is its own living organism, each with its own norms, capacities and culture that are more than the sum of the individuals who comprise it. Communities may or may not reflect the average of these individual capacities. For a community to unearth the secret sauce of synergy, they have to be able to unleash the diverse mixture of talents, passions and viewpoints of individual members, and harness these into innovative and productive endeavors. How do they do this?

What capacities or characteristics do innovative communities possess that others do not? Linda Hill and her colleagues wrote *Collective Genius: The Art and Practice of Leading Innovation* to investigate this very question. They examined companies, such as Pixar and Google, to see what made them so successfully and repeatedly innovative. What they found is that innovative organizations have three capabilities: 1) creative abrasion; 2) creative agility; and 3) creative resolution.[386]

Creative abrasion

Creative abrasion is the capacity to share ideas through dialogue that amplifies differences, rather than minimizes them. It is not about brainstorming, where ideas are put forth without judgement or debate. To the contrary, innovative groups have heated arguments over the alternatives presented. The participants are fully invested and passionate about the possibilities they present. They actively listen, advocate and debate. They know that diversity and conflict are crucial for creativity.

Creative agility

Creative agility refers to the ability to test and refine the diversity of ideas through quick pursuit, reflection and adjustment, where you act, as opposed to plan your way into the future. It is *discovery-driven learning* that is a combination of scientific method and artistic processes. They run a series of experiments with increasingly refined iterations of their efforts, but they do not use a series of pilots that might water down, or slow down, the process.

Creative resolution

The final capability, *creative resolution*, is the synergistic component. It is the integration of any number of diverse, even opposing, ideas into a *new* combination that produces the solution. It is not a solution that requires every person's original idea to be preserved as was originally presented. It is not a compromise solution in an effort to appease those who want their ideas included. Rather, it is a novel expression of ideas reconfigured into both/and solutions whose author is the group itself.[387]

Like many communities these innovative organizations value *inclusivity*. They want everyone's full-throated participation and do not allow any one group or individual to dominate, not even the *boss* or the *expert*. Unlike many communities however, this does not mean that every individual's voice should carry the same weight, have equal airtime, or whose specific words should somehow be represented in the solution. It simply means everyone had a chance to be heard.

Innovative organizations do not operate by compromise, majority rule, Robert's Rules, or the superior's rules. It is not a go-along-to-get-along method. It demands that participants are strong enough to voice what they think and feel, agile enough to be influenced by what others think and feel, and able to integrate the differing thoughts into a new solution that is not *my baby*, but ours. And, unlike many communities, they are not paralyzed by analysis. They are willing and able to act their way into the next iteration of the vision and into a new way of being.

Make room for the new

> *"If you want to go fast, go alone. If you want to go far, go together." African Proverb*

If you want to go far, go together

Neurons by themselves are very fast (firing off impulses at speeds up to 200 miles per hour), but by themselves are not very smart. Together, a brain has nearly 100 million neurons and nearly as many synapses as there are stars in the heavens. When the neurons in our brain work together we have enormous capacity to adapt, imagine, and create anew. The same is true for a community. Individuals alone can go very fast, but when individuals in a community connect and become a learning community the synergy is tremendous. They can go far and possibilities are endless.

Open your boundaries, collaborate and partner

If your community is to transform itself and avert the ravages of entropy it must open its boundaries. Bringing new people into the conversation about your plans for the future will not only bring new energy to counter the entropy, it will change the conversation. It will bring a new dynamic and new ideas to the conversations. Communities that close in on themselves out of fear of *outsiders* will close down in short order. In order to transform your community, you must be willing to move your mental fences, open the doors, and welcome the stranger and their strange ideas.

Robert Putnam, in *Bowling Alone*,[388] examined the difference between healthy and less healthy civic communities. He found that healthier communities, those defined as happier and more productive, had a strong sense of cohesion and cooperation. He found that our world is becoming increasingly polarized and segregated. Our choices to live in gated communities and create our own virtual worlds of like-minded people have reduced the frequency of our having to rub shoulders with people who are different. It has diminished our capacity to handle differences. It stems, he believes, from a strong desire for *belonging* which reinforces our need to go along to get along.

For example, when meeting a new group, in order to fit in, we tend to say, "Me too", affirming whatever the group says and does in order to fit in. We might even amplify our response to make a solid impression, agreeing with the group and adding a bit of our own extra punch. This dynamic leads to a mutually amplifying set of responses, a sort of "Can you top this?" mentality, that results in the group escalating its rhetoric to the extreme. The group spirals inward with its mentality, tightening its mental fences, and treating anyone who thinks otherwise as an alien other.

As a society, we need to learn to rub shoulders with those who think, act and look differently than ourselves. Communities can help to counter the propensity by refusing to live in a *gated community* or *virtual world* of like-minded people. Communities can counter the cultural norms of polarization and competition by demonstrating cooperation and collaboration. If communities are to transform, they will need to open their boundaries and learn to partner.

Cross-disciplinary learning

A key to opening up transformative possibilities is *cross-disciplinary learning*. Communities attempting to go it alone in their planning will end up stewing in their own juices. They are unable to bootstrap themselves into thinking and acting beyond what they already know. Bringing new people into the conversations, as in a *charrette*, is one way to accomplish this.

The word charrette is a French word meaning "chariot" or "cart." It was originally used among architects who came together in collaborative sessions to seek solutions for design problems. It is a term resurrected today among groups that collaborate for the purpose of gathering the collective wisdom and to better address issues they hold in common. It rests on the premise that we can accomplish more together than we can separately.

I have been in numerous planning sessions with communities, hearing very similar conversations across them. Of course, each community has a different culture and set of circumstances, but some questions are common to all. For example, when discussing healthcare plans I typically hear communities ask:

- How do we address the healthcare needs of our members with our diminishing financial and human resources?

- How do we help our members get past the denial of their own aging and understand the urgent need for change?

- How do we involve our members in planning, to develop their ownership and ready them for the changes they will have to implement and endure?

- How do we work through their fears and resistance to these changes?

- How do we care for our own health and wellbeing as leaders amidst all the stress, and will we have a future after all is said and done?

- How do we plan for life, not death, during this season of our life?

Rather than communities working in silos, reinventing the same wheel, why not put your collective heads, hearts, imaginations and resources together? That's why I have conducted a number of charrettes with these broad goals:

- Explore what you might do better together rather than separately;

- Learn from one another how you might better address the challenges and open up new opportunities;

- Determine how you might partner, resource or assist one another in addressing the healthcare needs among women religious.

Gathering a mixed group of people together who share common interests brings energy and excitement. Margaret Mead famously said, "Never doubt that a small group of thoughtful, committed citizens can change the world; indeed, it's the only thing that ever has."[389] Charrettes allow for a cross-fertilization and synergy of ideas among thoughtful, committed people. People can share their learnings from prior successes and failures. They can share fresh ideas and discover new ones. All of these things push communities beyond their ordinary silos. It allows new possibilities to emerge and brings forth new resources to tap that otherwise would not have been available. It often jump-starts a new vision for communities.

Creative Fidelity

"Wisdom lies neither in fixity nor in change, but in the dialectic between the two." Octavio Paz

Some people interpret the *new* as being unfaithful to the past. They hear a proposal for a new direction as a criticism of current or past leaders. Others, upon hearing a proposed new approach to Chapter, react by exclaiming, "This is against canon law!" Some consider certain topics as "sacred cows" that ought not be discussed. Still others see proposed new directions as being unfaithful to the Church, tradition, or their founding charism or mission.

The Dalai Lama once said, "Learn and obey the rules very well, so you will know how to break them properly." Transformation will mean breaking a few rules or at least suspending them. Law follows life, not the other way around. By the time the laws are written, life has moved on. In order to make room and create something new, you will need to look at change not as an indictment of the past or an act of infidelity, but as the next evolutionary step that builds upon and honors the best of all that preceded it. There needs to be room for *creative fidelity* to the traditions, laws, customs and all that has held value for a community. Creative fidelity is the dialectic between fixity and change, between what has been and what is yet to be.

Some people couch their resistance to change as *obedience* to their Constitutions, canon law or the Church and are satisfied to claim what they perceive to be the higher moral ground. They will insist that their Constitutions prohibit certain changes when, in fact, there is more wiggle room in these documents than some might see. For example, most communities have moved beyond *proposals* as part of Chapter. However, some resist this change saying, "canon law gives every individual the right to submit proposals." When, in fact, canon law says no such thing. It allows for every member to express their "wishes," but how this is done is up to the community.

Another example is when members believe canon law gives them the "right to vote," *carte blanche*. In fact, this right carries certain responsibility. Members must earn this right by whatever is further stipulated in their Constitutions, Directory or by the Chapter planning committee. For instance, they might need to be of a certain age, have the mental capacity or have attained solemn vows. They might be required to complete some preparatory study or attend pre-Chapter meetings. If these conditions are not met, they will not be able to vote. This is no different than the stipulations on our civic rights: to vote, drive a car or own a home. We have these rights as long as we meet the stipulated requirements.

Creative fidelity is key to the work of transformation. It is working with the tension, the dialectic, between the past you wish to honor and the future you wish to create. Transformation requires creative fidelity to law, norms and traditions, as well as new approaches to spirituality, structures, technologies and visions for the future. As Cardinal Newman famously said: "To live is to change, and to be perfect is to have changed often." Joan Chittister explains the notion of creative fidelity this way:

> "The soul only grows as a result of the changes that tax and test our tolerance for the present, of the ability to find God where God is rather than where we think God should be for us. Change of mind, change of heart, change of hopes, change of insights require us over and over again to sort through all the pseudo-certainties of our lives, keeping some things, altering others, discarding the rest of the notions that were once its convictions, its absolutes, the very staples of our souls."[390]

Communities that fail to innovate simply won't survive. You will need to harness the imagination and creative potential of your community in order to innovate and transform. You will need to raise your collective IQ by learning to harness the richness of diversity. If you want to go far you will need to open your boundaries, partner and collaborate. You will need to embrace the notion of creative fidelity and honor both the richness of your traditions and the yearning to become new again.

Develop the Courage to Risk

"No one can make history who is not willing to risk everything for it, to carry the experiment with his own life through to the bitter end and to declare that his life is not a continuation of the past, but a new beginning."
Carl Jung

Learning and experimentation, like every new venture into the unknown, involve risk. Communities who are taking the path of transformation have more courage to take risks than most. They have developed this courage over time, not all at once but with each successful experience. When Gerald

Arbuckle first wrote, *Out of Chaos: Refounding Religious Congregations*, he warned that refounding means "putting aside our kingdoms of false security."[391] Certainty and security must be replaced with courage in the face of ambiguity if you are to go down this path of transformation.

Courage is as contagious as fear

In general, communities, like any mature organization, have accumulated resources, earned esteemed reputations, developed successful practices, and put in place structures and leaders that support their mission. The have garnered the knowledge and power to make things work. The more they have accumulated, the more successful they have been, and the more power they have had, the more they have to lose. And the more they have to lose, the more they become risk-adverse. Fear is a companion to communities facing a crossroads and the courage needed to take risks can be in short supply.

However, communities that are low in the supply of courage are not doomed to failure. Over time, they can summon the courage needed for transformation. I've seen it happen: *courage is as contagious as fear*. The more leaders and members demonstrate courage by taking risks, the more others are inspired and encouraged to do the same. Credible leaders are those who inspire us, not merely in their rhetoric, but by their courageous actions and willingness to take risks. Courageous members who are willing to take the risk to self-initiate, think outside the box, speak truth to power, will inspire others to do the same.

Being-in-it-together

One of the greatest antidotes to fear and a source of courage is the experience of being-in-it-together. Communities that make a serious collective commitment to the work of transformation develop a tremendous sense of camaraderie. This all-hands-on-deck commitment fosters a sense of urgency to the situation. The community knows it is facing an existential threat and members know the future depends on everyone's efforts, not just the efforts of a few.

This is akin to what soldiers experience when facing battle. Sebastian Junger studied the causes of Post-Traumatic Stress Disorder (PTSD) on soldiers returning from war. He found that the severity of PTSD symptoms was not directly tied to the atrocities they witnessed or experienced. Instead, he found that soldiers returning home experienced the trauma of losing the intense bonds they had experienced in war, the experience of *being in-it-together*. It was the sense of being-in-it-together during the intensity of war that enabled soldiers to carry out extraordinary acts of courage and to risk and sacrifice their own lives.[392]

It is this same sense of being-in-it-together that gives members of a community, who commit themselves to the intense work of transformation, the courage needed to take risks and sacrifice. When a community faces a crossroads, makes a collective decision to the do the hard work of transformation, and follows through with collective action, courage grows over time. Each courageous act instills more courage, bonds them, and lessens the grip of fear.

Resiliency

"We may encounter many defeats, but we must not be defeated. It may even be necessary to encounter the defeat, so that we can know who we are. So that we can see, oh, that happened and I rose. I did get knocked down flat in front of the whole world, and I rose. I didn't run away – I rose right where I'd been knocked down. And then that's how you get to know yourself. You say, hmm, I can get up! I have enough of life in me to make somebody jealous enough to want to knock me down. I have so much courage in me that I have the effrontery, the incredible gall to stand up. That's it." Maya Angelou

If you are going to take risks, sooner or later you are going to stumble. It is important to learn how to recover from a fall and get back up. Shortly after I learned to fly a plane, I decided to take aerobatic lessons, in part, to help me know how to get out of a mess should I ever get into one.

To help me learn how to fall and recover, the instructor first talked me through a couple of loops and barrel rolls, helping me know how to keep my bearings through these nauseating maneuvers. He then had me close my eyes while abruptly twisting the ailerons from side to side, pushing the rudder back and forth and turning the plane upside down. Then he calmly announced, "We are now falling through 10,000 feet. You have the controls." Terrified, nauseous and sweating profusely, it took a moment for me to get my bearings and regain control of the plane. We did it again and again. The terror of falling out of the sky was gradually transformed into confidence. I knew I could survive falling from the sky.

I have to say that most communities I know don't do failure very well. They have had a lot of experience with success but limited experience with failure. When leaders or members do happen to fail or make mistakes, often there is judgement and blame. Leaders and members learn not to take risks in order to avoid these consequences. They have grown increasingly leery of taking risks for fear of the potential consequences if they fail. Communities need to learn how to fail, fall and get back up. They need to help each other recover from their mistakes and treat these as learning experiences. Communities would do well to take in the encouraging words of Winston Churchill: "Success is not final, failure is not fatal: it is the courage to continue that counts."

Lifelong Learning and the Will to Live

"To exist is to change, to change is to mature, to mature is to go on creating oneself endlessly." Henri Bergson

Communities that transform at this stage in their life are life-long learners with a tenacious will to live. While their average age may be in the 70's or 80's, this has not deterred them from choosing life and continuing to learn. They have learned patience, acquired wisdom, transformed their lives and opened up seeds of new life. They have grown to recognize transformation as a lifelong journey, not a quick fix with the deadline being their next Chapter. Rather than growing weary over the course of the journey their will to live has grown stronger. They are lifelong learners with a deep desire for the fullness of life.

Life-Long Learning

My father died of vascular dementia at the age of 69 after years of gradual decline. During those same years, my sister had been through the revolving door of hospitals, group homes and the streets of Boston, suffering from a most intractable form of schizophrenia. Those were dark days in my family, especially for my mother who felt utterly alone and responsible for us all. She was working as a nursing home administrator while searching for any treatment that might help my sister and caring for my father at home until his death. When he died, she was completely worn to the nub and facing her own graced crossroads.

A year after my father died my mother packed up her grief and worn out soul and embarked on a bicycle tour of Europe. She came home some months later having fallen in love, then eloped and married in Hawaii! She married a retired ophthalmologist, Frank, who had lost his wife to cancer a year earlier. Together they had 20 years of an incredible romance and encore marriage before my mother passed away just shy of 90.

Both Frank and my mother grew more deeply in love with each other and the fullness of life during those 20 years. They took courses at nearby Stamford University, and then traveled the world visiting the places they studied. They were rapacious readers, loved foreign films and competing with other couples at bridge. They were engaged with local politics and did volunteer work in their civic community. Frank, at age 100, only recently retired from golf and tennis but still plays bridge, the stock market, and reads the New York Times cover to cover every morning.

My mother successfully navigated one of the most difficult crossroads of her life. Just when she was brought to her knees, utterly exhausted and lost at age 69, she set out on a path not knowing where it would lead. She fell in love and began to grow again. She took lessons and became adept at golf, tennis and bridge. She carefully planted and nurtured her backyard garden. In the process, she learned how to let go and make room for new life to bloom.

She was, and Frank still is, the epitome of a life-long learner. Together they learned how to love again. It wasn't easy. They didn't have a roadmap for their encore marriage. Undoubtedly, they both brought some baggage from their first marriages that needed to be unpacked and sorted through. But they did it. Through it all, by choice and determination, they each reclaimed a sense of home again. They might agree with T.S. Eliot and say that they came full circle through the spiral of life to know love and home as if for the first time.

Communities that are engaged in the work of transformation are not planning for death. They are planning for life. They are lifelong learners who refuse to stagnate. They are curious, studying, growing, and helping others grow. In one community with whom I work, when I enter their dining area between meals, their senior members are scattered about the tables in small groups. It is a study hall. They are tutoring younger members, teaching foreign students and helping neighbors with projects. It is a room full of laughter and life. It is amazing. The members are receiving as much as they are giving. They are continuing to learn, to grow and transform, even in their senior years.

The will to live

"The difference between a successful person and others is not a lack of strength, not a lack of knowledge, but rather a lack in will." Vince Lombardi

The will to live streams forth from our soul from our first breath to our last. While God promises an abundance of life, God does not choose life for us. What we do with our own gift of life, our own soul's desire, is left to each one of us to choose. It is from our own free will and the choices we make that our soul will either grow or diminish in stature.

We live our lives in direct proportion to the size of our soul and our will to live. You might liken the soul to a lung through which we breathe in and out, the *breath of life*. The larger our soul, the more of life we can draw in and give back to others. So how large is your soul? How much of life can you breathe in and out again to others? How strong is your will to live?

Some people have large souls and indomitable spirits. We know them in all walks of life from Ann Frank, Malala Yousafzai[iii] and Greta Thunberg[iv] to our family members and friends who demonstrate astonishing courage in the face of adversity. From the unsinkable Molly Brown to Rocky Balboa their spirits are infectious. These are the heroes in real life, or in movies, who lift our spirits and enlarge our souls.

It is amazing to watch an incredibly skilled athletes in the flow of it, performing at the top of their game, like Simone Biles, Venus Williams, or LeBron James. It reminds us of those times when our lives have been aligned with the flow of grace. We love to see a comeback from a past champion, like when Tiger Woods came back from his fall from grace to win the Tour Championship in 2018. It gives testimony to transformation and redemption. And we go nuts when an underdog wins, like when the Red Socks won the World Series in 2004. Our universal love of the underdog recognizes that we, too, can be victorious against all odds. Underdogs may have less talent but they have more *heart* than their opponent. It gives us hope that we too can overcome adversity.

Communities who will transform and thrive into the future will be those that beat the odds with an unshakable will to live. They live in alignment with grace, believe in transformation and redemption, and have heart to overcome adversity. These are communities with large souls whose spirits are alive, breathing life in and out with large breaths. They have learned to cooperate and live in the flow of grace. They are agents of transformation.

---

iii Children Rights activist, Malala Yousafzai became the youngest person to earn the Nobel Peace Prize at age 17.

iv Climate activist, Greta Thunberg became the youngest person to earn Time Magazine's 2019 Person of the Year at age 16.

Reflection: Becoming a Learning Community

---

1. *How might your community better harness its creativity and become a learning community?*

2. *What might strengthen your community's courage and willingness to take risks?*

Summary

> *"We are not what we know but what we are willing to learn."* Mary Catherine Bateson

Experimentation and learning comprise the fourth dynamic element, an essential process, in the Journey of Transformation. This requires the willingness of your community to act your way into a new way to being even in the face of ambiguity and with no guarantees. Your community needs to become a learning community and muster the courage to take risks and experiment. You will need to adopt a beginner's mindset and be willing to make mistakes and learn from them. You will need to harness your collective imagination and creativity, and raise your collective IQ. You will need to open your boundaries, collaborate and partner. If you can become learners again and make the road while you walk, you can transform your lives and continue the creative work of evolution.

CHAPTER 16:
TRANSFORMATIVE
VISIONING

Gather the wisdom, weave a dream

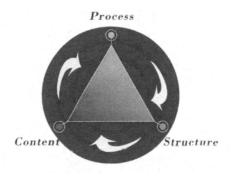

"We don't have to wait for some grand utopian future. The future is an infinite succession of presents, and to live now as we think human beings should live, in defiance of all that is bad around us, is itself a marvelous victory."
Howard Zinn

Gather the Wisdom, Weave a Dream

The purpose of Transformative Visioning is to *gather the wisdom and weave a dream* powerful enough to awaken a community's soul and inspirational enough to unleash its passion, both of which are needed to make real the vision claimed. Transformative Visioning is the dynamic element within the Journey of Transformation that invites your community to create, articulate and activate a prophetic vision for the future. What gives it its transformative potential however is not some grand vision you might create at the end of it all. Rather, it is what happens to you while you are creating it that makes all the difference. *Its power is not in a future that awaits you, but in the sort of people you are becoming and the very purpose for your existence.*

Of the five dynamics elements, Transformative Visioning is the one that drives the overall Journey of Transformation through its focus on visioning. It provides the overarching movement and the linchpin into which the other four dynamic elements are woven and given expression. Transformative Visioning engages leaders and members in visioning and planning, along with the deeper work of transformation.

Transformative Visioning includes conventional planning methods with which you are familiar and need to use in order to plan the operational changes pertaining to your land, buildings, healthcare and the like. It incorporates the conventional approaches along with new processes that invite *depth, integration* and *partnership*. It includes these conventional methods but takes things to another level in order to bring forth deep change. The intent of creating a new vision is not simply to make surface changes that extend your years of survival. Rather, it is more for crafting a vision based upon your deepest longings with the hope of bringing forth new life. In this sense, Transformative Visioning is not merely operational but *aspirational*.

Transformative Visioning is a process for creating a shared vision of the future that is distinct from the past. It transcends and includes the past but is focused squarely on the future. It is not about forecasting the future or eliminating risk. It is not about creating new vision statements to hang on the wall or strategic plans for three-ring binders. It is about opening up a variety of possible futures and taking substantial risks to bring forth new life. It invites members to dialogue in new ways, participate in new forums and gather with new partners.

Transformative Visioning is a journey that will test your readiness to live authentically out of your deepest beliefs and leave behind all that has become bereft of meaning or is made more of nostalgia than of your call to further the reign of God. It is a journey that seeks to transform the very soul of community through holy and intimate conversations, loving and reconciling exchanges, and communal discernment of God's call. It is less about strategic plans than who you are growing to become and the very purpose you claim for your existence.

In this Chapter I will discuss the keys to Transformative Visioning, namely the kinds of *processes*, *content* and *structures* that bring Transformative Visioning to life. I will also discuss the tensions between conventional planning methods and Transformative Visioning as a source of generativity.

Transformative Visioning Processes

"The future enters into us in order to transform itself in us long before it happens." Rainer Maria Rilke

Transformative Visioning is part and parcel of the larger Journey of Transformation. It is a process that engages communities in planning and visioning which integrates conventional planning approaches with the deeper work of transformation. At the heart of it, Transformative Visioning is an organic, emergent and iterative process. Let me explain.

Organic, emergent, iterative

"Take the first step in faith. You don't have to see the whole staircase, just take the first step." Martin Luther King, Jr.

Transformative Visioning is an *organic* process. The vision grows from the soul of community to the surface and all its forms. It is not contrived, engineered or delivered from on high. The future is already in us, already tugging at us and growing in us long before we will ever see its completion. Only in retrospect do we see how it was emerging all along. The anguish of this ambiguity can be eased a bit if, rather than trying to force it, we trust our ability to intuit, discern and enable the future to unfold.

Transformative Visioning is an *emergent* process. Emergence, defined by Peggy Holman, is "higher-order complexity arising out of chaos in which novel, coherent structures coalesce though interactions among the diverse entities of a system."[393] Chaos, novelty, coalescence and mystery are key. "We don't control emergence," says Holman, "Yet we can engage it confident that unexpected and valuable breakthroughs can occur."[394]

In her recent book, *Who Do We Choose To Be*, Margaret Wheatley spoke of it this way: "I used to joke that calling something 'an emergent process' was just a scientific term for 'making it up as we go along,' or 'flying by the seat of our pants'. . . . Working with emergence means we are fully engaged, carefully observing what's going on as we do our work, learning from experience, applying those learnings, adapting, changing. In other words, behaving like everything else alive does."[395]

Emergence and how we work with it is another example of *cooperating with grace*. It is not flying by the seat of our pants. To the contrary, it involves substantial planning and preparation, then listening to the Spirit and adjusting our plans accordingly. Conventional methods help us plan, set goals, timelines and budgets; all of which we must do. But we also need to hold these lightly and choose to engage the inevitable chaos rather than avoid it or tamp it down. We need to actively look for the new, different and dissonant voices on the margins, rather than whitewash these and only focus on the majority. We need to embrace the mystery, follow the energy, learn and adapt along the way.

Conventional methods of organizational change are typically top-down, leadership-driven. Leaders usually hold tightly to their well-crafted plans, to known and familiar approaches and predictable outcomes. They advocate and declare the vision and avoid the chaos of transformation as much as possible. Transformative Visioning, in contrast, emphasizes shared leadership and is

Spirit-driven. It engages all members in the exploration of mystery and the search for novelty. Conflict and resistance are understood as not only inevitable but integral to fashioning a new vision.

Transformative Visioning is an *iterative* process, meaning the vision is continually a "work in progress." The vision is not something that is established all at once or once and for all. At first it is hard to see the newness emerging. It is like trying to see new green shoots of grass amidst a familiar field. The first impulse is to put any newness into an old frame of reference and see only what we have seen in the past. It takes a while for the new to be recognized as "new." It requires continual vigilance, listening to the Spirit and tracking what seems to be a new coherence of energy and ideas.

The vision does not arrive all at once, not even on the second or third *drafts*. It is a continual, reciprocal process of articulating the vision, making decisions, implementing, evaluating, modifying and re-articulating the vision. Once a step in the right direction is identified, it is important to put a stake in the ground and commit to moving toward it. Commit to taking a step, experiment, and learn from the experience. Each step taken reveals new insights, further enlightens the *next best step* and further elucidates the next iteration of the vision.

Harnessing tension as a source of generativity

The nature of transformation is inherently dynamic and full of tension. You will need to learn how to not just tolerate the tension but harness it as a source of generativity. This won't be easy. You will have urges to abort the chaos, get things done and over with and avoid the tension. These urges are understandable but you must not succumb to them. You will need to strengthen your capacity to use tension and conflict as sources of creativity, insight and learnings. These will help you know what adjustments to make in your approach and the next steps to take. Working through these tensions is the very work of transformation. Here are a few examples of the kinds of dynamic tensions you will face throughout the journey:

1. Change vs. transformation
2. Existing vs. emerging paradigm

3. The chicken vs. the egg

Change vs. transformation

There will be ongoing tension between the planning you will need to do in order to develop and implement pragmatic changes versus your ongoing discernment of the deeper invitations and the inner work of transformation. The inner work of transformation and the outer work of change involve two very different kinds of processes. They each demand very different kinds of mindsets and skillsets. They each demand their own time and energy. These conflicting demands are frequently in tension. You will need to find a way to integrate and work with the tension between change and transformation.

As we learned, speed can be a defense against depth and so can the press to get things done. The drive to get things done in a speedy and uncomplicated manner lives in constant tension with the needed depth of transformation which is slow and complex. Time is money, and the longer things take the more expensive things can become. Things can also cost more if they are not done well in the first place. Impatience can easily drive communities to bypass the deeper work of transformation and simultaneously put at risk the quality of task accomplishment. The slow work of God lives in tension with our endless to-do lists and the need to get things done.

The challenge is in getting things done *and* knowing when to slow down and go deeper. How much emphasis you place on the strategic planning versus the inner work is entirely up to you. Keep in mind, however, that the balance of emphasis will determine: how fast or slow you move, how simple or complex the planning becomes and how comfortable or unpredictable your experience becomes. It will determine how much wisdom and ownership is harnessed and how shallow or deep the resultant change will be. These are all trade-offs. They are values in tension. Ideally, instead of opting for one set of values over another, you might come to experience this tension as a creative and generative force. No matter where you start, these trade-offs will need to be continually rebalanced as your visioning efforts move along.

Existing vs. emerging paradigms

*"Truly creative people use the gap between vision
and current reality to generate energy for change."*
Peter Senge

There is inherent tension between the perception of today's reality and the emerging vision of the future. Peter Senge described this tension metaphorically as a rubber band stretched between reality and vision saying, there are only two ways this tension will resolve: "pull reality toward the vision or pull the vision toward reality."[396] "Truly creative people," he suggests, "use the gap between vision and current reality to generate energy for change."[397]

The Journey of Transformation by its very nature will disrupt the status quo and cause a radical shift in your life and mission. Recall that during times of transition, *what got you to today, won't get you to tomorrow.* The very things that brought you to today are the things you'll need to let go of in order to transform. This means that the existing mind-sets, heart-sets and skill-sets of your leaders and members will need to shift. It demands that the normative patterns, practices and ways of doing things will need to change. It requires that your existing values and organizational structures that have undergirded your life will need to adapt. This collision of paradigms will shake the community to its very soul, as it must, if transformation is to happen.

This also means that the people in key positions who have supported the community as it exists today will be in tension with these new changes. Ironically, these tensions can exist within the very leaders who initiated the call to transformation. Leadership often embodies the conflict between supporting what has been while creating the new. They will be challenged to change the very structure in which they are embedded. Leadership, or those in administrative positions, might end up out of a job or having to drastically change what they are used to doing.

The successful completion of a system's developmental phase triggers its demise by generating challenges that the organization is not equipped to handle. The current system needs to break down in order to break through to a new system. A direct implication here is that your current structures and the people who faithfully serve them to maintain life as it is will be met with increased tension. The tension between your wish to maintain the status quo and your desire for new life that disrupts the status quo will be with you throughout the journey. How well you hold and harness this tension will be a test of your skills, resolve and discipline.

Chicken vs. egg

Which comes first, creating a vision and then making decisions about your life or making decisions out of which a new vision emerges? From a practical standpoint, you cannot wait 10 years to make certain decisions, despite the fact that there is no clear vision. At the same time, it would be unwise to make decisions without an eye toward the future, toward some kind of emerging vision. Decision-making and visioning need to happen simultaneously and reciprocally inform each other throughout the journey. Decisions that must be made now will inform your emerging vision, and processes geared toward visioning your future will inform decisions that you must make now.

To illustrate this more concretely, it would be hard to determine what to do with your properties and buildings without some kind of vision of the future. Any real estate consultant whom you would ask to evaluate your property and offer you options will ask, "What is your vision?" "Where do you hope to be in 5 or 10 years?" You will have to articulate an initial vision of some kind, recognizing that it will continue to emerge and shift as things progress. It will become clearer as you make more specific decisions. This will be a reciprocal process of articulating a vision, making decisions aligned with your developing vision, discovering more insights, articulating new iterations of a vision, and so on.

In summary, truly creative communities must learn to hold and harness all of these tensions between what has been and can be as generative forces. If these tensions are ignored, communities run the risk of fragmenting. If these tensions are too quickly and arbitrarily resolved with either/or solutions, communities run the risk of aborting the creative potential. The challenge is in learning to hold the tension, search for new solutions, and keep working with these as the journey progresses.

Concretely, this means working with the other four dynamic elements as you engage in Transformative Visioning: 1) working toward a shift in conscious-ness, 2) claiming your inner voice, 3) reconciling and working through conflicts, as well as 4) experimenting, learning and taking risks. These tensions represent the leading edge of change and working through them is what will transform you. Do this work while in small groups and large assemblies. Ideally, these tensions and your work with them can become a source of energy, creative and growth *if* it is handled well.

Transformative Visioning Content

"Close both eyes to see with the other eye." Rumi

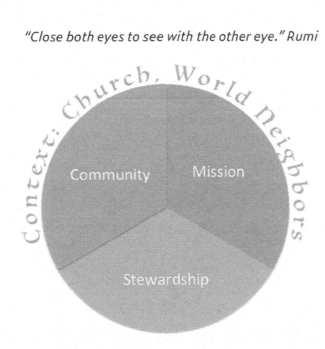

Visioning Content and Big Questions

What's in a vision? In other words, what will be the content that will inform the substance of your new vision? Every community is different but let me offer a general template for you to consider and then you can tailor this to fit your own circumstances. Consider these three domains of content as a focus for your visioning efforts: 1) Mission, 2) Community, and 3) Stewardship.

Let me also suggest a number of *big questions* within each of these domains. These are a sampling of key questions with which most communities grapple in developing their vision. When you ponder these questions, imagine where your community might be five to ten years from now. Following a survey of this content, I will describe the *structures* you might use to address this content and shape your vision for the future.

Mission

Ideally, your mission flows from your charism, is nourished by life in community and responds to the needs of the world. It is not the sum total of what you do (i.e., your ministries); rather, it is a synergistic expression of your being. Religious communities are not a collection of individual vocations. You have a collective purpose, a reason for existing, which is greater than the sum of your individual ministries – your mission.

It is essential to create a vision for how your mission will be carried forth into the future. In creating this vision, it will be important to discuss how your mission and vision need to adapt to the changing times and urgent needs of the world. It will be important to shape how your mission will be carried forth by those who will live on, your partners in mission and all those whose lives you touch.

Big questions

1. **To what degree is your charism a lived reality in your community and how does this inform your mission?**

2. **What are the urgent needs in our world today to which you are called and best suited to respond?**

3. **In light of the internal changes taking place in your community and the external changes in our world, what shifts are necessary in order to transform and support your future mission:**

a. What values do you want to preserve, let go, and claim as new?

b. What practices do you want to preserve, let go, and foster as new?

c. What structures do you want to preserve, let go, and create as new?

d. What mind-sets, heart-sets and skill-sets do you want to preserve, let go, and claim as new?

4. What succession plans are needed to sustain your mission in the future?

5. What ministries will you own or operate, sponsor or co-sponsor, partner in, let go, or claim as new?

Community

Creating a vision for your future means birthing a new way of being community, a new way of creating home. Who you say you are, how you live and organize your life, and the quality of your relationships are keys to any future you create. Choosing life, creating new life and forging a new vision for the future will necessitate transforming your community's way of life.

Big questions

1. In light of the internal changes taking place in your community and the external changes in our world, what shifts are necessary in order to transform and support your future life in community:

a. What values do you want to preserve, let go, and claim as new?

b. What practices do you want to preserve, let go, and foster as new?

    c.   **What structures do you want to preserve, let go, and create as new?**

    d.   **What mind-sets, heart-sets and skill-sets do you want to preserve, let go, and claim as new?**

2.   **How would you describe the greatest strengths that exist in your community and how will you build on these?**

3.   **How would you describe the greatest challenges that exist in your community and how will you address these?**

4.   **Where and how will you create a sense of home or belonging among your members?**

5.   **What are the gaps between who you say you are and how you behave toward one another or others? What does this tell you about who you are growing to become?**

Stewardship

Sustaining your life and mission requires stewardship of your human, financial and material resources. You have resources and options to consider in order to be proactive and responsible stewards. The central goal here is to align your resources with your emerging vision.

Big questions

1.   **In light of the internal changes taking place in your community and the external changes in our world, what shifts are necessary for you to sustain your life and mission into the future:**

    a.   **What values do you want to preserve, let go, and claim as new?**

    b.   **What practices do you want to preserve, let go, and foster as new?**

    c.   **What structures do you want to preserve, let go, and create as new?**

d. **What mind-sets, heart-sets and skill-sets do you want to preserve, let go, and claim as new?**

2. **What buildings and houses might you require and what space do you want to own, rent, consolidate, renovate, repurpose, relinquish or develop?**

3. **What land might you require and what do you want to own, rent, consolidate, repurpose, purchase, or relinquish (e.g., sell, donate, put in trust)?**

4. **How will you address your healthcare and retirement needs?**

5. **What human, financial and material resources will you need in order to support both the care of your members and your developing vision for the future?**

Context and partners in mission

Your evolving context

Your life does not exist in a vacuum or for its own sake. You live in an evolving world and in relationship with others in Religious Life and the broader Church, as well as others in the neighborhoods in which you reside. In addition to addressing the three core domains (Mission, Community and Stewardship), it will be important to understand the evolving context in which you live. It will be important, for any vision you create, that you discern the relevant signs of the times and align your efforts accordingly.

Big questions

Recall your reflections from Chapter 2: The World in which We Live:

1. **What are the trends in the world, Religious Life, the Church and life in your own neighborhoods and how might these evolve over the next 5 to 10 years?**

2. **What are the aching, gaping needs of our world to which you are called and best suited to respond?**

Partners in mission

Your partners in mission include anyone who resonates with your mission and charism and who wants to share in bringing this to our world. This extended family of yours could include: associates, affiliates, auxiliaries, co-journers, co-ministers, companions, board members, other religious, staff and employees.

Your partners in mission have the potential of bringing a tremendous variety of gifts to the table: wisdom, energy, skills and new ways of thinking, along with tremendous loyalty and love. How you shape these partnerships in the future will be part and parcel of your developing vision. In other words, who you choose and why says something about where you want to go in the future, with whom, and how you might get there. It says something about your identity and the beliefs you hold regarding living in our interdependent world.

Big questions

1. **Which partnerships seem especially important in helping you shape your future?**

2. **Which partnerships resonate less with who you are becoming and are less central to your emerging vision?**

3. **What are your concerns about sharing your life with others?**

4. **In what ways do you want your partners in mission to be involved in your visioning efforts?**

Transformative Visioning Structures

"True vision always is a gift. When it graces us, therefore, we do not experience 'sight' as much as being 'sighted,' being drawn, being enticed into depth. Our answers then will emerge out of that depth." Barbara Fiand

How do you involve your entire community in the work of Transformative Visioning and the larger Journey of Transformation? How can you address the content of what goes into a vision in such a way that it aids in your community's transformation? Again, recognizing that the circumstances of each community are different, let me offer a template and some general guidelines to help you get started. You can then adapt these to fit your own situation.

There are any number of ways to go about this, so as I describe the rationale, guidelines and templates imagine what might work for your community. Then imagine how you might tailor these to better fit your circumstances.

Rationale and considerations

The primary purpose for creating new structures is to help a community engage in the Journey of Transformation with the Transformative Visioning process as its driving element. The structures I will describe are visioning structures. The very act of creating these can be transformative in that it disrupts the status quo and challenges you to think and act differently.

These new structures I'm proposing are not "governance" structures (although some decisions may overlap with governance). Nor are they meant to replace all of your existing community structures (although they will replace some). Life will need to go on with many of your existing structures and plans while new structures and plans are developed. It will be a process of evolution in your existing structures, along with the mind-sets, skill-sets and personnel that support them.

Every member's whole-hearted commitment to participate in this journey is essential for your individual and collective growth, conversion and transformation. All members will be needed and valued for whatever their contributions can be. Each of the personal and collective contributions will make a difference in what this Journey of Transformation can mean for all of the members and for our world.

Inclusivity and efficiency

Inclusivity and efficiency are two values with which you will need to grapple in shaping your structures. In order to engage in communal transformation, you will need to tap *everyone's* talents and wisdom. You will need maximal participation to capitalize on your pool of talent and to develop the owner-ship you will need for engendering a cooperative spirit. The more members and others who are included in shaping the vision, the more creativity and wisdom will be generated.

On the other hand, a value that often competes with this maximal *inclusivity* is *efficiency*. The more people that are involved, the more cumbersome and inefficient the process becomes. Additionally, not everyone can do planning well. Not everyone understands or appreciates process. Not everyone can grasp the complexities of properties, finances and building assessments. But everyone can do something. The challenge is to find a place for everyone at the table so that each person can bring his or her best self to the process. Balancing inclusivity and effectiveness is key to shaping your structures and approaches.

Small and large group work

Transformative Visioning and the Journey of Transformation cannot all be done on the few occasions you might meet as a whole community and it cannot all be done only by small groups. You need both. Large gatherings (e.g. assemblies and Chapters) are critical for cross-conversations among differing groups, making major decisions, building a common framework of understanding, amassing communal ownership and transforming normative patterns that occur in these venues. Small group work is equally critical for engaging in in-depth conversations, research, writing, working through details of a plan and making decisions that need not involve the entire community.

Most communities have a large assembly once or twice a year, a Chapter every four to six years, with committees doing the legwork in-between. This frequency does not encourage depth, integration or partnership. Having one or two assemblies per year does not promote a continual integration and deepening of member's participation. Members will not remember what happened a year ago and there is no momentum. The work of transformation needs to be fluid and some decisions can't wait years before implementing. The capacity to build upon each step is often lost with one-and-done assemblies. Committees too often work in silos with only the leadership seeing the big picture. You will need to find ways to meet more frequently in large groups and better connect and integrate the smaller group work.

In addition, when engaged in this work it will be important that it becomes ongoing and open-ended, not artificially constrained by Chapter-to-Chapter deadlines. Too often, electing new leaders means a whole new approach to things. This kind of stop-start pausing for Chapter then switching gears and directions with a new team is very disruptive, even demoralizing, when a community has been on a roll and gaining momentum. It helps when this transformative work becomes a primary mandate that bridges across Chapters. In this way Chapters elect leaders who express a passion and have the ability to keep it going. This provides greater continuity and deepening of the community's efforts.

Personal work of every member

Beyond the group work, there is the all-important personal work required for reading, studying, reflecting, praying and journaling. And everyone will need to engage in the personal inner work of transformation, the visioning processes and the overall Journey of Transformation. At the end of the day, transformation is an inside-out process that occurs within the minds and hearts of every individual in the community. Communal transformation takes place to the degree that each person is committed to the personal and communal work.

Guiding principles

What will the visioning groups be asked to do and how might that help you determine the makeup of these groups? In order to guide your thinking, consider the following three guiding principles for creating the structures you will use for the Journey of Transformation: *depth*, *integration* and *partnership*.

Depth

The various groups you put together will need to get beyond surface ideas and invite in-depth conversations. In addition to sharing ideas, these groups will need time to reflect, explore and be creative. Participants will need to build safety in order to be honest, vulnerable and real. They will need to get into conflict and have the time to work it through. This way of interacting is a shift from the typical "committee" work that focuses only on the "agenda" and typically ignores the relationship dimension of meetings. These visioning groups are intended to focus on both the tasks and the relationships. Examples of depth work might include periodic use of the following:

a. Have ample time for in-depth sharing and reflection during your meetings (beyond opening prayer). For example, start meetings with a *check-in* or reflection asking people to share how they are coming to the meeting. This would not be weather reporting. Rather, they would be asked to share how they are physically, emotionally and spiritually that might be affecting their quality of *presence*. Additionally, the group might pause along the way, and do a *check-out* at the end. A check-out might ask them to reflect not only on what they accomplished, but how they felt about their partnership and participation.

b. Use contemplative engagement and communal discernment at key junctures in your planning, as a means of searching for the deeper, collective wisdom of the group.

c. Encourage the expression of emotions, intuition, imagery, and more personal sharing that helps you get beyond the *heady* work of ideas and opinions.

d. Working with conflict and resistance is also key, which might require professional facilitation.

Integration

The shift from silos to synergy is also key. Integrating and cross-fertilizing your efforts will work against the tendency for groups to become overly possessive of their ideas and their turf. Create structures that bring people together who are working in different areas and who hold different perspectives and talents. This will help you bring creativity and energy to your discussions. Encourage cooperation and coordination of your efforts.

Beyond structures that promote integrative efforts across groups, are integrative conversations that take place within groups. Invite the integration of *head and heart* (thoughts and feelings). Invite the integration of planned agenda with the unplanned agenda (important issues) that emerges throughout the conversation. Integrate your plans with the energy of the Spirit moving in real-time. Integrate the individual and group reflections ("I" and "We"). Integrate the work of the small group with other small groups and the *big picture*. Again, these kinds of integrative efforts are different than the more heady, narrow and siloed focus of most *committees*.

Partnership

Partnership and collaboration are also key. Invite greater collaboration among leaders and members, members and staff, members and associates, members and other religious, consultants and companions in mission. Pragmatically, having more people involved helps to ease the burden for any one person or group. Creating more flexible and permeable boundaries prevents loss of energy and inward focus. It allows new energy and ideas to emerge. It shifts the *same-old* narratives into new narratives needed for transformation. It's important to move toward the values of greater interdependence, mutuality, partnership, and opening up new narratives.

Caveats

Having named a few guidelines, let me also mention a couple of caveats. Involving every member in this work comes with a price in terms of your calendar and *it can't be an add-on*. Also, when you begin to create these structures you will have a great many unanswered questions. It won't be perfect, especially right out of the gate. Just *get started and let it evolve*.

It cannot be an add-on

The maintenance needs in community can leave little time left to vision and plan for the future. Yet if you are to engage in this work of transformation, you will need time to do it. Lots of time. It can't be an add-on to what you are already doing. Your desire for transformation will be tested by your willingness to actually allocate the necessary resources: your money, personnel and, most challenging of all, your calendar. Therefore, you will need some serious discernment, after you have taken everything into account, regarding where you want to place your time and other resources.

Get started and let it evolve

The logistics of setting up new structures and approaches is one of the first steps in moving you from theory to practice. I would urge you to discuss and *work through* the tension and confusion that these departure points might evoke, as well as the differences of opinion you might hold regarding how to adapt these to fit your needs. Please don't swallow the structures I'm about to offer hook, line and sinker, or toss them out lightly and revert to the status quo (i.e., using current structures and approaches) because of their novelty. Take what I am offering and mold it to fit your circumstances. Shape it to fit your values and make it right for you. Don't try to perfect it or create it all at once. Just get started, live into it, learn from your experience and let it evolve.

Who participates and how?

What new structures might facilitate the Transformative Visioning process and overall Journey of Transformation? Using the familiar people in the existing structures reinforces the same mindsets and practices that have existed in the past. New structures are needed to help bring forth a new vision for the future and to engage more fully in the Journey of Transformation.

What follows is a description of structures that I typically recommend as a departure point for discussion when first exploring with leadership what might be useful for their community. Remember, there are any number of ways to go about this. Therefore, as these are described, imagine which ones might work for your community. Then imagine how you might modify and tailor these to better fit your circumstances, and continue to modify these along the way.

Here, I will describe one approach that uses these three building blocks as a possibility: Core Groups, Guiding Team and Integration Team. For additional illustrations, see *Appendix D: Examples of Transformative Visioning Structures.*

Core Groups

Figure 21: Three Core Groups

Core Groups involve every member of the community. In this way, all are welcomed, and everyone has a place at the table. Every member would be invited to participate in a Core Group of their interest. Thus, the total membership of a community would be divided up across each of the Core Groups.

The purpose of the Core Groups is to engage every member in the Transformative Visioning processes. Each Core Group would address the corresponding issues in the primary domains of the content. In this example, it shows the three domains discussed eariler: Mission, Community and Stewardship. For example, if a community has 100 members, there might 40 in the Mission Core Group, 35 in Community and 25 in Stewardship.

Again, there could be four or five Core Groups with different names and content focus, depending upon the size and interests of the particular community. In general, unless your community is very large, fewer Core Groups is better so that it does not become too complex and cumbersome. Part of your initial planning will be to have your community determine the number of Core Groups, their particular focus and names. Again, for purposes of illustration, let's stick with these three.

I typically suggest inviting every member of the community to commit to participating in one of these Core Groups (at whatever level they are capable). Each member would contribute to the work of a specific Core Group according to his or her interests and talents. It is important to discern who could contribute in what ways to the work that needs to be accomplished in each Core Group. Even your elders can participate to some degree.

Each Core Group would include two components: a **Core Team** to lead the group and a **Wisdom Circle** to include the involvement, ownership and wisdom of all members.

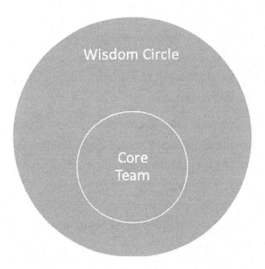

Figure 22: Core Group with two subgroups

Core Teams

Each Core Group has a Core Team to lead its efforts. Core Teams could consist of four to seven people. Four is a rather small number for a good mix of talents and dialogue. Having more than seven members can become cumbersome, making it more difficult to have spontaneous, free-flowing and in-depth discussions. You could use any number of combinations from the following categories of people to be on the Core Team.

Core Team Coordinators

I recommend that two people on each Core Team act as "Coordinators." The Coordinators coordinate and facilitate the work of their Core Team and Wisdom Circle. The coordinators partner in setting the agenda and facilitating the meetings of their Core Team and Wisdom Circle. Having two coordinators is to encourage partnership and ease the burden on any one person. Additionally, it is an effort to shift away from having a *committee chair* which encourages the traditional top-down mindset rather than a more mutual way of interacting.

425

Leadership as liaisons

Where is leadership? At least one person from leadership ought to be involved in each Core Team. This strengthens the coordination and integration of efforts across the Core Teams because leadership regularly meets and is in touch with all of the moving parts.

It works best if a leader in a Core Team function as a *liaison*, rather than the Coordinator. This shifts the primary responsibility for leading the Core Teams to the members, encouraging subsidiarity. Leaders do not abnegate their role as community leaders, but they are not *in charge* of the Core Team. By virtue of their role as congregational leaders, they set certain parameters (e.g., budget, broad directions, and deadlines), and help coordinate the moving parts within the larger community agenda.

Resource People

Resource People could be tapped, as needed, to help the Core Teams. These Resource People could be other members, other religious or laity. These are people who have the expertise and ability to stretch the thinking of a Core Team and help it accomplish its agenda. These might be relators, financial advisors, architects, developers, healthcare professionals, attorneys, farmers, artists, or people who are known for their capacity to think outside the box. They would meet with the Core Team on an as needed basis (i.e., not as Core Team members).

Involvement of key people across Core Teams

You likely have some key people (e.g., in administration or other offices) who could easily contribute to tasks that cut across two or three Core Teams. They could either float across the Core Teams or be placed in one as their primary Core Team. If they are placed in a Core Team, I usually suggest they become a member of the Core Team that best fits their primary job responsibility (e.g., the Treasurer might join the Stewardship Core Team). They can always consult with other Core Teams as needed. Having key people as members of a Core Team stretches them to think more integratively and act more collaboratively than if they were simply left in their current positions to carry out their usual responsibilities.

Wisdom Circles

In addition to Core Teams, each Core Group has a Wisdom Circle, comprised of the broader membership. In the illustration we have been using, there would be three Wisdom Circles (Mission, Community and Stewardship). Each member would choose to participate in one of the three Wisdom Circles to share their passions and talents.

The purpose of Wisdom Circles is to promote the values of *inclusivity, collaboration, shared wisdom* and to develop a wider base of *ownership* for their efforts. Using these Wisdom Circles you can tap the wisdom of members in any number of ways. You do not have to have only face-to-face Wisdom Circle meetings which can be hard for senior members or those who would have to travel a long distance. You might have an occasional meeting with the whole Wisdom Circle, however, you might also use video conferencing, surveys, or small focus groups. Core Teams could share information, seek consultation and make decisions within their respective Wisdom Circles.

Integration Team

The primary purpose of the Integration Team is to integrate efforts across the Core Groups while encouraging in-depth, integrative dialogue and partnership among leaders and members. To accomplish this, the Guiding Team, Leadership Team, and Core Team Coordinators comprise the Integration Team. Some communities have chosen to include only the Coordinators from each Core Team, and others have included all members of the Core Teams. Ideally, this is the pool of the most motivated and capable people in your community.

The Integration Team might meet every couple of months, give or take, depending upon your circumstance and the work they are expected to do. The Integration Team deals with agenda brought to it by the Core Teams, Guiding Team and Leadership Team. They, in turn, send work back to those teams. The

Integration Team, along with leadership, and, to a lesser extent, the Guiding Team determine the agenda for assemblies and Chapters. The Guiding Team would then design specific goals and processes for accomplishing this agenda.

Leadership

Leadership's primary role is to inspire and empower membership to engage in the overall Journey of Transformation. They are the primary hub for integrating and coordinating the entire journey. Leadership provides encouragement and support for members' efforts. They convene the conversations that matter and shape new ways to partner as leaders and members. They challenge the status quo and orchestrate working through the chaos, conflict, and resistance that must be addressed. Leadership also provides the financial, material and human resources necessary to give members the greatest opportunity to succeed in their efforts.

Guiding Team

The primary purpose of a Guiding Team is to guide the community through the Transformative Visioning processes and overall Journey of Transformation. They would work with a facilitator to design processes as well as plan and implement the goals for community assemblies, Chapters and other gatherings. The Guiding Team works closely with leadership and the Integration Team. This might be similar to the familiar Chapter Planning Committee, however, the Guiding Team is a *new structure*, not an ad hoc group.

The Guiding Team is composed of a combination of leaders and members working together as partners. It helps to have one Coordinator from each Core Team on the Guiding Team. This bolsters the coordination and integration of Core Team efforts. The Guiding Team might meet every 6 to 8 weeks to design, coordinate and integrate the various processes.

Reflection: Transformative Visioning

---

1. *What might help your community appreciate and work with Transformative Visioning as an organic, emergent and iterative process?*

2. *In what ways might you want to experiment with new structures to help you gather the wisdom and weave a new dream?*

Summary

In this chapter I introduced the fifth dynamic element, Transformative Visioning, defining its purpose and its connection to the larger Journey of Transformation. I emphasized Transformative Visioning as an organic, emergent and iterative process. We looked at a few of the tensions that are inherent in the process and are ideally held as generative forces. We surveyed the major content areas for visioning – mission, community, and stewardship – and some of the big questions associated with each. We then looked at how Transformative Visioning might be implemented and the structures that could be created to aid in its implementation, structures based on the values of depth, integration and partnership.

Epilogue: Ever Ancient, Ever New

Who are you called to become?

> *"Stand at the crossroads and look; ask for the ancient paths, ask where the good way is, and walk in it, and you will find rest for your souls."*
> **Jeremiah 6:16**

A Deeper Invitation

There is a Great Turning taking place across our planetary home that is bringing all life to a crossroads. Humanity might choose the path of least resistance, which we know will lead inevitably to death and destruction. Or we, together, might choose the ancient path, the path of deep change and transformation that could potentially lead us to our next evolutionary leap. It remains to be seen what path we will ultimately choose, but the hour of our existential crisis is at hand.

Religious Life itself is situated in this same Great Turning and is facing its own crossroads. All mainline religions, and especially the Catholic Church, are viewed by society as increasingly out of touch, out of sync and anachronistic.

You might choose the path of least resistance and reinforce the official future with its numbing narrative of aging and diminishment. Or you might choose the ancient path of transformation that could potentially lead Religious Life to its next evolutionary leap. It remains to be seen.

Most everyone is banking on the fact that Religious Life has cycled throughout history and *seems* destined to rise again. However, history also tells us that most communities will become extinct during this downturn. Most will make small, safe, predictable changes instead of radical changes. They will focus on the external changes and avoid the inner work of transformation. They will, in a variety of ways, respond predominately out of fear and not out of the kind of courage, creativity and forbearance that is needed to perdure, transform and give birth to new life.

History further suggests that if a new cycle in Religious Life is to emerge it is certainly not going to happen on its own. Religious men and women will need to do their part. History demonstrates that religious must do more than adapt. They will need a transformative response to our changing times. Religious will need to offer a prophetic alternative to society, not mirror it or continue to live as they have in the past. Religious will need to bring forth bold, new, contemporized expressions of the Gospel. Those who have studied this history tell us that breathing new life into Religious Life requires nothing less than personal and communal conversion.

Communities are facing a *graced crossroads*. Grace, of course, is in every nook and cranny of creation. But when we as individuals or communities of faith hit bottom, we have a unique accessibility to grace that otherwise eludes us in ordinary times. During times of transition when all hope seems to vanish, the veil between ordinary life and the Divine Presence becomes thin, and grace does more abound. Here, at a graced crossroads, there is a *deeper invitation*: listen to God's call to choose life, not only for ourselves but for all those to whom we profess our love, our descendants and future generations.

Most communities will approach these graced crossroads by employing conventional change methods like strategic planning. Unfortunately, the research tells us that conventional approaches are not suited for unconventional times such as these. They are woefully inadequate to bring about deep change in a community's culture. The Dirty Dozen represent the most common pitfalls communities will encounter when attempting to transform their lives. Out of fear, they will attempt to avoid the conflict, chaos, ambiguity, intimacy and inner work that are integral to transformation.

Communities will need to use some form of strategic planning when it comes to the pragmatic changes that are demanding their attention (e.g., buildings, property, healthcare, etc.). However, alone, such conventional approaches will not suffice to transform communities. These approaches will need to be adapted, used flexibly, and incorporated creatively into other processes. In order to transform your lives, you will need to integrate these conventional planning and visioning methods into processes aimed specifically at deep change and the inner work of transformation.

Toward this end, I introduced the Journey of Transformation to describe the principles and processes of this inner work. It is a method and means for cooperating with grace. The foundation for the Journey of Transformation is based upon three sets of knowledge: 1) *empirical knowledge* acquired from contemporary science and the humanities; 2) *experiential knowledge* gleaned from our own life experiences of transformation; and, 3) *soul knowledge* gathered from ancient and contemporary faith traditions shedding light on what it means to be on a faith journey. It is from these foundations that I proposed five key principles of transformation:

1. Maturation is a lifelong opportunity

2. Growth and transformation move in spirals

3. We plateau for a time, then transform

4. We breakdown to breakthrough

5. It is pain that brings us to the graced crossroads, but it is Love that pulls us through.

I further proposed five dynamic elements that when woven together constitute the key processes used in the Journey of Transformation:

1. Shift in consciousness: creating a new narrative

2. Reclaim our inner voice: the seat and soul of everything that lives

3. Reconciliation and conversion: the womb of our becoming

4. Experimentation and learning: acting our way into a new way of being

5. Transformative visioning: listening to our deepest longings

These five dynamic elements comprise the inner work of transformation that communities will need to do in order to cooperate with grace and transform their lives. The fifth element, Transformative Visioning, drives the entire Journey of Transformation with its focus on creating a future. The other four dynamic elements are wrapped around the fifth element throughout the Journey of Transformation. These five dynamic elements are the transformative processes into which the more conventional processes are incorporated and used to shape a vision for a community's future.

The Journey of Transformation is a comprehensive approach that addresses your entire life and mission, not just the bricks and mortar of your lives. It engages and integrates the heart and soul of your members as you plan and shape your vision for the future. It is multidimensional in that it addresses not only the organizational dimensions of your community but also the personal and interpersonal dimensions. It is multilayered in that it goes beyond what you can see on the surface to also address the patterns, structures, worldview, and indeed the very culture and soul of your community.

The Divine Mystery of transformation can partially be understood from our human perspective and the rest is left to mystery. Indeed, we sought to understand what we could of this mystery, so that we know what is our part to play. We need to dispose ourselves to grace and learn how to cooperate with grace. The parts we can't see (grace of ambiguity) and can't control (grace of chaos) are integral to any faith journey. These underlying and unnerving aspects of a transformative journey require that your communities grow in their capacity to use their instruments of faith (e.g., prayer, contemplation and discernment). Even so, at the end of all your planning, praying, organizing, discerning, implementing and evaluating, transformation will require you to take a leap of faith. The rest is grace.

This leap of faith and the path of transformation are ancient paths of peril and promise. I and others can offer guidance, but the choices are yours to make. Your choices will determine not only your own future but will have a hand in determining the fate of Religious Life and our planet. You could choose to sit on the sidelines, be bystanders or observers of all that is happening. Or you could choose to actively partner with others and participate as agents of transformation. You could choose the ancient path, a heroic journey.

Many people fret about the dwindling stream of vocations and fidelity of newer members. I have no doubt that men and women will continue to come forth to shape the emergence of a new Religious Life. They will find their role to play. The newer members I know seem genuinely called, full of energy and hope, and are bringing new understandings and ways of fulfilling their call. They are opening their hearts and minds, collaborating across congregations, partnering with laity and are eager to shape the future of Religious Life. In a book written by newer members entitled *In Our Own Words*, Teresa Maya, said "Sisters before us planted; we must tend to the harvest."[398] They are tending the garden and its harvest.

Frankly, I worry more about the elders who seem a bit lost in determining their own role to play. This struggle is not surprising given our Western society's bias toward youth and productivity. We have placed our seniors in a "role-less" status. Many religious speak about a shift from *doing* to *being* at this stage in life. It sounds good in theory, but few seem satisfied with this hard-to-grasp shift. What exactly does *being* do all day long, anyway? What's on a *being's* to-do list? Ram Dass, when grappling with his own role-less aging, came to a shift in consciousness: "Don't be a wise elder, be an incarnation of wisdom." He believes, "That changes the whole nature of the game. That's not just a new role, it's a new state of being."

Young or old, you are not role-less! What could be more needed now than incarnating *wisdom* in a world that increasingly discounts facts and truth. What could be more needed now than your *compassionate presence* in our wounded world so prone to shaming and blaming? What could be more needed now than being *models of living community* in a world that seems more interested in building walls than bridges? What could be more needed now than the presence of men and women who are incarnating the gospel values of love, kindness, inclusivity, justice, forgiveness and mercy in a world so polarized and prone to violence? Who better than you to bring the message of restorative justice in a world so ready to exact retribution? Who will bridge these tragic gaps but you?

Religious of all ages are needed as agents of transformation. There are plenty of so-called leaders in our world who are challenging the status quo by tearing down institutions and stoking the fears of the disenfranchised for their own political gain. They are *disturbers* of the status quo, but they are not *transformers*. We need people who can not only challenge the status quo and systems that are no longer working, but who offer alternatives that include, transcend and transform the past into a viable future.

The world needs agents of transformation who, as Richard Rohr suggests, are those who live and love as Jesus did: "Those who agree to carry and love what God loves – which is both the good and the bad – and to pay the price for its reconciliation within themselves.... They are the leaven, the salt, the remnant, the mustard seed that God uses to transform the world."[399] No matter your age, your ministry, or whatever is on your to-do list, you can be a presence that transforms.

One month before signing the Emancipation Proclamation, December 1, 1862, President Abraham Lincoln addressed Congress, saying: "The dogmas of the quiet past, are inadequate to the stormy present. The occasion is piled high with difficulty, and we must rise with the occasion. As our case is new, so we must think anew, and act anew. We must disenthrall ourselves, and then we shall save our country."[400]

Our world and Religious Life need those who will rise to the occasion and disenthrall themselves of the past. We cannot travel to the future without honoring our past, our ancestors and traditions, but these will not lead us there. We need to loosen our grip on nostalgia and the ways we've always understood and done things. What leads us into the future is our courage to take risks and our creative fidelity to the values and beliefs we treasure most. What leads us to the future is having the will, skills and discipline to stay in the struggle in order to harness the generative potential of conflict and chaos that is the crucible of transformation. If we truly wish to honor the past, we must do for the next generation what our ancestors did for us: we must make room for the new.

At these graced crossroads, there exists a profound opportunity to engage the Divine Mystery of transformation and respond to God's call to new life. If you can cooperate with grace by doing the inner work of transformation, you can transcend the past. You can give life to your deepest longings, called forth by the lure and love of God, and help humanity take the next best step in its evolutionary spiral. Stand at the crossroads and discern the ancient paths where the good way lies. Walk in it and find rest for your souls.

APPENDICES

Appendix A: Continuum of Lifecyle Viability

DIMENSIONS OF COMMUNITY	Continuum of Lifecycle Viability Community Characteristics				NEW LIFE
	Strong Communities	Typical Communities	Marginal Communities	Near Death Communities	Transformative Communities
Mission and Charism	Leveraging resources mostly aligned with mission	Maintenance overshadows mission; resources misaligned	Maintenance grossly overshadows mission	Life is seen in the review mirror; maintaining what was in the past	Resources fully leveraged and aligned with mission
Ministries	A mixture of new ministries and succession plans for other ministries	Cautiously exploring new ministries and/or succession planning	"Founder's Syndrome," few new ministries	No new ministries, few active, external ministries	Embracing an abundance of future opportunities
Partnerships with Laity	Exploring affiliations, acquisitions and opportunities	Thinking more strategically about affiliations, but with ambivalence	Internally focused; reluctant to partner	*Cultural lock* and fear of *outsiders*; unwilling to collaborate	Creating new affiliations and partnerships in mission
Partnerships with Religious	Collaborating and creating new partnerships	Pursuing alliances, strategic collaborations, mergers or unions	Considering custodial completion or covenants	No custodial arrangements made	Initiating new forms of life and collaborative efforts
Community Life	Meaningful, relational, real and healthy	Some meaningful relationships and some camps	Fragmented, camps, doing your own thing	Stifling, apathetic, disconnected, distant, lifeless	"See how they love one another" – and they do
Membership Departures/ Arrivals	Active and energetic vocation & formation efforts, averaging 1 new member/yr	Active vocation & formation efforts with much anxiety and tension, no new members	Vocation & formation efforts are mired in conflict and no new members	Inactive vocation, formation efforts, no new members or hope for vocations	Active vocation & formation efforts, new forms of membership, > 1 new member/yr
Planning	Developing new directions for allocating resources and membership	Developing new goals to do better what's been done in the past	Crisis/survival mode; succession planning	Reactive, failure to plan; no hope for the future	Risking to birth new visions and being transformed by the journey
Leadership	Energizing and effective leadership team	Administrative focus on the status quo more than future visions	Maintenance oriented, focused on fixing problems, recycled leadership, little synergy	Suffocating under maintenance demands; ineffective; conflicted; low trust	Charismatic, courageous, innovative, and inspiring
Resources: Human, Financial and Spiritual	Adequate resources applied toward mission and community	There are enough resources if changes are made in how they are used	Resources are inadequate and viewed as "scarce," they are driven by fear and have periodic crises	Resources are grossly inadequate; they have frequent crises and are unable to resolve these	Resources are seen as "abundant" and are well leveraged to plan for the future

DIMENSIONS OF COMMUNITY	Strong Communities	Typical Communities	Marginal Communities	Near Death	Transformative Communities
Mission and Charism	Mission and maintenance needs are at great odds; human, material and financial resources are fairly leveraged and aligned with mission; innovative and courageous actions fall short of the rhetoric; even so, there is a sense of being-in-it-together for mission	Maintenance pressures supersede mission efforts; human, material and financial resources are misaligned and not leveraged toward mission; the work is toward greater efficiencies ("belt-tightening") and doing things better, rather than innovating new ways	Maintenance needs and keeping things going *as is* grossly overshadows mission efforts; human, material and financial resources are neither aligned nor leveraged toward mission; there is little sense of being-in-it together for mission	The heydays of mission efforts are viewed through the rearview mirror; nearly all resources (human, material and financial) are aimed toward maintaining buildings or caring for members with few, if any, going to mission; a sense of mission is all but a memory	An integrative and proactive response to mission and maintenance needs; human, material and financial resources are fully leveraged and aligned with mission; mission fully aligned with charism and needs of world; members full of zeal for mission and have a strong sense of being-in-it-together
Ministries	Future ministry opportunities are explored and sometimes emerge; members serve on several boards and the community has several sponsored ministries; ministry efforts and succession planning is done in the context of a strategic plan	New ministries are cautiously explored and seldom initiated; no succession planning is done; few members are in direct service, though several are on boards; there are some sponsored ministries, but no overall plan for the future.	"Founders' syndrome" (i.e., *This is my baby*) is commonplace; few new ministries have been initiated in the last 5 years and, if so, these were mostly individual endeavors (when the member leaves, the ministry shuts down); "slot-filling" is common	There have been no new ministries initiated in the last 5 to 10 years; there are no plans for new ministries and no meaningful ministry options for senior members; nearly all members are retired and typically do non-remunerative, part-time ministries (if at all); few external ministries	Ministry opportunities arise and address emerging needs of the world and our neighbors; members are fully engaged in direct service, systemic change, boards and succession plans; new ministries flow from a clear focus for mission and a vision for the future

441

DIMENSIONS OF COMMUNITY	Strong Communities	Typical Communities	Marginal Communities	Near Death	Transformative Communities
Partnerships with laity	There are explorations regarding affiliations, acquisitions and opportunities with the laity and lay organizations; associations are fairly comfortable, though equal partnership remains a challenge	There are periodic discussions and thought given to strategic affiliations with the laity, but little action; there are periodic reunions with former members and celebrations with lay co-ministers, but rarely more than collaboration	The community, by and large, is internally focused and highly reluctant to partner with the laity; they are seen as "outsiders," "not one of us" and a threat to the community's fragile sense of identity, security and self-sufficiency	"Cultural lock-in" exists as members are greatly threatened by "outsiders;" the boundaries are rigid around community; "outsiders" are a threat to the fragile identity, security and self-esteem of the members which is tied to past success	There are active pursuits and successful partnerships with lay persons and organizations as part of an overall vision for the future; there are many mutually desirable and welcomed partnerships, strategic and structural alliances
Partnerships with other religious	There are several project-related or programmatic efforts to collaborate with other religious (Inter-novitiate programs; sharing resources, sharing of "best practices"); however, pursuing strategic alliances or combining structures for mutual benefit seldom occurs	There may be one or two project-related or programmatic efforts done jointly with another community; mostly they function independently from other religious; pursuing alliances and strategic collaborations is not done; however, the possibility of union or merger, is on the horizon	There are currently discussions regarding covenants or completion; they know they cannot go on as is because of a shrinking pool of leaders or financial crises; they are more dependent than they wish to be and are challenged at the prospect of forming equal partnerships	The community is past the point of mergers; they are no longer able to care for their own mission, finances or members but are not actively pursuing custodial arrangements to care for themselves	There are active pursuits and successful partnerships with other religious organizations (Catholic and other) as part of the overall vision for the future; there are many mutually desirable and welcomed partnerships, strategic and structural alliances

DIMENSIONS OF COMMUNITY	Strong Communities	Typical Communities	Marginal Communities	Near Death	Transformative Communities
Community	Members for the most part experience a sense of community and care for one another; they can have meaningful conversations during assemblies, though honest, intimate and challenging conversations are rare; some growth takes place inside community but mostly beyond the walls of community	Some members have meaningful relationships inside community, but the majority do not; substantive conversations take place among like-minded people; camps and cliques are common around contentious issues; personal growth and development takes place outside of community	The community is fragmented and split along issues; the sense of being community is marginal; camps abound and most members do their own thing with little accountability to the whole; tension at assemblies is high and unresolved; conflicts pile up creating more and more baggage; there is a chronic malaise among members	Community is stifling; members dislike coming together; many rules/spoken and unspoken expectations; it is hard to be your authentic self in community; members feel disconnected from one another; the elders are shelved and passing time, while the younger members do their own thing	"See how they love one another." The gospel <u>call</u> to "love one another" is real and evident by behavior; they have intimate conversations about things that matter; they can reach across the differences, affirm and challenge one another; community is a place of growth where all are welcomed
Membership; Ratio of Departures to Arrivals	There is around 1 new member joining every year or so; there are active and energetic vocation and formation efforts; new forms of membership are discussed but not seriously pursued; identity is stronger on paper than it is in life	There are no new members; there is some active vocation/ formation efforts, <u>but these</u> are fraught with anxiety; often there is a desperation to recruit new members which confounds discernment and results in blame when no one arrives	There are no new members; if there are active vocation/formati on, efforts these are mired in conflict leaving identity and boundaries unclear; there is a mixture of despair and wishful thinking	There have been no new members in the last 10 years; there is little hope and even less discussion regarding new members; prayers for new vocations may persist, but no action is taken	The ratio of members leaving/joining is irrelevant; there is zeal for life and mission; identity is strong; boundaries are clear and permeable while experimenting with new forms of membership

DIMENSIONS OF COMMUNITY	Strong Communities	Typical Communities	Marginal Communities	Near Death	Transformative Communities
Planning for the future	The community is developing new directions for allocating resources and member to be involved; Chapters are directional (though not transformative) in nature; strategic (pastoral) planning is done as needed; leadership does most of the planning, but actively collaborates with membership	The community develops new goals at Chapter, as this is the primary planning forum; goals are typically geared toward doing things better, rather than doing new things; efficiency in getting tasks done is valued over depth and substance; leadership over-functions, while membership under-functions	The community is intermittently or frequently in crisis mode; they are so busy trying to "put out fires" and simply survive that proactive planning is nearly impossible; expediency trumps depth or substance; leadership over-functions while membership under-functions; risks are avoided	The community is frequently or continually in crisis mode and is highly reactive; there is a failure to plan; leadership is swamped with responsibility for the whole, while members are disengaged, passive and dependent; high denial of impending demise; too internally conflicted to cooperate effectively	The community is shaping a new *vision*; planning is an ongoing and a valued function of these *learning communities*; it is a transformative and emergent process as much as it is strategic and goal directed; depth and discernment are values that inform the planning; leaders and members are partners in a shared vision
Leadership	Leadership is fairly energizing and effective; they function as a team with everyone pitching in to the best of his or her abilities	Leadership is largely administrative; it focuses on keeping the status quo more than change or any future vision;	Leadership is maintenance oriented, focused on fixing problems, leadership is recycled because there are no other viable members; there is little or no synergy	Suffocating under maintenance demands; ineffective, conflicted; low trust; frequently one or more leaders on a team departs due to stress, illness or death	Leadership charismatic, courageous, innovative, and inspiring; there is great synergy on the team, high trust from the members and a great deal of partnership between leaders and members
Resources: Human, Financial and Spiritual	There are adequate resources to apply toward mission and to use to develop community	There are enough resources for the community if it makes the necessary changes to plan for the future	Resources are inadequate and viewed as "scarce;" the community is driven by fear of not having "enough;" periodic crises reinforce this fear	Resources are grossly inadequate to sustain the life of community; there are frequent crises and no clear plans to address these	Resources are adequate and viewed as "abundant;" they are seizing opportunities to plan well to leverage these for their future

Appendix B: Alignment of Life

Alignment of Life at All Levels

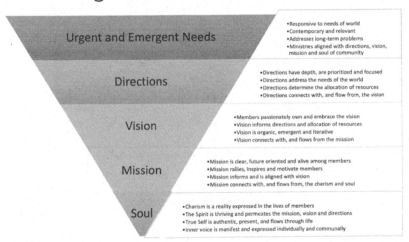

Urgent and Emergent Needs
- Responsive to needs of world
- Contemporary and relevant
- Addresses long-term problems
- Ministries aligned with directions, vision, mission and soul of community

Directions
- Directions have depth, are prioritized and focused
- Directions address the needs of the world
- Directions determine the allocation of resources
- Directions connects with, and flow from, the vision

Vision
- Members passionately own and embrace the vision
- Vision informs directions and allocation of resources
- Vision is organic, emergent and iterative
- Vision connects with, and flows from the mission

Mission
- Mission is clear, future oriented and alive among members
- Mission rallies, inspires and motivate members
- Mission informs and is aligned with vision
- Mission connects with, and flows from, the charism and soul

Soul
- Charism is a reality expressed in the lives of members
- The Spirit is thriving and permeates the mission, vision and directions
- True Self is authentic, present, and flows through life
- Inner voice is manifest and expressed individually and communally

Misalignment of Life at All Levels

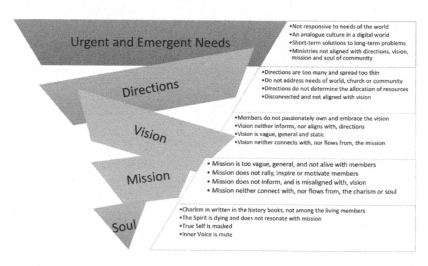

Appendix C: Back to the Future

Example of an instructional letter given to a women's community

As you journey more deeply into shaping your future, I am asking you to prepare a letter. This letter will be shared during your upcoming assembly in order to kindle your spirits and provide food for the journey. This letter will likely also be shared in the months and years to come as you engage in ongoing visioning and the Journey of Transformation.

I hope that you will consider this letter as one of the most important letters you will ever write, that the shaping of your very future depends on it. I ask that you take this invitation into prayer and let it ripen, pouring new wine into new wineskins, until you are sure of what you want to say. Take it down into the depths of your soul and speak of your deepest longings for the future of your community.

What am I asking you to write? We have been engaged in a planning and visioning process for a while, exploring what we might create. In the last assembly, you were introduced to the possibilities of transformation and a way of visioning that builds upon our prior work, incorporates strategic planning and invites us to discern God's call to new life as you shape your future together. We want this next phase of our work to build upon our prayerful reflections. Where do you imagine you are being led as a congregation? Having listened to the dreams of the future from some of our sisters and associates, what are yours?

I want you to walk with your cherished ancestors in prayer and talk with them about the future of your community. Choose one or two spiritual companions who are dearest in your heart and with whom you could have a prayerful, soul-to-soul conversation. It might be Saint _____ , or perhaps you want to pray and talk with your founder _____ , or Jesus. Choose the one who knows you, knows your life and who you know, deep inside, would only want what is good and right for you, your community and those you serve.

For example, if you chose to pray with Jesus, ask what he sees for you in the depths of his soul. What are his deepest longings for you? What might you look like ten years from now if you look through his eyes? What does he see happening? What might be your mission in the future if you are listening to his deepest desires? How might you be living community? How might the spirit of your charism come alive for you in today's world? In his heart-of-hearts, how does he hope this journey will transform you? Pray with Jesus as you walk with your ancestors, as disciples on the road to Emmaus.

Once you've had time to let your dream ripen, write a letter to your members as if you are writing it 10 years hence, looking back from the future on all that has happened. Write to your members as if you are the voice of the one you chose to pray with or use your own voice having taken his to heart. Write from the depths of your soul a very personal letter that speaks of your deepest longings. Write to your members telling them what you see as the future of your community ten years from now. Write it out of unwavering faith, audacious hope and most especially with love for your members, associates, companions in mission and a wounded world in need of your charism.

Appendix D: Examples of Transformative Visioning Structures

What follows are four examples of structures I have used, arranged here from the simplest to the more complex. There are endless permutations that could be created using various combinations of theses structural building blocks. However, these four broad templates should give you a rough idea of what might work for your community. Then it would be a matter of tailoring these to fit your circumstances.

Example 1

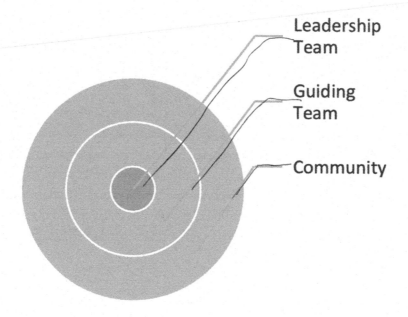

This example is the simplest structure, best for communities that are small, with 25 or fewer members that are willing and able to do this complex work. Notice that there are no Core Groups, nor is there an Integration Team. The Guiding Team caries the primary responsibility of the work and brings as much as possible to the community as a whole. The community might meet three times per year and the Guiding Team might meet six times per year.

Example 2

Leadership
Team

Guiding
Team

Visioning
Group

Community

This example adds another layer and is also best for communities that are relatively small and with few members who are willing and capable of doing this complex work. However, it has a "Visioning Group" comprised of the more able members of a community. The elderly and infirm are exempt. There are no Core Groups, nor is there an Integration Team. The Guiding Team

caries the primary responsibility of the work and brings as much as possible to the Visioning Group. The Visioning Group might meet three times per year and the Guiding Team might meet six times per year. Those not participating in the Visioning Group, could be included in local community conversations or meet one-on-one with members of the Guiding Team to be kept abreast.

Example 3

This example adds yet another layer and is best suited for communities that are larger, with at least 75 members who are willing and able to this work. This illustration includes an Integration Team and three Core Teams. The community could meet three times per year. The Guiding Team could meet six times per year. The Integration Team could meet up to six times per year and Core Teams and Wisdom Circles as needed.

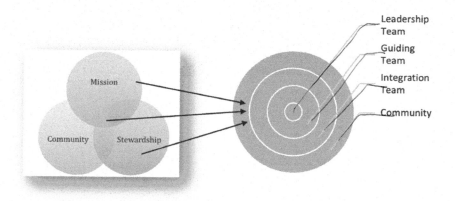

Example 4

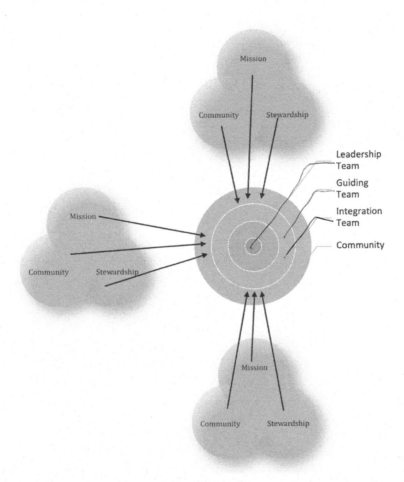

This example adds even more complexity, which is best reserved for large communities in multiple regions or countries. This illustration shows three regions or countries, each having three Core Groups. Representatives from these regions or countries would comprise the Integration Team, which meets three times a year or so. I have used this with communities spanning different continents and it is very effective for enhancing a truly international, intercultural experience of the whole. There are a variety of ways to organize each region or country. Options would need to be explored in the initial planning that would honor the particular culture of each region and country.

About The Author

Dr. Ted Dunn is a clinical psychologist and has worked with men and women religious across the globe since the 1980's. Early in his career he worked as a psychotherapist providing psychological, neuropsychological and vocation evaluations as well as therapy services to hundreds of men and women. He has worked with leadership, vocation, formation and other teams. He has provided training for inter-novitiate programs and supervision to novice directors. He facilitates Chapters, assemblies, communal discernment processes, and conducts workshops on a variety of topics in the United States and internationally.

In the 1990s Dr. Dunn was heavily involved in guiding communities through processes of reconfiguring (e.g., mergers), restructuring (e.g., new models of governance) and forays into refounding (e.g., novel approaches to new life). His focus for the past 20 years, though, has been to assist Catholic and other faith-based communities in processes of deep change and transformation. Over the past 15 years he has come to develop this approach to communal transformation presented in this book.

Dr. Dunn's integration of spirituality, psychology, and organizational change are keys to his success. Though the approaches and populations he has served have varied over the years, his *compassionate approach to healing, belief in the natural resiliency of the human spirit, and personal commitment to life-long learning* remain the foundation of all his professional endeavors. These are the bedrock of his current call to minister to religious communities and other value-based organizations

ENDNOTES

1 Gerald A. Arbuckle, *Strategies for growth in religious life* (New York: Alba House, 1987), p.33.

2 Eckhart Tolle, *A new earth: awakening to your life's purpose* (New York, N.Y.: Dutton/Penguin Group, 2005), p.20.

3 Sandra Marie Schneiders, *Finding the treasure: locating Catholic religious life in a new ecclesial and cultural context*, Religious life in a new millennium (New York: Paulist Press, 2000), p.360.

4 Ted Dunn, "Gather the wisdom, weave a dream: Transformative visioning as a refounding process," *Human Development* 31, no. 2 (2010): p.15.

5 John W. Gardner, *Self-renewal: the individual and the innovative society*, Rev. ed. (New York: Norton, 1981), p.45.

6 David Wechsler, *The measurement of adult intelligence* (Baltimore,: The Williams & Wilkins Company, 1939), p.229.

7 Christine Valters Paintner, *The soul's slow ripening: 12 Celtic practices for seeking the sacred* (Notre Dame: Sorin Books,, 2018), p.1.

8 Ronald Rolheiser, *The holy longing: the search for a Christian spirituality*, 1st published ed. (New York: Image, 2014), p.147.

9 Jr. Martin Luther King, "Letter from a Birmingham Jail," *African Studies Center* (1963), https://www.africa.upenn.edu/Articles_Gen/Letter_Birmingham.html.

10 Adapted from Ted Dunn, "Refounding Religious Life: A choice for transformational change," *Human Development* 30, no. 4 (2009): p.12.

11 Thomas Merton, *The ascent to truth*, A Harvest/Harcourt Brace Jovanovich book (New York ; London: Harcourt Brace Jovanovich, 1981), p.5.

12 Ilia Delio, *The emergent Christ: exploring the meaning of Catholic in an evolutionary universe* (Maryknoll, N.Y.: Orbis Books, 2011), p.13.

13 Albert Gore, *The future: six drivers of global change*, First edition. ed. (New York: Random House, 2013), p.xvii.

14 Brian Swimme and Mary Evelyn Tucker, *Journey of the universe* (New Haven: Yale University Press, 2011), p.14.

15 David J. Rothkopf, *The great questions of tomorrow*, First TED Books hardcover edition. ed., Ted books (New York: TED Books, Simon & Schuster, 2017), p.17.

16 Julia Boorstin, "Google's Eric Schmidt Kicks Off 'Techonomy' Conference," CNBC, https://www.cnbc.com/id/38565740.

17 Anderson Cooper, "Voyagers," in *60 Minutes* (2018).

18 Nassim Nicholas Taleb, *The black swan: the impact of the highly improbable*, 2nd ed. (New York: Random House Trade Paperbacks, 2010), p.xxxii.

19 Ibid., p.135.

20 Burton Gordon Malkiel, *A random walk down Wall Street: the time-tested strategy for successful investing*, Revised and updated edition . ed. (New York: W.W. Norton & Company, 2015), p.157.

21 Thomas L. Friedman, *The world is flat: a brief history of the twenty-first century*, 1st further updated and expanded hardcover ed. (New York: Farrar, Straus and Giroux, 2007).

22 Chris Anderson, *The long tail: why the future of business is selling less of more*, Rev. and updated ed. (New York: Hyperion, 2008).

23 Daryl Conner, "The next generation of fire," in *The change management handbook: a road map to corporate transformation*, ed. Lance Berger, Martin Sikora, and Dorothy Berger (Burr Ridge, Ill: Irwin Professional Pub, 1994), p.259.

24 Ibid., p.267-68.

25 Amy Webb, *The signals are talking: why today's fringe is tomorrow's mainstream*, First edition. ed. (New York: PublicAffairs, 2016), p.2.

26 Rachel Carson, *Silent spring*, 1st Fawcett Crest ed. (New York: Fawcett Crest, 1964).

27 Peter Senge et al., *The necessary revolution: Working together to create a sustainable world* (New York, NY: Random House, 2010), p.16-18.

28 Richard Wike, "What the world thinks about climate change in 7 charts," Pew Research Center, http://www.pewresearch.org/fact-tank/2016/04/18/what-the-world-thinks-about-climate-change-in-7-charts.

29 Friedman, *The world is flat: a brief history of the twenty-first century*, p.10-11.

30 Ben Parr, "The number of books in the world," Mashable, Inc, https://mashable.com/2010/08/05/number-of-books-in-the-world/#8HkZdSDf-GmqC.

31 Barak Shoshany, "If the entire internet were printed in a single book, how many pages would it be?," Quora, https://www.quora.com/If-the-entire-internet-were-printed-in-a-single-book-how-many-pages-would-it-be.

32 Esteban Ortiz-Ospina and Max Roser, "Global health," Our world in data, https://ourworldindata.org/health-meta.

33 Phil Hay, "World undergoing major population shift with far-reaching implications for migration, poverty, development: WB/IMF Report," The world bank, worldbank.org/en/news/press-release/2015/10/07/world-un-

dergoing-major-population-shift-with-far-reaching-implications-for-mi-gration-poverty-development-wbimf-report.

34 Ken Robinson, "Bring on the learning revolution!," in *TED2010*, ed. TED (TED Conference2010).

35 Ray Kurzweil, "Get ready for hybrid thinking," in *TED2014*, ed. TED Talk (2014).

36 Jennifer A. Doudna and Samuel H. Sternberg, *A crack in creation: gene editing and the unthinkable power to control evolution* (Boston: Houghton Mifflin Harcourt, 2017), p.xvi.

37 John Bagot Glubb, *The fate of empires and Search for survival* (Edinburgh: Blackwood, 1978).

38 Margaret J. Wheatley, *Who do we choose to be?: facing reality, claiming leadership, restoring sanity*, First edition. ed. (Oakland, CA: Berrett-Koehler Publishers Inc., 2017), p.8.

39 Catholic Church. Pope (2013: Francis) and Catholic Church. United States Conference of Catholic Bishops., *On care for our common home: Laudato si': encyclical letter*, Publication, USCCB Communications (Washington, DC: United States Conference of Catholic Bishops, 2015), p.14.

40 Gerald A. Arbuckle, *Out of chaos: refounding religious congregations* (New York: Paulist Press, 1988).

41 Ibid., p.134.

42 Ibid., p.186.

43 Lawrence Cada et al., *Shaping the coming age of religious life* (New York: Seabury Press, 1979), p.5.

44 Ibid., p.11.

45 Ibid., pp.51-60.

46 Ibid., p.59.

47 Ibid., p.60.

48 David J. Nygren and Miriam D. Ukeritis, *The future of religious orders in the United States: transformation and commitment* (Westport, Conn.: Praeger, 1993).

49 David Nygren and Miriam Ukeritis, "The future of religious orders in the United States," *Origins* 22, no. 15 (1992): pp.257-72.

50 Diarmuid O'Murchu, *Reframing religious life: an expanded vision for the future* Revised ed. (London, England: St. Pauls, 1998), p.26.

51 Ibid., pp.27-28.

52 Ibid., p.25.

53 Diarmuid O'Murchu, *Religious Life in the 21st Century: The Prospect of Refounding* (Maryknoll, NY: Orbis Books, 2016), p.14.

54 Ibid., p.13.

55 Ibid., p.54.

56 Diarmuid O'Murchu, *Inclusivity: A Gospel Mandate* (Maryknoll, NY: Orbis Books, 2015).

57 Michael Crosby, *Repair my house: becoming "Kindom" Catholics* (Maryknoll, N.Y.: Orbis Books, 2012), pp.vii – ix.

58 Ibid., p.50.

59 Patricia Wittberg, *Pathways to re-creating religious communities* (New York: Paulist Press, 1996), p.9.

60 Ibid., p.14.

61 Raymond L. Fitz and Lawrence J. Cada, "The recovery of religious life," *Review for Religious* 34, no. 5 (1975): p.690.

62 Lawrence Cada et al., *Shaping the coming age of religious life*, p.2.

63 Nygren and Ukeritis, *The future of religious orders in the United States: transformation and commitment.*

64 O'Murchu, *Reframing religious life: an expanded vision for the future* p.130.

65 Ted Dunn, "Discerning choices for new life: A survey of options," *Human Development* 32, no. 2 (2011): pp.16-26.

66 Raymond Hostie, *Vie et mort des ordres religieux; approches psycho-sociologiques,* Bibliothèque d'études psycho-religieuses (Paris: Desclée de Brouwer, 1972), p.82.

67 Lawrence Cada et al., *Shaping the coming age of religious life,* p.59.

68 Patricia Wittberg, *The rise and decline of Catholic religious orders: a social movement perspective,* SUNY series in religion, culture, and society (Albany: State University of New York Press, 1994), p.194.

69 Cada, "The recovery of religious life," p.706.

70 George Wright and George Cairns, *Scenario thinking : practical approaches to the future* (Houndmills, Basingstoke, Hampshire, UK ; New York, NY: Palgrave Macmillan, 2011), p.1.

71 Michael Renner, "Corporate mergers skyrocket," *Vital Signs* 2019, no. March (2000), www.globalpolicy.org/socecon/tncs/mergers/renner.htm.

72 KPMG, "Mergers and acquisitions: global research report," *Unlocking sharholder value: keys to success* (1999), http://people.stern.nyu.edu/adamodar/pdfiles/eqnotes/KPMGM&A.pdf.

73 Kim S. Cameron and Robert E. Quinn, *Diagnosing and Changing Organizational Culture: Based on the Competing Values Framework,* Third edition. ed. (San Francisco, CA: Jossey-Bass, 2011), p.9.

74 Kathleen Sprows Cummings, "Understanding U.S. Catholic sisters today," Foundation and Donors Interested in Catholic Activities, Inc. (FADICA), http://www.nationalcatholicsistersweek.org/_resources/FDC_001_Report.pdf.

75 Sandra Marie Schneiders, *Prophets in their own country: women religious bearing witness to the Gospel in a troubled church* (Maryknoll, NY: Orbis Books, 2011), pp.42.43.

76 Ibid., p.101.

77 Mary Pellegrino, "The future enters us long before it happens: opening space for an emerging narrative of communion," in *Leadership Conference of Women Religious* (Orlando, FL: LCWR, 2017), pp.3-4.

78 Schneiders, *Prophets in their own country: women religious bearing witness to the Gospel in a troubled church*, p.41.

79 Ibid., pp.18,76.

80 Pew Research Center, "The Global Religious Landscape," (2012), http // www.pewforum.org /2012/12/18/global-religious-landscape-exec.

81 "Religion and Education Around the World," (2016), http://www.pewforum.org/2016/12/13/religion-and-education-around-the-world.

82 "The gender gap in religion around the world," 2018, no. April 23 (2016), http://www.pewforum.org/2016/03/22/the-gender-gap-in-religion-around-the-world.

83 Pew Research Center, "The Future of World Religions: Population Growth Projections, 2010-2050," (2015), https://assets.pewresearch.org/wp-content/uploads/sites/11/2015/03/PF_15.04.02_ProjectionsFullReport.pdf.

84 Gene Veith, "Where Christianity is growing the fastest," 2018, no. April 24, 2018 (2016), http://www.patheos.com/blogs/geneveith/2016/08/where-christianity-is-growing-the-fastest.

85 Pew Research Center, "Trends in Global Restrictions on Religion," (2016), https://www.pewforum.org/2016/06/23/trends-in-global-restrictions-on-religion.

86 "The Global Catholic Population," 2018, no. April 23 (2013), http://www.pewforum.org/2013/02/13/the-global-catholic-population.

87 Josephine McKenna, "Number of priests and nuns in marked decline," *The Telegraph* (2013), https://www.telegraph.co.uk/news/worldnews/europe/vaticancityandholysee/10103961/Number-of-priests-and-nuns-in-marked-decline.html.

88 National Religious Vocation Conference, "Vocations to religious life fact sheet," February (2013), https://cara.georgetown.edu/CARAResearch/Vocation_Fact_Sheet.pdf.

89 Robert D. Putnam and David E. Campbell, *American grace: how religion divides and unites us,* 1st Simon & Schuster hardcover ed. (New York: Simon & Schuster, 2010), pp. 140-41.

90 Pew Research Center, "America's Changing Religious Landscape," (2015), http://www.pewforum.org/2015/05/12/americas-changing-religious-landscape/pf_15-05-05_rls2_1_310px.

91 Robert Jones and Daniel Cox, "America's changing religious identity: Findings from the 2016 American Values Atlas," (2017), www.publicreligion.org.

92 Pew Research Center, "The Future of World Religions: Population Growth Projections, 2010-2050".https://assets.pewresearch.org/wp-content/uploads/sites/11/2015/03/PF_15.04.02_ProjectionsFullReport.pdf

93 700 Club, "Mormans are fatest growing religion.," The Christian Broadcasting Network, http://www1.cbn.com/churchandministry/mormons-are-fastest-growing-religion.

94 Betty Clermont, "Why the U.S. Catholic Church has lost more members than any other major denomination.," Open Tabernacle, https://opentabernacle.wordpress.com/2017/10/01/why-the-u-s-catholic-church-has-lost-more-members-than-any-other-major-denomination.

95 Pew Research Center, "A portrait of American catholics on the eve of Pope Benedict's visit to the U.S.," Pew Research Center, http://www.pewforum.org/2008/03/27/a-portrait-of-american-catholics-on-the-eve-of-pope-benedicts-visit-to-the-us.

96 Pew Research Center, "America's changing religious landscape: Full Report," *Full Report* (2015), www.pewresearch.org.

97 Putnam and Campbell, *American grace: how religion divides and unites us*, p.146.

98 Robert Jones and Cox, "America's changing religious identity: Findings from the 2016 American Values Atlas".www.publicreligion.org.

99 Pew Research Center, "America's changing religious landscape: Full Report".www.pewresearch.org.

100 Ibid.

101 Clermont, "Why the U.S. Catholic Church has lost more members than any other major denomination.".

102 Pew Research Center, "The Shifting Religious Identity of Latinos in the United States," 2018, no. April 23 (2014), http://www.pewforum.org/2014/05/07/the-shifting-religious-identity-of-latinos-in-the-united-states.

103 Mary L. Gautier and C. Joseph O'Hara, "New Sisters and Brothers in Perpetual Vows. A Report to the Secretariat of Clergy, Consecrated Life and Vocations United States Conference of Catholic Bishops.," (Washington D.C.: Center for Applied Research in the Apostolate, Georgetown University, 2011), p.6.

104 Mary Johnson, *New generations of Catholic sisters: the challenge of diversity* (New York: Oxford University Press, 2014), p.134.

105 Erick Berrelleza, Mary L. Gautier, and Mark M. Gray, "Population trends among religious institutes of women," *Special Report* Fall (2014), https://cara.georgetown.edu/wp-content/uploads/2018/06/Women_Religious_Fall2014_FINAL.pdf.

106 Ibid.

107 Santiago Sordo Palacios, Thomas Gaunt, and Mary Gautier, "Population Trends among Religious Institutes of Men," Fall (2015), https://cara.

georgetown.edu/wp-content/uploads/2018/06/Men_Religious_Fall2015_FINAL.pdf.

108 Erick Berrelleza, Mary L. Gautier, and Gray, "Population trends among religious institutes of women".https://cara.georgetown.edu/wp-content/uploads/2018/06/Women_Religious_Fall2014_FINAL.pdf

109 Patricia Wittberg and Mary Gautier, "Emerging U.S. Communities of Consecrated Life since Vatican II," (Washington DC: Center for Applied Research in the Apostolate, 2017), p.5.

110 Ibid., p.19.

111 Ibid., p.21.

112 Erick Berrelleza, Mary L. Gautier, and Gray, "Population trends among religious institutes of women".https://cara.georgetown.edu/wp-content/uploads/2018/06/Women_Religious_Fall2014_FINAL.pdf

113 Mary L. Gautier and Jonathan Holland, "A profile of the Associate-Religious relationship in the United States and Canada," ed. Center for the Applied Research in the Apostolate (Washington, DC: Georgetown University, 2016).

114 Matthew F. Kohmescher, *Catholicism today: a survey of Catholic belief and practice*, 3rd ed. (New York: Paulist Press, 1999), p.8.

115 Ibid., p.15.

116 Ibid., p.93.

117 Ibid., p.109.

118 James D. Davidson, *The search for common ground: what unites and divides Catholic Americans* (Huntington, Ind.: Our Sunday Visitor Pub. Division, 1997), pp.16-19.

119 Pew Research Center, "U.S. Catholics open to non-traditional families," (2015), https://www.pewforum.org/2015/09/02/u-s-catholics-open-to-non-traditional-families.

120 Ibid.

121 Davidson, *The search for common ground: what unites and divides Catholic Americans*, p.48.

122 Pew Research Center, "U.S. Catholics open to non-traditional families".https://www.pewforum.org/2015/09/02/u-s-catholics-open-to-non-traditional-families.

123 Caryle Murphy, "Most U.S. Christian groups grow more accepting of homosexuality," PEW Research Center, http://www.pewresearch.org/fact-tank/2015/12/18/most-u-s-christian-groups-grow-more-accepting-of-homosexuality.

124 Putnam and Campbell, *American grace: how religion divides and unites us*, pp.148-53.

125 Pew Research Center, "U.S. Catholics open to non-traditional families".https://www.pewforum.org/2015/09/02/u-s-catholics-open-to-non-traditional-families.

126 Mark Gray, Paul Perl, and Tricia Bruce, "Marriage in the Catholic Church: a survey of U.S. Catholics," (2007), https://cara.georgetown.edu/?s=Marriage+in+the+Catholic+Church%3A+a+survey+of+U.S.+-Catholics%22.

127 Pew Research Center, "U.S. Public Continues to Favor Legal Abortion, Oppose Overturning Roe v. Wade," (2019), https://www.people-press.org/2019/08/29/u-s-public-continues-to-favor-legal-abortion-oppose-overturning-roe-v-wade.

128 "Public Opinion on Abortion," (2019), https://www.pewforum.org/fact-sheet/public-opinion-on-abortion.

129 Davidson, *The search for common ground: what unites and divides Catholic Americans*, p.201.

130 Joanna Piacenza, "Support for Death Penalty by Religious Affiliation," (2015), https://www.prri.org/spotlight/support-for-death-penalty-by-reli-

gious-affiliation.

131 Pew Research Center, "Americans of all ages divided over doctor-assisted suicide laws," (2014), https://www.pewresearch.org/fact-tank/2014/10/22/americans-of-all-ages-divided-over-doctor-assisted-suicide-laws.

132 Putnam and Campbell, *American grace: how religion divides and unites us*, p.243.

133 Davidson, *The search for common ground: what unites and divides Catholic Americans*, p.26.

134 Mark M. Gray and Mary L. Gautier, "Catholic Women in the United States: beliefs, practices, experiences and attitudes," Report, 2018, no. August 6 (2018), https://cara.georgetown.edu/CatholicWomenStudy.pdf.

135 Pew Research Center, "'Strong' Catholic Identity at a Four-Decade Low in U.S.," 2018, no. April 22 (2013), https://www.pewforum.org/2013/03/13/strong-catholic-identity-at-a-four-decade-low-in-us.

136 Pew Research Center, "U.S. Catholics open to non-traditional families".https://www.pewforum.org/2015/09/02/u-s-catholics-open-to-non-traditional-families.

137 Gautier, "Catholic Women in the United States: beliefs, practices, experiences and attitudes".https://cara.georgetown.edu/CatholicWomenStudy.pdf.

138 Davidson, *The search for common ground: what unites and divides Catholic Americans*, p.45.

139 Toby Lester, "Catholic confession's steep price," Boston Globe, https://www.bostonglobe.com/ideas/2014/02/16/catholic-confession-steep-price/NbMVFfYljv26Gcphu17yPJ/story.html.

140 Gautier, "Catholic Women in the United States: beliefs, practices, experiences and attitudes".https://cara.georgetown.edu/CatholicWomenStudy.pdf.

141 Pew Research Center, "U.S. Catholics open to non-traditional families".https://www.pewforum.org/2015/09/02/u-s-catholics-open-to-non-traditional-families.

142 Pew Research Center, "Public's Views on Human Evolution," (2013), https://www.pewforum.org/2013/12/30/publics-views-on-human-evolution.

143 Putnam and Campbell, *American grace: how religion divides and unites us*, pp.111-12.

144 Davidson, *The search for common ground: what unites and divides Catholic Americans*, p.201.

145 Ibid., p.45.

146 Pew Research Center, "The Shifting Religious Identity of Latinos in the United States".http://www.pewforum.org/2014/05/07/the-shifting-religious-identity-of-latinos-in-the-united-states.

147 Gautier, "Catholic Women in the United States: beliefs, practices, experiences and attitudes".https://cara.georgetown.edu/CatholicWomenStudy.pdf.

148 Davidson, *The search for common ground: what unites and divides Catholic Americans*, p.201.

149 Daniel Cox and Robert P. Jones, "One-Quarter Say God Will Determine the Super Bowl's Winner—but Nearly Half Say God Rewards Devout Athletes," (2017), https://www.prri.org/research/poll-super-bowl-women-sports-god-athletes-marijuana/.

150 Putnam and Campbell, *American grace: how religion divides and unites us*, p.550.

151 Ibid., p.493.

152 John L. Allen, *The future church: how ten trends are revolutionizing the Catholic Church*, 1st ed. (New York: Doubleday, 2009), p.456.

153 Parker J. Palmer, "The Broken- Open Heart: Living with faith and hope in the tragic gap," *Weavings: A Journal of the Christian Spiritual Life* xxiv (2009), https://www.couragerenewal.org/PDFs/PJP-WeavingsArticle-Broken-OpenHeart.pdf.

154 Anthony J. Gittins, *Living mission interculturally : faith, culture, and the renewal of Praxis* (Collegeville, Minnesota: Liturgical Press, 2015), pp.150-51.

155 Shakil Choudhury, *Deep diversity: overcoming us vs. them* (Toronto: Between the Lines, 2015).

156 Bennett Milton, "Toward ethnorelativism: a developmental model of intercultural sensitivity," in *Education for the intercultural experience*, ed. R. Michael Paige (Yarmouth, ME: Intercultural Press, 1993).

157 Schneiders, *Finding the treasure: locating Catholic religious life in a new ecclesial and cultural context*, p.84.

158 Dunn, "Discerning choices for new life: A survey of options," p.19-20.

159 National Religious Retirement Office, "Lack of funds," National Religious Retirement Office, https://retiredreligious.org/the-need.

160 Wheatley, *Who do we choose to be?: facing reality, claiming leadership, restoring sanity*, p.19.

161 Wittberg, *Pathways to re-creating religious communities*, p.108.

162 *The rise and decline of Catholic religious orders: a social movement perspective*, p.214.

163 Nygren and Ukeritis, *The future of religious orders in the United States: transformation and commitment.*

164 Barbara Fiand, *Refocusing the vision: religious life into the future* (New York: Crossroad Pub. Co., 2001), p.79.

165 Lawrence Cada et al., *Shaping the coming age of religious life*, p.86.

166 Wittberg, *Pathways to re-creating religious communities*, p.11.

167 Christopher Lasch, *The culture of narcissism: American life in an age of diminishing expectations*, 1st ed. (New York: Norton, 1978).

168 Ted Dunn, "Transformation of Religious Life: Contemplative reflections of 'younger' members," *The Ocsasional Papers*, no. Winter (2017): p.28.

169 Juliet Schor, *The overworked American: the unexpected decline of leisure* (New York, N.Y.: Basic Books, 1991).

170 Dean Schabner, "Americans: overworked, overstressed," (2006), https://abcnews.go.com/%20US/story?id=93604.

171 David Emanuele, "Work-cations," in *Sunday Today with Willie Geist* (New York: NBC Today Show, 2018).

172 Joan Chittister, *The way we were: a story of conversion and renewal* (Maryknoll, N.Y.: Orbis Books, 2005), p.32.

173 Sandra Marie Schneiders, *Buying the field: Catholic religious life in mission to the world*, Religious life in a new millennium (New York: Paulist Press, 2013), p.148.

174 Ibid.

175 Ibid., p.151.

176 Paula Reed Ward, "A playbook for concealing the truth' -- Grand jury's investigative report identifies over 300 abusive priests," *Pittsburgh Post-Gazette*, August 14 2018.

177 John Jay College of Criminal Justice, ""Executive Summary", The Nature and Scope of Sexual Abuse of Minors by Catholic Priests and Deacons in the United States 1950–2002," (United States Conference of Catholic Bishops, 2004).

178 Ilia Delio, "Schism or Evolution," The Omega Center, https://www.omegacenter.info/schism-or-evolution.

179 Johnson, *New generations of Catholic sisters: the challenge of diversity*, p.135.

180 Wittberg, *Pathways to re-creating religious communities*, p.58.

181 O'Murchu, *Reframing religious life: an expanded vision for the future* p.28.

182 Ibid., p.30.

183 David Kinnaman, "Six Reasons Young Christians Leave Church," Barna Group, https://www.barna.com/research/six-reasons-young-christians-leave-church.

184 Betsy Cooper et al., "Exodus: Why Americans are Leaving Religion— and Why They're Unlikely to Come Back," (2016), http://www.prri.org/research/prri-rns-poll-nones-atheist-leaving-religion.

185 Gautier, "Catholic Women in the United States: beliefs, practices, experiences and attitudes". p.10.https://cara.georgetown.edu/Catholic-WomenStudy.pdf.

186 Pew Research Center, "America's Changing Religious Landscape". http://www.pewforum.org/2015/05/12/americas-changing-religious-landscape/pf_15-05-05_rls2_1_310px

187 Desmond Murphy, *The death and rebirth of religious life* (Alexandria, NSW, Australia, Ridgefield, CT: E.J. Dwyer; Morehouse Pub. distributor, 1995).

188 Schneiders, *Finding the treasure: locating Catholic religious life in a new ecclesial and cultural context*, p.228.

189 Michael Crosby, *Can religious life be prophetic?* (New York: Crossroad Pub. Co., 2005), p.15.

190 Joan Chittister, *The fire in these ashes: a spirituality of contemporary religious life* (Kansas City: Sheed & Ward, 1995), p.26.

191 Walter Brueggemann, *The prophetic imagination* (Philadelphia: For-

tress Press, 1978), p.59-60.

192 Diarmuid O'Murchu, *Religious life: A prophectic vision* (Notre Dame, IN: Ave Maria Press, 1991), p.40.

193 Crosby, *Can religious life be prophetic?*, p.125.

194 Anthony J. Gittins, *A presence that disturbs: a call to radical discipleship*, 1st ed. (Liguori, Mo.: Liguori/Triumph, 2002), p.75.

195 Ibid., p.3.

196 Barbara Fiand, *From religion back to faith: a journey of the heart* (New York: Crossroad Pub. Co., 2006), p.47.

197 *Refocusing the vision: religious life into the future*, p.51.

198 *From religion back to faith: a journey of the heart*, p.33.

199 Chittister, *The fire in these ashes: a spirituality of contemporary religious life*, p.62.

200 Crosby, *Can religious life be prophetic?*, p.50.

201 Chittister, *The fire in these ashes: a spirituality of contemporary religious life*, p.71.

202 Ibid., p.78-79.

203 Ibid., p.4.

204 Schneiders, *Finding the treasure: locating Catholic religious life in a new ecclesial and cultural context*, p.106.

205 Amy Hereford, *Navigating Change: The role of law in the life-cylce of a religious institute* (Saint Louis, MO: Religious Life Project, 2014).

206 Ibid., p.197.

207 Pope Paul VI, "Ecclesiae Sanctae," Typis Polyglottis Vaticanis (Rome1966).

208 "A critical juncture:Assessing the viability of religious institutes. A self-evaluation instrument," (Silver Spring, MD: Leadership Conference of Women Religious (LCWR) National Association for Treasurers of Religious Institutes (NATRI)

National Religious Retirement Office (NRRO) 2000).
209 LCWR and NRRO A joint effort of NATRI, "The collaborative Viability Project," (Joint effort of NATRI, LCWR and NRRO, 2000), pp.ii-iii.

210 Edgar H. Schein, *Organizational culture and leadership*, 2nd ed., A joint publication in the Jossey-Bass management series and the Jossey-Bass social and behavioral science series (San Francisco: Jossey-Bass, 1992), p.9.

211 Wittberg, *The rise and decline of Catholic religious orders: a social movement perspective*, p.31.

212 Hereford, *Navigating Change: The role of law in the life-cylce of a religious institute*, pp.198-99.

213 Ibid., p.200.

214 Arbuckle, *Out of chaos: refounding religious congregations*, p.134.

215 Ted Dunn, "The role of meaning-making in transitional times," *The Ocsasional Papers* 48, no. 2 (2019): p.5.

216 Sharon Euart, "25 Q & A's—Commisary for Religious Institutes," in *News in Brief* (Resource Center for Religious Institutes, 2018), p.4.

217 Ibid., p.5.

218 Ted Dunn, "Circular models of leadership: Birthing a new way of being," *Human Development* 27, no. 4 (2006).

219 Nelson Mandela, *Long walk to freedom : the autobiography of Nelson Mandela*, 1st ed. (Boston: Little, Brown, 1994), p.624-25.

220 Ira Chaleff, *The courageous follower : standing up to and for our leaders*, 1st ed. (San Francisco: Berrett-Koehler Publishers, 1995), p.13.

221 Peter Block, *Stewardship: choosing service over self-interest*, Second edition, revised and expanded. ed. (San Francisco: Berrett-Koehler Publishers, 2013), pp.29-31.

222 *The answer to how is yes : acting on what matters*, 1st ed. (San Francisco, CA: Berrett-Koehler Publishers, 2002), p.34.

223 "Visionary leadership in community building," ed. Nicole Farkouh (Abundant Community, 2018).

224 Dunn, "Discerning choices for new life: A survey of options," p.21.

225 Block, *The answer to how is yes : acting on what matters*, p.35.

226 *Community: the structure of belonging* (San Francisco: Berrett-Koehler Publishers, 2008), p.129.

227 Dunn, "Discerning choices for new life: A survey of options," pp.21-22.

228 Dietrich Bonhoeffer, *The cost of discipleship*, 1st Touchstone ed. (New York: Touchstone, 1995).

229 Malcolm Gladwell, *David and Goliath : underdogs, misfits, and the art of battling giants*, First Edition. ed. (New York: Little, Brown and Company, 2013), p.6.

230 Philip E. Tetlock, *Expert political judgment: how good is it? How can we know?* (Princeton, N.J.: Princeton University Press, 2005).

231 Wittberg, *Pathways to re-creating religious communities*, p.198.

232 Dunn, "Discerning choices for new life: A survey of options," pp.25-26.

233 Jason Jennings, *The reinventors: how extraordinary companies pursue radical continuous change* (New York: Portfolio/Penguin, 2012), p.45.

234 Thomas J. Chermack, *Scenario planning in organizations: how to create, use, and assess scenarios* (San Francisco, CA: Berrett-Koehler, 2011),

p.3.

235 Henry Mintzberg, *The rise and fall of strategic planning: reconceiving roles for planning, plans, planners* (New York, Toronto: Free Press; Maxwell Macmillan Canada, 1994), p.158.

236 Ibid., pp.403,13.

237 Cameron and Quinn, *Diagnosing and Changing Organizational Culture: Based on the Competing Values Framework*, p.12.

238 Ibid., p.11.

239 Ibid., p.1.

240 Ibid., p.13.

241 Ibid., p.11.

242 Mintzberg, *The rise and fall of strategic planning: reconceiving roles for planning, plans, planners*, pp.415-16.

243 Leonard David Goodstein, Timothy M. Nolan, and J. William Pfeiffer, *Applied strategic planning : a comprehensive guide* (New York: McGraw-Hill, 1993), p.188.

244 Peter M. Senge, *The fifth discipline: the art and practice of the learning organization*, 1st ed. (New York: Doubleday/Currency, 1990), p.214.

245 Richard Rohr and John Feister, *Hope against darkness: the transforming vision of Saint Francis in an age of anxiety* (Cincinnati, Ohio: St. Anthony Messenger Press, 2001), p.25.

246 Andrew Norman, *Charles Darwin : destroyer of myths* (Barnsley, South Yorkshire: Pen & Sword Discovery, 2013), p.261.

247 C. G. Jung, "Structure and Dynamics of the Psyche," in *The Collective Works of C. G. Jung*, ed. Michael Fordham Herbert Read, Gerhard Adler, William McGuire, Bollingen Series (New Jersey: Princeton University, 1969; reprint, Third), p.787.

248 Harry R. Moody and David Carroll, *The five stages of the soul: charting the spiritual passages that shape our lives*, 1st Anchor Books ed. (New York: Anchor Books, 1997), pp. 27-34.

249 Ibid., p.34.

250 Joseph Campbell, *The hero with a thousand faces*, 3rd ed., Bollingen series XVII (Novato, Calif.: New World Library, 2008), p.80.

251 Robert C. Atchley, *Spirituality and aging* (Baltimore: Johns Hopkins University Press, 2009), p.67.

252 George E. Vaillant, *Aging well: surprising guideposts to a happier life from the landmark Harvard study of adult development*, 1st ed. (Boston: Little, Brown, 2002), p.50.

253 Gail Sheehy, *Passages: predictable crises of adult life*, 1st ed. (New York: Dutton, 1976).

254 Daniel J. Levinson, *The Seasons of a man's life*, 1st ed. (New York: Knopf, 1978).

255 Judith Viorst, *Necessary losses: the loves, illusions, dependencies and impossible expectations that all of us have to give up in order to grow*, 1st Ballantine Books trade ed. (New York: Simon and Schuster, 1986).

256 Lars Tornstam, *Gerotranscendence: a developmental theory of positive aging* (New York: Springer Pub. Co., 2005).

257 Richard Rohr, *Falling upward: a spirituality for the two halves of life*, 1st ed. (San Francisco: Jossey-Bass, 2011).

258 Parker J. Palmer, *A hidden wholeness: the journey toward an undivided life*, 1st ed. (San Francisco, CA: Jossey-Bass, 2008).

259 Joan Chittister, *The gift of years: growing older gracefully* (New York, NY: BlueBridge, 2008).

260 Ronald Rolheiser, *Sacred fire: a vision for a deeper human and Christian maturity*, First Edition. ed. (New York: Image, 2014).

261 Diarmuid O'Murchu, *Adult Faith: Growing in wisdom and understanding* (Maryknoll, NY: Orbis Books, 2010).

262 Erik H. Erikson, *Identity and the life cycle* (New York: Norton, 1980).

263 Thomas S. Kuhn, *The structure of scientific revolutions* (Chicago: University of Chicago Press, 1962).

264 Ludwig von Bertalanffy, *Perspectives on general system theory: scientific-philosophical studies*, The International library of systems theory and philosophy (New York: G. Braziller, 1975).

265 Elizabeth A. Carter and Monica McGoldrick, *The Family life cycle: a framework for family therapy* (New York: Gardner Press : distributed by Halsted Press, 1980).

266 Senge, *The fifth discipline: the art and practice of the learning organization*, pp.6-11.

267 Ibid., p.14.

268 Claus Otto Scharmer, *Theory U: leading from the future as it emerges : the social technology of presencing*, Second edition. ed. (San Francisco, California: Berrett-Koehler Publishers, Inc., a BK Business Book, 2016).

269 Margaret J. Wheatley, *Leadership and the new science: learning about organization from an orderly universe*, 1st ed. (San Francisco: Berrett-Koehler Publishers, 1992).

270 Peter Block, *Stewardship: choosing service over self-interest*, 1st ed. (San Francisco: Berrett-Koehler Publishers, 1993).

271 Arthur F. Burns and Wesley C. Mitchell, *Measuring business cycles*, National Bureau of Economic Research Studies in business cycles (New York,: National Bureau of Economic Research, 1946).

272 Ichak Adizes, *Managing corporate lifecycles*, Rev. and enl. ed. (Paramus, N.J.: Prentice Hall Press, 1999).

273 Arbuckle, *Out of chaos: refounding religious congregations.*

274 Lawrence Cada et al., *Shaping the coming age of religious life.*

275 Dunn, "Refounding Religious Life: A choice for transformational change."

276 Don Beck and Christopher C. Cowan, *Spiral dynamics: mastering values, leadership, and change: exploring the new science of memetics*, Developmental management (Cambridge, Mass., USA: Blackwell Business, 1996), p.18.

277 Brian Swimme and Thomas Berry, *The universe story: from the primordial flaring forth to the ecozoic era--a celebration of the unfolding of the cosmos*, 1st ed. (San Francisco, Calif.: HarperSan Francisco, 1992), p.71.

278 Pierre Teilhard de Chardin, *The phenomenon of man* (New York,: Harper, 1959).

279 Barbara Marx Hubbard, *Conscious evolution: awakening the power of our social potential* (Novato, Calif.: New World Library, 1998), p.63.

280 "Mystery Unfolding: Leading in the Evolutionary Now," in *LCWR Assembly* (St. Louis, MO: Leadership Conference of Religious Women, 2012).

281 Ilia Delio, *Making all things new : catholicity, cosmology, consciousness*, Catholicity in an evolving universe (Maryknoll, New York: Orbis Books, 2015), pp.191-200.

282 Elizabeth A. Johnson, *Ask the beasts: Darwin and the god of love* (London: Bloomsbury, 2014), p.285.

283 Robert E. Quinn, *Deep change: discovering the leader within*, Jossey-Bass business & management series (San Francisco, Calif.: Jossey-Bass Publishers, 1996), p.3.

284 Nygren and Ukeritis, *The future of religious orders in the United States: transformation and commitment*, p.259.

285 Edward Teller, Goodreads, Inc., https://www.goodreads.com/quotes/69423-when-you-come-to-the-end-of-all-the-light.

286 Thomas Merton, *Thoughts in solitude* (New York,: Farrar, 1958), p.83.

287 Marcia Allen, "Transformation – an experiment in hope," in *Leadership Conference of Religious Women* (Orlando, 2016), p.5-7.

288 Ken Untener, "A Future Not Our Own: In Memory of Oscar Romero (1917–1980)," *The mystery of the Romero Prayer* (1979), https://www.journeywithjesus.net/PoemsAndPrayers/Ken_Untener_A_Future_Not_Our_Own.shtml.

289 Václav Havel and Karel Hvížďala, *Disturbing the peace : a conversation with Karel Hvížďala*, 1st American ed. (New York: Knopf : Distributed by Random House, 1990), p.181.

290 Joan Chittister, *Scarred by struggle, transformed by hope* (Grand Rapids, Mich.: William B. Eerdmans Pub. : Ottawa Novalis, Saint Paul University, 2003), p.2.

291 Ibid., p.19.

292 Joanna Macy and Chris Johnstone, *Active hope : how to face the mess we're in without going crazy* (Novato, Calif.: New World Library, 2012).

293 Tina Turner, "What's Love Got to Do with It," in *What's Love Got to Do with It* (Parlophone, 1993).

294 Richard Rohr, *The naked now: learning to see as the mystics see* (New York: Crossroad Pub. Co., 2009), p.122.

295 Jean Pierre Medaille, *Maxims of the Little Institute*, Writings of Jean Pierre Medaille, Maxim 84 (Toronto, CA: Sisters of St. Joseph of Toronto, 1985), p.139.

296 Thomas Merton, *Conjectures of a guilty bystander*, 1st ed. (Garden City, N.Y.,: Doubleday, 1966), p.145.

297 National Transportation Safety Board, "Aircraft Accident Report," (Washington D.C.: National Transportation Safety Board, 1979), p.1.

298 Taleb, *The black swan: the impact of the highly improbable*, p.xxii.

299 Ibid., p.199.

300 Chittister, *The fire in these ashes: a spirituality of contemporary religious life*, p.2.

301 Diarmuid O'Murchu, *Religious life in the 21st century: the prospect of refounding* (Maryknoll, New York: Orbis Books, 2016), p.3.

302 Ibid., p.24.

303 Fiand, *From religion back to faith: a journey of the heart*, p.33.

304 Crosby, *Repair my house: becoming "Kindom" Catholics*, p.51.

305 Schneiders, *Prophets in their own country: women religious bearing witness to the Gospel in a troubled church*, p.100.

306 John Dear, *The God of peace: Toward a new theology of nonviolence* (Eugene, Oregon: Wipf & Stock Publishers, 1994).

307 D Couturier, "Religious life at a crossroads," *Origins: CNS Documentary Service* 36, no. 12 (2006).

308 E.M. Prevallet, "In the service of life: widening and deepening religious commitment" (paper presented at the A series of presentation of earth spirituality presented at a conference sponsored by The Loretto Earth Network, Nerinx, KY, 2002).

309 Tolle, *A new earth: awakening to your life's purpose*, p.102.

310 Ibid., p.23.

311 Ken Wilber, *Integral psychology ; Transformations of consciousness ; Selected essays*, 1st ed., The collected works of Ken Wilber (Boston: Shambhala, 1999), pp.15-16.

312 Ted Dunn and Beth Lipsmeyer, "Tranforming Communities through CARE," in *Conversational Approach to Relational Effectiveness (CARE)* (Unpublished2020).

313 Wilber, *Integral psychology ; Transformations of consciousness ; Select-*

ed essays, pp.11-12.

314 Ken Wilber, Jack Engler, and Daniel P. Brown, *Transformations of consciousness: conventional and contemplative perspectives on development*, 1st ed. (Boston

New York: New Science Library ;
Distributed in the U.S. by Random House, 1986), p.68.
315 Wilber, *Integral psychology* ; *Transformations of consciousness* ; *Selected essays*, p.44.

316 *Integral spirituality: a startling new role for religion in the modern and postmodern world*, 1st ed. (Boston: Integral Books, 2006), p.196.

317 Wilber, Engler, and Brown, *Transformations of consciousness: conventional and contemplative perspectives on development*, p.266.

318 Ibid., pp.20-21.

319 Cynthia Bourgeault, *The heart of centering prayer: nondual Christianity in theory and practice*, First Edition. ed. (Boulder: Shambhala, 2016), p.14.

320 Wilber, Engler, and Brown, *Transformations of consciousness: conventional and contemplative perspectives on development*, p.21.

321 Richard Rohr, "Living with paradox, uncertainty and mystery," *The Ocsasional Papers* Summer (2017): p.11.

322 Tolle, *A new earth: awakening to your life's purpose*, p.18.

323 Catherine Bertrand, "The transforming power of contemplative engagement," *The Ocsasional Papers* Summer (2016): p.8.

324 Ted Dunn, "Where two or more are gathered," *Review for Religious* 64, no. 3 (2005): pp.2-3.

325 Tolle, *A new earth: awakening to your life's purpose*, p.295.

326 William Stafford and Kim Robert Stafford, *Ask me : 100 essential*

poems (Minneapolis, Minnesota: Graywolf Press, 2014).

327 Thomas Moore, *Care of the soul: a guide for cultivating depth and sacredness in everyday life*, 1st ed. (New York, NY: HarperCollins, 1992), p.129.

328 Richard Rohr, *Immortal diamond: the search for our true self*, 1st ed. (San Francisco, CA: Jossey-Bass, 2013), p.vii.

329 Ibid., p.5.

330 R. Ruth Barton, *Strengthening the soul of your leadership: seeking God in the crucible of ministry* (Downers Grove, Ill.: IVP Books, 2008), p.13.

331 Palmer, *A hidden wholeness: the journey toward an undivided life*, pp.58-59.

332 Ibid., pp.33-34.

333 David G. Benner, *Spirituality and the awakening self: the sacred journey of transformation* (Grand Rapids, Mich.: Brazos Press, 2012), p.122.

334 Pierre Teilhard de Chardin, *The divine milieu: an essay on the interior life*, 1st ed. (New York,: Harper, 1960).

335 Swimme and Berry, *The universe story: from the primordial flaring forth to the ecozoic era--a celebration of the unfolding of the cosmos.*

336 Harrison Owen, *Riding the tiger: doing business in a transforming world* (Potomac, Md.: Abbott Pub., 1991), p.93.

337 Ibid., p.91.

338 P. R. Régamey and Paul, *Paul VI donne aux religieux leur charte : exhortation "Evangelica testificatio"*, Problèmes de vie religieuse, (Paris: Éditions du Cerf, 1971), par.11.

339 *Dogmatic constitution on the Church: Lumen gentium, solemnly promulgated by His Holiness, Pope Paul VI on November 21, 1964,* (Boston: St. Paul Editions, 1965), par.12.

340 Régamey and Paul, *Paul VI donne aux religieux leur charte : exhortation "Evangelica testificatio"*, par.10.

341 John Carroll Futrell, "Discorvering the Founder's Charism," *The Way Supplement* 14 (1971): pp.64.65.

342 Anthony J. Gittins, "Sows' Ears and Silk Purses: The Limitations of Charisms and Communities," *Review for Religious* 43 (1984): p.707.

343 Moore, *Care of the soul: a guide for cultivating depth and sacredness in everyday life*, pp.xi- xii.

344 Francis Weller, *The wild edge of sorrow: rituals of renewal and the sacred work of grief* (Berkeley, California: North Atlantic Books, 2015), p.56.

345 Rolheiser, *The holy longing: the search for a Christian spirituality*, p.98.

346 Thomas Merton, Naomi Burton Stone, and Patrick Hart, *Love and living* (New York: Farrar, Straus, and Giroux, 1979), pp.11-12.

347 Rohr, *Immortal diamond: the search for our true self*, pp.27-28.

348 Campbell, *The hero with a thousand faces*.

349 Ibid., pp.101.02.

350 Ibid., p.32.

351 Parker J. Palmer, *Let your life speak: listening for the voice of vocation* (San Francisco: Jossey-Bass, 2000), p.61.

352 Viktor E. Frankl, *Man's search for meaning* (Boston: Beacon Press, 2006), p.66.

353 Dunn, "The role of meaning-making in transitional times," pp.4-8.

354 John O'Donohue, *Anam cara: a book of Celtic wisdom*, 1st ed. (New York: Cliff Street Books, 1997), pp.90-91.

355 Moore, *Care of the soul: a guide for cultivating depth and sacredness in everyday life*, p.94.

356 Block, *Community: the structure of belonging*, p.30.

357 Chris Hedges, "What every person should know about war," New York Times, https://www.nytimes.com/2003/07/06/books/chapters/what-every-person-should-know-about-war.html.

358 Nicholas Kristof, "Why 2017 was the best year in human history," New York Times, https://www.nytimes.com/2018/01/06/opinion/sunday/2017-progress-illiteracy-poverty.html.

359 Martin Luther King Jr., "Pilgrimage to Nonviolence," *Martin Luther King, Jr. Papers Project* (1960), http://okra.stanford.edu/transcription/document_images/Vol05Scans/13Apr1960_PilgrimagetoNonviolence.pdf.

360 Patricia Wittberg, *Creating a future for religious life: a sociological perspective* (New York: Paulist Press, 1991), p.31.

361 Richard Rohr, *What the mystics know: seven pathways to your deeper self* (New York: Crossroads, 2015), p.49.

362 Norman Mailer and Michael Lennon, *Conversations with Norman Mailer*, Literary conversations series (Jackson: University Press of Mississippi, 1988), p.389.

363 Chittister, *Scarred by struggle, transformed by hope*, p.23.

364 Arbuckle, *Out of chaos: refounding religious congregations*, p.184.

365 Cada, "The recovery of religious life," p.706.

366 Ted Dunn, "Triangulation and the misuse of power: A dance of victims, villains and rescuers," *Human Development* 27, no. 2 (2006): p.22.

367 Palmer, "Standing in the tragic gap". p.3.https://www.couragerenewal.org/PDFs/PJP-WeavingsArticle-Broken-OpenHeart.pdf

368 Dunn and Lipsmeyer, "CARE."

369 John Gottman, "The Four Horsemen: criticism, contempt, defensiveness, and stonewalling," The Gottman Institute, https://www.gottman.

com/blog/the-four-horsemen-recognizing-criticism-contempt-defensive-ness-and-stonewalling.

370 Desmond Tutu, *No future without forgiveness*, 1st ed. (New York: Doubleday, 1999).

371 Beatrice Bruteau and Ilia Delio, *Personal transformation and a new creation : the spiritual revolution of Beatrice Bruteau* (Maryknoll, New York: Orbis Books, 2016), p.125.

372 Richard Rohr, *Things hidden: scripture as spirituality* (Cincinnati, Ohio: St. Anthony Messenger Press, 2008), p.37.

373 Francis Jansen, "Monument to Forgiveness: a soul's invitation to all our ancestors," *Kosmos Journal*, no. Fall/Winter (2016): p.15.

374 Wittberg, *Creating a future for religious life: a sociological perspective*, p.35.

375 Arbuckle, *Strategies for growth in religious life*, p.42.

376 Peter M. Senge, *The fifth discipline: the art and practice of the learning organization*, Rev. and updated. ed. (New York: Doubleday/Currency, 2006), p.1.

377 Moore, *Care of the soul: a guide for cultivating depth and sacredness in everyday life*, pp.121-29.

378 Malcolm Gladwell, *Outliers: the story of success*, 1st ed. (New York: Little, Brown and Co., 2008), pp.35-68.

379 Rohr, *Falling upward: a spirituality for the two halves of life*, P.154.

380 Jeremy Gutsche, *Exploiting chaos: 150 ways to spark innovation during times of change* (New York: Gotham Books, 2009), p.96.

381 Kathryn Schulz, *Being wrong: adventures in the margin of error*, 1st ed. (New York: Ecco, 2010), pp.3-24.

382 Richard Rohr, *The universal Christ: how a forgotten reality can change*

everything we see, hope for, and believe, First edition. ed. (New York: Convergent, 2019), p.72.

383 Brené Brown, "The power of vulnerability," in *TEDxHouston*, ed. Ted Talk (Ted.com, 2010).

384 Block, *Community: the structure of belonging*, p.4.

385 Ken Robinson, *Out of our minds: the power of being creative*, Third edition. ed. (Chichester, West Sussex: John Wiley & Sons, Ltd, 2017).

386 Linda A. Hill, *Collective genius: the art and practice of leading innovation* (Boston: Harvard Business Review Press, 2014), p.4.

387 Ibid., pp.121-89.

388 Robert D. Putnam, *Bowling alone: the collapse and revival of American community* (New York: Simon & Schuster, 2000).

389 Nancy Lutkehaus, *Margaret Mead : the making of an American icon* (Princeton: Princeton University Press, 2008), p.261.

390 Chittister, *The fire in these ashes: a spirituality of contemporary religious life*, pp.78-79.

391 Arbuckle, *Out of chaos: refounding religious congregations*, pp.185-86.

392 Sebastian Junger, *Tribe: on homecoming and belonging*, First edition. ed. (New York: Twelve, 2016).

393 Peggy Holman, *Engaging emergence : turning upheaval into opportunity*, 1st ed. (San Francisco: Berrett-Koehler Publishers, 2010), p.18.

394 Ibid., p.9.

395 Wheatley, *Who do we choose to be?: facing reality, claiming leadership, restoring sanity*, p.231.

396 Senge, *The fifth discipline: the art and practice of the learning organization*, p.150.

397 Ibid., p.153.

398 Teresa Maya, "Called To Leadership: Challenges And Opportunities For Younger Members In Leadership," in *In Our Own Words: Religious Life in a Changing World*, ed. Juliet Mousseau and Sarah Kohles (Collegeville, MN: Ligurgical Press, 2018), p.170.

399 Rohr, *The universal Christ: how a forgotten reality can change everything we see, hope for, and believe*, p.153.

400 Abraham Lincoln, "Annual Message to Congress - Concluding Remarks," http://www.abrahamlincolnonline.org/lincoln/speeches/congress.htm.